Financial Reporti
Unlisted Companies in
the UK and Republic of
Ireland

Financial Reporting for Unlisted Companies in the UK and Republic of Ireland

Steve Collings FMAAT FCCA

Paul Gee BA (Econ) FCA

Bloomsbury Professional

Bloomsbury Professional Ltd, Maxwelton House, 41–43 Boltro Road, Haywards Heath, West Sussex, RH16 1BJ

© Bloomsbury Professional Ltd 2014

Bloomsbury Professional, an imprint of Bloomsbury Publishing Plc

A CIP Catalogue record for this book is available from the British Library.

ISBN: 978 1 78043 229 8

Typeset by Phoenix Photosetting, Chatham, Kent
Printed and bound by Hobbs the Printers, Totton, Southampton, SO40 3WX

Foreword

Generally accepted accounting practice in the UK and Republic of Ireland has developed over the last 40 years, first in the form of Statements of Standard Accounting Practice and then as Financial Reporting Standards augmented by Abstracts (collectively 'UK Accounting Standards'). While most of the standards made reference to international accounting, particularly in the later FRSs, they were essentially 'UK' rules. Those standards, and their practical application, have become embedded in the financial reporting of our unlisted companies and woven into the professional lives of both accounts preparers and auditors.

The introduction of a new regime that has its roots firmly in International Financial Reporting Standards through the IFRS for Small and Medium Entities (the IFRS for SMEs), therefore, presents a potentially significant culture shock. It is not just the differences in terminology, recognition, measurement and presentation that will provide a challenge, but also the fact that 3,000-plus pages of 'old' UK GAAP are replaced with just 350 pages of FRS 102. A lot of detailed exposition that has guided accounts preparers has disappeared and new areas of interpretation have opened up.

Understandably, accountants will seek guidance on how FRS 102 differs from 'old' UK GAAP, how to implement the new regime, the areas where judgement and interpretation will be required, and how to approach those judgements. In this book, the authors take us through each aspect of FRS 102, providing signposts to key issues and practical worked examples to demonstrate its 'real life' implications. While I believe there is no substitute for reading the Standard, I am sure this book will act as a valuable reference tool and support as we work towards applying FRS 102 for the first time.

Stephanie Henshaw
Technical Partner
Francis Clark LLP
November 2013

Preface

This is the first edition of *Financial Reporting for Unlisted Companies in the UK and Republic of Ireland*. This book has been designed to give a clear, concise and comprehensive reference to all aspects of the new UK GAAP.

Financial reporting has evolved considerably over the years as a result of diversity in business and the changing world in which the profession lives. The UK and Republic of Ireland are about to witness one of the most significant changes in the history of UK GAAP: the abolition of FRSs/SSAPs/UITFs and the introduction of a modern set consisting initially of three standards which will form a new UK GAAP for companies not eligible to apply the FRSSE and which do not report under EU-adopted IFRS. The UK and Republic of Ireland has undergone a rigorous programme to bring financial reporting into a modern age and this has been achieved by the issuance of three new standards, all of which apply to accounting periods commencing on or after 1 January 2015, with early adoption permitted:

FRS 100   *Application of Financial Reporting Requirements*

FRS 101   *Reduced Disclosure Framework*

FRS 102   *The Financial Reporting Standard applicable in the UK and Republic of Ireland*

UK GAAP has been overhauled to enable financial statements prepared under the new UK GAAP to be transparent and at the same time meeting users' needs. Balancing these needs out for preparers has resulted in a significantly-reshaped financial reporting framework that is comprehensive, far less voluminous and not disjointed unlike the previous UK GAAP. The sheer reduction in volume of the new UK GAAP will be a welcome change amongst practitioners and preparers of financial statements in all business sectors. For companies at the smaller end of the scale, the FRSSE (effective January 2015) will still be applicable although it is expected that the FRSSE will see changes in the future to further align it with the concepts and principles laid down in FRS 102.

Key features of this publication include 'Signposts' at the start of each chapter which are designed to highlight, at a glance, the contents of the chapter. There are also 'Focus' boxes throughout each chapter which flag up important concepts and points that preparers of financial statements should take on board. Comprehensive, real-life worked examples are an integral feature of this publication as the authors firmly believe in bringing theory to life using practical illustrations to help preparers to thoroughly understand some of the complex issues embedded within each section of the new UK GAAP. At the end of each chapter are disclosure requirements that are needed within a set of financial statements prepared under the new regime, together with an overview of how the new UK GAAP differs from its predecessor.

I hope that you find this book helpful in your dealings with UK GAAP and we would welcome any comments or suggestions for future editions.

The authors would like to extend a special thanks to Caroline Fox BA FCA, who did a remarkable job as the technical editor of this publication.

Steve Collings
FMAAT FCCA
September 2013

Contents

Contents

Table of Cases

Table of Statutes

Table of Statutory Instruments

Table of Financial Reporting Standards

References are to paragraph number. References in *italics* refer to the page numbers of the Appendix.

Table of Examples

Table of Examples

Table of Examples

Table of Examples

Chapter 1

The development of FRS 102

SIGNPOSTS

- It was acknowledged several years ago that the old UK GAAP had become overly complicated and voluminous which contributed to extensive disclosure requirements and complications within the profession. It was further acknowledged that the old UK GAAP was based on standards that lacked cohesive principles and that the old UK GAAP had failed to keep up with evolving, and increasingly complex, business transactions (see **1.1**).

- To overhaul the old UK GAAP would have been too costly for the UK and such costs would have essentially outweighed the benefits of doing so, hence the (now defunct) Accounting Standards Board (ASB) decided to go back to the drawing board and adopt a reporting regime that was essentially based on the International Accounting Standards Board's *IFRS for SMEs*. These proposals were contained in FREDs 43, 44 and 45 (see **1.2**).

- Significant concerns were raised by interested parties during the comment period relating to the concept of public accountability and the prohibition of various accounting methods previously contained in the old UK GAAP which preparers of financial statements had become accustomed to and were enshrined within the old regime (see **1.3**).

- FREDs 46, 47 and 48 were issued in January 2012. These addressed the concerns raised about the previous FREDs 43 to 45 which eliminated the 'tier system'; they incorporated both accounting methods that were in previous UK GAAP and guidance relating to public benefit entities (see **1.4** and **1.5**).

- FREDs 46 and 47 have become FRS 100 and 101 respectively. They are applicable for accounting periods commencing on or after 1 January 2015, with earlier adoption permissible. FRED 48 (now FRS 102) was approved for issue on 5 March 2013 and this is also applicable for accounting periods commencing on or after 1 January 2015 with earlier adoption permissible. FRS 103 *Insurance Contracts* will apply to companies that operate in the insurance industry (though at the time of writing this standard had not been finalised by the Financial Reporting Council (FRC)) (see **1.6** and **1.7**).

- There is still a three-tier approach to financial reporting following the introduction of FRSs 100, 101 and 102 (see **1.8**).

- FRS 102 is structured in 'sections' rather than individual accounting standard numbers and has been greatly reduced in size (the old UK GAAP was over 3,000 pages long – FRS 102 is 335 pages long including the Appendices). The FRC views FRS 102 as being fit for purpose, providing a comprehensive set of principles-based standards that will enable financial statements to be more meaningful for users (see **1.9**).

- Companies based in the Republic of Ireland will have to prepare financial statements in accordance with Irish companies' legislation. A table outlining the provisions in Companies Acts 1963 to 2012 is contained in FRS 100 *Application of Financial Reporting Requirements* (see **1.10**).

DEVELOPMENT OF THE FINANCIAL REPORTING STANDARD FOR MID-SIZED ENTITIES TO FRS 102

1.1   The UK's (now defunct) Accounting Standards Board (ASB) concluded several years ago that the old UK GAAP (FRSs, SSAPs and UITFs) had become overly complicated in many areas as well as voluminous. Many in the profession had complained about the sheer volume and extensive disclosure requirements commanded by the old UK GAAP and it was also acknowledged that the previous standards were in desperate need of an overhaul because UK GAAP consisted of a blend of dated standards that lacked cohesive principles, together with additional standards that had merely been adopted from International Financial Reporting Standards (IFRS) as well as a failure to keep pace with evolving, and increasingly complex, business transactions.

1.2   The ASB (now the Accounting Council of the Financial Reporting Council) agreed that instead of going back and overhauling existing standards, they would effectively start 'from scratch' and develop a new UK GAAP. This was mainly due to the fact that to 'overhaul' the old UK GAAP would be inappropriate and the cost of doing so would essentially outweigh the benefits. This led to the following Financial Reporting Exposure Drafts (FREDs) being issued by the ASB on 29 October 2010:

- FRED 43 *Application of Financial Reporting Standards* originally set out a new three-tier financial reporting framework based on the Consultation Paper issued by the ASB in August 2009. It also set out the reporting criteria which were based on the concept of 'public accountability' and size as well as introducing the concept of a public benefit standard in relation to not-for-profit organisations.

• FRED 44 *Financial Reporting Standard for Medium-Sized Entities* was coined the 'FRSME' and the plan was to replace the previous UK GAAP with this particular standard for those entities that were neither publicly accountable, nor small. The deviation from the International Accounting Standards Board's (IASB) *IFRS for SMEs* was very marginal.

• FRED 45 *Financial Reporting Standard for Public Benefit Entities* dealt with a number of common issues within the not-for-profit sector, but was not a comprehensive standard which would have resulted in not-for-profit organisations referring to the relevant GAAP applicable to them.

1.3   During the commentary period, the ASB received 293 responses and there were several concerns raised by interested parties relating to FREDs 43, 44 and 45. These primarily related to the use of the 'public accountability' approach as well as the three-tier structure which was proposed in FRED 43. The three-tier proposal originally said that only 'non-publicly accountable' bodies could adopt FRED 44 which would have resulted in publicly accountable entities such as pension funds, insurance companies and public sector entities being required to switch from UK GAAP in its previous form to EU-adopted IFRS. This would have resulted in small entities such as small pension funds, insurance companies and public sector entities having to make additional disclosures in their financial statements which would have been inappropriate and overwhelming for the user of those financial statements. In addition to the concerns relating to public accountability, additional concerns were raised concerning:

• the prohibition of the revaluation model in FRED 44 for tangible and intangible fixed assets;

• the use of the 'temporary difference' approach to deferred tax calculations rather than a 'timing difference' approach;

• writing off of borrowing costs incurred on loans for self-constructed assets resulting in a prohibition of the option to capitalise such costs as part of the cost of the asset; and

• hedge accounting of a net investment in a foreign operation in consolidated financial statements.

FRS 102: The Financial Reporting Standard applicable in the United Kingdom and the Republic of Ireland

1.4   In January 2012, following detailed reviews of feedback on their original proposals contained in FREDs 43 to 45, the ASB issued revised exposure drafts as follows:

1.5   *The development of FRS 102*

- FRED 46 *Application of Financial Reporting Requirements*
- FRED 47 *Reduced Disclosure Framework*
- FRED 48 *The Financial Reporting Standard applicable in the UK and Republic of Ireland.*

If adopted, FREDs 46 to 48 would take effect for accounting periods commencing on or after 1 January 2015. FRED 46 would outline which reporting entity would use which standard; FRED 47 offered a reduced disclosure framework for subsidiaries of parents that prepare financial statements under EU-adopted IFRS. The objective here was to enable subsidiaries to take advantage of reduced disclosure requirements to enable them to take advantage of cost savings in the preparation of their financial statements, but without reducing the quality of financial reporting; FRED 48 contained the new UK accounting standards.

1.5   The revised exposure drafts addressed the following concerns raised on the publication of FREDs 43 to 45. They:

- eliminated the tier system for large, small-medium and micro companies;
- introduced accounting treatments that were permissible under the old UK GAAP; and
- incorporated guidance for public benefit entities into FRED 48 rather than having a separate standard.

The new standards

1.6   FREDs 46 to 48 were to become:

- FRS 100 *Application of Financial Reporting Requirements*;
- FRS 101 *Reduced Disclosure Framework*; and
- FRS 102 *The Financial Reporting Standard applicable in the United Kingdom and Republic of Ireland.*

FRS 100 and 101 were issued by the Financial Reporting Council (FRC) on 22 November 2012, but FRS 102 was delayed due to the reexposure of certain areas of the draft standard – notably in respect of defined benefit pension schemes and service concession arrangements.

At its board meeting on 5 March 2013, the FRC finally approved FRS 102 and this will take mandatory effect for accounting periods commencing on or after 1 January 2015, although earlier adoption is permissible (as is the case with FRS 100 and 101). FRS 103 *Insurance Contracts* will also be published as a separate standard (at the time of writing this was still in the development stage).

Both FRS 100 and 101 are mandatorily effective for accounting periods commencing on or after 1 January 2015. However, group entities are being encouraged to adopt these standards earlier as they can be applied for year-ends ending on or after 1 October 2012 due to legislation being introduced which allows companies that are not required to apply EU-adopted IFRS by the *IAS Regulation* more flexibility to change their accounting framework to FRS 101 or FRS 102. This may be advantageous to groups that had a 31 December 2012 year-end considering that the disclosure requirements in EU-adopted IFRS are quite vast.

Implementation date

1.7   For reporting entities that do not wish to adopt FRS 102 earlier, it becomes applicable for accounting periods commencing on or after 1 January 2015. However, reporting entities falling under the scope of FRS 102 will have to think about the impact it will have as the first balance sheet to be prepared under the new FRS will be as at 1 January 2014 (assuming a December year-end). There are additional disclosure requirements needed in the year to transition to FRS 102. There is more on these issues in **Chapter 40** which deals with the first-time adoption of FRS 102.

1.8   The structure of financial reporting in the UK and Republic of Ireland will essentially be as follows:

Size of company	FRSSE (January 2015)	FRS 102	EU-adopted IFRS
Small	✓	✓	✓
Medium and unlisted		✓	✓
Listed (including AIM-listed)			✓

The Structure of FRS 102

1.9   Old UK GAAP was split into FRSs, SSAPs and UITF Abstracts all numerically listed, for example FRS 1 *Cash Flow Statements*, FRS 2 *Accounting for Subsidiary Undertakings* and so forth. FRS 102 takes a different approach and lists everything in 'sections' so essentially we have a single FRS with the previous accounting standards contained within separate sections as follows:

1.9   *The development of FRS 102*

Section	Content
1	Scope
2	Concepts and pervasive principles
3	Financial statement presentation
4	Statement of financial position
5	Statement of comprehensive income and income statement
	Appendix: Example showing presentation of discontinued operations
6	Statement of changes in equity and statement of income and retained earnings
7	Statement of cash flows
8	Notes to the financial statements
9	Consolidated and separate financial statements
10	Accounting policies, estimates and errors
11	Basic financial instruments
12	Other financial instruments issues
13	Inventories
14	Investments in associates
15	Investments in joint ventures
16	Investment property
17	Property, plant and equipment
18	Intangible assets other than goodwill
19	Business combinations and goodwill
20	Leases
21	Provisions and contingencies
	Appendix: Examples of recognising and measuring provisions
22	Liabilities and equity
	Appendix: Example of the issuer's accounting for convertible debt
23	Revenue
	Appendix: Examples of revenue recognition
24	Government grants
25	Borrowing costs
26	Share-based payment

The following are contained in FRS 102 as Appendices:

Focus

Contrast FRS 102 with the old UK GAAP in which each standard/SSAP and Task Force Abstract were numbered sequentially. Structuring FRS 102 in 'sections' rather than by standard number makes it more accessible and much easier to refer to.

Although Appendix II outlines the significant differences between FRS 102 and IFRS for SMEs, FRS 102 does not give a clear table of comparison with the old UK GAAP. Indeed, a new financial reporting framework brings with it new accounting methodologies and preparers will need an appreciation of how FRS 102 differs from the old UK GAAP as there are some quite significant variations between the two. **Chapter 4** outlines the differences.

Reporting Entities in the Republic of Ireland

1.10   As companies in the Republic of Ireland will be mandated under Irish companies legislation, Appendix IV to FRS 100 *Application of Financial Reporting Requirements* contains a useful table which outlines the provisions in the *Companies Act 1963–2012* and related Regulations which implement EC Accounting Directives (Irish company law) and correspond to the provisions of the UK's *Companies Act 2006* and the *UK Large and Medium-sized Companies and Groups (Accounts and Reports) Regulations 2008 (SI 2008/410)*.

SUMMARY – WHAT IS DIFFERENT FROM THE PREVIOUS UK GAAP?

- The fundamental principles within UK GAAP remain largely unchanged, but in some areas they have become more principle based; this, in turn, will require more judgement on the part of management.

- FRS 102 is a standalone standard. In the rare instance that it does not cover a transaction or event, management is to develop an accounting policy having reference to Section 2, Concepts and Pervasive Principles (see **Chapter 2**).

- Previous standards in the UK and Republic of Ireland were set by the Accounting Standards Board. However this has been superseded by the Accounting Council of the Financial Reporting Council (FRC). The FRC is responsible for the final approval standards.

Chapter 2

The concepts and pervasive principles

SIGNPOSTS

- The *Concepts and Pervasive Principles* outline the qualitative characteristics of financial statements and explains how items are classified among assets, liabilities, income, expenses and equity (see **2.1** and **2.7**).

- FRS 102 requires reporting entities to report the commercial *substance* of a transaction and not its legal form. This is particularly prevalent among leasing transactions where the substance of the transaction is an asset which is legally owned by the lessor (see **2.2**).

- The *Concepts and Pervasive Principles* do not have the same force of any sections of FRS 102 and where there is conflict between the *Concepts and Pervasive Principles* and any specific requirements of a section of FRS 102, the section will prevail (see **2.3**).

- General purpose financial statements prepared under FRS 102 are prepared with the user in mind and not what those charged with stewardship of a company wish to report. This is to avoid the financial statements being manipulated to achieve a desired outcome (see **2.5**).

- There are ten qualitative characteristics which general purpose financial statements must possess to ensure they give a true and fair view and enable the user of the financial statements to make rational, economic decisions based on the financial information (see **2.6**).

- Transactions are reported in the financial statements when it is probable that any future economic benefits associated with the item will flow to or from the entity and the item has a cost or value that can be measured reliably and can be subsequently measured using the historical cost model or the revaluation model (see **2.8** and **2.10**).

- Contingent assets and contingent liabilities are never recognised in the financial statements, but are instead disclosed as appropriate in the notes to the financial statements (with the exception of contingent liabilities of an acquiree in a business combination) (see **2.11** and **2.12**).

- Assets and liabilities and income and expenses should never be offset against each other unless specifically required by a relevant section of FRS 102 (see **2.17**).

- The concept of going concern is critical in the preparation of financial statements and management must assess the entity's ability to continue as a going concern for a period which is at least, but is not limited to, 12 months from the date when the financial statements are authorised for issue (see **2.18**).

INTRODUCTION

2.1　The *Concepts and Pervasive Principles* underpin the preparation of financial statements. In the previous UK GAAP such concepts were found in the Statement of Principles and Section 2 essentially has the same objective. The *Concepts and Pervasive Principles* sets out the objective of financial statements, outlines the qualitative characteristics of information present in the financial statements and explains how items in the financial statements should be classified among assets, liabilities, income, expense and equity.

2.2　One of the main fundamental principles is the concept of *substance over form*. This is a principle that has been established in UK GAAP for many years and works on the basis that a reporting entity must report the economic substance of transactions – that is a transaction's *commercial reality* – and not its legal form. This is best illustrated in **Chapter 15** which deals with leasing where an asset subject to a finance lease is treated as an *owned* asset because the characteristics of the lease suggest the entity has the benefit of using an asset to generate economic benefits for the entity whilst at the same time being obliged to pay the lessor periodic rentals to use that asset. The concept of substance over form, therefore, is not to report the legal structure of transactions, but to report the commercial reality of transactions.

2.3　Whilst the *Concepts and Pervasive Principles* is essentially the 'backbone' of financial statement preparation, it does not have the force of an accounting standard. Where conflicts arise between the requirements of a section within FRS 102 and the *Concepts and Pervasive Principles*, the relevant section within FRS 102 will always prevail.

> **Focus**
>
> The *Concepts and Pervasive Principles* essentially serve to enable the Financial Reporting Council to introduce new accounting standards, as well as to amend existing ones, by embedding a principle that financial statements are prepared for the purposes of providing financial information to users that enables them to arrive at rational decisions. In addition to this principle, it enables those preparing financial statements to apply standards to transactions and events and to deal with issues which are not covered by an accounting standard.

OBJECTIVE OF FINANCIAL STATEMENTS

2.4   The *Concepts and Pervasive Principles* outline the objective of financial statements, purely from the perspective of the *user* of the financial statements. In essence, the *Concepts and Pervasive Principles* is not interested in the results that management and those charged with stewardship of the entity want to report – it is concerned with what stakeholders (such as shareholders, HM Revenue and Customs, financiers, and other such third parties) – want to see reported. It is for this reason that the *Concepts and Pervasive Principles* is explicit on what should be reported as assets, liabilities, income, expenses and equity in an attempt to prohibit management and those charged with stewardship of the entity from manipulating the financial statements.

2.5   The overall objective of financial statements according to the *Concepts and Pervasive Principles* is to provide information about the financial position, performance and cash flows of the reporting entity which is useful to enable third parties to make rational decisions about the entity where those users are not in a position to demand reports that are tailored to meet particular information needs.

Whilst internal management accounts may take a particular 'house style' and contain certain information relevant to the reporting entity, *general purpose* financial statements must follow a prescribed format laid down in both *Companies Act 2006* and FRS 102. This not only ensures compliance with legislation and accounting standards, but also ensures consistent financial reporting among entities within the scope of FRS 102.

THE QUALITATIVE CHARACTERISTICS

2.6   The *Concepts and Pervasive Principles* contain ten key characteristics which must be present in all general purpose financial statements that are prepared under FRS 102 as follows:

- understandability;
- relevance;
- materiality;
- reliability;
- substance over form;
- prudence;
- completeness;
- comparability;
- timeliness; and
- balance between benefit and cost.

Understandability

2.7   Clearly financial statements must be presented in an understandable manner. The *Concepts and Pervasive Principles* acknowledge that information should be presented in such a way so as to make it comprehensible by users who have an adequate degree of knowledge about the entity and economic activities as well as accounting and who are prepared to study the information presented with reasonable diligence. An important point within this particular concept is that information should not be omitted on the grounds that it may be too complicated for some users to understand.

Relevance

2.8   Information presented in general-purpose financial statements must be relevant to aid the decision-making of users. The *Concepts and Pervasive Principles* acknowledge that information is relevant when it is capable of influencing the economic decisions of users by helping them to evaluate past, present or future events or confirming, or correcting, their past evaluations.

Materiality

2.9   The concept of materiality has been an important principle for many years and is as important today as it was many years ago. The *Concepts and Pervasive Principles* confirm that information is material – and therefore has relevance – if its omission or misstatement, both individually or collectively, could influence the economic decisions of users taken on the basis of the financial statements.

Materiality is not something that can be pre-determined or quantified as a whole – it is purely entity specific. How material an item is will depend on the size and nature of the entity and the size and nature of the omission or misstatement. The *Concepts and Pervasive Principles* state that it is inappropriate to make, or leave uncorrected, immaterial departures from FRS 102 to achieve a particular presentation of an entity's financial position, financial performance or cash flow.

Reliability

2.10   Reliability is influenced by materiality in that the *Concepts and Pervasive Principles* consider information to be reliable when it is free from material error and bias and represents faithfully that which it either purports to represent or could reasonably be expected to represent. To achieve reliability, financial statements must not be manipulated in such a way as to achieve a desired outcome (eg by employing methods to achieve off-balance sheet finance).

Substance over form

2.11   This concept was looked at earlier in the chapter and is one of the key qualitative characteristics of financial statements. In essence, financial statements must report the commercial reality of transactions and not their legal form. The *Concepts and Pervasive Principles* acknowledge that such a characteristic will enhance the reliability of financial statements.

Prudence

2.12   Prudence is a long-established principle in financial reporting and is the inclusion of a degree of caution in the preparation of financial statements. It works on the basis that assets and income are not overstated whilst liabilities and expenses should not be understated (one could argue that it works on the 'worst case scenario' approach). A key example of this is in relation to construction contracts. If losses are foreseen on a construction contract, they must be recognised within the financial statements as soon as they are foreseen, not when they are actually incurred.

Completeness

2.13   Information presented within the financial statements must be complete within the boundaries of materiality and cost. The *Concepts and Pervasive Principles* acknowledge that financial information will be misleading and unreliable in terms of its relevance if the information presented in the financial statements is not complete.

Comparability

2.14   In order to make rational, economic decisions, users of the financial statements must be able to compare the results from one period to another or between different entities in the same sector to evaluate the financial position, performance and cash flows of the entity. It is for this very reason that financial statements must also disclose the reporting entity's critical accounting policies as well as details of any changes in those accounting policies, together with the effects of such changes.

Timeliness

2.15   The *Concepts and Pervasive Principles* acknowledge that *timeliness* involves providing the information within the decision timeframe. It works on the basis that information is more relevant the sooner it is presented (eg financial information may well lose its relevance if a significant period of time has elapsed). However, in contrast, some financial information may well become more relevant with the passage of time (eg assessing trends).

Balance between benefit and cost

2.16   The costs of providing information to users should not exceed the benefits of such provision. The *Concepts and Pervasive Principles* acknowledge that such evaluations of cost and benefit is substantially a judgemental process. It also acknowledges that financial reporting information assists capital providers in making better decisions, which in turn, results in more efficient functioning of capital markets and a lower cost of capital for the economy as a whole. From an individual-entity level, such entities will enjoy improved access to capital markets and perhaps also lower costs of capital. Benefits may also include better management decisions on the grounds that financial information prepared for internal use is essentially based on (at least partly) information that is prepared for general purpose financial reporting purposes.

Focus

The *accruals* basis of preparing financial statements is a central theme in financial reporting. Financial statements must recognise all transactions as and when they happen, not when they are paid or received in cash or other assets. The financial statements must be prepared on a *going concern* basis when it is presumed that the entity will remain in business for at least 12 months from the date of approval of the financial statements. The going concern presumption is *not* appropriate if management intends to cease trading or liquidate the business, or has no realistic alternative but to do so.

THE ELEMENTS OF FINANCIAL STATEMENTS

2.17   The *elements* of financial statements are split between those reported in a company's statement of financial position (the balance sheet), those reported in the company's income statement (profit and loss account) and those reported in the statement of cash flows (cash flow statement) and are classified as follows:

- assets
- liabilities
- equity
- income
- expenses.

Focus

FRS 102 uses international terminology such as statement of financial position for the balance sheet, statement of comprehensive income for the profit and loss account, statement of cash flows for the cash flow statement and other comprehensive income for the statement of total recognised gains and losses. There is flexibility allowed in the titles given to the primary financial statements as per FRS 102, paragraph 3.22 provided that the titles given are not misleading.

Assets

2.18   Assets are those items that contribute directly to economic-benefit-generating items and can be both tangible (ie they possess a physical form) or intangible (ie they do not possess a physical form). Cash flows that arise from assets can come primarily from two forms: use of the asset or the disposal of the asset. The definition of an asset has become wider in its scope over the years and is not simply something an entity owns. The concept of ownership is not essential in determining whether an item qualifies for recognition in an entity's balance sheet – indeed finance leases are a particularly good example of such assets where the asset's legal ownership remains with one party – whilst the substance of the transaction at individual entity level says that the company does have the right to recognise an asset on its balance sheet because the *risks and rewards* of ownership of such an asset lies with the entity.

The key principle in asset recognition under FRS 102 is to determine who controls the benefits that are expected to flow from the asset in question. If it is the entity itself, then recognition on the company's balance sheet is appropriate.

15

Liabilities

2.19   Likewise, with liabilities, the definition has become much wider in its scope over the years. The key to recognising whether or not a liability exists is to determine whether the entity has a present obligation to act or perform in a particular way. Usually it is fairly clear when a reporting entity has a liability, however, there are occasions when it is not as clear cut – such as determining whether events give rise to a provision being recognised in the balance sheet, or whether disclosure as a contingent liability is more appropriate (see **Chapter 5**). There are generally two situations that will give rise to a liability on the part of the reporting entity:

- a legal obligation; and

- a constructive obligation.

A *legal* obligation is legally enforceable as part of a binding contract or a statutory requirement, whereas a *constructive* obligation is an obligation that derives from an entity's actions because of:

- an established pattern of past practice, published policies or a sufficient specific current statement; and

- as a result the entity has created a valid expectation in the minds of those other parties that it will discharge its responsibilities.

Example 2.1 – A constructive obligation

The Bury Corporation has been in existence for more than 30 years and buys and sells retail merchandise. The company has always enjoyed market domination and has been rapidly expanding, quite successfully, over recent years. A few years after the company commenced trading, the directors offered a bonus incentive to its management. Where pre-tax profit was over a certain benchmark figure, the company would pay a 1% bonus to the management and staff for profits in excess of the benchmark. The management accounts for the year ended 28 February 2014 currently show that profitability is over the benchmark. The last meeting of the management team occurred on 31 January 2014, where it was announced that profitability would be over the benchmark threshold. The reporting accountant is, therefore, proposing to recognise a provision for a bonus in the 2014 year-end financial statements.

The fact that the company has – based on a pre-determined formula – always paid bonuses and that in the meeting held on 31 January 2014 it was

---

announced that the company was already over the benchmark figure, creates an expectation in the minds of the management team that they will be receiving a bonus. The creation of this expectation gives rise to a constructive obligation and – provided the provision can be estimated reliably and there will be an outflow of economic benefits required to settle the liability – the company can recognise the bonus in the financial statements of the company for the year ended 28 February 2014.

Equity

2.20   Equity is simply the residual left over in the net assets of an entity after all its liabilities have been deducted (eg the retained earnings of a company that are reinvested back into the company).

Income

2.21   Income is split between two components:

- income from revenue; and

- income from gains.

It is important to emphasise that the two components are very different. Revenue is income that arises through the entity undertaking ordinary business activities. For example, a motor dealership would derive revenue from the sale of cars and a clothing retailer would derive revenue from selling clothes to its customers.

Income from gains arises when an entity enters into transactions that are not revenue-based transactions. For example, a manufacturer of office furniture may sell an item of machinery used in the production of office furniture at a profit. The profit made on this disposal would be reported as a gain on disposal of plant and machinery and not as a revenue transaction.

Expenses

2.22   Likewise with income, expenses can be split into two major component parts:

- expenses in the ordinary course of activities; and

- losses.

Expenses incurred in the ordinary course of activities would include items such as cost of sales, wages and salaries, depreciation, motor expenses and such like and would be reported in the profit and loss account under their relevant line item headings. The *Concepts and Pervasive Principles* confirm that expenses usually take the form of an outflow or depletion of assets. An outflow would be considered an outflow of cash, whereas a depletion of assets would normally take the form of depreciation or amortisation.

Losses are transactions that the company enters into that are not part of ordinary business activities. Such losses are normally reported separately in the profit and loss account, or statement of changes in equity.

Example 2.2 – Losses

The Breary Group is a manufacturer of plastic masterbatches that are used for colouring plastics. It is a very plant-intensive company and has a year-end of 31 December 2013. On 20 October 2013, it sold an item of machinery with a net book value of £7,000 for £6,200.

The difference between the net book value of the equipment (£7,000) and the sales proceeds (£6,200) is £800. This represents a loss on disposal of the equipment and will be reported separately within the profit and loss account as 'Loss on disposal of fixed assets'.

RECOGNITION AND MEASUREMENT OF ITEMS WITHIN THE FINANCIAL STATEMENTS

2.23   Transactions should be recognised in the financial statements when the transaction satisfies the following criteria:

- it is probable that any future economic benefit associated with the item will flow to or from the entity; and

- the item has a cost or value that can be measured reliably.

Focus

It is important to appreciate that a failure to recognise transactions within the financial statements is not rectified by the disclosure of accounting policies or by way of explanatory note in the financial statements.

2.24   If an item does not qualify at the time for recognition within the financial statements, it may qualify at a later date. Such items, whilst not being recognised in the financial statements, may well warrant additional disclosure in the notes or explanatory material or in supplementary schedules.

2.25 *Measurement* refers to the process of determining the monetary amounts at which an entity measures assets, liabilities, income and expenses within its financial statements. There are two permissible measurement techniques in FRS 102:

- historical cost; and

- fair value.

Historical cost is the amount of cash or cash equivalents that an entity pays, or the fair value of the consideration given, to acquire assets at the time of acquisition. For liabilities, historical cost is the amount of proceeds, cash or cash equivalents received or the fair value of non-cash assets received in exchange for the obligation at the time the obligation is incurred. The phrase *amortised historical cost* refers to the historical cost of an asset or liability plus or minus that portion of its historical cost previously recognised as an expense or income.

Fair value is the amount for which an asset could be exchanged, a liability settled or an equity instrument granted between knowledgeable and willing parties in an arm's-length transaction.

2.26 An *asset* must be recognised in an entity's balance sheet when it is probable that the future economic benefits associated with the asset will flow to the entity and the entity can place a reliable value on the asset. *Contingent assets* are never recognised in an entity's balance sheet, but are instead disclosed, as appropriate, in the notes to the financial statements.

2.27 A *liability* is recognised when three criteria have been met:

- the entity has an obligation at the end of the reporting period as a result of a past event;

- it is probable that the entity will be required to transfer resources embodying economic benefits in settlement; and

- the settlement amount can be measured reliably.

As with *contingent assets*, a *contingent liability* is never recognised in the financial statements because such liabilities fail to meet the recognition criteria. Instead, such contingent liabilities are disclosed as appropriate in the notes to the financial statements. However, contingent liabilities of an acquiree in a business combination are recognised in accordance with FRS 102, paragraph 2.4.

Focus

The definition of a liability is featured quite heavily in Section 21, Provisions and Contingencies. This is covered in **Chapter 22**.

2.28 *Income* is recognised in the statement of comprehensive income (or income statement, if presented) when an increase in future economic benefits related to an increase in an asset, or the decrease of a liability has arisen and the amount of the income can be measured reliably.

2.29 *Expenses* are recognised in the entity's income statement when a decrease in future economic benefits related to a decrease in an asset or the increase in a liability has arisen and the amount of the expense can be measured reliably.

SUBSEQUENT MEASUREMENT OF ITEMS WITHIN THE FINANCIAL STATEMENTS

2.30 Paragraphs 2.47 and 2.48 to FRS 102 outline the subsequent measurement of both financial assets and financial liabilities. The two paragraphs require basic financial assets and basic financial liabilities to be measured at amortised cost less impairment with the following exceptions:

- investments in non-convertible preference shares and non-puttable ordinary and preference shares that are *publicly traded* or whose fair value can otherwise be measured reliably, which are measured at fair value with changes in fair value recognised in profit or loss; and

- any financial instruments that upon their initial recognition were designated by the entity as at fair value through profit or loss.

2.31 Paragraphs 2.49 to 2.50 deal with the subsequent measurement of non-financial assets and paragraph 2.49 acknowledges that most non-financial assets that are initially recognised under the historical cost model are then subsequently measured under another basis. For example:

- some fixed assets are initially recognised at historic cost, but are then subsequently measured using the fair value model; and

- stocks are measured at the lower of cost and net realisable value less costs to complete and sell.

FRS 102 also permits (or even requires) measurement of some non-financial assets at fair value such as:

- Investments in associates and joint ventures which an entity measures at fair value (see **Chapter 31**).

- Investment property that is valued at fair value (see **Chapter 13**).

- Biological assets that an entity will measure at fair value less estimated costs to sell and agricultural produce that an entity measures, at the point of harvest, at fair value less estimated costs to sell (see **Chapter 16**).

- Property, plant and equipment that an entity measures under the revaluation model (see **Chapter 12**).

- Intangible assets that an entity measures under the revaluation model (see **Chapter 14**).

OFFSETTING ASSETS AND LIABILITIES AND INCOME AND EXPENSES

2.32   Reporting entities are prohibited from offsetting assets against liabilities and income against expenses unless required or permitted by a section of FRS 102. Paragraph 2.52 (a) and (b) confirms that:

- measuring assets net of valuation allowances (eg allowances for inventory obsolescence and allowances for uncollectible receivables) is not offsetting; and

- if an entity's normal *operating activities* do not include buying and selling *fixed assets*, including investments and operating assets, then the entity reports gains and losses on disposal of such assets by deducting from the proceeds on disposal the *carrying amount* of the assets and related selling expenses.

Example 2.3 – Offsetting

Cahill Corp Limited (Cahill) is a company based in the UK that has adopted FRS 102 for its accounting year-end to 31 December 2015. Cahill purchased an item of machinery for £60,000 cash and received a government grant towards the cost of this asset for £20,000. The useful economic life of the item of machinery is ten years, with an estimated residual value of zero. The finance director has offset the grant against the original cost of the machine and is recognising the grant in profit or loss by way of reduced depreciation charges.

The offsetting of the grant against the cost of the machine is in contravention of paragraph 24.5G of FRS 102 which states:

'Where part of a grant relating to an asset is deferred it shall be recognised as deferred income and not deducted from the *carrying amount* of the asset.'

In addition to this prohibition, the Companies Act 2006 prohibits offsetting because the statutory definitions of 'purchase price' and 'production costs' do not make any provision for any deduction from that amount in respect

---

of a grant. As a result, Cahill must recognise any unamortised grants as a liability within the balance sheet as deferred income as follows:

On initial recognition

DR fixed asset additions	£60,000
CR cash at bank	£60,000

Being initial recognition of new machine

Grant receipt

DR cash at bank	£20,000
CR deferred income	£20,000

Being receipt of grant

Depreciation

DR depreciation charges	£6,000
CR accumulated depreciation	£6,000

Being depreciation charge for one year

Grant release over life of the asset

DR deferred income	£2,000
CR grant income	£2,000

Being one year's worth of grant income

Focus

The fact that a general bad debt provision may be offset against trade debtors; or a write-down of inventory might be credited from inventory in the balance sheet does not constitute offsetting in this context. These are merely allowances against the carrying amount rather than offsetting a liability against an asset.

GOING CONCERN

2.33 The concept of going concern is critical in the preparation of financial statements. Paragraphs 3.8 and 3.9 cover the issue of going concern and these paragraphs require management of an entity to make an assessment of the entity's ability to continue as a going concern. The presumption is that an entity will continue to be a going concern unless management intends to liquidate the entity or to cease trading, or has no realistic alternative but to do so.

Example 2.4 – Assessing going concern

Whatmough Enterprises Ltd has prepared financial statements to 31 October 2013 and is due to authorise these for issue on 4 January 2014. Management has undertaken an assessment of the company's ability to continue as a going concern and has used the period from 1 November 2013 to 31 October 2014 by reviewing current order levels, forecasts and internal management accounts.

Management is incorrect in assessing a going concern for the period 1 November 2013 to 31 October 2014 as paragraph 3.8 to FRS 102 states that '... management takes into account all available information about the future, which is at least, but is not limited to, twelve months from the date when the financial statements are authorised for issue'. As a result, management needs to conduct a going concern review for the 12 months from 4 January 2014 in order to comply with paragraph 3.8.

2.34   There may be situations when management is uncertain as to whether the entity is a going concern. Such situations can occur, for example, during times of financial distress, economic recession, retraction in the market or when banks or financial institutions indicate their unwillingness to renew borrowing facilities. Paragraph 3.9 requires management to disclose uncertainties when it is aware of events or conditions that cast significant doubt upon the entity's ability to continue as a going concern.

In addition, paragraph 3.9 also says that when management deems the going-concern basis to be inappropriate (in other words the financial statements are not prepared on a going concern basis), disclosure must be made in the financial statements of the basis on which management have prepared the financial statements (such as the 'break up' basis) and also disclose the reasons why the entity is not regarded as a going concern. There may also be a need for the entity to make provisions for closure costs and losses to the date of termination, including redundancies and penalties for early termination of various contracts that may be in subsistence.

Example 2.5 – Going concern basis inappropriate

Scanlon Limited has a year-end of 31 October each year and is currently preparing the financial statements to 31 October 2013. The company's profitability has declined at a rapid rate over the last few months and the company is suffering from cash flow difficulties. The company's bankers have indicated that they are unwilling to renew borrowing facilities (which are to be reviewed on 6 November 2013) and have also informed management that they intend to 'call in' its overdraft and a loan. The directors have failed to secure finance to meet this repayment and they, themselves, have no resources available to enable the company to meet such repayments. As a consequence, management has concluded that it has no realistic alternative but to liquidate the company with immediate effect.

Management has declared the going concern basis inappropriate for the financial statements as at 31 October 2013 and has prepared the financial statements on a 'break up' basis. All fixed assets have been reclassified as current assets at fair values and all long-term liabilities have been reassigned as current liabilities. Disclosure has been made as follows in the explanatory notes to the financial statements:

Going concern

The financial statements have not been prepared on a going concern basis, but have been prepared under the break-up basis. The entity is not regarded as a going concern as the company has failed to negotiate renewed borrowing facilities to enable it to continue as a going concern. Under the break-up basis, all fixed assets have been reclassified as current assets at their market value and all long-term liabilities have been reclassified as current liabilities.

SUMMARY – WHAT IS DIFFERENT FROM THE PREVIOUS UK GAAP?

- FRS 102 contains more 'qualitative characteristics' than previous UK GAAP which focused on:
    - relevance;
    - reliability;
    - comparability;
    - understandability; and
    - materiality.

- In FRS 102, there are additional qualitative characteristics as follows:
    - substance over form;
    - prudence;
    - completeness;
    - timeliness; and
    - balance between benefit and cost.

- The elements of the financial statements are defined differently in FRS 102 than in the previous *Statement of Principles*, although the effect is still the same.

Chapter 3

Accounting policies, estimates and errors

SIGNPOSTS

- Reporting entities must select accounting policies that are appropriate to the entity's specific requirements and apply them consistently and make disclosure of such within their financial statements (see **3.5**).

- FRS 102, paragraphs 8.4 and 8.5 require disclosure of significant accounting policies.

- FRS 102, paragraphs 8.6 and 8.7 require disclosure of judgements and key sources of estimation uncertainty – this was not required under previous UK GAAP (see **3.12–3.14**).

- There are two conditions that have to be considered before a reporting entity can change their accounting policy (see **3.15**).

- Changes in accounting policies are not the same as changes in accounting estimates. Accounting policy changes are applied retrospectively while accounting estimate changes are applied prospectively (see **3.17** and **3.24**).

- Material prior period errors must be corrected by way of a retrospective prior year adjustment while immaterial errors can be corrected in the current year (see **3.25**).

- A reporting entity is required to make additional disclosures concerning changes to their accounting policies, estimates and error correction (see **3.27** onwards).

INTRODUCTION

3.1   Accounting policies, estimates and errors are dealt with in Section 10 of FRS 102. This particular section outlines the need for a reporting entity to select appropriate accounting policies and estimations, apply them consistently and make certain disclosures within their financial statements. This enables the user of the financial statements to evaluate the effect that the entity's chosen accounting policies and estimation techniques have on the financial statements.

3.2   Section 10 also covers the matter of error correction and outlines the situation when errors must be corrected retrospectively; that is when the prior year/period reported in the financial statements is restated and the balance on the opening profit and loss reserves is amended to take account of the error. It is generally accepted within the accountancy profession that over- or under-estimations of figures such as accruals, taxation provisions and stock provisions will often occur. Generally these estimations are immaterial to the financial statements themselves and will simply be adjusted in the current year's financial statements without the need for a prior year adjustment.

However, Section 10 refers to *material* errors which will need correction by way of a prior period adjustment. In the previous UK GAAP, FRS 3 *Reporting Financial Performance* referred to *fundamental errors* which were defined as those errors which effectively destroy the truth and fairness of the financial statements. Section 10 merely refers to *material* errors and therefore judgement on the part of the accountant will be required to ascertain whether an error is material or immaterial.

DEFINITIONS

3.3   FRS 102, paragraph 10.2 defines *accounting policies* as the specific principles, bases, conventions, rules and practices applied by an entity in preparing and presenting financial statements.

3.4   FRS 102, paragraph 10.19 defines *prior period errors* as omissions from, and misstatements in, the entity's financial statements for one or more prior periods arising from a failure to use, or misuse of, reliable information that:

(a)   was available when financial statements for those periods were authorised for issue; and

(b)   could reasonably be expected to have been obtained and taken into account in the preparation and presentation of those financial statements.

Selecting and Applying Accounting Policies

3.5   Reporting entities are required to select accounting policies that are appropriate in their specific circumstances. An example of an accounting policy that may involve different practices is the capitalisation of borrowing costs – some entities may capitalise the borrowing costs while others may write them off immediately to profit or loss as and when they are incurred.

3.6 Measurement bases are the way in which monetary attributes are measured, such as at depreciated historic cost or at revaluation, lower of cost or net realisable or recoverable amount. Some typical examples of accounting policies which may involve different measurement bases are measuring:

- the entity's fixed assets at cost or at fair value; and

- inventories (stock) using first-in first-out or weighted average cost.

Different entities will present items within the financial statements in different places, for example some entities may disclose depreciation charges within cost of sales, while others may disclose depreciation charges within administrative expenses.

3.7 Disclosure of a company's material accounting policies should be made within the financial statements. The level of disclosure must be sufficient in order for users to understand the accounting policies that the reporting entity has adopted.

3.8 FRS 102, paragraphs 8.4 and 8.5 require disclosure of a summary of significant accounting policies (see **Example 3.7** below).

3.9 There are some situations when a transaction or event may arise within a reporting entity that may not be specifically covered by FRS 102. In such situations, paragraph 10.4 requires management to exercise judgement in developing and applying an accounting policy. In doing so, management are required to ensure that the accounting policy they develop and apply is:

(a) *relevant* to the economic decision-making needs of users; and

(b) *reliable* in that the financial statements:

    (i) represent faithfully the *financial position,* financial *performance* and *cash flows* of the entity;

    (ii) reflect the economic substance of transactions, other events and conditions, and not merely the legal form;

    (iii) are neutral (ie free from bias);

    (iv) are prudent; and

    (v) are complete in all material respects.

3.10 In addition to the above, paragraph 10.5 requires management to consider other sources (in descending order) to develop and apply an appropriate accounting policy. These sources are:

(a) the requirements and guidance in FRS 102 dealing with similar and related issues;

(b)   where an entity's financial statements are within the scope of a *Statement of Recommended Practice* (SORP) the requirements and guidance in that SORP dealing with similar and related issues; and

(c)   the definitions, *recognition* criteria and *measurement* concepts for assets, liabilities, income and expenses and the pervasive principles in Section 2, Concepts and Pervasive Principles (see **Chapter 2**).

3.11   When a reporting entity has chosen accounting policies that are specific to its individual circumstances, FRS 102, paragraph 10.7 requires such policies to be applied consistently from one accounting period to the next.

Information about judgements and key sources of estimation uncertainty

3.12   FRS 102, paragraphs 8.6 and 8.7 require specific disclosures (these are new and were not required by UK GAAP).

3.13   An entity should disclose the judgements (apart from those involving estimations – see immediately below) that management has made in the process of applying the entity's accounting policies and which have the most significant effect on the amounts recognised in the financial statements (FRS 102, paragraph 8.6). These disclosures must be given either in the statement of accounting policies or in the notes to the financial statements

3.14   The notes to the financial statements should provide information regarding certain key assumptions (FRS 102, paragraph 8.7). These are assumptions concerning the future and assumptions regarding key sources of estimation uncertainty at the reporting date. The particular focus is those assumptions that have a significant risk of causing a material adjustment to the carrying amounts of assets and liabilities within the next financial year.

As regards those assets and liabilities, the notes should give details of:

●   their nature; and

●   their carrying amount as at the end of the reporting period.

Example 3.1 – Judgements and key sources of estimation uncertainty

Extract from notes to the financial statements

Key assumptions and significant judgements

The preparation of financial statements under the Financial Reporting Standard applicable in the UK and the Republic of Ireland requires the

---

company to make estimates and assumptions that affect the application of policies and reported amounts.

Estimates and judgements are continually evaluated and are based on historical experience and other factors including expectations of future events that are believed to be reasonable under the circumstances. Actual results may differ from these estimates.

The estimates and assumptions which have a significant risk of causing a material adjustment to the carrying amount of assets and liabilities within the next financial year are discussed below:

Impairment of assets

Non-current assets, including goodwill and property, plant and equipment are reviewed for impairment if events or changes in circumstances indicate that the carrying amount may not be recoverable.

When a review for impairment is conducted, the recoverable amount of an asset or cash-generating unit is determined based on value-in-use calculations prepared on the basis of management's assumptions and estimates.

Allowances for doubtful debts

The company maintains allowances for doubtful accounts for estimated losses resulting from the subsequent inability of customers to make required payments. If the financial conditions of customers were to deteriorate, resulting in an impairment of their ability to make payments, additional allowances may be required in future periods.

Inventory provisions

The company periodically reviews inventory for excess amounts, obsolescence and declines in market value below cost and records an allowance against the inventory balance for any such declines. These reviews require management to estimate future demand for products. Possible changes in these estimates could result in revisions to the valuation of inventory in future periods.

Changes to Accounting Policies

3.15　　There are two conditions that must be considered before a reporting entity can change an accounting policy or policies. Paragraph 10.8 outlines these conditions as follows:

(a)　　the change in policy is required because of a change to FRS 102; or

(b)   the change in policy is required because such a change will result in the financial statements providing reliable and more relevant information about the effects of transactions, other events or conditions on the entity's financial position, financial performance or cash flows.

3.16   Paragraph 10.9 outlines three issues which FRS 102 considers *not* to be changes in accounting policy:

(a)   The application of an accounting policy for transactions, other events or conditions that differ in substance from those previously occurring.

(b)   The application of a new accounting policy for transactions, other events or conditions that did not occur previously or were not material.

(c)   A change to the cost model when a reliable measure of fair value is no longer available (or vice versa) for an asset that this FRS would otherwise require or permit to be measured at fair value.

Example 3.2 – Change in accounting policy

Company A Limited provides social housing throughout the United Kingdom. It has previously had an accounting policy that all borrowing costs incurred during the construction of its houses are capitalised within the cost of the fixed assets. However, the directors have considered that it would be more reliable and provide more relevant information if such costs were to be written off to the profit and loss account as and when they are incurred.

In such a situation, paragraph 10.10 would apply and this change would be considered a change in accounting policy because the capitalisation of borrowing costs may be written off to profit or loss or may be capitalised as part of the construction of a qualifying asset.

Applying Changes to an Accounting Policy

3.17   All changes to accounting policies are done by way of *retrospective application*. This means that all changes must be made to all prior periods presented within the financial statements. Changes in accounting policy are made retrospectively so as to provide consistency to the financial statements in order that they portray the fact that the new accounting policy had always been applied.

3.18   To determine whether or not a change in accounting policy has occurred, accountants should ask the following three questions:

1. Has there been a change in the way the entity recognises amounts in the financial statements?

2. Has there been a change in the way the entity measures amounts in the financial statements?

3. Has there been a change in the way the entity presents amounts in the financial statements?

If the answer to any of the above three questions is *yes*, then there has been a change in accounting policy.

3.19   A change to a recognition policy could be if:

● the reporting entity decides to capitalise borrowing costs rather than writing them off to profit or loss as and when they are incurred; or

● there have been changing revenue recognition practices relating to the sale of goods or rendering of services.

3.20   A change to a measurement policy could be where the reporting entity decides to carry buildings in the balance sheet at fair value as opposed to depreciated historic cost.

3.21   A change to a presentation policy would be where a reporting entity decides to present depreciation charges within administrative expenses as opposed to cost of sales. The only effect of this change is to restate the comparative amounts on a comparable basis.

Example 3.3 – Change in accounting policy

Company A Limited has a year-end of 31 July 2013 and is the manufacturer of disposable clothing. In 2012 it valued its inventory on an individual basis. However, 2013 has seen the company expand at a rapid rate, therefore the directors feel that the method of first-in first-out (FIFO) would be more appropriate.

Had the 2012 inventory valuation been valued under FIFO, this would have produced an inventory valuation £10,000 higher than was originally calculated. Profit and loss reserves prior to the accounting policy change amounted to £260,000.

In this example the impact of the adjustment can be shown as follows:

	Financial statements 31 July 2012		
	Pre-adjustment	*Adjustment*	*As restated*
	£	£	£
Turnover	340,000	–	340,000
Cost of sales	115,000	(10,000)	105,000
Administrative expenses	49,000	–	49,000
Net profit *	176,000	(10,000)	186,000

* Taxation implications have been ignored.

To deal with the retrospective application the opening balance of each account shown within reserves (usually profit and loss account reserves) is adjusted for the earliest prior period presented as if the new accounting policy had always been in existence.

When it is impracticable to determine the individual period effects of a change in accounting policy on comparative information, entities should apply the requirements to the carrying amounts of the earliest period where it is practicable (FRS 102, paragraph 10.12).

Applying Changes to Accounting Estimates

3.22   A *change to an accounting estimate* is not the same as a change in accounting policy. This term is defined in the Glossary to FRS 102 as follows:

'A change in accounting estimate is an adjustment of the carrying amount of an asset or a liability, or the amount of a periodic consumption of an asset, that results from the present status of, and expected future benefits and obligations associated with assets and liabilities. Changes in accounting estimates result from new information or new development and, accordingly are not corrections of errors.'

3.23   An example of a common change to an accounting estimate is when a company may change its depreciation rates from say 25% on a reducing balance basis to three years on a straight-line basis. The three questions detailed above are not affected (in other words there is no change to recognition criteria, measurement bases or methods of presentation when depreciation rates are changed) because:

- the fixed assets are still carried at cost less accumulated depreciation;

- the depreciation is still allocated to individual accounting periods which reflect the consumption of the economic benefits of the fixed assets concerned; and

- the fixed assets and depreciation are still presented in the same way in the entity's balance sheet and profit and loss account.

3.24   Paragraph 10.15 says that a change in accounting estimate is an adjustment of the carrying value of an asset or a liability, or the amount of the periodic consumption of an asset that results from the assessment of the present status of, and expected future benefit and obligations associated with, assets and liabilities.

3.25   An important point to emphasise about the nature of accounting estimate changes is that they are *not* correction of errors. Financial statements inherently contain a degree of estimations (such as accruals, tax provisions or bad debt provisions). Paragraph 10.15 acknowledges that changes in accounting estimates that result from new information or developments are not the correction of errors.

Changes in accounting estimates are applied *prospectively*. This means that retrospective application of the accounting estimate change is not required; reporting entities merely apply the change in the current and succeeding accounting periods.

Example 3.4 – Change in accounting estimate

Company A Limited has a policy of depreciating their motor vehicles on a five-year straight-line basis and the financial statements for the year ended 31 October 2013 are in the process of being completed. Management of Company A have decided to change the method of depreciating their motor vehicles to a 25% reducing-balance basis.

Company A will apply the change in the 2013 financial statements and subsequently go forward with their new policy. The 2012 financial statements will not need adjusting as the change is not a change in accounting policy.

Error Correction

3.26   Errors, in the context of Section 10, are the effects of mathematical mistakes, errors in applying the reporting entity's accounting policies, oversights, misinterpretation of facts and fraud. *Material* prior period errors are corrected by retrospective application, whereas *immaterial* prior period errors can be corrected in the current period. Immaterial errors could include over- or under-estimations in respect of accruals, prepayments, tax provisions, stocks and bad debt provisions. Paragraph 10.21 outlines the appropriate accounting treatment for the correction of prior period material errors as follows:

(a)   by restating the comparative amounts for the prior period(s) presented in which the error occurred; or

(b)   if the error occurred before the earliest prior period presented, restating the opening balances of assets, liabilities and equity for the earliest prior period presented.

In some situations the above approach may be impracticable (eg where the error has arisen from a computer systems breakdown). Where retrospective application is impracticable, the correction of the error should be reflected in the financial statements of the current period, with full disclosure of the facts and impact.

Example 3.5 – Correction of immaterial error

Company B Limited is preparing its financial statements for the year ended 30 November 2013. Extracts from the previous year's financial statements are as follows:

	30 November 2012
	£
Turnover	4,325,012
Pre-tax profit	274,201
Net assets	2,774,231

During the preparation of the 2013 financial statements the accountant discovered an electricity bill that had been received on 6 January 2013 amounting to £4,000 (excluding VAT) and which related to the period 1 October 2012 to 31 December 2012.

The materiality of the transaction has to be deciphered and such a bill is clearly immaterial to the financial statements as a whole. Certainly at 0.09% of revenue (£4,000 ÷ £4,325,012 × 100) and 1.5% of pre-tax profit, the fact that a £4,000 electricity bill has been overlooked is not going to have a significant impact on the financial statements. It can simply be corrected in the current year.

Example 3.6 – Correction of material error

The financial statements of Company C Limited for the year ended 31 December 2012 are in the process of being completed. These financial statements are shown below:

Company B Ltd

Profit and Loss Account for the year ended 31 December 2012

	2012	2011
	£'000	*£'000*
Turnover	4,000	3,500
Cost of sales	(950)	(820)
Gross profit	3,050	2,680
Administrative expenses	(1,200)	(800)
Profit on ordinary activities before taxation	1,850	1,880
Tax on profit on ordinary activities	(700)	(600)
Profit for the financial year	1,150	1,280

Company B Ltd

Balance Sheet as at 31 December 2012

	31.12.12		31.12.11	
	£	£	£	£
Tangible fixed assets		5,325,000		4,000,000
Current assets				
Stocks	400,000		300,000	
Trade debtors	175,000		100,000	
Cash at bank	250,000		200,000	
	825,000		600,000	
Creditors: amounts falling due within one year		750,000		350,000
Net current assets		75,000		250,000
Total assets less current liabilities		5,400,000		4,250,000

Capital and reserves

Called up share capital	100,000	100,000
Profit and loss account	5,300,000	4,150,000
	5,400,000	4,250,000

During the preparation of the financial statements for the year ended 31 December 2012, it was noticed that a large item of plant and machinery that had been purchased on 20 December 2011 had been allocated to repairs and renewals within the profit and loss account (shown within administrative expenses) amounting to £325,000. The financial statements above do not contain any amendments to the financial statements in respect of this error, which the partner in charge has deemed to be material. This error will need to be corrected by way of a prior period adjustment.

The administrative expenses in the 2011 financial statements will need to be reduced by £325,000 and the tangible fixed assets will also increase by this amount. However, the depreciation element will also have to be considered so, for the purposes of this illustration, assume that the client writes off the value of all its plant and machinery over five years on a straight-line basis (£325,000 ÷ 5 years) = £65,000 worth of depreciation (note: the tax implications have been ignored for the purposes of this illustration).

Company B Ltd

Profit and loss account for the year ended 31 December 2012

	2012	2011
		(as restated)
	£	£
Turnover	4,000,000	3,500,000
Cost of sales	950,000	820,000
Gross profit	3,050,000	2,680,000
Administrative expenses	1,265,000	540,000
Profit on ordinary activities before taxation	1,785,000	2,140,000
Tax on profit on ordinary activities	700,000	600,000
Profit for the financial year	1,085,000	1,540,000

Company B Ltd

Balance sheet as at 31 December 2012

	31.12.12		31.12.11 (as restated)	
	£	£	£	£
Tangible fixed assets		5,520,000		4,260,000
Current assets				
Stocks	400,000		300,000	
Trade debtors	175,000		100,000	
Cash at bank	250,000		200,000	
	825,000		600,000	
Creditors: amounts falling due within one year		750,000		350,000
Net current assets		75,000		250,000
Total assets less current liabilities		5,595,000		4,510,000
Capital and reserves				
Called up share capital		100,000		100,000
Profit and loss account		5,495,000		4,410,000
		5,595,000		4,510,000

Company B Ltd

Extract from Statement of Changes in Equity for the year ended 31 December 2012

	2012	2011 (as restated)
	£	£
Profit for the financial year	1,085,000	1,540,000
Prior year adjustment		
(as explained in Note 5)	260,000	
Total gains and losses recognised		
since the last annual report	1,345,000	

Note 5	2012
At beginning of the year as previously stated	4,150,000
Prior year adjustment*	260,000
At beginning of year as restated	4,410,000
Profit for the year	1,085,000
At the end of the year	5,495,000
* This has been calculated as:	
Cost of asset capitalised	325,000
Depreciation (5 years)	(65,000)
Prior year adjustment	260,000

DISCLOSURE REQUIREMENTS

3.27   The following disclosures are required to be made within a reporting entity's financial statements concerning changes in accounting policies, changes in accounting estimates and the correction of prior period errors.

Accounting policies

3.28   FRS 102, paragraphs 8.4 and 8.5 require the disclosure of significant accounting policies.

Example 3.7 – Disclosure of significant accounting policies

Note 2 – Basis of preparation and significant accounting policies

These financial statements have been prepared in accordance with the Financial Reporting Standard applicable in the UK and Republic of Ireland (the FRS) issued by the Financial Reporting Council. They are presented in £ sterling.

They have been prepared using the historical cost convention except that as disclosed in the accounting policies below certain items, including property, plant and equipment, and derivatives, are shown at fair value.

The preparation of the financial statements requires management to make estimates and assumptions that affect the reported amounts of revenues, expenses, assets and liabilities and the disclosure of contingent liabilities at the date of the financial statements. If, in the future, such estimates and assumptions, which are based on management's best judgement at the date of the financial statements, deviate from the actual circumstances, the original estimates and assumptions will be modified as appropriate in the year in which the circumstances change. Where necessary, the comparatives have been reclassified or extended from the previously reported results to take into account presentational changes.

The company has applied the following accounting policies:

Revenue

Revenue comprises the fair value of the sale of goods and services net of value added tax, rebates and discounts.

Revenue is recognised as follows:

Sale of goods

Sales of goods are recognised when the company has delivered products to the customer, the customer has accepted the products, and collectibility of the related receivables is fairly assured.

In respect of products sold with a right of return, accumulated experience is used to estimate and provide for such returns at the time of sale.

In respect of products sold with a right of return, accumulated experience is used to estimate and provide for such returns at the time of sale.

Sale of services

Service revenues are recognised as those services are provided to customers. Turnover in respect of service contracts is recognised when the company obtains the right to consideration.

Inventories

Inventories are stated at the lower of cost or net realisable value. Cost is determined on a first-in first-out (FIFO) basis. Net realisable value is the amount that can be realised from the sale of the inventory in the normal course of business after allowing for the costs of realisation.

In addition to the cost of materials and direct labour, an appropriate proportion of production overheads is included in the inventory values.

An allowance is recorded for obsolescence.

Property, plant and equipment

Items of property, plant and equipment are measured at cost or revalued amount less accumulated depreciation and accumulated amortisation. Depreciation is charged so as to allocate the cost or revalued amount of assets, less their residual value over their estimated useful lives, using the straight-line method. Land has an indefinite useful life and is therefore not depreciated. The estimated useful lives of other items of property, plant and equipment are:

- Buildings 60 years

- Machinery 10 years

- Office equipment 3 years.

Revaluation of properties

Freehold and leasehold properties are revalued every five years. Any overall surplus over book value is credited to the revaluation reserve and any overall deficit in excess of historic cost is charged to the profit and loss account in the year of revaluation. In subsequent years transfers are made to retained profits in order to amortise surpluses over the remaining useful lives of the properties. On disposal the profit or loss is calculated by reference to the net book value and any unamortised revaluation surplus is transferred from revaluation reserves to retained profits.

Impairment of assets

Property, plant and equipment are reviewed for impairment if events or changes in circumstances indicate that the carrying amount may not be recoverable. When a review for impairment is conducted, the recoverable amount of an asset or cash-generating unit is determined based on value-in-use calculations prepared on the basis of management's assumptions and estimates.

Goodwill

Goodwill is amortised over its useful life, restricted to a maximum of five years where a reliable estimate of useful life cannot be made.

Internally developed intangibles

Development costs incurred on software development are capitalised when all of the following conditions are satisfied:

- completion of the software module is technically feasible so that it will be available for use;

- the group intends to complete the development of the software module and use it;

- the software will be used in generating probable future economic benefits;

- there are adequate technical, financial and other resources to complete the development and to use the software; and

- the expenditure attributable to the software can be measured reliably.

Management applies judgement based on information available at each balance sheet date when deciding whether the recognition criteria have been met, as the economic success of any development is uncertain and may be subject to future technical problems at the time of recognition. All development activities are subject to continual monitoring by management.

The costs of internally generated intangibles comprises all directly attributable costs necessary to create, produce and prepare the intangible asset to be capable of operating in the manner intended by management. These costs include employee costs specifically incurred on software development.

Amortisation commences upon completion of the intangible asset and the charge is shown within administrative expenses. Development expenditure is amortised over the period expected to benefit.

Prior to completion of the intangible asset, costs capitalised are tested for impairment. After completion, the carrying amount is reviewed at each reporting date in accordance with the group's impairment review procedures.

Development costs not meeting the criteria for capitalisation are expensed as incurred.

Intangibles acquired in a business combination

An intangible asset acquired in a business combination is deemed to have a cost to the group of its fair value as at the acquisition date. This fair value reflects market expectations about the probability that the future economic benefits related to the intangible asset will flow to the group.

Leases

Where assets are financed by leasing agreements that give rights approximating to ownership (finance leases) the assets are treated as if they had been purchased outright. The amount capitalised is the present value of the minimum lease payments payable over the term of the lease. The corresponding liability to the leasing company is included as an obligation under finance leases.

Depreciation on leased assets is charged to the profit and loss account on the same basis as shown above.

Leasing payments are treated as consisting of capital and interest elements, and interest is charged to profit or loss over the lease term using the effective interest method.

The rental cost of properties and other assets held under operating leases are charged to profit and loss account on a straight-line basis. Benefits received as an incentive to sign a lease, whatever form they take, are credited to the profit and loss account on a straight-line basis over the lease term.

Cash and cash equivalents

Cash and cash equivalents comprises cash on hand and time, call and current balances with banks and similar institutions, which are readily convertible to known amounts of cash and which are subject to insignificant risk of changes in value. This definition is also used for the cash flow statement.

Taxes

Income taxes include all taxes based upon the taxable profits of the company. Other taxes not based on income, such as property and capital taxes, are included within operating expenses or financial expenses according to their nature.

Deferred tax is recognised in respect of all timing differences that have originated but not reversed at the reporting date and which will result in an obligation to pay more, or a right to pay less or to receive more tax.

Provision is made for deferred tax on gains arising from the revaluation (and similar fair value adjustments) of fixed assets.

Deferred tax assets are recognised only to the extent that the directors consider that it is more likely than not that there will be suitable taxable profits from which the future reversal of the underlying timing differences can be deducted.

Deferred tax is measured on an undiscounted basis at the tax rates that are expected to apply in the periods in which the timing difference reverses, based on tax rates and laws that have been enacted, or substantively enacted, by the reporting date.

Current and deferred income tax assets and liabilities are offset when the income taxes are levied by the same taxation authority and when there is a legally enforceable right to offset them.

Pensions

The company's contributions to defined contribution plans are charged to the profit and loss account in the period to which the contributions relate.

Provisions

Provisions are recognised where a legal or constructive obligation has been incurred which will probably lead to an outflow of resources that can be reasonably estimated. Provisions are recorded for the estimated ultimate liability that is expected to arise, taking into account the time value of money. A contingent liability is disclosed where the existence of the obligations will only be confirmed by future events, or where the amount of the obligation cannot be measured with reasonable reliability.

Fair values

Fair value is the amount for which a financial asset, liability or instrument could be exchanged between knowledgeable and willing parties in an arm's-length transaction. It is determined by reference to quoted market prices adjusted for estimated transaction costs that would be incurred in an actual transaction, or by the use of established estimation techniques. The fair values at the balance sheet date are approximately in line with their reported carrying values unless specifically mentioned in the notes to the financial statements.

Foreign currency translation

Individual financial statements of entities within the group

Transactions in foreign currencies are recognised in the individual entity's functional currency at the exchange rates at the transaction dates. At the year-end, monetary items denominated in foreign currencies are retranslated at the year-end exchange rate. Non-monetary items measured in terms of historical cost in a foreign currency are not retranslated. Non-monetary items carried at fair value that are denominated in foreign currencies are re-translated at the year-end exchange rate.

All exchange differences are recognised in profit or loss.

Consolidated financial statements

For the purposes of the consolidated financial statements, the results and financial position of each group entity are expressed in £ Sterling which is the functional currency of the parent company and the presentation currency for the consolidated financial statements.

Exchange differences arising from the translation of the financial statements of foreign operations are recognised in other comprehensive income. Exchange differences arising on a monetary item that forms part of the reporting entity's net investment in a foreign operation are also recognised in other comprehensive income. All other exchange differences are recognised in consolidated profit or loss in the period in which they arise.

Financial instruments

Financial assets and financial liabilities are recognised on the balance sheet when the company becomes party to the contractual provisions of the financial instrument.

Trade debtors and trade creditors are initially measured at fair value. Subsequent to initial valuation, they are carried at amortised cost using the effective interest method, less any impairment losses.

Interest-bearing borrowings are recognised initially at fair value less directly attributable transaction costs. Subsequent to initial recognition, interest-bearing borrowings are stated at amortised cost with any difference between cost and redemption value being recognised in the profit and loss account using the effective interest method.

Investments in equity shares which are publicly traded or where the fair value of the shares can otherwise be measured reliably are initially measured at fair value. Transaction costs are charged to profit or loss. The investments are subsequently remeasured in the balance sheet at fair value with changes in fair value are recognised through profit or loss.

Investments in equity shares which are not publicly traded and where the fair value of the shares cannot be measured reliably are initially measured at cost, including transaction costs. The investment is not remeasured except where impairment has been identified.

The company primarily uses forward foreign currency contracts to manage its exposure to fluctuations in foreign exchange rates. The group does not hold derivative financial instruments for trading purposes.

Derivatives are initially recognised at fair value on the date a contract is entered into and are subsequently measured at fair value. The fair values of derivatives are measured using observable market prices, or where market prices are not available, fair values are calculated by reference to forward exchange rates for contracts with similar maturity profiles, or by using discounted expected future cash flows at prevailing interest and exchange rates.

The company does not adopt hedge accounting.

Changes in accounting policy

3.29   A reporting entity can change an accounting policy either if it is required to do so because of a change to FRS 102, or if the change in accounting policy will result in providing reliable and more relevant information for users.

3.30   For accounting policy changes which have arisen because of a change to FRS 102, a reporting entity needs to disclose:

(a)   the nature of the change in accounting policy;

(b)   for the current and each prior period presented, to the extent practicable, the amount of the adjustment for each financial statement line affected;

(c)   the amount of the adjustment relating to periods before those presented, to the extent practicable; and

(d)   an explanation if it is impracticable to determine the amounts to be disclosed in (b) or (c) above.

Paragraph 10.13 to FRS 102 confirms that the financial statements or prior periods do not need to repeat these disclosures.

3.31   For accounting policy changes which have arisen because of voluntary changes due to the change providing reliable and more relevant information for users, the following are required to be disclosed:

(a)   The nature of the change in accounting policy.

(b)   The reasons why applying the new policy provides reliable and more relevant information.

(c)   To the extent practicable, the amount of the adjustment for each financial statement line item affected, shown separately:

(i)   for the current period;

(ii)   for each prior period presented; and

(iii)   in aggregate for periods before those presented.

(d)   An explanation if it is impracticable to determine the amounts to be disclosed in (c) above.

Paragraph 10.14 to FRS 102 confirms that the financial statements of subsequent periods need not repeat the above disclosures.

Changes in accounting estimates

3.32   Reporting entities applying changes to accounting estimates are required to disclose the nature of any change in an accounting estimate together with the effect the change has on assets, liabilities, income and expenses for the current period. These disclosures are necessary to comply with paragraph 10.18 to FRS 102.

Where it is practicable for the entity to estimate the effect of the change in accounting estimate in one or more future periods, the entity shall disclose those estimates.

Correction of prior period errors

3.33   Paragraph 10.23 to FRS 102 requires the following disclosures to be made concerning prior period errors:

(a)   the nature of the prior period error;

(b)   for each prior period presented, to the extent practicable, the amount of the correction for each financial statement line item affected;

(c)   to the extent practicable, the amount of the correction at the beginning of the earliest period presented; and

(d)   an explanation if it is not practicable to determine the amounts to be disclosed in (b) or (c) above.

Paragraph 10.23 also confirms that the financial statements of subsequent periods need not repeat these disclosures.

SUMMARY – WHAT IS DIFFERENT FROM THE PREVIOUS UK GAAP?

The UK GAAP equivalents here are FRS 18 *Accounting Policies* (dealing with accounting policies and estimation techniques), and FRS 3 *Reporting Financial Performance* (which included a reference to correction of fundamental errors – see FRS 3.63).

In practical terms, there are few differences between FRS 102 and the previous UK GAAP, apart from differences of detail noted in the text above and those highlighted below.

Under FRS 102, retrospective restatement is required for errors which are material, whereas previous UK GAAP only required this for errors which were regarded as fundamental. This could result in more retrospective statements under FRS 102 as compared with previous UK GAAP.

Note, the new disclosure requirement regarding information about judgements and key sources of estimation uncertainty (see **3.12–3.14**). Whilst this will inevitably result in a certain amount of boiler-plating, it is important that entities focus on issues which are specific to their particular business.

Chapter 4

The differences between FRS 102 and the previous UK GAAP

SIGNPOSTS

- It had always been the intention of the previous Accounting Standards Board that the UK and Republic of Ireland would report under a financial reporting framework *based on* International Financial Reporting Standards (IFRS) (see **4.1**).

- The introduction of FRS 102 *The Financial Reporting Standard applicable in the UK and Republic of Ireland* brings with it some *new accounting practices* which were not seen in the old UK GAAP (see **4.2**).

- There are many *terminology changes* within FRS 102 which are outlined both in this chapter and in the **Appendix** (see **4.3** and **4.4**).

- There are many notable changes in accounting practice in relation to *accounting policies*; the statement of cash flows; deferred taxation; defined benefit pension plans; employee benefits; fair value accounting; fixed assets; investment properties; leases; prior period adjustments; revenue recognition and stock valuations (see **4.5** to **4.29**).

- There have been consequential amendments to the Financial Reporting Standard for Smaller Entities (the FRSSE) and the Financial Reporting Council have issued *FRSSE (effective January 2015)* (see **4.30**).

INTRODUCTION

4.1   When the Accounting Standards Board (ASB) – now the Accounting Council of the Financial Reporting Council (FRC) – decided that both the UK and the Republic of Ireland would report under an international-based financial reporting framework, it ensured that UK GAAP was aligned, as far as possible, to EU-adopted IFRS. This was a deliberate attempt by the ASB to ensure that when the UK and the Republic of Ireland eventually adopted an IFRS-based framework, there were no significant deviations from the previous UK GAAP.

4.2   Financial reporting has evolved considerably over the years and new practices have also developed. Take, for example, financial instruments (these are discussed in **Chapters 35** to **38**). The accounting for financial instruments has developed considerably over the years to reflect the development and increased use of the instruments themselves. To this day, work is still being undertaken to further enhance and improve the ways in which entities report financial instruments in their financial statements.

With the passage of time, the needs of users have also changed. This is recognised in the UK and the Republic of Ireland with attempts by the standard-setters to enhance corporate reporting and reduce 'clutter' within the financial statements. Cutting 'clutter' is merely one aspect of the ways in which financial reporting has evolved over the years and FRS 102 *The Financial Reporting Standard applicable in the UK and Republic of Ireland* has brought with it some alternative accounting practices that may not be familiar to some accountants. Whilst the ways in which financial statements will be prepared under FRS 102 will largely remain the same, there are some changes that are inherent with a new financial reporting regime.

Focus

At the transitional stage, it is vital that preparers of general purpose financial statements are aware of the key differences between old UK GAAP and FRS 102. Without adequate knowledge of these differences, it will become difficult to ensure that an entity's accounting policies are compliant with the requirements in FRS 102 and, hence, result in errors applying FRS 102 at the conversion stage.

TERMINOLOGY CHANGES

4.3   FRS 102 is based on an international financial reporting regime (IFRS for SMEs) and adopts the use of certain terminology that is found in EU-adopted IFRS. However, it is important to note that financial statements prepared under FRS 102 must use caption headings prescribed in Schedule 1 of the Regulations to CA 2006 (see examples in **8.4** and **9.27**).

4.4   *The differences between FRS 102 and the previous UK GAAP*

Focus

Whilst international terminology is used in FRS 102, particularly in the titles of the primary financial statements, FRS 102, paragraph 3.22 does allow flexibility in the titles given to financial statements, provided the titles given are not misleading (hence 'balance sheet' would still be permissible).

4.4   Appendix III to FRS 102 contains a very useful analysis of the terminology differences contained in FRS 102 versus the terminology used in the *Companies Act 2006* (see also **4.3** above). The varying terminology is shown in the following table:

Companies Act 2006	*FRS 102*
Accounting reference date	Reporting date
Accounts	Financial statements
Associated undertaking	Associate
Balance sheet	Statement of financial position
Capital and reserves	Equity
Cash at bank and in hand	Cash
Debtors	Trade receivables
Diminution in value (of assets)	Impairment
Financial year	Reporting period
Group (accounts)	Consolidated (financial statements)
IAS	EU-adopted IFRS
Individual (accounts)	Individual (financial statements)
Interest payable and similar charges	Finance costs
Interest receivable and similar income	Finance income/investment income
Minority interests	Non-controlling interest
Net realisable value (of any current asset)	Estimated selling price less costs to complete and sell
Parent undertaking	Parent
Profit and loss account	Income statement (under the two-statement approach)
	Part of the statement of comprehensive income (under the single-statement approach)

Companies Act 2006	*FRS 102*
Related undertakings	Subsidiaries, associates and joint ventures
Stocks	Inventories
Subsidiary undertaking	Subsidiary
Tangible assets	Includes: property, plant and equipment; Investment property
Trade creditors	Trade payables

ACCOUNTING CHANGES

4.5   There are some changes that reporting entities preparing financial statements under FRS 102 will have to adopt. For users of the Financial Reporting Standard for Smaller Entities (FRSSE), there are also some consequential amendments to that standard because of FRS 102. A summary of these changes is outlined at the end of this chapter.

FRS 102 has brought about some notable changes in the following areas:

- accounting policies
- cash flow statement
- consolidated financial statements
- deferred taxation
- defined benefit pension plans
- employee benefits
- fair value accounting
- financial instruments
- fixed assets
- goodwill and intangible assets
- investment properties
- leases
- prior period adjustments
- revenue recognition and
- stock valuations.

Accounting policies

4.6   Accounting policies are covered in more detail in **Chapter 3** and in FRS 102, Section 10, Accounting Policies, Estimates and Errors. Paragraph 10.4 to Section 10 tells those preparing financial statements that if FRS 102 does not specifically address a transaction, other event or condition, an entity's management must develop and apply an accounting policy that is:

- *Relevant* – information is relevant to aid the decision-making process of the users.

- *Reliable* – will result in the financial statements faithfully representing the financial position, performance and cash flows. In addition, the policy must also reflect the economic substance of the transaction(s)/ event(s)/condition(s) rather than reflecting the legal form. To achieve reliability, the policy adopted must also be neutral, prudent and complete in all material respects.

FRS 18 *Accounting Policies* was very similar, but in some cases, the end result and impact on profit or loss would not have been necessarily the same.

Under FRS 3 *Reporting Financial Performance*, the correction of errors by way of a prior-year adjustment is only undertaken if the error is deemed to be 'fundamental'. The term 'fundamental error' is defined as an error which destroys the truth and fairness of the financial statements. Under Section 10, an error is corrected by way of a prior-year adjustment if it is considered 'material' hence there may be more errors corrected by way of a prior-year adjustment under FRS 102 than would have been the case under FRS 3.

Focus

Whilst the concept of accounting policies is broadly similar to that of old UK GAAP, there are some accounting treatments in FRS 102 (eg the correction of errors by way of prior-period adjustment) that will have an impact on profit or loss.

Differences with the old UK GAAP standards

4.7   FRS 3 *Reporting Financial Performance* and FRS 18 *Accounting Policies*.

Statement of cash flows (Cash flow statement)

4.8   Under previous UK GAAP (specifically FRS 1 *Cash Flow Statement*), those preparing a cash flow statement would have prepared the statement under the following standard headings:

- operating activities
- dividends from joint ventures and associates
- returns on investments and servicing of finance
- taxation
- capital expenditure and financial investments
- acquisitions and disposals
- equity dividends paid
- management of liquid resources
- financing.

Section 7, Statement of Cash Flows requires the statement of cash flows to be prepared under three types of cash flow classification:

- operating activities
- investing activities
- financing activities.

4.9   *Operating activities* are the day-to-day revenue-producing activities that are not related to either investing or financing activities. This category is essentially a 'default' category, encompassing all cash flows that do not fall within investing or financing classifications and paragraph 7.4 to Section 7 gives examples of what it considers cash flows from operating activities are, including:

(a)   cash receipts from the sale of goods and the rendering of services;

(b)   cash receipts from royalties, fees, commissions and other revenue;

(c)   cash payments to suppliers for goods and services;

(d)   cash payments to and on behalf of employees;

(e)   cash payments or refunds of *income tax,* unless they can be specifically identified with financing and investing activities;

(f)   cash receipts and payments from investments, loans and other contracts held for dealing or trading purposes, which are similar to *inventory* acquired specifically for resale; and

(g)   cash advances and loans made to other parties by *financial institutions.*

4.10   *Investing activities* are those activities that involve the acquisition and disposal of long-term assets (eg monies used for the purchase of fixed assets and cash receipts from the disposal of fixed assets). Paragraph 7.5 to FRS 102 gives examples of what it considers to be cash flows arising from investing activities:

- cash payments to acquire *property, plant and equipment* (including self-constructed property, plant and equipment), *intangible assets* and other long-term assets. These payments include those relating to capitalised development costs and self-constructed property, plant and equipment;

- cash receipts from sales of property, plant and equipment, intangibles and other long-term assets;

- cash payments to acquire *equity* or debt instruments of other entities and interests in *joint ventures* (other than payments for those instruments classified as cash equivalents or held for dealing or trading);

- cash receipts from sales of equity or debt instruments of other entities and interests in joint ventures (other than receipts for those instruments classified as cash equivalents or held for dealing or trading);

- cash advances and loans made to other parties (except those made by financial institutions);

- cash receipts from the repayment of advances and loans made to other parties;

- cash payments for futures contracts, forward contracts, option contracts and swap contracts, except when the contracts are held for dealing or trading, or the payments are classified as financing activities; and

- cash receipts from futures contracts, forward contracts, option contracts and swap contracts, except when the contracts are held for dealing or trading, or the receipts are classified as financing activities.

4.11   *Financing activities* are those activities that change the equity and borrowing structure of a company. For example, if a company issues shares in the year to raise cash, the proceeds from the share issue would be a financing activity. Similarly, where the client raises a loan, the proceeds from the loan would be classified as a financing activity.

Paragraph 7.6 to FRS 102 gives the following examples of cash flows from financing activities:

(a)   cash proceeds from issuing shares or other equity instruments;

(b)   cash payments to *owners* to acquire or redeem the entity's shares;

(c)   cash proceeds from issuing debentures, loans, notes, bonds, mortgages and other short-term or long-term borrowings;

(d)   cash repayments of amounts borrowed; and

(e)   cash payments by a lessee for the reducing of the outstanding *liability* relating to a *finance lease*.

Focus

There are likely to be many presentational changes on transition from the old UK GAAP to FRS 102 where the statement of cash flows is concerned. For example, taxation paid would have appeared under the 'Taxation' heading in previous FRS 1. Taxation paid is now incorporated within operating activities and only included within investing or financing activities if any of the corporation tax paid can be specifically identified with investing or financing cash flows.

Differences with the old UK GAAP standards

4.12   FRS 1 *Cash Flow Statements.*

Consolidated financial statements

4.13   Section 9, Consolidated and Separate Financial Statements, deals with the preparation of consolidated financial statements. There are few significant changes from the old UK GAAP although, where subsidiaries are held for resale, FRS 102 generally allows an accounting policy choice relating to measurement which is at cost less impairment provisions or at fair value. These elements of the investment portfolio must be excluded and measured at fair value, which will result in more subsidiaries being excluded.

In addition, where a change in non-controlling interests (minority interests) occurs, but does not result in the parent losing control of the subsidiary, this is treated as a transaction with equity holders and hence no impact on profit or loss.

Differences with the old UK GAAP standards

4.14   FRS 2 *Accounting for Subsidiary Undertakings*

Deferred taxation

4.15   Section 29 deals with income tax issues and requires deferred tax to be recognised in respect of all timing differences at the balance sheet date. This was similar to the requirements in the previous FRS 19 *Deferred Tax*. However, Section 29 has been aligned more closely to its international counterpart, IAS 12 *Income Tax* and recognises additional circumstances in which deferred tax issues can arise. These 'additional circumstances' are known as the timing difference 'plus' approach and deferred tax now arises on:

- revaluations of non-monetary assets, including investment property;

- fair values on business combinations; and

- unremitted earnings on overseas subsidiaries or associates.

In addition, Section 29 now prohibits reporting entities from discounting deferred tax assets and liabilities to present-day values. However in reality, hardly any entities discount deferred tax balances to present-day values and so this new prohibition (which follows IAS 12 principles) will generally go unnoticed.

Focus

Under Section 29, it is highly likely that more deferred tax provisions are going to be required than under old UK GAAP.

Differences with the old UK GAAP standards

4.16   FRS 19 *Deferred Tax.*

Defined benefit pension plans

4.17   Defined benefit pension plans (or 'final salary pension schemes' as they are often coined in the UK) are dealt with in Section 28, Employee Benefits. Paragraph 28.18 provides a number of simplifications where the valuation basis (the Projected Unit Credit Method) would require undue cost or effort. Section 28 does not require the use of an independent actuary to provide a valuation as FRS 17 *Retirement Benefits* did. However, the entity must be able to measure its obligation and cost under defined benefit plans without undue cost or effort. Therefore, unless the reporting entity employs an actuary or the preparer of the financial statements is an actuary also, the entity will still have to use the services of an independent actuary to include the defined benefit pension plan's surplus or deficit and associated accounting input and disclosures within the financial statements.

> **Focus**
>
> It is unlikely that reporting entities will be able to take advantage of the relaxed approach in Section 28 where actuarial valuations are concerned and hence entities that have defined benefit pension plans will still be required to obtain actuarial information to allow the accounting input and relevant disclosures to take place in the financial statements.
>
> In addition, the net interest on the net defined benefit plan liability is calculated as a single item by multiplying the net defined benefit plan's liability by the discount rate used to determine the present value of the plan's liabilities. Under FRS 17, a calculation of an expected return on plan assets and an interest cost relating to the plan's liabilities would have been made and this revised approach in Section 28 may have a potential impact on earnings.

Differences with old UK GAAP standards

4.18   FRS 17 *Retirement Benefits.*

Employee benefits

4.19   Employee benefits are dealt with in Section 28. Emphasis is placed on the fact that reporting entities should make accruals at the year-end for short-term employee benefits that have been accrued by the employee, but will be paid by the reporting entity in the next accounting period. In reality, many entities did not make accruals for such short-term employee benefits (such as holiday pay and sick pay) despite the fact that this was technically incorrect. Under the previous UK GAAP, FRS 12 *Provisions, Contingent Liabilities and Contingent Assets*, cited an example of holiday pay accrued, but not paid by the reporting entity until the next accounting period, as meeting the definition of a provision (hence a liability). The difficulty is potentially in the calculation of holiday pay that is to be carried over for future use and pulling this information together, particularly in transition to FRS 102 from the old UK GAAP.

> **Focus**
>
> There is no specific requirement in the old UK GAAP to recognise short-term employee benefits (such as accrued holiday pay at the year-end). A good planning tip could be to align the company's holiday year with the financial year to minimise any complications in calculating holiday pay accruals at the year-end.

Differences with the old UK GAAP standards

4.20   There are no specific standards in the old UK GAAP that are affected; however, reference was made to an example of unpaid holiday pay at the year-end being a provision in FRS 12 *Provisions, Contingent Liabilities and Contingent Assets* so, technically, entities should have made provision for this under the old UK GAAP.

Fair value accounting

4.21   There are two fundamental changes in FRS 102 relating to the increased use of fair value accounting and the number of accounting policy choices that are available. There are a number of areas within the financial statements that are likely to be affected by the increased use in fair value accounting which can be identified as follows:

- *Biological assets* (living animals and plants) (**Chapters 16** and **40**) can be measured using fair values (where such values can be obtained reliably) with fluctuations in those fair values being passed through profit or loss. Such policies must be applied consistently to each class of biological asset and its related agricultural produce. The use of the fair value model is not mandatory – the cost model may be used instead (see **Chapter 16**).

- *Business combinations* (**Chapters 29** to **34**)) where intangible assets are acquired and whose values can be reliably measured need to be separate from goodwill at acquisition (such as intellectual property, in-process research and development and customer lists).

- *Financial instruments* (**Chapters 35** to **38**) including derivatives and investments in equity shares, must be carried at fair value, with changes in fair values going through profit or loss. Examples of derivatives include forward foreign currency contracts, interest rate swaps and options, and commodity contracts.

- *Investments* in subsidiaries, associates and jointly controlled entities (**Chapters 35** to **38**) can be held in the separate financial statements of the parent company at either cost less impairment or at fair value with changes in fair value going through either profit or loss or through other comprehensive income (FRS 102, paragraph 9.26).

- *Investment property* (**Chapter 13**) whose fair value can be measured reliably should be carried at fair value at each reporting date with changes in that fair value going through profit or loss.

- *Property, plant and equipment* (**Chapter 12**) can be measured using the revaluation model or the depreciated historic cost model. On transition to FRS 102, a reporting entity could use fair value as 'deemed cost' on transition to FRS 102 and then choose to carry those assets under the cost model going forward.

> **Focus**
>
> The Financial Reporting Council has stated that it does not intend to amend FRS 102 until at least three years have elapsed from its issue. However, changes are anticipated to the way financial instruments are accounted for before this three-year period has elapsed. This is primarily due to the ongoing work by the international standard-setters in the area of financial instruments.

Differences with the old UK GAAP standards

4.22   FRS 2 *Accounting for Subsidiary Undertakings*, FRS 15 *Tangible Fixed Assets*, FRS 26 *Financial Instruments: Recognition and Measurement* and SSAP 19 *Accounting for Investment Properties*.

Financial instruments

4.23   FRS 102 splits financial instruments into two elements: 'Basic Financial Instruments' and 'Other Financial Instruments Issues'. The current UK GAAP deals with financial instruments in FRS 25 *Financial Instruments: Presentation*, FRS 26 *Financial Instruments: Recognition and Measurement* and FRS 29 *Financial Instruments: Disclosures*.

Basic financial instruments include items such as trade debtors, trade creditors and straightforward bank loans and are measured usually at amortised cost, with certain types being measured at cost or fair value. Most debtors and creditors that are classified as current assets or current liabilities will still be measured at the undiscounted amount of cash expected to be received or paid.

Other financial instruments will include instruments such as foreign exchange forward contracts and loans that have complex terms attached to them. Under FRS 102, these will all be measured at fair value at each balance sheet date with movements recognised in profit or loss. The key difference here is that, under the old UK GAAP, many of these instruments would not have been recognised on the balance sheet, but merely disclosed.

> **Focus**
>
> The requirement to include instruments such as foreign exchange forward contracts and loans with complex terms attached will affect entities' balance sheets.

Differences with the old UK GAAP standards

4.24   FRS 25 *Financial Instruments: Presentation,* FRS 26 *Financial Instruments: Recognition and Measurement* and FRS 29 *Financial Instruments: Disclosures.*

Fixed assets

4.25   FRS 15 *Tangible Fixed Assets* went into a lot of detail concerning the capitalisation criteria for *subsequent expenditure.* As a general rule, FRS 15 required subsequent expenditure to be written off to profit or loss unless the expenditure:

- provided an enhancement of the economic benefits of the asset in excess of the previously assessed standard of performance;

- related to a component of a tangible asset that had been treated separately for depreciation purposes which was replaced or restored; or

- related to a major inspection or overhaul of the tangible fixed asset that restored the economic benefits of the asset(s) that had been used up by the entity and that have already been reflected in the depreciation charge.

Section 17, Property, Plant and Equipment deals with this issue at paragraph 17.15 but merely states that day-to-day servicing of property, plant and equipment must be recognised in profit or loss in the periods which the costs are incurred. Those preparing financial statement would therefore be directed to the *Concepts and Pervasive Principles* in Section 2 of FRS 102 to determine whether any subsequent expenditure does, in fact, meet the definition and recognition criteria of an asset outlined in FRS 102, paragraphs 2.15(a) and 2.27(a) and (b).

4.26   Paragraph 17.15 also deals with 'spare parts and servicing equipment'. FRS 15 did not deal with such equipment, therefore many reporting entities carried this in the financial statements as inventory with recognition taking place as and when such parts/equipment were used in the business. Section 17, at paragraph 17.5, requires 'major' spare parts and standby equipment to be included within the cost of the fixed asset(s) to which the equipment relates when the business is expected to use them for more than one accounting period. The treatment under FRS 102 would essentially mean that the cost of major spare parts/servicing equipment would be recognised within the depreciation charge rather than in the profit and loss account through the consumption of stock (ie cost of sales).

4.27   Where fixed assets are acquired under a deferred payment arrangement (in other words deferred beyond normal credit terms), the cost of the asset must be the present value of all future payments in accordance with FRS 102, paragraph 17.13. Such issues were not specifically covered in FRS 15 and would have resulted in the value of assets capitalised being understated, giving rise to a lower depreciation charge. FRS 102 addresses this issue, so the net book value of fixed assets accounted for in accordance with paragraph 17.13 would be higher. This would also have a consequential increase in the depreciation charge.

Focus

The revised accounting treatment for various items such as spare parts and servicing and fixed assets acquired under a deferred payment arrangement is likely to have an impact on depreciation charges, gross profit margins and profitability.

Differences with the old UK GAAP standards

4.28   FRS 15 *Tangible Fixed Assets*.

Goodwill and intangible assets

4.29   Intangible assets (other than goodwill) are dealt with in Section 18, Intangible Assets other than Goodwill. The key difference between FRS 102 and the old UK GAAP is in relation to the presumed maximum life. The old UK GAAP presumed a maximum useful life of 20 years, with an option to rebut this period if a longer (or indefinite) life can be justified. Under FRS 102, intangible assets and goodwill will always have a finite life and if no reliable estimate can be made, the useful life is deemed to be a maximum of five years.

Focus

There will potentially be large write-downs of goodwill on transition to FRS 102 where management cannot assign a reliable estimate for useful economic lives; this is going to affect a reporting entity's profit (or loss) with potential tax consequences. At the transition date, reporting entities should use the written down value of goodwill under old UK GAAP FRS 10. This balance will then be amortised prospectively over its remaining useful life. In some cases the transition to FRS 102 will result in an accelerated write-off of goodwill.

Differences with the old UK GAAP standards

4.30   FRS 10 *Goodwill and Intangible Assets.*

Investment properties

4.31   SSAP 19 *Accounting for Investment Properties* required such properties to be classified in the balance sheet at their market value with any changes in this market value being recognised through a revaluation reserve account within equity and reported via the statement of total recognised gains and losses.

Section 16, Investment Property, at paragraph 16.7, essentially extinguishes the use of the revaluation reserve and requires all changes in the fair value of an investment property to be recognised in profit or loss. The upshot of this treatment is that the reported profit or loss would be different than would otherwise have been the case under the old SSAP 19 (although no tax effect would be triggered until the asset was sold).

Focus

A key issue to consider is that any fair value gains that are reported in profit or loss are *not* distributable as a dividend to shareholders because the gain is not realised.

4.32   It is worth noting that Section 16 requires fair values to be obtained where obtaining such values can be done without 'undue cost or effort', whereas SSAP 19 did not make this exception. In Section 16, if obtaining fair values would result in undue cost or effort, the entity accounts for such investment property in accordance with Section 17, Property, Plant and Equipment until a reliable measure of fair value becomes available. In reality, the entity would commission a surveyor to undertake the fair value exercise and, in the opinion of the authors, it is difficult to envisage how obtaining such fair values for investment property would result in undue cost or effort.

Accounting for fair value gains and losses in investment property is markedly different under FRS 102 than its previous counterpart, SSAP 19. While accounting standards do not have specific reasoning behind their methodologies, investment property is not subjected to depreciation or impairment testing because they are valued at fair value at each reporting date, hence any changes in fair value are taken directly to profit or loss.

An entity's interest in a property that is held under a lease and classified as an investment property may be classified as a finance lease regardless of the fact that the lease may have been accounted for under an operating lease if it was in the scope of Section 20, Leases. In this respect, the asset is recognised at the *lower* of the fair value of the property and the present value of the minimum lease payments with an equivalent amount being recognised as a liability. This is an accounting policy option under FRS 102, paragraph 16.3.

Differences with the old UK GAAP standards

4.33   SSAP 19 *Accounting for Investment Properties* and SSAP 21 *Accounting for Leases and Hire Purchase Contracts.*

Leasing

4.34   SSAP 21 *Accounting for Leases and Hire Purchase Contracts* set out a specific numeric benchmark when determining whether a lease is either a finance, or an operating, lease (this could be found in paragraph 22 to the Guidance Notes to SSAP 21). This benchmark was where the minimum lease payments equated to 90% or more of the fair value of the asset subjected to the lease.

The classification in Section 20, Leases does not refer to a 90% benchmark, but the equivalent is within the term 'substantially all'. Section 20 also offers examples of the various situations that either individually, or in combination, would give rise to lease being classified as a finance lease. These classifications are based on IAS 17 *Leases* and are as follows:

(a)   The lease transfers ownership of the asset to the lessee by the end of the lease term.

(b)   The lessee has the option to purchase the asset at a price that is expected to be sufficiently lower than the fair value at the date the option becomes exercisable for it to be reasonably certain, at the inception of the lease, that the option will be exercised.

(c)   The lease term is for the major part of the economic life of the asset, even if title is not transferred at the end of the lease.

(d)   At the inception of the lease, the present value of the minimum lease payments amounts to at least substantially all of the fair value of the leased asset.

(e)   The leased asset is of such a specialised nature that only the lessee can use them without major modifications.

In addition, Section 20 contains three other indicators that the lease could be a finance lease:

(a)   If the lessee can cancel the lease, the lessor's losses associated with the cancellation are borne by the lessee.

(b)   Gains or losses from the fluctuation in the residual value of the leased asset accrue to the lessee (eg in the form of a rent rebate equalling most of the sales proceeds at the end of the lease).

(c)   The lessee has the ability to continue the lease for a secondary period at a rent that is substantially lower than market rent.

Focus

The emphasis here is on judgement being required to determine the correct classification of a leasing transaction. This is essentially a new 'theme' in the new standard.

4.35   The classification criteria are based upon the risks and rewards of ownership of the associated asset and which party retains those risks and rewards. There are a number of factors that can determine whether or not risks and rewards have been transferred from the lessor to the lessee. Paragraph 20.7 acknowledges that the examples of indicators contained in FRS 102, paragraphs 20.5–20.6 will not be conclusive in every respect, so consideration must be given to other indicators that risks and rewards may (or may not) have transferred from lessor to lessee. More judgement is needed in this subjective area.

4.36   In some cases, lessees may receive an incentive payment to take up a lease. Paragraph 20.15 does not make reference to the effect of incentive payments relating to operating leases. The previous UK GAAP stated in paragraph 8 of UITF 28 *Operating Lease Incentives* that any incentive should be allocated to match the effect of the increased rentals in later periods so that the financial statements reflect the true effective rental for premises – in other words, an incentive is not recognised immediately.

4.37   A new IFRS, due in 2014/2015, will govern the way in which leases will be accounted for. Essentially, this new IFRS would exonerate many operating leases, so these will now default to be treated as finance leases and must be reported on the balance sheet of such entities. In the authors' opinion, it is important that those preparing financial statements in the UK are aware of the International Accounting Standard Board's proposals because it may have a future impact in the UK and the Republic of Ireland. The new standard aims to minimise opportunities for 'off-balance sheet finance' and is based on a 'right of use'. Only very short leases would qualify for classification as an operating lease. At the time of writing, there had not been any mention by the Financial Reporting Council that the UK and Republic of Ireland would follow this proposal, but it is likely to have an impact in the future.

Differences with the old UK GAAP standards

4.38   SSAP 21 *Accounting for Leases and Hire Purchase Contracts.*

Prior period adjustments

4.39   Prior-period adjustments are dealt with in Section 10, Accounting Policies, Estimates and Errors and there is a notable difference between Section 10 and the previous FRS 3 *Reporting Financial Performance*. FRS 102, paragraph 10.21 requires an entity to correct a 'material' prior period error retrospectively in the first financial statements which are authorised for issue after discovery of the error by way of a prior period adjustment.

The previous FRS 3, paragraph 63, required the correction of 'fundamental' errors. Fundamental errors were those which were so significant that they destroyed the true and fair view of the financial statements as well as their validity.

4.40   The terms 'material' and 'fundamental' could be interpreted differently among preparers of general purpose financial statements, but they amount to the same thing. This interpretation aspect may mean that more errors are corrected by way of a prior period adjustment.

Focus

The method in which a material error is corrected has not changed from the mechanics contained in the previous FRS 3. They will still be corrected by restating the previous year's financial statements and then restating the balance on opening profit and loss account reserves.

Differences with the old UK GAAP standards

4.41   FRS 3 *Reporting Financial Performance*.

Revenue recognition

4.42   FRS 102 contains slight variations in the wording relating to the measurement of revenue compared to its previous counterpart, Application Note G to FRS 5 *Reporting the Substance of Transactions*. Paragraph 23.3 in FRS 102 refers to revenue being the fair value of the consideration *'received or receivable'*. Application Note G to FRS 5 at paragraph G4 said that a seller recognises revenue under an exchange transaction with a customer when, and to the extent that, it obtains the *'right to consideration'* in exchange for its performance.

This subtle difference in wording could potentially allow for later recognition of profit which would result in a potentially different tax treatment as the tax treatment would follow the accounting treatment.

Paragraph 23.15 to FRS 102 also refers to a 'specific act' and a 'significant act'. The paragraph states that when a specific act is much more significant than any other act, the entity postpones revenue recognition until the significant act is executed. Application Note G to FRS 5 was much more prohibitive in that it required revenue to be recognised in line with performance (passing a 'milestone' or a 'critical event' occurring) and earning the right to consideration. Hence there is the potential here for the possibility of recognising profit later than would otherwise be the case under the old Application Note G to FRS 5. This would also have a direct effect on the tax as the tax treatment would follow the accounting treatment.

Paragraph 23.16 to FRS 102 states that if an entity cannot estimate the outcome of a service contract then it should only recognise revenue to the extent of the expenses recognised that are recoverable. In contrast, paragraph 10 to SSAP 9 *Stocks and Long-Term Contracts* stated that where the outcome of long-term contracts could not be assessed with reasonable certainty, no profit should be reflected in the profit and loss account and suggested showing as turnover a proportion of the total contract value using a zero estimate of profit.

Differences with the old UK GAAP standards

4.43   FRS 5 *Reporting the Substance of Transactions.*

Valuations of inventory (Stock)

4.44   SSAP 9 *Stocks and Long-Term Contracts* allowed stock to be valued using the 'last-in first-out' (LIFO) cost-flow assumption. Whilst this method was permissible in SSAP 9, the standard itself did not like it and acknowledged that there must be justifiable circumstances for the use of LIFO.

Paragraph 13.18 in Section 13, Inventories follows the same stance as its international counterpart, IAS 2 *Inventories*. Reporting entities are no longer permitted to use LIFO as a cost-flow assumption and are limited to the use of the 'first-in first-out' or weighted average cost method.

The FRSSE (effective January 2015)

4.45   The Financial Reporting Standard for Smaller Entities (FRSSE) is here to stay and there are no immediate proposals to withdraw it, although it is inevitable that there will be changes in the future to the FRSSE so that there are no significant deviations away from mainstream UK GAAP. Users of the FRSSE can find the consequential amendments in FRS 100 *Application of Financial Reporting Requirements.*

The FRSSE (effective April 2008) has been amended as a consequence of FRS 102 and a summary of these amendments are as follows:

The status of the FRSSE

4.46

- The status of the FRSSE becomes effective January 2015. Paragraph 1 is also amended to remove inapplicable text.

- Paragraph 5 is amended for transactions and events not covered by the FRSSE. It is amended so that entities must *first* have regard to their own accounting policies. It is then amended to guide users to FRS 102 in developing a new accounting policy.

- Paragraph 5A is inserted which refers to public benefit entities.

- Paragraph 10 is amended requiring entities not eligible to use the FRSSE to report under EU-adopted IFRS, apply FRS 101 *Reduced Disclosure Framework* in the individual financial statements of qualifying entities, or apply FRS 102 in accordance with the requirements of FRS 100 *Application of Financial Reporting Requirements*. A footnote has also been included in paragraph 10 that refers to company law in the Republic of Ireland requiring certain companies to prepare Companies Act accounts using a financial reporting framework based on accounting standards other than those issued by the FRC.

- Paragraph 11 is amended to remove reference to the first issuance of the FRSSE in November 1997 and also to make reference to FRS 102 and SORPS.

Main body of the FRSSE

4.47

- Paragraph 2.6 is amended to refer to the FRSSE (effective January 2015).

- The footnote to paragraph 2.6 is amended to include provisions *applicable* rather than *relating to* small companies and amendments are made to change the effective date to January 2015.

- Paragraph 6.13 is amended to make reference to capitalised goodwill and intangible assets have a finite useful life and amending the economic useful life of goodwill and intangible assets that cannot be assigned a reliable estimated useful life from 20 years to five years.

- Paragraph 6.45 is amended to remove the suggestion of obsolescence or fall in the demand for a product.

- Paragraphs 6.45A to C are inserted as follows:

'6.45A:

At each reporting date an assessment shall be carried out of whether there is any indication that an asset should be written down (ie whether its carrying amount is more than its recoverable amount). If any such indication exists, the recoverable amount of the asset shall be estimated. If there is no indication that an asset should be written down, it is not necessary to estimate the recoverable amount.

6.45B:

In assessing whether there is any indication that an asset should be written down, the following might be considered:

(a)   During the period, an asset's market value has declined significantly more than would be expected as a result of the passage of time or normal use.

(b)   Significant changes with an adverse effect on an asset, or the entity, have taken place during the period, or will take place in the near future, (eg external factors such as technological, market, economic or legal changes or internal factors such as the asset becoming idle, or plans to dispose of an asset before the previously expected date).

(c)   Market interest rates have increased during the period, and those increases are likely to affect materially the asset's recoverable amount.

(d)   Evidence is available of obsolescence or physical damage of an asset.

(e)   Evidence is available from internal reporting that indicates that operating results or cash flow from the use of the asset are, or will be, worse than expected.

6.45C:

If there is an indication that an asset should be written down, this may indicate that the entity should review the remaining useful economic life, the depreciation method or the residual value of the asset and adjust it in accordance with paragraph 6.40 even if no loss is recognised for writing down the asset.'

- Paragraph 15.7 is amended to include paragraph (d) which says that related party transactions entered into between two or more members of a group, provided that any subsidiary which is a party to the transaction is wholly owned by such a member, does not require a related party disclosure.

Part C amendments to 'Definitions'

4.48

- The definitions of 'close family' are amended and now include that person's children, spouse or domestic partner; children of that person's spouse or domestic partner and dependents of that person or that person's spouse or domestic partner.

- The definition of 'key management personnel' is inserted.

- The definition of 'public benefit entities' is inserted.

- The current definition of a related party is deleted and replaced with the following text:

  A related party is a person or entity that is related to the entity that is preparing its financial statements (in this Standard referred to as the 'reporting entity').

  (a) A person or a close member of that person's family is related to a reporting entity if that person:

    (i) has control or joint control over the reporting entity;

    (ii) has significant influence over the reporting entity; or

  (b) Is a member of the *key management personnel* of the reporting entity or of a parent of the reporting entity. An entity is related to a reporting entity if any of the following conditions applies:

    (i) the entity and the reporting entity are members of the same group (which means that each parent, subsidiary and fellow subsidiary is related to the others);

    (ii) one entity is an associate or joint venture of the other entity (or an associate or joint venture of a member of a group of which the other entity is a member);

    (iii) both entities are joint ventures of the third party;

    (iv) one entity is a joint venture of a third entity and the other entity is an associate of the third entity;

    (v) the entity is a retirement benefit scheme for the benefit of employees of either the reporting entity or an entity related to the reporting entity. If the reporting entity itself is such a scheme, the sponsoring employers are also related to the reporting entity;

    (vi) the entity is controlled or jointly controlled by a person identified in (a);

(vii)   a person identified in (a)(i) has significant influence over the entity or is a member of the key management personnel of the entity (or of a parent of the entity).

In addition, the FRC explained that, where an entity applying the FRSSE undertakes a new transaction for which it has no existing accounting policy, it should have regard to FRS 102, not as a mandatory document, but as a means of establishing current practice. The FRC removed the reference to the accounting standards applicable to consolidated financial statements because the general requirements in the FRSSE for developing accounting policies for transactions or events that are not dealt with in the FRSSE are equally applicable to consolidated financial statements.

The FRC made two further amendments to the FRSSE:

(a)   it introduced a requirement which is consistent with EU Directives, that if an entity is unable to make a reliable estimate of the useful life of goodwill or intangible assets, the life shall be presumed not to exceed five years.

(b)   It clarified that an entity shall assess annually whether there is any indication that an asset should be written down. This will assist entities applying the existing requirement for fixed assets and goodwill to be carried at no more than their recoverable amount.

These amendments relate to applying existing company law requirements.

- Paragraph 42 has also been amended to make reference to FRS 102 and remove reference to 'auditors', 'the Board' and citation of an example of marking to market fixed interest instruments.

Focus

At the time of writing, the European Parliament has just announced changes to its accounting rules which would enable Member States to be given the ability to introduce significantly simplified reporting requirements for micro businesses. These changes would result in significant matters to be considered before they are introduced into UK legislation and a review of the disclosure requirements contained within the FRSSE would have to be undertaken.

Chapter 5

Events after the reporting period

SIGNPOSTS

- Recognition in the financial statements: Preparers must be aware that only 'adjusting' events can ever be recognised within the financial statements. 'Non-adjusting' events must be disclosed within the financial statements (see **5.4** and **5.8**).

- Payment of dividends to shareholders: These can only be provided for within the financial statements if they have been declared prior to the year-end date. Dividends that have not been declared by the year-end date must not be recognised as a liability within the current year's financial statements (see **5.9**).

- Disclosure requirements: There are additional disclosure requirements relating to events that occur after the reporting period that either affect the current year's financial statements or require disclosure based on their materiality (see **5.11**). It is also important to disclose the date of authorisation for issuance of the financial statements.

INTRODUCTION

5.1 It is generally accepted within the accountancy profession that it is not practicable to be able to finalise an entity's financial statements immediately after the year-/period end. There has to be an element of time between an entity's accounting year-/period-end and the date on which the financial statements are authorised for issue. The time that will elapse between a company's year-end and the date on which the financial statements are authorised for issue will depend on a varying degree of factors such as the nature and complexity of the company, any deadlines that have been imposed on the company by third parties such as financiers or stock markets as well as statutory deadlines such as Companies House and HM Revenue and Customs filing deadlines.

5.2   *Events after the reporting period*

Focus

There are no significant differences between Section 32, Events after the End of the Reporting Period and the old UK GAAP at FRS 21 *Events after the Balance Sheet Date*.

Those preparing financial statements must be aware of events or conditions that exist at the year-end date and where there are uncertainties that are subject to future outcomes. Some of these events or conditions may become adjusting events or they may be non-adjusting events depending on the facts of each particular case. There are also situations that may arise during the course of an assignment that occur after the year-end date but which are considered to be so material in the context of the financial statements that disclosure may be considered necessary to alert those reading the financial statements.

5.2   The *Financial Reporting Standard applicable in the UK and the Republic of Ireland* deals with events after the reporting period at Section 32. Section 32 is based on the principles contained in IAS 10 *Events after the Reporting Period*. The IAS uses the terminology 'events after the reporting period' though many professional accountants in the United Kingdom will be familiar with alternative terminology such as 'events after the balance sheet date' or 'post-balance sheet events'. The remainder of this chapter will refer to 'events after the end of the reporting period' to be consistent with the technical contents of Section 32 to FRS 102.

The classification of an event after the end of the reporting period as an adjusting or non-adjusting event will depend on whether the event gives additional information relating to conditions which exist at the reporting date, or if the event gives additional information relating to conditions that arose after the reporting date.

Focus

An *adjusting* event is an event whose conditions existed at the reporting date. A *non-adjusting* event is an event whose conditions did not exist at the reporting date. If a non-adjusting event is material it should be disclosed, not adjusted for, in the financial statements.

DEFINITIONS

5.3   Section 32 of FRS 102 defines events after the end of the reporting period as those events, favourable and unfavourable, that occur between the end of the reporting period and the date when the financial statements are authorised for issue. There are two types of events: (FRS 102, paragraph 32.2):

(a)   those that provide evidence of conditions that existed at the end of the reporting period (adjusting events after the end of the reporting period), (FRS 102, paragraph 32.2(a)); and

(b)   those that are indicative of conditions that arose after the end of the reporting period (non-adjusting events after the end of the reporting period). (FRS 102, paragraph 32.2(b)).

Example 5.1 – An adjusting event

Company A Ltd is preparing financial statements to 31 March 2013. It has extracted an aged debtors listing as at that date which shows one of its customers is significantly overdue in settlement of its account. The final (unapproved) draft financial statements are completed on 27 June 2013 by the external accountants and, on that date, a letter was received by a firm of Insolvency Practitioners confirming that the customer had gone into liquidation. The letter from the Insolvency Practitioners confirmed that it was highly unlikely there would be any surplus proceeds, after realising assets and paying off preferential creditors, to pay a dividend to unsecured creditors.

The letter from the Insolvency Practitioner is evidence that Company A Ltd will not receive payment from its customer and as a consequence it must write this debt off. In other words, this is an 'adjusting' event after the end of the reporting period as it is evidence that the debt will not be settled.

Section 32 of FRS 102 gives guidance to preparers of financial statements as to the timelines they should be working towards between the date of the financial statements and the date on which the financial statements are authorised for issue. FRS 102 says that events after the end of the reporting period include all events up to the date when the financial statements are authorised for issue, even if those events occur after the public announcement of profit or loss of other selected financial information (FRS 102, paragraph 32.3).

RECOGNITION AND MEASUREMENT

Adjusting events

5.4   By their definition, adjusting events give rise to a change in the amounts that are included within an entity's financial statements, whether favourable or unfavourable. The entity should also make any required disclosures within the notes to the financial statements.

Example 5.2 – Discovery of a fraud

A company operates in the 'Do-it-Yourself' trade with a year-end of 30 April. The company has prepared its financial statements for the year ended 30 April 2013 and the auditors completed their detailed on-site fieldwork on 27 June 2013. During the audit work the audit senior noticed large cash discrepancies throughout the year which had been written off to sundry expenses within the profit and loss account to agree the bank reconciliation. The audit manager and audit senior calculated that the value of the cash discrepancies amount to £75,000 which is considered material to the financial statements. It was later found that the cashier had been stealing the cash on a regular basis due to a distinct lack of segregation of duties within the cash office.

The financial statements will need to be adjusted to reflect the discovery of the fraud. This accords with the requirements in Section 32 of FRS 102 at paragraph 32.5(e) which says that the discovery of fraud or errors are adjusting events after the end of the reporting period and therefore should be adjusted within the financial statements.

Section 32 recognises various examples of adjusting events which may occur after the end of the reporting period and which would require an entity to adjust its financial statements accordingly. Such examples are:

- the settlement of a court case after the end of the reporting period that confirms that the entity had a present obligation at the reporting date. The entity must adjust any existing provision for the obligation, or create a new provision (provisions are dealt with in Section 21, Provisions and Contingencies);

- the receipt of information after the reporting period indicating that an asset was impaired as at the year-end; for example, the bankruptcy of a customer that occurs after the reporting period or the sale of inventories after the reporting period that gives evidence about their net realisable value at the year-end; reporting period of the consideration for assets sold or purchased before the end of the reporting period;

- the determination after the end of the reporting period of profit-sharing or bonus arrangements if the entity had an obligation to make such payments as a result of events before the end of the reporting period; and

- as in the example above, the discovery of fraud or errors that show the financial statements are incorrect.

Settlement of a court case

5.5   The settlement of a court case after the end of the reporting period is an adjusting event. If an entity's legal advisers had previously indicated that the reporting entity may unsuccessfully defend the legal case, then ordinarily a provision for settlement together with associated legal costs would be made within the financial statements, provided the provision met the definition of a provision as per Section 21.

In some cases, an entity may not have recognised a provision because to do so would have been in breach of the requirements contained in Section 21. In such cases, the entity would ordinarily have to make disclosure of a contingent liability. Where the entity is required to settle a court case after the end of the reporting period this is deemed to be evidence that such conditions existed at the reporting date and the entity would be required to create a new provision if the outcome of the court case confirms that such an outflow of economic benefit was probable at the reporting date.

If a reporting entity has already created a provision at the reporting date which was based on a reliable estimate of an outflow of future economic benefits, then the entity would be required to adjust the provision following settlement of the court case.

Example 5.3 – Settlement of a court case after the year-end

A company has a year-end date of 31 March 2013. At that date the company was in dispute with one of its customers who had brought a legal claim against the company. The customer alleged that the company had damaged their property during works carried out on it. At the year-end date the legal advisers were not able to confirm whether the company would be successful in its defence and, as such, the accountant made a disclosure of a contingent liability.

On 23 June 2013 (some three days before the financial statements were to be authorised for issue) the court found in favour of the customer and ordered the company to pay damages of £20,000 plus legal costs of £7,000. The accountant has suggested that the contingent liability disclosure remain within the financial statements and the damages and costs be accounted for in the 2014 financial statements.

Paragraph 32.5(a) is specific on such issues. The settlement of a court case after the end of a reporting period is an adjusting event. While the company was not able to recognise a provision in accordance with

FRS 102, Section 21 due to the recognition criteria not being met, the company is now required to create a new provision in accordance with FRS 102, paragraph 32.5(a). This particular paragraph is also specific in that the entity must not merely disclose a contingent liability because the settlement provides additional evidence to be considered in determining whether the recognition criteria for a provision has been met in accordance with Section 21 to FRS 102.

Asset impairment

5.6 Section 32 would require an entity to consider an impairment loss on an asset when it becomes aware of conditions that exist at the end of the reporting period and which would fall to be treated as an adjusting event. It is generally a rule within the accountancy profession that an entity's assets should not be carried in the statement of financial position (balance sheet) at any more than their recoverable amount. In recognition of this principle, it is common for entities to undertake a review of carrying values at the end of a reporting period to verify if there is any evidence of impairment of such assets.

The most common adjusting event where assets are concerned is the bankruptcy of a customer after the end of the reporting period. If information comes to light before the financial statements are authorised for issue that monies are not going to be received from a customer (eg confirmation from an insolvency practitioner shown in the example in **5.1**) then the reporting entity is required to write down the value of its current assets to recoverable amount. This is usually achieved by a specific bad debt provision being made, though it is not uncommon for many entities to err on the side of caution and make general bad debt provisions by arriving at a best estimate of a blanket percentage of debtors that will not be recovered at the reporting period.

Example 5.4 – Write-down of inventory to net realisable value

Company A Limited supplies various components to a manufacturer of hi-tech computer equipment and has a year-end date of 31 January. On 31 January 2013, an inventory count was undertaken by Company A and it had a batch of parts for a hi-tech mini laptop computer called the 'MiniComp UltraLite X8'. The value of these parts amounted to £17,600 and was included in the inventory valuation at that amount.

On 2 February 2013, no component parts had been used from inventory and it was announced by the manufacturer of the MiniComp UltraLite X8 that this model would be discontinued from production with immediate effect and the manufacturer would no longer be placing any further orders for the component parts manufactured by Company A Ltd. The board of directors have estimated that the net realisable value of these component parts is now zero.

The announcement by the manufacturer of the immediate discontinuance of the laptop and the fact that the component parts no longer have an available market will trigger a potential write-down of this inventory. The value of the components is currently valued at £17,600 in the inventory valuation, but as there is no longer a market for these components, the directors' estimate of their net realisable value of zero will become an adjusting event. As a result, the component parts must be reduced from £17,600 to £nil in the financial statements for the year ended 31 January 2013.

Example 5.5 – Impairment of an asset as an adjusting event

Company B Limited operates in the construction industry and has a head office and five branches across the country. The company's year-end is 30 April and they are currently in the process of preparing the financial statements for the year-ended 30 April 2013. On 1 April 2013, the company successfully tendered for a contract to build luxury three- and four-bedroom properties in a vibrant city centre location. The terms of the contract are that the company will purchase materials and equipment and source their own labour in order to commence the contract. The contractor has said that when the contract is 25% complete they will release their first-stage payment. Company B Ltd has estimated that it will take a period of four months to get the contract 25% complete and has approached their bank for a loan for working capital and equipment.

The bank has agreed to the loan in principle, subject to the company pledging their head office and five branches' properties as security for the finance. The company has agreed to this clause and has instructed a valuation agency to carry out a valuation of their properties. Prior to the valuation the properties had a carrying value in the statement of financial position (balance sheet) of £1 million. The valuation agency carried out their valuation on 31 May 2013 and valued the properties at £875,000 in total.

This valuation would provide evidence of an impairment in value from £1 million to £875,000, particularly as the valuation was carried out one month after the company's year-end. The value of the impairment would therefore be (£1m – £875,000) = £125,000 and this would fall to be classified as an adjusting event under Section 32 of FRS 102.

Cost of assets sold or purchased prior to the year-end

5.7   In cases where the cost of assets purchased, or the proceeds from assets sold, before the end of the reporting period become known after the end of the reporting period, it is absolutely vital to determine whether or not an event existed at the reporting date, or whether a new event is created after the reporting date.

Example 5.6 – Sale of an asset

Company A Limited is in the process of selling one of its properties to an unconnected third party, Company B Limited. Company B Limited wants to extend the property to house large items of plant and machinery; to do this Company B must apply to the local authority for planning permission. The terms of the sale agreement are that the sale will only go ahead if Company B obtains planning permission because, if this is refused, Company B will have to source an alternative property. Company A's year-end is 28 February 2013 and the financial statements are due to be approved for issuance on 29 April 2013. On 27 April 2013, the local authority granted Company B planning permission and the sale duly completed. The accountant for Company A Ltd is proposing to recognise the sale proceeds as a debtor from Company B in the financial statements as at 28 February 2013.

The fact that the planning permission has been granted and the sale duly completed after the year-end date of 28 February 2013 is not, in itself, evidence that conditions existed at the reporting date. No sale had taken place at the year-end date and the fact that Company B would have had to obtain planning permission in order for the sale to be successful is an event in its own right that causes the sale.

There are situations when the sale of an asset may take place unconditionally and the value of the sale proceeds will be determined based on various factors. In the example above, had the value of the sale proceeds of the property been subjected to the successful outcome of the planning permission, then the seller would have to consider the probability that planning permission would be granted when determining the value of the sales proceeds and the resulting receivable at the year-end date. The company accountant would have to calculate the receivable in accordance with Section 11, Basic Financial Instruments and/or Section 12, Other Financial Instruments Issues. Any adjustments relating to the receivable's value arising from the granting or refusal of planning permission after the reporting period would be a non-adjusting event.

Fraud

5.8   Section 32 recognises that the discovery of fraud or errors that confirm the financial statements are incorrect are adjusting events; as such, these should be recognised within the financial statements.

Fraud, by its very nature, is designed to be concealed and, more often than not, will involve schemes which have been carefully designed and engineered in such a way that the perpetrators may not be found out. However, even the most sophisticated and carefully engineered frauds have been exposed. Some companies have been involved in investments with entities, sometimes offshore entities, whose values have suffered a decline due to instances of fraudulent activity which have only been exposed after the end of the reporting period. The issue here is whether such instances of fraud are adjusting or non-adjusting events.

The first issue to establish in cases where fraud in relation to an investment has been discovered after the end of the reporting period is whether (or not) the investment itself is actually in existence. It has not been unheard of that companies have invested in entities (usually offshore entities) only to find out later that these entities do not, in fact, exist and they have been a victim of fraud.

If the underlying investment does exist and did have a value attributed to it at the end of the reporting period, then the decline in value (the loss) due to fraud would be a non-adjusting event due to the fact that the reporting entity had the option of selling their investment at the year-end date without suffering a loss due to fraud.

If, however, the investment does not exist and never did, then clearly the entity would never have been able to avoid the loss due to fraud and the discovery of the fraud after the end of the reporting period would thus become an adjusting event due to the fact that the discovery of the fraud provides evidence that the investment did not exist at the reporting date.

NON-ADJUSTING EVENTS

5.9   Non-adjusting events are not recognised within the financial statements themselves; instead, they are disclosed within the notes to the financial statements.

Paragraph 32.7 cites two examples of typical non-adjusting events after the reporting period:

5.9 *Events after the reporting period*

(a) A decline in market value of investments between the end of the reporting period and the date when the financial statements are authorised for issue. The decline in market value does not normally relate to the conditions of the investments at the end of the reporting period, but reflects circumstances that have arisen subsequently. Therefore, an entity does not adjust the amounts recognised in its financial statements for the investments. Similarly, the entity does not update the amounts disclosed for the investments as at the end of the reporting period, although it may need to give additional disclosure in accordance with paragraph 32.10 (FRS 102, paragraph 32.7(a)).

(b) An amount that becomes receivable as a result of a favourable judgement or settlement of a court case after the *reporting date* but before the financial statements are issued. This would be a contingent asset at the reporting date (see paragraph 21.13), and disclosure may be required by paragraph 21.16. However, agreement on the amount of damages for a judgement that was reached before the reporting date, but was not previously recognised because the amount could not be measured reliably, may constitute an adjusting event (FRS 102, paragraph 32.7(b)).

Example 5.7 – Decline in market value of investments

A company has a year-end of 30 June 2013 and has invested in Company B PLC which is listed on the London Stock Exchange. The value of the investment in Company B at the year-end date was £10,000. However, on 2 August 2013, the market value of the shares in Company B declined to such an extent that the value of the investment was only £2,000; this share price is not expected to rise for the foreseeable future. The directors are concerned about the impact that the sharp fall in the market value of Company B's share price will have on the financial results for the year-ended 30 June 2013 which are due to be authorised for issue on 10 August 2013.

Paragraph 32.7(a) states that a decline in the market value of investments between the end of the reporting period and the date when the financial statements are authorised for issue is a non-adjusting event because the condition (the fall in share price) did not exist at the year-end date. As a result, the financial statements amounts for the value of the investment at the year-end will remain at £10,000. However, the company will make a disclosure in the financial statements relating to the fall in share price of Company B.

Example 5.8 – Contingent asset

Company A Ltd instigated legal proceedings against Company B Ltd on 20 April 2013 because Company B had failed to comply with the terms of a contract to supply goods. As a result of its failure to adhere to the terms of the contract, Company A Ltd has suffered significant losses due to its customers sourcing alternative goods elsewhere. Company A has a year-end date of 31 July 2013.

Company B Ltd has filed a defence with the court and the case was heard on 2 August 2013. Prior to the court case, Company A's legal advisers were not able to reliably estimate any potential costs that may become refundable if Company A was successful in its case. However, the court ordered that Company B pay costs of £15,000. The finance director of Company A Ltd is proposing to recognise this reimbursement of costs as a receivable in the financial statements as at 31 July 2013.

Paragraph 32.7(b) states that an amount that becomes receivable as a result of a favourable judgement or settlement of a court case after the reporting date, but before the financial statements are issued, is a contingent asset at the reporting date. As a result, the finance director would be unable to recognise a receivable, but would instead make disclosure of a contingent asset.

In the example above, if Company A and Company B reached agreement before Company A's year-end of 31 July 2013 as to the amount of damages/ costs that Company B would pay, but the damages/costs were not previously recognised in Company A's financial statements because such amounts could not be reliably measured, then this would be an adjusting event because an obligating event did exist at the year-end (Company B agreeing to pay damages/costs).

DIVIDENDS

5.10   Section 32 of FRS 102 takes a very strict balance sheet approach in respect of dividends. Dividends can only be recognised as a liability in the financial statements if the dividend has been declared on, or by, the end of the reporting period. Paragraph 32.8 to FRS 102 states:

'If an entity declares dividends to holders of its equity instruments after the end of the reporting period, the entity shall not recognise those dividends as a liability at the end of the reporting period because no obligation exists at that time. The amount of the dividend may be presented as a segregated component of retained earnings at the end of the reporting period.'

5.11 *Events after the reporting period*

When an entity declares a dividend to shareholders after the reporting period, the entity must not recognise a liability in the current period financial statements, regardless of the fact that it may have an established practice of paying dividends to equity holders.

5.11   A reporting entity must make a disclosure in the financial statements relating to dividends that have been proposed and declared after the reporting date, but before the financial statements are authorised for issue in the notes to the financial statements.

DISCLOSURE REQUIREMENTS

5.12   Paragraph 32.6 prohibits non-adjusting events being recognised in a reporting entity's financial statements. Instead a reporting entity must make disclosures concerning non-adjusting events as follows:

- the nature of the event; and

- an estimate of its financial effect, or a statement that such an estimate cannot be made.

The standard requires consideration to be given to events that occur up to the date the financial statements are authorised for issue. It is crucial that the users of the financial statements are aware that they do not reflect events after that date. In view of this aspect, paragraph 32.9 requires the date the financial statements were authorised for issue to be disclosed, as well as disclosure of who authorised the financial statements to be issued. Where the owners of the reporting entity have the power to amend the financial statements after issue, this fact must also be disclosed.

SUMMARY – WHAT IS DIFFERENT FROM THE PREVIOUS UK GAAP?

There are no significant differences between FRS 102 and the previous UK GAAP other than in terminology (FRS 102 refers to *events after the reporting period* whereas FRS 21 refers to *events after the balance sheet date*).

Chapter 6

Related party disclosures

SIGNPOSTS

- The definition of a 'related party' in FRS 102 is identical to that in FRS 8 (as revised in December 2008).

- Compared to FRS 8 *Related Party Disclosures* there are differences of detail in the disclosure requirements of FRS 102, including the requirement to disclose the total key management personnel compensation.

- The disclosure exemption in FRS 8 for transactions between members of a group is retained in FRS 102.

- FRS 102 includes disclosures exemptions for state-controlled entities – these exemptions are not contained in FRS 8.

INTRODUCTION

6.1   Section 33 is concerned with disclosures which are necessary to draw attention to the possibility that an entity's financial position and profit or loss have been affected by:

- the existence of related parties; and

- transactions and balances with related parties.

SCOPE

6.2   There is a disclosure exemption for transactions entered into between two or more members of a group, provided that any subsidiary undertaking which is a party to the transaction is wholly owned by a member of the group.

6.3   There is a further disclosure exemption for certain transactions where a state has involvement with the reporting entity. The term 'state' refers to a national, regional or local government.

The disclosure exemption in the financial statements of the reporting entity applies in the following situations:

- where a state has control, joint control or significant influence over the reporting entity;

- with another entity that is a related party because the same state has control, joint control or significant influence over both the reporting entity and the other entity.

DEFINITION OF RELATED PARTY

6.4 A related party is a person or entity that is related to the entity that is preparing its financial statements (referred to in the FRS as 'the reporting entity'). The guidance behind this definition requires one of the longest sections in the Glossary to FRS 102.

(a) A person or a close member of that person's family is related to a reporting entity if that person:

    (i) has control or joint control over the reporting entity; or

    (ii) has significant influence over the reporting entity; or is a member of the key management personnel of the reporting entity or a parent of the reporting entity.

Focus

Close members of the family of a person are those family members who may be expected to influence, or be influenced by, that person in their dealings with the entity and include:

- that person's children and spouse or domestic partner;

- children of that person's spouse or domestic partner; and

- dependants of that person or that person's spouse or domestic partner.

Key management personnel is defined as those persons having authority and responsibility for planning, directing and controlling the activities of the entity, directly or indirectly, including any director (whether executive or otherwise) of that entity.

(b) An entity is related to a reporting entity if any of the following conditions apply:

    (i) the entity and the reporting entity are members of the same group (which means that each parent, subsidiary and fellow subsidiary is related to the others);

    (ii) one entity is an associate or joint venture of a member of a group of which the other entity is a member;

(iii)   both entities are joint ventures of the same third party;

(iv)   one entity is a joint venture of a third entity and the other entity is an associate of the third entity;

(v)   the entity is a post-employment benefit plan for the benefit of employees of either the reporting entity or an entity related to the reporting entity. If the reporting entity is itself such a plan, the sponsoring employers are also related to the reporting entity;

(vi)   the entity is controlled or jointly controlled by a person identified in (a) above; and

(vii)   a person identified in (a)(i) above has significant influence over the entity or is a member of the key management personnel of the entity (or a parent of the entity).

(Glossary and paragraph 33.2)

6.5   Where the terms 'associate' and 'joint venture' appear above, these include also subsidiaries of the associate and subsidiaries of the joint venture.

Example 6.1 – Who is a related party?

A Limited is owned and controlled by John who is the sole director. A Limited has transactions with the following parties:

- Pauline – who is John's domestic partner.

- George – who is Pauline's brother. George lives with John and Pauline.

- Sally – who is Pauline's daughter from a previous relationship. Sally lives in Australia and has never met John.

- B Limited – a company owned and controlled by John.

- C Limited – a company in which John is one of five directors but not a shareholder.

- D Limited – a company owned and controlled by Pauline.

Which of the above are related parties of A Limited?

- Pauline is a close member of John's family and is a related party if she has significant influence over A Limited (unlikely here as John is the sole director).

- George is not a related party except in the circumstances where George is a dependant of Pauline or John.

- Sally is a close member of John's family but would only be a related party if she had significant influence over A Limited (unlikely here as she lives in Australia).

- B Limited is a related party of A Limited as both companies are owned by John.

- C Limited is a related party of A Limited because John controls A Limited and is a member of the key management personnel of C Limited.

- D Limited is a related party of A Limited because it is controlled by a close member of John's family.

6.6   An entity should assess the substance of each possible related party relationship, and *not* merely the legal form.

DEFINITION OF RELATED PARTY TRANSACTION

6.7   A related party transaction is defined as a transfer of resources, services or obligations between a reporting entity and a related party, regardless of whether a price is charged (Glossary and paragraph 33.8).

EXAMPLES OF RELATED PARTY TRANSACTIONS

6.8   Typical examples in paragraph 33.8 include:

- transactions between an entity and its principal owners;

- transactions between an entity and another entity when both entities are under the common control of a single entity or person; and

- transactions in which an entity or person that controls the reporting entity incurs expenses directly that would otherwise have been borne by the reporting entity.

6.9   Further examples in paragraph 33.12 are:

- purchases or sales of goods (finished or unfinished);

- purchase or sales of property and other assets;

- rendering or receiving of services;

- leases;

- transfers of research and development;

- transfers under licence agreements;

- transfers under finance arrangements (including loans and equity contributions in cash or in kind); and

- provision of guarantees or collateral.

6.10 Dividends paid to directors and related parties with significant influence continue to be discloseable, even though they are not explicitly referred to in FRS 102.

FROM SCOPE OF DEFINITION

6.11 Paragraph 33.4 points out that the following are *not* related parties:

(a) two entities simply because they have a director or other member of key management personnel in common *or* because a member of key management personnel of one entity has significant influence over the other entity;

(b) two venturers simply because they share joint control over a joint venture;

(c) any of the following simply by virtue of their dealings with an entity (even though they may affect the freedom of action of an entity or participate in its decision-making process):

- providers of finance;

- trade unions;

- public utilities; and

- government departments and agencies.

(d) a customer, supplier, franchisor, distributor or general agent with whom an entity transacts a significant volume of business, merely by virtue of the resulting economic dependence.

DISCLOSURE REQUIREMENTS

Parent–subsidiary relationships

6.12 Relationships between a parent and its subsidiaries must be disclosed whether or not there have been related party transactions. The following should be disclosed:

- the name of the entity's parent; and

- the ultimate controlling party if different from the parent.

6.13   *Related party disclosures*

6.13   In cases where neither the entity's parent, nor its ultimate controlling party, produce financial statements available for public use, disclosure is required of the next most senior parent that does produce financial statements for public use.

Key management personnel compensation

6.14   The definition of key management personnel is stated in **6.4** above. Disclosure is required of the total amount of key management personnel compensation. This includes all elements of employee benefits, defined in the Glossary as all forms of consideration given by an entity in exchange for service rendered by employees.

6.15   The term 'employee benefits' is broad and includes the four types specified in Section 28 of FRS 102 (see **Chapter 23**) as well as share-based payments in Section 26 of FRS 102 (see **Chapter 28**).

6.16   Employee benefits include all forms of consideration paid, payable or provided by the entity, or on or behalf of the entity (eg by parent or subsidiary) in exchange for services provided by the entity;

Disclosure details

6.17   Where an entity has related party transactions, it should disclose:

- the nature of the related party relationship;

- information about the transactions, outstanding balances and commitments necessary for an understanding of the potential effect of the relationship on the financial statements.

Although the requirements below make no specific reference to disclosure of the name of the individual related party (as has been required by paragraph 8(a) of FRS 8), in some cases this will be necessary to comply with the above requirements.

6.18   Minimum disclosures required are:

(a)   the amount of the transactions;

(b)   the amount of outstanding balances; their terms and conditions, including whether they are secured and the nature of the consideration to be received in settlement; details of any guarantees given or received;

(c)   provision for uncollectible receivables related to the amount of outstanding balances; and

(d) the expense recognised during the period in respect of bad or doubtful debts due from related parties.

Disclosure categories

6.19   The disclosures in **6.18** above should be given separately for each of the following four categories:

(a) entities with control, joint control or significant influence over the entity;

(b) entities over which the entity has control, joint control or significant influence;

(c) key management personnel of the entity or its parent (in the aggregate); and

(d) other related parties.

Example 6.2 – Disclosure example

Note 22: Related party transactions

During the year the group entered into transactions, in the ordinary course of business, with related parties. Sales to and from related parties are made on terms equivalent to those that prevail in arm's-length transactions.

The group provides e-procurement services to its customers for which it pays an annual fee on a commercial basis to a related party, Hampstead Limited, which makes the service available. Two of the group's directors, G Holmes and W Smithson, are directors of Hampstead Limited and have a material interest in it.

The fees payable during the year to Hampstead Limited amounted to £4.3m (2014: £3.6m) and the amounts owed at the end of the year were £1.2m (2014: £0.8m).

The total key management personnel compensation during the year amounted to £567,500 (2014: £434,200).

Dividends paid to directors during the year amounted to £235,700 (2014: £198,670).

The company has been controlled throughout the current and the previous year by G Holmes, a director and controlling shareholder.

Example 6.3 – Disclosure example

Note 24: Related party transactions

Transactions between the group and its joint venture undertakings are disclosed below, with the relevant proportion being eliminated on consolidation.

During the year, Group companies entered into the following material transactions with joint ventures:

Royalties and management fees receivable £1.9m (2014: £2.1m) and dividends receivable £0.8m (2014: £0.6m).

The following receivable balances relating to joint ventures were included in the consolidated balance sheet:

Trade debtors £0.56m (2014: £0.44m).

The total key management personnel compensation during the year amounted to …

Dividends paid to directors during the year amounted to …

The company has been controlled throughout the current and previous year by …

Further considerations in FRS 102

6.20   Disclosures should not make reference to related party transactions being made on terms equivalent to those prevailing in arm's-length transactions unless such terms can be substantiated (see **Example 6.2** above).

6.21   Items of a similar nature may be disclosed on an aggregated basis, except where separate disclosure is necessary for an understanding of the effects of the related party transactions on the entity's financial statements.

Regulations to CA 2006

6.22   *Schedule 1, paragraph 72* refers to disclosures of related party transactions. The definition of related party is as set out above and the disclosure requirements above should be sufficient to comply with paragraph 72.

6.23 *Regulation 4(2)* states that medium-sized companies need not comply with paragraph 72 but, in practice, this is unlikely to have any great significance because of the equivalent requirements of Section 33 of FRS 102.

Focus

FRS 102 is not intended to be a one-stop-shop (see Appendix IV, paragraph A4.10, which states that 'preparers will continue to have regard to the requirements of company law in addition to accounting standards'). An example of this is the requirement in *CA 2006, s 413* to disclose details of advances, credits and guarantees to directors.

SUMMARY – WHAT IS DIFFERENT FROM THE PREVIOUS UK GAAP?

- Following amendments to FRS 8 in 2008, identifying related parties should be familiar.

- The wording of disclosure requirements is different compared with FRS 8 but, in practice, for most companies and groups, the level of disclosure is likely to be much the same as previously.

- The new disclosure to watch out for is the aggregate total of key management personnel compensation. Note carefully the elements which make up this aggregate total (see **6.15** above) and that the compensation includes that relating to directors, executive and non-executive, including in some cases senior management with specific responsibilities (see definition in **6.14** above).

- FRS 102 does not give comment in relation to materiality – the term 'material', is defined in the Glossary to FRS 102, in FRS 102, paragraph 2.6 and in FRS 102, paragraphs 3.15–3.16A (see **2.6** and **7.22–7.23**). Materiality, as regards related party disclosures, is defined in detail in FRS 8.

Chapter 7

Financial statement presentation

SIGNPOSTS

- Section 3 of FRS 102 sets out what a complete set of financial statements should comprise (see **7.1**) and covers related requirements such as materiality (see **7.17**) and when comparative information should be provided (see **7.16**).

- Appendix VI of FRS 102 sets out relevant legislative requirements for companies in the Republic of Ireland (see **7.5** and **7.29**).

- FRS 102, paragraphs 3.8 and 3.9 refer to going concern (FRS 102, paragraphs 3.8, 3.9)) – this is dealt with in **Chapter 2**.

- Note the requirement for a statement of compliance with FRS 102, paragraph 3.3 (see **7.13**).

- FRS 102, paragraphs 8.6 and 8.7 deal with new disclosures regarding judgements and key sources of estimation uncertainties – these are relevant to accounting policy disclosures referred to in FRS 102, paragraph 3.17(e) and are dealt with in **Chapter 3.**

- An important planning point is that detailed disclosures should be carefully noted in the first year of adopting FRS 102 (see **Chapter 39**).

INTRODUCTION AND SCOPE

Complete set of financial statements

7.1   A complete set of financial statements includes all of the following (FRS 102, paragraph 3.17):

(a)   A statement of financial position as at the reporting date. This statement may continue to be referred to as the balance sheet, if desired (see Section 4 of FRS 102 and **Chapter 8**);

(b)   A comprehensive income statement for the reporting period which should deal with both profit or loss items as well as items of other comprehensive income. FRS 102 offers a choice of two formats (see Section 5 of FRS 102 and **Chapter 9**);

(c) A statement of changes in changes in equity for the reporting period (see Section 6 of FRS 102 and **Chapter 10**);

(d) A statement of cash flows for the reporting period (see Section 7 of FRS 102 and **Chapter 11**); and

(e) Notes, comprising a summary of significant accounting policies and other explanatory information (see Section 8 of FRS 102, **7.6** below and **Chapter 3**).

Each of the above should be presented with equal prominence.

7.2 Some entities may be entitled to present a combined version of (b) and (c) – this is referred to in **Chapters 9** and **10**.

Can alternative titles be used for the financial statements?

7.3 An entity may use titles for the financial statements other than those used in this FRS as long as they are not misleading (FRS 102, paragraph 3.22).

Where relevant, this is referred to in **Chapters 8** and **9** where UK companies may wish to use titles that are as consistent as possible with existing reporting practice.

Statutory regulations – UK companies

7.4 Because of European Accounting Directives, the formats of the statement of financial position (or balance sheet) and the income statement (or profit and loss account) must comply with the format rules to the *Companies Act 2006*. These rules are set out in the Large and Medium-sized Companies and Groups (Accounts and Reports) Regulations 2008 (SI 2008/410) ('the Regulations').

Statutory regulations – Companies in the Republic of Ireland

7.5 The requirements of FRS 102 apply equally to entities in the Republic of Ireland and the UK.

Relevant legislation for Irish companies is contained in Appendix VI of FRS 102 which contains a 22-page summary of provisions in the Companies Acts 1963 to 2012, and related Regulations which implement EC Accounting Directives.

Notes to the financial statements

7.6 The notes to the financial statements should:

- present information about the basis of preparation of the financial statements and the specific accounting policies used (see **Chapter 3**);

- disclose the information required by FRS 102 that is not presented elsewhere in the financial statements; and

- provide information that is not provided elsewhere in the financial statements but is relevant to an understanding of them.

(FRS 102, paragraph 8.2.)

7.7 Items in the financial statements should be cross-referenced to related information in the notes, which should normally be presented in the following order:

- a statement that the financial statements have been prepared in compliance with FRS 102 (see **7.13**);

- a summary of significant accounting policies applied (see **Chapter 3**);

- supporting information for each item presented in the financial statements, in the sequence in which each statement and each line item is presented; and

- any other disclosures.

Disclosure of accounting policies

7.8 The following should be disclosed in the summary of significant accounting policies (see **Chapter 3**):

- the measurement basis (or bases) used in preparing the financial statements; and

- the other accounting policies used that are relevant to an understanding of the financial statements.

(FRS 102, paragraph 8.4.)

Information about judgements and key sources of estimation uncertainties

7.9 The disclosure requirements of FRS 102, Sections 8.6 and 8.7 are dealt with in **Chapter 3**.

FAIR PRESENTATION AND COMPLIANCE WITH THE FRS

Fair presentation

7.10 FRS 102 requires the financial statements to present fairly the financial position, financial performance and cash flows of an entity.

7.11 *'Fair presentation'* is defined in the Glossary as: 'faithful representation of the effects of transactions, other events and conditions in accordance with the definitions and recognition criteria for assets, liabilities, income and expenses.'

7.12 Additional disclosures over and above those required by FRS 102 may be needed when compliance with FRS 102 is insufficient to enable users to understand the effect of particular transactions, other events and conditions on the entity's financial position and performance.

Compliance with FRS 102

7.13 Where an entity has complied fully with FRS 102, it should include a statement of compliance within the notes to the financial statements (FRS 102, paragraph 3.3). (See **Chapter 39, Examples 39.2** and **39.10**, which give suggested wordings, including that which is appropriate in the first year of adopting FRS 102).

A public benefit entity (see **Chapter 40**) that has applied the 'PBE' prefixed paragraphs is required to make an explicit and unreserved statement that it is a public benefit entity.

7.14 In what paragraph 3.4 of FRS 102 refers to as 'extremely rare circumstances', where management concludes that compliance with the FRS would be so misleading as to conflict with the objectives of financial statements, the entity shall depart from that requirement.

7.15 In such rare cases, FRS 102, paragraphs 3.5 and 3.6 set out the required disclosures.

SOME IMPORTANT CONSIDERATIONS

Changes in reporting year-ends

7.16 The following disclosures are required when an entity changes its reporting period and presents financial statements for a period of longer or shorter than a year (FRS 102, paragraph 3.10):

- the fact that the reporting period has changed;

- the reason for using a longer or shorter period; and

- the fact that comparative amounts and notes presented in the financial statements are not entirely comparable.

Presentation and classification of items

7.17 An entity should be consistent between one reporting period and the next as regards presentation and classification of items except when either of the following applies:

(a) significant changes in the nature of the entity's operations or a review of the financial statements indicate that another presentation or classification would be more appropriate; or

(b) FRS 102 requires a change in presentation.

Example 7.1 – Change of presentation

Company A has changed its business model within the past 12 months. Previously it was a manufacturing company and presented its profit and loss expenses analysed by function of expense (cost of sales etc).

The business has now ceased manufacturing and instead receives most of its income by way of royalties. The directors have decided that analysis by nature of expense (FRS 102, paragraph 5.11(a)), including line items such as staff costs, depreciation, operating charges is more appropriate and relevant for the company's new business model.

7.18 When there is a change in classification or presentation, comparatives should be restated except where this is impracticable. Applying a requirement is impracticable when the entity cannot apply it after making every reasonable effort to do so (Glossary). Note that where an entity considers reclassification is 'impracticable', it should disclose the reason why.

7.19 When comparatives are reclassified, the following should be disclosed:

- the nature of the reclassification;

- the amount of each item or class of items that is reclassified; and

- the reason for that reclassification.

Comparatives

7.20   A complete set of financial statements should, as a minimum, present comparatives for each of the required financial statements and the related notes.

Comparative information should be given for all amounts presented in the current period's financial statements, *except where the FRS permits or requires otherwise.*

As regards narrative and descriptive information, comparative information should be provided when it is relevant to an understanding of the current period's financial statements.

Focus

This is a crucial requirement and should be borne in mind when considering all disclosure areas. Where exemption is available in particular cases, this will be clearly indicated in the text.

Implementing FRS 102 – planning ahead

7.21   Restated comparatives will be required in the first year of adopting FRS 102 – this is dealt with in **Chapter 39**.

Materiality

7.22   The term 'material' is defined in the Glossary as:

'Omissions or misstatements of items are material if they could, individually or collectively, influence the economic decisions of users taken on the basis of the financial statements. Materiality depends on the size and nature of the omission or misstatement judged in the surrounding circumstances. The size or nature of the item, or a combination of both, could be the determining factor.'

7.23   An entity need not provide a specific disclosure otherwise required by the FRS if the information is not material (FRS 102, paragraph 3.16A).

Focus

This is a long-standing feature of UK GAAP – for example SSAPs contained the phrase 'the provisions of this Statement of Standard Accounting Practice … need not be applied to immaterial items'.

This provision is not contained within the IFRS for SMEs – it was added in to maintain the status quo as compared with existing UK GAAP.

Aggregation

7.24   A line item which is not individually material should be aggregated with other items either in the particular financial statement or in the notes.

7.25   An item which is not sufficiently material to warrant separate presentation in the particular financial statement, may warrant separate presentation in the notes.

IDENTIFICATION OF THE FINANCIAL STATEMENTS

7.26   Each of the financial statements and notes should be clearly identified and distinguished from other information in the same document.

7.27   The following information should be displayed properly and repeated when necessary for an understanding of the information presented (FRS 102, paragraph 3.23):

- the name of the reporting entity and any change in its name since the end of the preceding reporting period;

- whether the financial statements cover the individual entity or a group of entities;

- the date of the end of the reporting period and the period covered by the financial statements;

- the presentation currency (see **Chapter 32**); and

- the level of rounding, if any, used in the financial statements.

7.28   Other disclosures required are (FRS 102, paragraph 3.24):

- the domicile and legal form of the entity;

- the entity's country of incorporation;

- the address of its registered office;

- its principal place of business if this is different from its registered office; and

- a description of the nature of the entity's operations and its principal activities (unless this is disclosed by cross-reference to the business review or similar statement accompanying the financial statements).

ADDITIONAL LEGAL REQUIREMENTS

7.29   FRS 102, Appendix IV: A4.10 makes the following important comment:

'However, FRS 102 is not intended to be a one-stop shop for all accounting and legal requirements, and although the FRC believes the FRS 102 is not inconsistent with company law, compliance with FRS 102 alone will often be insufficient to ensure compliance with all the disclosure requirements set out in the Act and the Regulations. As a result preparers will continue to be required to have regard to the requirements of company law in addition to accounting standards.'

INTERIM FINANCIAL REPORTS

7.30   FRS 102 does not address presentation of interim financial reports, but requires that entities which prepare such reports should describe the basis for preparing and presenting the information.

7.31   Where relevant, UK entities should refer to the following statement issued in July 2007 by the former ASB: 'Half-yearly financial reports'. Note that that this statement will *not* be withdrawn for periods commencing on or after1 January 2015.

SUMMARY – WHAT IS DIFFERENT FROM THE PREVIOUS UK GAAP?

- The good news is that a large part of Section 3 of FRS 102 contains similar requirements to those in existing UK GAAP, but there are some differences to note:

    - The complete set of financial statements contains a number of changed requirements (see **7.1**). These are referred to in detail in **Chapters 8 to 11**.

    - FRS 102 requires a statement of compliance (see **7.13**).

    - There are some options for alternative titles to the financial statements (see **7.3**).

    - FRS 102 refers to 'fair presentation' (see **7.10–7.11**).

- In relation to accounting policy disclosures, FRS 102, paragaraphs 8.6 and 8.7 require the disclosure of information about judgements and key sources of estimation uncertainties (see **Chapter 3**).

Chapter 8

Statement of financial position (Balance sheet)

SIGNPOSTS

● The statement can alternatively continue to be referred to as the balance sheet, if desired (see **8.1**).

● The balance sheet should continue to be presented in the same way as at present (same caption headings) as it must comply with the Regulations to CA 2006 (see **8.2**).

● There is a new disclosure requirement relating to a description of each reserve within equity (see **8.7**).

● Section 4 refers to binding sales agreements (see **8.8** below and **Chapter 33**).

● Section 4 refers to situations where an entity does not have an unconditional right to defer settlement of a liability for at least 12 months after the reporting date, which will affect whether the liability is classified as 'creditors: amounts falling due within one year' (see **8.5**).

● There is a new requirement to give a description of each reserve within equity (see **8.7**).

INTRODUCTION

8.1   The term 'statement of financial position' is commonly used in full IFRS. As paragraph 3.22 of FRS 102 effectively allows the term 'balance sheet' to be used instead, this chapter uses this familiar UK terminology.

FORMAT AND CONTENT

The Regulations to CA 2006

8.2   The balance sheet should be presented in accordance with Schedule 1 of the Regulations to CA 2006 (see **7.4**). The Regulations offer a choice of two balance sheet formats. An example of the more commonly used format is given below (see **Example 8.1**).

8.3 *Statement of financial position (Balance sheet)*

Relevant company law regulations for companies in the Republic of Ireland were referred to in Chapter 7 (see **7.5**).

8.3 Transition issues, for example restatement of comparatives, in the first year of applying FRS 102 are dealt with in **Chapter 39** of this book.

Further requirements

8.4 An entity is required to present additional line items, headings and subtotals in the balance sheet when such presentation is relevant to an understanding of the entity's financial position.

Example 8.1 – Balance sheet format

Balance sheet as at 31 December 2015

	Notes	2015 £	2015 £	2014 £	2014 £
Fixed assets					
Tangible assets – property, plant and equipment			x		x
Investments	7		x		x
			x		x
Current assets					
Stocks		x		x	
Debtors		x		x	
Prepayments and accrued income		x		x	
Cash at bank and in hand		–		x	
		x		x	
Creditors: Amounts falling due within one year	9	(x)		(x)	
Net current assets			x		x
Total assets less current liabilities			x		x
Creditors: Amounts falling due after more than one year	10		(x)		(x)

102

Provisions for liabilities		(x)	(x)
Taxation, including deferred taxation	11	(x)	(x)
Net assets		x	x
Capital and reserves			
Called-up equity share capital	13	x	x
Capital redemption reserve	14	x	x
Profit and loss account	15	x	x
Shareholders' funds		x	x

SPECIFIC ISSUES

Classification of creditors as current

8.5   This refers to a situation where an entity does not have an unconditional right to defer settlement of a liability for at least 12 months after the reporting date. Such a liability should be classified under 'Creditors: amounts falling due within one year' (FRS 102, paragraph 4.7).

Focus

This maintains the requirement previously in UK GAAP FRS 25, paragraphs 50A–50E (but in considerably less detail).

Note also post-balance sheet event disclosure implications under Section 32 (see **Chapter 5**).

Example 8.2 – Breach of loan covenant: agreement with bank not reached before balance sheet date

Company A has a balance sheet date of 31 December 2011. The company has a bank loan which was originally due to be repaid on 31 December 2013 but the company breached its loan covenant in November 2011. Agreement was subsequently reached with the bank in May 2012 before the accounts were signed off and a revised repayment date of 31 December 2014 agreed.

In accordance with FRS 102, paragraph 4.7, the entity should classify the liability as current because, at the balance sheet, it does not have an unconditional right to defer its settlement for at least 12 months after that date. Post-balance sheet event disclosure will be required in accordance with Section 32.

Example 8.3 – Breach of loan covenant: agreement with bank reached before the balance sheet date

An alternative scenario to that above is where the lender agrees *before* the balance sheet date not to demand payment as a consequence of the breach and allows a payment period of at least 12 months beyond the balance sheet date. Alternatively the lender may provide a period of grace ending at least 12 months after the balance sheet date within which the entity can rectify the breach and during which the lender cannot demand immediate repayment.

In these circumstances the liability may be classified as non-current.

Notes relating to share capital and reserves

8.6   The following should be disclosed, either on the face of the balance sheet, or in the notes, in respect of each class of share capital (FRS 102, paragraph 4.12):

- the number of shares issued and fully paid, and issued but not fully paid;

- par value per share, or the fact that the shares have no par value;

- a reconciliation of the number of shares outstanding at the beginning and at the end of the period;

- the rights, preferences and restrictions attaching to that class of shares including restrictions on the distribution of dividends and the repayment of capital;

- shares in the entity held by the entity or its subsidiaries, associates or joint ventures; and

- shares reserved for issue under options and contracts for the sale of shares, including the terms and amounts.

8.7   The notes should include a description of each reserve within equity.

Example 8.4

Share premium account

This reserve represents the premium on shares issued at a value that exceeds their nominal value.

Capital redemption reserve

The reserve is a non-distributable reserve and represents the nominal value of shares purchased and cancelled.

Merger reserve

The merger reserve represents the excess of the fair value over the nominal value of shares issued by the company to acquire at least 90% in an acquiree company. A purchaser company acquiring at least 90% equity interest in an acquiree company under an arrangement which provides for the allotment of equity shares by the purchaser in return for the equity interest in the acquire must apply *section 612* of the *Companies Act 2006*.

When applicable, *section 612* requires that the premium on the issue of equity shares by the purchaser be disregarded. Therefore, the company did not record a premium on the shares it issued but recognised a merger reserve in the consolidated balance sheet.

Binding sales agreements

8.8   An entity may, at the reporting date, have a binding sale agreement for a major disposal of assets, or a disposal group. Disclosure requirements for this situation are dealt with in **33.2**.

SUMMARY – WHAT IS DIFFERENT FROM THE PREVIOUS UK GAAP?

- Financial statements prepared in accordance with FRS 102 must comply with the format rules in the Regulations to CA 2006. This effectively means entities may continue to follow existing format requirements, or take the opportunity to choose an alternative format (provided it is consistent with the Regulations).

- Some entities that previously did not come under *CA 2006* may need to review their formats to ensure compliance with FRS 102.

- Entities will be required to disclose a description of each reserve within equity (see **8.7**).

- FRS 102 specifies explicit disclosure requirements relating to binding sales agreements (see **8.8**).

Chapter 9

Statement of comprehensive income and income statement

SIGNPOSTS

- FRS 102 offers a choice of two formats for the Statement of comprehensive income (see **9.10**).

- Some companies with relatively straightforward circumstances may have the option of a single statement of income and retained earnings (see FRS 102, paragraph 5.1 and **Chapter 10**).

- This part of FRS 102 contains some terminology that may be unfamiliar to existing UK GAAP users – in particular the use of the term 'other comprehensive income' (see **9.28–9.29**).

- **Chapter 7** referred to FRS 102, paragraph 3.22 which states that 'an entity may use titles for the financial statements other than those used in this FRS as long as they are not misleading'.

- UK companies may wish to use titles that are as consistent as possible with existing reporting practice as long as this complies with the Regulations to CA 2006 – this approach is followed in this chapter and acceptable alternatives are indicated where applicable.

- FRS 102 does not refer to the term exceptional item – this chapter gives guidance on acceptable practice (see **9.18**).

INTRODUCTION AND SCOPE

Introduction

9.1 Section 5 of FRS 102 requires an entity to present its total comprehensive income – this is effectively its total financial performance. Total comprehensive income includes two main elements:

- the profit or loss for the period – this is essentially the profit after tax as currently reported in the profit and loss account; and

- other comprehensive income – items permitted or required to be recognised outside of profit or loss, for example surpluses on the revaluation of fixed assets.

Profit or loss + other comprehensive income = Total comprehensive income.

Other comprehensive income is further referred to below (see **9.28** and **9.29**).

9.2   Section 5 gives a choice of two presentation formats – these are referred to below.

Scope

9.3   All entities, whether or not they report under *CA 2006*, must comply with the requirements of Section 5, and in addition:

- companies which report under *CA 2006* must comply with the general rules and format requirements of Schedule 1 (companies other than banking and insurance companies), or Schedule 2 (banking companies) or Schedule 3 (insurance companies) to the Regulations to CA 2006; or Schedule 6 for groups.

- LLPs must comply with the general rules and formats of *Schedule 1* or *Schedule 3* to the *LLP Regulations*.

9.4   Legislation relating to companies in the Republic of Ireland is dealt with in Appendix VI of FRS 102 (see **Appendix**).

9.5   Entities which report under Regulations other than those referred to above, should comply with the relevant requirements of FRS 102 except to the extent that these conflict with Regulations applicable to the entity.

CA 2006 Regulations

9.6   The Regulations to CA 2006 (see **7.4**) require that every profit and loss account must show the items listed in any one of the profit and loss account formats (analysis of expenses by function or analysis of expenses by nature (see **9.13**)), and also that:

- any item required to be shown in a company's balance sheet or profit and loss account may be shown in greater detail than required by the particular format used; and

- every profit and loss account must show the amount of a company's profit or loss on ordinary activities before taxation.

9.7   Ordinary activities are described in Section 5 as: 'any activities which are undertaken by a reporting entity as part of its business and such related activities in which the reporting entity engages in furtherance of, or incidental to, or arising from, those activities.'

9.8   Paragraph 5.10 of FRS 102 states that: 'ordinary activities include any effects on the reporting entity of any event in the various environments in which it operates, including the political, regulatory, economic and geographical environments, irrespective of the frequency or unusual nature of the events.'

Focus

As regards Section 5 of FRS 102, there have been a number of changes to the text in the IFRS for SMEs.

Paragraphs 5.10 and 5.10A dealing with ordinary activities and extraordinary items have been added in order to ensure that FRS 102 is fully compliant with EU Directives.

These paragraphs are unlikely to result in any changes to existing UK reporting practices as the added text is based on the definitions in FRS 3 *Reporting Financial Performance* which deliberately limited the usage of extraordinary items, in order to prevent the profit and loss account from being manipulated.

9.9   Although FRS 102 uses terminology based on the IFRS for SMEs (statement of comprehensive income; income statement), UK companies adopting FRS 102 must nevertheless comply with the above requirements in the Regulations to CA 2006 as well as additional requirements of FRS 102. FRS 102 effectively requires a 'Regulations plus' approach.

(Note: Section 3, paragraph 3.22 regarding alternative financial statement titles.)

FORMAT OPTIONS

9.10   FRS 102 requires that a complete set of financial statements should include either of the following:

(a)   a single statement of comprehensive income displaying all items of income and expense recognised in determining profit or loss (effectively the profit and loss account) and items of other comprehensive income; or

(b)   two separate statements: a separate income statement (profit and loss account) and a statement of comprehensive income.

9.11   Both options are referred to below. The second option has proved to be more popular for UK groups who have adopted EU-endorsed IFRS, and so may also prove to be the more popular option under FRS 102.

9.12   The text below deals with the two-statement option first, followed more briefly by the single statement option. Before dealing with the format options, there are a number of issues which apply whichever format option is selected. These are dealt with immediately below.

GENERAL REQUIREMENTS

Analysis of expenditure

9.13   Expenses should be analysed either by function of expense (the more popular option currently used in the UK) or by nature of expense. Strictly the choice should be determined by reference to 'whichever provides information that is reliable and more relevant':

● analysis by function aggregates expenses under headings including cost of sales, distribution costs and administrative expenses; or

● analysis by nature aggregates expenses under headings such as staff costs, depreciation, raw materials and consumables, other operating charges.

(See the Regulations to CA 2006, Schedule 1, Section B.)

9.14   Examples of each of the above are included below – see **Examples 9.3** and **9.4**.

Profit or loss on ordinary activities before tax and operating profit

9.15   As indicated above, the Regulations require disclosure of a company's profit or loss on ordinary activities before taxation.

9.16   However, FRS 102 does not require disclosure of operating profit and the term, although used in the FRS (paragraph 5.9B), is not a defined term in the Glossary. However, the FRS does not prohibit use of the term and it is used in the example in the Appendix to Section 5 of FRS 102 (note that the Appendix provides guidance on Section 5 but is not part of the section). **Example 33.2** in **Chapter 33** is based on the example in the Appendix to Section 5.

9.17   If the term 'operating profit' is used, it is important that items such as reorganisation expenses or inventory write-downs which relate to the entity's operations are not excluded on the grounds that they occur infrequently or irregularly.

By way of illustration, in the example referred to above, the operating profit includes profit on disposal of operations and the effect of discontinued operations (see **9.25** below and **33.7–33.9**).

Exceptional items

9.18   Paragraph 5.9A requires separate disclosure of the nature and amount of items of income or expense which are material.

Example 9.1 – Items which might require separate disclosure

Examples of items which would require separate disclosure if considered material include:

- inventory and plant write-downs/reversals of write-downs;
- restructuring cost;
- disposals of property, plant and equipment items;
- disposals of investments;
- litigation settlements; and
- other reversals of provisions.

9.19   Although FRS 102 does not use the term 'exceptional item', it may continue to be used provided the term is defined, for example in the summary of significant accounting policies.

The Accounting Councils Advice to the FRC paragraph 43 noted the former Accounting Standards Board's policy of supplementing company law formats to highlight a range of important components of financial performance in order to aid users' understanding.

Example 9.2 – Accounting policy extract: exceptional items

Extract from statement of accounting policies

Exceptional items are defined as items of income and expenditure which are material and which are considered to be of such significance that they require separate disclosure, either on the face of the profit and loss account, or in the notes to the financial statements.

9.20   Presentation options for exceptional items include:

● separate disclosure on the face of the profit and loss account/income statement, supplemented by explanatory note (see **Example 9.3**);

● disclosure in a note to the profit and loss account/income statement without separate disclosure on the face of the profit and loss account/ income statement; and

● use of a multi-column approach – first column profit before exceptional items, second column exceptional items, third column for total income and expenses.

Investment properties

9.21   Where the fair value model is used (see **13.17, 13.18**), changes in fair value are taken through profit or loss, not through other comprehensive income. For a non-property company, these changes could be presented as other operating income.

Extraordinary items

9.22   FRS 102 contains paragraph 5.10A referring to and defining extraordinary items. This was inserted to comply with EU Directive requirements. In practice, in the UK, as indicated above, it is highly unlikely that companies will wish to use this caption heading.

By contrast, full IFRS prohibits the use of extraordinary items.

Correction of material errors and changes in accounting policies

9.23   These should be presented as retrospective adjustments and should not be included within total comprehensive income (see **9.28** below).

Focus

This is a different presentation approach compared with existing UK GAAP FRS 3 which includes correction of fundamental errors and changes in accounting policies within the Statement of total recognised gains and losses.

Additional line items, headings and subtotals

9.24   FRS 102 requires additional line items, headings and subtotals, where such presentation is 'relevant to an understanding of the entity's financial performance'.

Discontinued operations

9.25   Disclosure requirements relating to discontinued operations (including the requirement to restate comparatives) are dealt with in Section 5, paragraphs 5.7D and 5.7E. These are not further referred to in this chapter as they are dealt with in detail in **Chapter 33**.

Consolidated financial statements issues

9.26   Presentation requirements specific to consolidated financial statements are dealt with in **Chapter 29** (see **29.24**) and those relating to associates and jointly controlled entities in **Chapter 31** (see **31.14**).

THE TWO-STATEMENT APPROACH

Introduction

9.27   The two separate statements comprise:

- an income statement or profit and loss account (either title may be used); and

- a statement of total comprehensive income.

Income statement (or profit and loss account)

Example 9.3 – Presentation of profit and loss account/income statement

Profit and loss account for the year ended 31 December 2015

	Notes	2015	2014
		£	£
Turnover	2	x	x
Cost of sales		(x)	(x)
Gross profit		x	x
Distribution costs		(x)	(x)
Administrative expenses (including exceptional costs of £392,000) (2014: £514,000)	6	(x)	(x)
Operating profit	3	x	x
Net interest receivable	7	x	x
Profit on ordinary activities before tax		x	x
Taxation	8	(x)	(x)
Profit for the year	13	x	x

The operating profit for both years arises from the company's continuing operations.

Statement of comprehensive income

9.28   Section 5, paragraph 5.7 requires that the statement of comprehensive income begins with profit or loss (ie the profit for the year as in **Example 9.2** above) as its first line, and then display as a minimum line items that present each item of other comprehensive income (OCI) classified by nature.

9.29   The following are examples of other comprehensive income:

(a)   some gains or losses arising on translating the financial statements of foreign operations (see **32.25, 32.45, 32.49**);

(b)   some actuarial gains and losses related to defined benefit pension schemes (see **Chapter 23**);

(c)   some changes in fair value of hedging instruments where the complex hedge accounting option is adopted (see **38.19**);

(d)   some changes in fair value of investments in subsidiaries, associates and joint ventures (see **31.28** and **31.50**); and

(e)   some gains and losses arising on revaluation of property, plant and equipments (see **12.18** but note comments regarding investment properties in **9.21** above).

Example 9.4 – Statement of comprehensive income (where separate profit and loss account presented)

Statement of comprehensive income for the year ended 31 December 2015

Profit for the year		x	x
Other comprehensive income:			
Revaluation of property (less deferred tax)	6	(x)	(x)
Total comprehensive income for the year		x	x

No items of other comprehensive income

9.30   If there are no items of other comprehensive income in either the current or the comparative period, the entity may present only a profit and loss account (income statement) where the bottom line is labelled profit or loss.

Material errors and changes in accounting policy

9.31   Corrections of errors and changes in accounting policies (see **Chapter 3**) should be presented as retrospective adjustments of prior periods rather than as part of the profit or loss in the period in which they arise.

9.32   These items are presented in either a statement of changes in equity or in a statement of income and retained earnings (see **Chapter 10**).

Combine with equity

9.33   The circumstances in which an entity may present a single statement of income and retained earnings are dealt with in **Chapter 10**.

THE SINGLE STATEMENT APPROACH

9.34   As an alternative to the two-statement approach referred to above, an entity may present a single statement of comprehensive income.

9.35   All of the considerations outlined above for the two-statement approach are applicable. The main difference is simply one of presentation – a single statement in two parts as illustrated immediately following.

Example 9.5 – Statement of comprehensive income (single statement approach)

Statement of comprehensive income

	Notes	2015	2014
		£	£
Turnover	2	x	x
Cost of sales		(x)	(x)
Gross profit		x	x
Distribution costs		(x)	(x)
Administrative expenses (including exceptional costs of £392,000) (2014: £514,000)	6	(x)	(x)
Operating profit	3	x	x
Net interest receivable	7	x	x
Profit on ordinary activities before tax		x	x
Taxation	8	(x)	(x)
		x	x
Profit for the year			
Other comprehensive income:			
Revaluation of property (less deferred tax)	13	x	x
Total comprehensive income for the year		x	x

Quick tip

Many straightforward business may be eligible under FRS 102, paragraph 3.18 to present a single statement of income and retained earnings – see **Chapter 10**.

SUMMARY – WHAT IS DIFFERENT FROM THE PREVIOUS UK GAAP?

- The two-statement approach is similar to UK GAAP – the income statement and the profit and loss account are identical. However, a key difference is that under FRS 3 the statement of total recognised gains and losses includes prior year adjustments, but these are excluded from the statement of comprehensive income under FRS 102

- FRS 102 does not use the term exceptional items, and all items go 'above the line' including profit on sale of land and buildings and discontinued operations (note the illustrative example in Appendix to Section 5).

- FRS 102 requires entities that do not report under *CA 2006* to comply with the Regulations to CA 2006 except to the extent that these requirements are not permitted by any statutory framework under which the entities operate. Some entities that previously did not come under *CA 2006* may need to review their formats to ensure compliance with FRS 102.

Chapter 10

Statement of changes in equity and statement of changes in retained earnings

---

SIGNPOSTS

There are two main issues in Section 6 of FRS 102:

- The statement of changes in equity – this is one of the four primary financial statements, all of which are given equal prominence (see **10.2**).

- FRS 102, Section 6.3 sets out the items that must be presented in the Statement of changes in equity (see **10.3**).

- FRS 102, Section 6.4 gives an option for some entities with straightforward circumstances to present a combined statement of income and retained earnings (see **10.5** and **10.6**).

SCOPE

10.1   Section 6 contains the requirements for presenting an entity's change in equity for the period.

There are two possible statement formats:

- A statement of changes in equity – this may be used in any circumstances.

- A statement of income and retained earnings – this may only be used in straightforward situations where certain conditions are met (see below) and if the entity so chooses.

117

STATEMENT OF CHANGES IN EQUITY

10.2   The aim of the statement is to present the movements in equity during the current and previous period relating to the following:

- profit or loss for the period;

- other comprehensive income for the period;

- the effects of changes in accounting policies and corrections of errors recognised in the period;

- investments by equity investors; and

- dividends and other distributions to equity investors during the period.

10.3   FRS 102, paragraph 6.3 requires the statement of changes in equity for the current and comparative period to show the following:

- total comprehensive income for the period, showing separately the total amounts attributable to owners of the parent and to non-controlling interests;

- for each component of equity:

   - the effects of changes in accounting policies;

   - the effects of correction of material errors;

   - a reconciliation between the carrying amount at the beginning and the end of the period, separately disclosing the changes resulting from:

      ○   profit or loss;

      ○   other comprehensive income;

      ○   issue of shares;

      ○   purchase of own shares;

      ○   dividends and other distributions to owners; and

      ○   changes in ownership interests in subsidiaries that do not result in a loss of control.

Focus

The statement of changes in equity must be presented as a primary statement. It cannot be presented as a note to the financial statements.

10.4 An analysis of other comprehensive income is required item by item (see **9.29** for examples). This analysis may either be shown on the face of the statement, or in a separate note.

Example 10.1 – Statement of changes in equity – no items of other comprehensive income

	Note	Share capital £	Share premium account £	Profit and loss reserves £	Total equity £
Balances at 1 January 2014		x	x	x	x
Profit for the year				x	x
Total comprehensive income for the year				x	x
Dividends paid	7			(x)	(x)
Issue of share capital	18	x	x		x
Balance at 31 December 2014		x	x	x	x
Profit for the year				x	x
Total comprehensive income for the year				x	x
Dividends paid	7			(x)	(x)
Issue of share capital	18	x	x		x
Balance at 31 December 2015		x	x	x	x

Example 10.2 – Statement of changes in equity – including item of other comprehensive income

	Note	Share capital	Revaluation reserve	Profit and loss reserves	Total equity
		£	£	£	£
Balances at 1 January 2014		x	x	x	x
Profit for the year				x	x
Other comprehensive income – surplus on revaluation of property (net of tax)					
Total comprehensive income for the year		x		x	x
Dividends paid	7			(x)	(x)
Issue of share capital	18	x	x		x
Balance at 31 December 2014		x	x	x	x
Profit for the year				x	x
Other comprehensive income – surplus on revaluation of property (net of tax)					
Total comprehensive income for the year				x	x
Dividends paid	7			(x)	(x)
Issue of share capital	18	x	x		x
Balance at 31 December 2015		x	x	x	x

STATEMENT OF INCOME AND RETAINED EARNINGS

10.5   This statement is an alternative to presenting a separate comprehensive income statement and a separate changes in equity statement but is only available in restricted circumstances.

FRS 102, paragraph 6.4 allows the alternative to be used where the *only* changes in equity for the periods presented (ie current period plus comparative) arise from:

● profit or loss;

● payment of dividends;

● correction of prior period errors; or

● changes in accounting policy.

10.6   The following is to be presented in the statement of income and retained earnings:

● profit or loss for the period in the income statement/profit and loss account;

● retained earnings at the beginning of the reporting period;

● dividends declared and paid or payable during the period;

● restatement of retained earnings for corrections of prior period errors;

● restatements of retained earnings for changes in accounting policy; and

● retained earnings at the end of the reporting period.

Example 10.3 – Statement of income and retained earnings

An entity has no items of other comprehensive income in either the current or the preceding period, nor are there any restatements in respect of correction of errors or changes in accounting policies.

The combined statement will be very simple – a profit and loss account which ends with the following line items:

Profit for the year	x
Retained earnings brought forward	x
Dividends paid	(x)
Retained earnings carried forward	x

SUMMARY – WHAT IS DIFFERENT FROM THE PREVIOUS UK GAAP?

FRS 3 does not require a detailed statement of changes in equity to be presented as a primary statement, but does require a summarised movement in shareholders' funds (which could be presented as a note to the financial statements).

Chapter 11

Statement of cash flows

SIGNPOSTS

- The statement of cash flows is a mandatory primary statement which must be presented with equal prominence to that of the statement of comprehensive income (profit and loss account) and statement of financial position (balance sheet) (see **11.1**).

- The statement of cash flows must be classified under three headings: operating activities, investing activities and financing activities (see **11.3**).

- The reconciliation of movement in cash and cash equivalents must also be presented as part of the statement of cash flows (see **11.13**).

- Disclosure shall be made of all significant cash and cash equivalent balances held by the reporting entity that are not available for use by the reporting entity, together with management commentary (see **11.14**).

- The statement of cash flows under FRS 102 is presented differently than how previous FRS 1 *Cash Flow Statements* required (see **11.15**).

INTRODUCTION

11.1   An entity's reporting profit is an important figure, but such profits must be cash-backed. Cash flow is thus of equal importance. Users of the financial statements will be interested for various reasons (eg suppliers will be interested in being paid for goods or services rendered to the reporting entity, shareholders will expect dividend payments, employees will require remunerating for their services to the reporting entity, financiers will want to ensure that the reporting entity can meet its funding obligations and HM Revenue and Customs (HMRC) will expect to receive appropriate levels of tax a company owes on the profits that it generates). For this reason, the standard mandates that the preparation of the statement of cash flows will take equal prominence to that of the statement of comprehensive income (profit and loss account) and the statement of financial position (balance sheet).

11.1 *Statement of cash flows*

The *Financial Reporting Standard applicable in the UK and the Republic of Ireland* deals with the statement of cash flows at Section 7. Section 7 requires a reporting entity to provide information about the changes in cash and cash equivalents for a reporting period. It does not, however, apply to the following entities:

- mutual life assurance companies;

- pension funds; and

- open-ended investment funds that meet all the following conditions:

  - substantially all of the entity's investments are highly liquid;

  - substantially all of the entity's investments are carried at market value; and

  - the entity provides a statement of changes in net assets.

DEFINITIONS

11.2   Section 7 of FRS 102 defines *cash equivalents* as 'short-term, highly liquid investments held to meet short-term cash commitments rather than for investment or other purposes' (FRS 102, paragraph 7.2).

This paragraph also confirms that an investment will qualify as a cash equivalent when it has a short maturity of three months or less from the date the reporting entity acquires such an investment. Bank overdrafts are also considered to be a component of cash and cash equivalents if they are repayable on demand and form an integral part of an entity's cash management.

PREPARATION OF THE STATEMENT OF CASH FLOWS

11.3   Section 7 of FRS 102 requires a reporting entity to prepare the statement of cash flows by categorising cash flows under three separate headings:

- operating activities;

- investing activities; and

- financing activities.

Operating Activities

11.4   Operating activities are considered to be the entity's revenue-producing activities. In other words, they are the cash flows that arise due to the day-to-day business activities the reporting entity undertakes.

Section 7.4 to FRS 102 provides the following examples of cash flows from a reporting entity's operating activities:

(a)   cash receipts from the sale of goods and rendering of services;

(b)   cash receipts from royalties, fees, commissions and other revenue;

(c)   cash payments to suppliers for goods and services;

(d)   cash payments to and on behalf of employees;

(e)   cash payments or refunds of *income tax*, unless they can be specifically identified with financing and investing activities;

(f)   cash receipts and payments from investments, loans and other contracts held for dealing or trading purposes, which are similar to *inventory* acquired specifically for resale; and

(g)   cash advances and loans made to other parties by *financial institutions*.

> **Example 11.1 – Reporting sales proceeds and a profit on disposal**
>
> Company A Limited manufactures roller shutters for commercial properties. The shutters are produced to order using a large item of plant in the manufacturing process. Company A has a year-end of 31 October 2013; on 20 October 2013 it sold the machine for £30,000, making a profit of £10,000 in exchange for a newer model.
>
> The £10,000 gain will be included within Company A's profit or loss as a profit on disposal of fixed asset. The sale proceeds of £30,000 (as opposed to the gain) will be reported in cash flows from investing activities, as opposed to cash flows from operating activities.

Method of Reporting Cash Flows from Operating Activities

11.5   Section 7 to FRS 102 provides for two possible methods for reporting cash flows from operating activities. Reporting entities can use either the:

● indirect method; or

● direct method

to prepare the statement of cash flows.

Indirect method

11.6   Under the indirect method, net cash flow from operating activities is arrived at by adjusting profit or loss for the effects of non-cash items reported in profit or loss and fluctuations during the accounting period in stock, debtors and creditors as well as all other items for which the cash effects relate to investing or financing activities of the reporting entity and an example of this method is as follows:

	2013	2012
	£'000	*£'000*
Operating profit	6,261	6,063
Depreciation charges	539	475
Loss on disposal of fixed assets	–	62
Gain on sale of subsidiary company	(125)	–
Equity-settled share-based payment expense	156	208
Decrease (increase) in trade and other debtors	(140)	139
Decrease (increase) in stock	27	(14)
(Decrease) increase in trade and other creditors	222	149
Cash generated from operations	6,940	7,082

	2013	2012
	£'000	*£'000*
Interest paid	(1,650)	(1,110)
Interest received	12	14
Corporation tax paid	(1,254)	(1,657)
Cash flow from operating activities	4,048	4,329

Direct Method

Focus

UK GAAP does prefer the use of the 'direct' method of preparing the statement of cash flows; however the reality is that, in practice, the indirect method is the method commonly used and is as equally acceptable.

11.7 Under the direct method, information is disclosed about the major classes of gross cash receipts and gross cash payments. In practice this method is less commonly used than the indirect method. An example of this method is as follows:

Example 11.2 – Illustration of the direct method

	2013	2012
	£'000	*£'000*
Collections from trade debtors	4,217	4,420
Payments to suppliers	(2,142)	(2,162)
Payments to employees	(657)	(569)
Payments of corporation tax	(64)	(138)
Payments relating to retirement benefits	(235)	(252)
Cash flow from operating activities	1,119	1,299

Investing Activities

11.8 Cash flows from investing activities arise from the acquisition and disposal of an entity's long-term assets and other investments which are not otherwise included in cash equivalents. Section 7.5 outlines various examples of investing activities which are:

(a) Cash payments to acquire property, plant and equipment (including self-constructed property, plant and equipment), intangible assets and other long-term assets. These payments include those relating to capitalised development costs and self-constructed property, plant and equipment.

(b) Cash receipts from sales of property, plant and equipment, intangible and other long-term assets.

(c) Cash payments to acquire equity or debt instruments of other entities and interests in joint ventures (other than payments for those instruments classified as cash equivalents or held for dealing or trading).

(d) Cash receipts from sales of equity or debt instruments of other entities and interests in joint ventures (other than receipts for those instruments classified as cash equivalents or held for dealing or trading).

(e) Cash advances and loans made to other parties.

(f) Cash receipts from the repayment of advances and loans made to other parties.

(g) Cash payments for futures contracts, forward contracts, option contracts and swap contracts, except when contracts are held for dealing or trading, or the payments are classified as financing activities.

(h) Cash receipts from futures contracts, option contracts and swap contracts, except when the contracts are held for dealing or trading, or the receipts are classified as financing activities.

Example 11.3 – Classification of investing activities

Company B Limited manufactures chemicals for use in domestic detergent products. It has four branches throughout the United Kingdom and has a year-end of 30 September 2013. Demand for the company's products has seen a sharp rise in the last two years and, on 1 July 2013, the company opened another branch in the south of the UK and purchased a building outright to house their operations which resulted in an outflow of cash amounting to £100,000.

Only expenditure that results in a recognised asset in the balance sheet is eligible to be classified as investing activities and therefore the cash payment of £100,000 will be treated as a cash flow from investing activities.

Example 11.4 – Disposing of fixed assets in ordinary course of business

Company C Limited is a vehicle rental company and hires cars for domestic and commercial use. It purchases fleets of vehicles to generate rental income for a limited period of time and then sells them.

Companies such as these that routinely sell items of property, plant and equipment that it has held for rental to others would recognise the gains on such disposals within revenue (as opposed to recognising a gain or loss on disposal of fixed assets). As a consequence, the proceeds from the disposal of such assets will be classed as cash flows from operating activities and not cash flows from investing activities.

Financing Activities

11.9 Paragraph 7.6 to Section 7 of FRS 102 states that financing activities are activities that result in changes in the size and composition of the contributed borrowings and equity of an entity. It gives five examples of what it deems to be financing activities which are:

(a) cash proceeds from issuing shares or other equity instruments;

(b) cash payments to owners to acquire or redeem the entity's shares;

(c) cash proceeds from issuing debentures, loans, notes, bonds, mortgages and other short-term or long-term borrowings;

(d) cash repayments of amounts borrowed; and

(e) cash payments by a lessee for the reduction of the outstanding liabilities relating to a *finance lease*.

Example 11.5 – Treatment of dividends

Company D Limited has a year-end of 30 June 2013. On 20 June 2013, the company declared a dividend to its ordinary shareholders which gave rise to a cash outflow of £75,000 which occurred on 23 June 2013.

Dividends are permitted to be treated as a financing cash flow because they are a cost of obtaining financial resources.

11.10 *Statement of cash flows*

11.10   The treatment of interest and dividends is covered in paragraphs 7.14 to 7.16 of Section 7 of FRS 102. Paragraph 7.14 confirms that a reporting entity must separately present cash flows from interest and dividends received and paid and treat them consistently from one accounting period to the next as operating, investing or financing activities.

Paragraph 7.15 permits a reporting entity to classify interest paid and interest and dividends received as operating cash flows on the basis that they are included within profit or loss. This particular section also permits an entity to classify interest paid and interest and dividends received as financing cash flows and investing cash flows respectively on the grounds that they are costs of obtaining financial resources or returns on investments.

Reporting entities that pay dividends to their shareholders may classify these as a financing cash flow on the grounds that they are a cost of obtaining financial resources. An alternative treatment would be to classify dividends paid as a component of cash flows from operating activities on the grounds that they are paid out of operating cash flows.

The key to these alternative treatments is to ensure that the treatment is consistent from one accounting period to the next in order to achieve consistency and comparability within the general purpose financial statements.

Taxes

11.11   Paragraph 7.17 of FRS 102 requires reporting entities to separately disclose cash flows arising from income taxes as cash flows from operating activities. The exception to this is when such a tax can be specifically identified with financing and investing activities. In circumstances where reporting entities have tax cash flows that are allocated over more than one class of activity, paragraph 7.17 requires disclosure of the total amount of taxation paid.

Non-Cash Transactions

11.12   The statement of cash flows is prepared, by its very nature, using a cash-based, rather than an accruals-based method to show the user of the financial statements how the entity has generated and used cash during the accounting period.

On this basis, the standard requires reporting entities to exclude investing and financing transactions that do not require the use of cash or cash equivalents. For such transactions, the standard requires disclosure of these transactions elsewhere within the financial statements in a way that provides all the relevant information about those investing and financing activities.

Example 11.6 – Disclosure of non-cash transactions

Company D Limited has a year-end of 30 September 2013. On 17 December 2012 it issued 150,000 new shares to convertible loan note holders in settlement of £100,000 of capital and interest outstanding on the loans. The remaining capital and interest liabilities were satisfied by a rights issue: £17,000 was raised in cash with the remainder being an exchange of shares.

Such transactions would be disclosed as a footnote to the statement of cash flows. Other examples of non-cash transactions, in addition to the conversion of debt to equity, are the acquisition of assets by assuming directly related liabilities or by means of a finance lease and issuing equity as consideration during a business combination.

Components of Cash and Cash Equivalents

11.13   Paragraph 7.20 to Section 7 of FRS 102 requires reporting entities to present the components of cash and cash equivalents as well as presenting a reconciliation of the amounts presented in the statement of cash flows to the equivalent items presented in the balance sheet. Paragraph 7.20 does not require reporting entities to present this reconciliation if the amount of cash and cash equivalents presented in the statement of cash flows is the same as the amount shown in the balance sheet.

Other Disclosure Requirements

11.14   When a reporting entity holds significant cash and cash equivalents but those cash and cash equivalents are not available for use by the entity, paragraph 7.21 of FRS 102 requires disclosure of such balances, together with management commentary. Paragraph 7.21 offers two examples of situations when a reporting entity may hold significant cash and cash equivalents that are not available to the entity such as foreign exchange controls or legal restrictions.

11.14   *Statement of cash flows*

Illustrative statement of cash flows (indirect method)

	£'000	£'000
Operating profit	5,630	
Adjustments for:		
Depreciation	2,172	
Loss on disposal of fixed assets	183	
Operating cash flows before movements in working capital		7,985
Increase in stock	(335)	
Increase in trade debtors	(266)	
Increase in trade creditors	84	
	(517)	7,468
Corporation tax paid	(854)	
Interest paid	(800)	
Net cash from operating activities	(1,654)	5,814
Investing activities:		
Proceeds from disposal of plant and machinery	509	
Purchases of fixed assets	(13,646)	
Net cash used in investing activities	(13,137)	(7,323)
Financing activities:		
New bank loan raised	3,000	
Proceeds from share issue	4,500	
Dividends paid	(700)	
Net cash used in/from financing activities	6,800	
Net increase/(decrease) in cash and cash equivalents		(523)
Cash and cash equivalents at beginning of the year		587
Cash and cash equivalents at end of the year		64

Focus

Various accounts production systems may have a different layout than the above. However, provided that the layouts conform to the principles in Section 7 there should not be any issues.

SUMMARY – WHAT IS DIFFERENT FROM THE PREVIOUS UK GAAP?

- Section 7 to FRS 102 requires the classification of cash flows under three categories (operating, investing and financing activities). Under the previous UK GAAP, FRS 1 *Cash Flow Statements* there were several additional headings required and the format was as follows:

  o   Operating activities

  o   Dividends from joint ventures and associates

  o   Returns on investments and servicing of finance

  o   Taxation

  o   Capital expenditure and financial investments

  o   Acquisitions and disposals

  o   Equity dividends paid

  o   Management of liquid resources

  o   Financing.

- The fact that FRS 102 requires classification of cash flows under three categories may require reporting entities to devote additional time in determining the appropriate categorisation for certain cash flow activities.

- In addition, FRS 102 requires a reconciliation of cash and cash equivalents as opposed to FRS 1 which merely requires a reconciliation of just cash.

Chapter 12

Property, plant and equipment

SIGNPOSTS

- Terminology: UK GAAP adopters will be familiar with the term 'tangible fixed assets' which must continue to be used as a balance sheet caption as required by the Regulations to CA 2006 (see **12.2**).

- Investment properties: FRS 102 requires investment properties whose fair value cannot be measured reliably without undue cost or effort to be accounted for in the same way as property, plant and equipment (see **12.1**).

- Cost or valuation: The FRS allows an accounting policy choice but this must be applied consistently between individual classes of property, plant and equipment (see **12.10**).

- Costs which should and should not be capitalised are dealt with in **12.7–12.8.**

- Detailed requirements regarding the revaluation model including the calculation of depreciation on revalued assets are dealt with in **12.14–12.23** and **12.27.**

- Impairment is referred to in **12.35–12.38** and **Chapter 18**.

INTRODUCTION

12.1 As well as applying to property, plant and equipment, Section 17 of FRS 102 also applies to investment property whose fair value cannot be measured reliably without undue cost or effort. (Investment property whose fair value *can* be measured reliably is dealt with in **Chapter 13**.)

> **Focus**
>
> 'Undue cost or effort' is not defined, but essentially refers to situations where applying a requirement of the FRS would involve excessive cost in relation to benefits obtained by users.
>
> Application under FRS 102 is unlikely to change as fair values can normally be obtained without undue cost or effort. It therefore seems likely that UK companies who have previously adopted SSAP 19 *Accounting for Investment Properties* and included the investment property in the balance sheet at open market value will fall within the scope of Section 16 of FRS 102 (see **Chapter 13**).

Definition of property, plant and equipment

12.2   Property, plant and equipment is defined as tangible assets that are held for use in the production or supply of goods or services, for rental to others, for investment, or for administrative purposes, and are expected to be used for more than one period.

The more familiar term to UK GAAP preparers, tangible fixed assets, must continue to be used on the face of the balance sheet and in the notes to the financial statements (a requirement of the Regulations to CA 2006 – see **7.4**).

Example 12.1 – A building operated as a care home

A company owns a building that is operated as a care home for elderly persons. The building would fall within the definition of property, plant and equipment in Section 17 of FRS 102.

Example 12.2 – Classification of assets in a holiday park

A holiday park operator owns a number of caravans. Most of these are rented out to holiday visitors. During the year, the company decides it will invest in five new caravans to replace five older ones which are to be put up for sale.

The caravans held for rental should be classified in the balance sheet as tangible fixed assets. Those held for sale should be reclassified from tangible fixed assets to inventories (at the lower of net book value before transfer, and net realisable value).

Another example of reclassification could be land previously held as a fixed asset but now held as inventory for sale to a property developer.

Focus

Where a company owns a property and makes parts of the property available to several users and in addition provides ancillary services for the users, it may be difficult in some cases to determine whether the property falls within the definition of property, plant and equipment or within the definition of investment property. An example would be serviced offices. This issue is referred to further in **13.1**.

Scope exclusions

12.3   The term property, plant and equipment does not include the following:

- biological assets related to agricultural activity (see **Chapter 16**);

- heritage assets (see **Chapter 40**); and

- mineral rights and mineral reserves (see **Chapter 40**).

RECOGNITION

12.4   The cost of an item should only be recognised as an asset if it is *probable* that future economic benefits associated with the item will flow to the entity and the cost of the item can be measured reliably.

12.5   Special considerations regarding major spare parts and replacement of components are referred to below (see **12.48–12.49**).

INITIAL MEASUREMENT

12.6   Property, plant and equipment may be:

- acquired from an external supplier;

- constructed by the entity itself; or

- obtained in an exchange transaction.

Which costs should be included?

12.7   These comprise:

- purchase price (including legal fees and import duties but after deducting trade discounts and rebates);

- any costs attributable to bringing the asset to its location and condition for operating as intended by management (eg costs of site preparation, assembly or testing of functionality);

- costs of dismantling, removing and restoration of sites (see **12.50** below); and

- any borrowing costs which are capitalised in accordance with Section 25 (see **Chapter 17**).

Which costs should not be capitalised?

12.8   The following do not qualify as assets and should be expensed as incurred:

- costs of opening a new facility;

- costs of introducing a new product or service (eg advertising or promotional services);

- costs of conducting business in a new location; and

- administration and general overheads.

Example 12.3 – Costs which should be capitalised

A company acquired a major item of equipment from a supplier in the USA and incurred expenditure relating to the following:

1.	Cost of purchase including import duties.
2.	Costs of transporting the equipment to its site in a factory in Birmingham.
3.	Labour and materials costs incurred in modifying the equipment to meet the specific needs of the entity's potential customers.
4.	Training costs relating to staff who will be directly involved in operating the machinery.
5.	Operating losses incurred between the time the equipment was ready for use, and when it was operating at full capacity (when customer order levels were on target).

Which of the above should be capitalised and recognised as an asset, and which should be expensed immediately to profit and loss account?

Items 1, 2 and 3 should be capitalised as they satisfy the crucial test of being necessary in bringing the item of equipment to its intended location and operating condition.

Items 4 and 5 do not satisfy the capitalisation criteria and should be recognised as expenses in the period in which they are incurred.

Exchanges of assets

12.9   This refers to situations where an item of property, plant and equipment is acquired in exchange for a non-monetary asset or assets or a combination of monetary and non-monetary assets.

The acquired asset should be measured at fair value except where either the exchange transaction lacks commercial substance or the fair value of neither the asset received nor the asset given up is reliably measurable.

Where the exception applies, the cost of the acquired asset is measured at the carrying amount of the asset given up.

MEASUREMENT AFTER INITIAL RECOGNITION

Accounting policy choice

12.10   After initial recognition, an entity may choose to measure all items of property, plant and equipment within a particular class (see **12.12**) at either:

- historical cost less subsequent depreciation (referred to as 'the cost model'); or

- revaluation less subsequent depreciation ('the revaluation model').

Companies Act 2006

12.11   Schedule 1 of the Regulations to CA 2006 deals with the historical cost accounting rules (see paragraphs 16–29) and the alternative accounting rules (see paragraphs 30–35).

Class of assets

12.12   This is defined as 'a grouping of assets of a similar nature and use in the entity's operations' – and this is also relevant for disclosure requirements (see **12.44**).

Example 12.4 – Individual classes of assets

The following are examples of potential individual classes of assets:

- land and buildings
- machinery
- ships
- aircraft
- motor vehicles
- furniture and fixtures
- office equipment.

The cost model

12.13 Items of property, plant and equipment are measured at historical cost less any accumulated depreciation and any accumulated impairment losses.

The revaluation model

12.14 Items of property, plant and equipment are carried at the revalued amount less any subsequent depreciation and any accumulated impairment losses.

The revalued amount is based on fair value at the date of revaluation (less subsequent *depreciation* and *impairment adjustments*).

The revaluation model should only be applied to items whose fair value can be measured reliably

Focus

Where an entity chooses to adopt the revaluation model, it must be applied consistently to all items of property, plant and equipment of the same class. This is the same as the requirement in previous UK GAAP FRS 15 *Tangible Fixed Assets*.

It is important that revaluations are made with 'sufficient regularity' so as to ensure that the carrying amount does not materially differ from that which would be obtained by determining fair value at the balance sheet.

Switching between the cost and revaluation models

12.15   Such a switch would amount to a change of accounting policy (see **Chapter 3**), requiring retrospective application, restatement of comparatives, and a prior period adjustment.

However, retrospective application may not be either possible or practicable where the switch would have been from the cost model to the revaluation model, as reliable comparative information may not be available.

Deferred tax

12.16   Where an entity adopts the revaluation model, deferred tax must be recognised in accordance with the requirements of FRS 102, paragraph 29.6 (see **Chapter 25**).

Fair value

12.17   This should be determined as follows:

- Land and buildings: market-based evidence usually obtained by appraisals by professionally qualified valuers.

- Plant and equipment: market value determined by appraisal.

Focus

Market-based evidence for items of plant and equipment such as motor vehicles may be readily obtainable.

This may not be possible for some items of a more specialised nature – it may be necessary to adopt an alternative approach to estimating fair value, for example an income approach (discounted estimated future cash flows) or a *depreciated replacement cost* approach.

Revaluation gains and losses – increases in carrying amount

12.18   Increases in an asset's carrying amount as a result of a revaluation shall be recognised in other comprehensive income (OCI) and accumulated in equity under the heading of revaluation reserve (see **Example 12.8** below).

12.19   In some cases, an increase in carrying amount reverses a previous revaluation decrease of the same asset, where such decrease was recognised in profit or loss. In these situations, the increase in carrying amount should be recognised in profit or loss to the extent it reverses the previous revaluation decrease.

Revaluation gains and losses – decreases in carrying amount

12.20   Decreases in an asset's carrying amount as a result of a revaluation shall be recognised in profit or loss.

12.21   In some cases, the asset may have been revalued upwards in a previous year resulting in a surplus in revaluation reserve.

In such situations, the decrease in carrying amount shall be recognised in OCI to the extent of any credit balance existing in the revaluation reserve in respect of that asset.

The decrease recognised in OCI reduces the amount accumulated in equity under the heading of revaluation reserve.

Transfers from revaluation reserve to profit and loss reserve

12.22   This issue is referred to in the Regulations to CA 2006, Sch 1, para. 35(3)(a)(i), and *CA 2006, s 842(5)* dealing with transfers between revaluation reserve and the profit and loss account reserve.

12.23   The 'excess depreciation' may be transferred out of revaluation reserve, and into retained profits reserve by annual transfers over the asset's remaining useful life.

The so-called 'excess depreciation' is the difference between the depreciation charge based on the revalued amount, and the charge that on a historical cost basis would have applied had the asset not been revalued.

DEPRECIATION

Definitions

12.24   Depreciation is defined as the systematic allocation of the *depreciable amount* of an asset over its *useful life*.

Depreciable amount is defined as 'the cost of an asset, or other amount substituted for cost (in the financial statements), less its residual value'.

'Other amount substituted for cost' covers situations where the revaluation model is adopted, or where an asset is written down to recoverable amount as a result of impairment.

Residual value is defined as 'the amount that an entity would *currently* [emphasis added] obtain from the disposal of an asset, after deducting the estimated costs of disposal, if the asset were already of the age and in the condition expected at the end of its useful life'.

Focus

This definition is different from that in the previous UK GAAP FRS 15 which requires residual value for an asset accounted for at historical cost to be assessed in terms of price levels at the date the asset was originally acquired.

Example 12.5 – Assessment of residual value

A building was acquired on 1 January 2011 at a cost of £500,000. The life of the building was assessed as 50 years with a residual value at the end of that period of £100,000. This latter amount reflected the condition of the building at the end of 50 years based on price levels as at 1 January 2011.

The annual depreciation charge was £8,000 [£500,000 – £100,000/50 years].

At 1 January 2020, after nine years depreciation charge, the net book value of the building was £428,000 [£500,000 – (9 × £8,000)].

On 31 December 2020, the remaining useful life was confirmed as 40 years but the residual value in terms of current prices (ie in terms of price levels at 31 December 2020) is £150,000. The residual value under FRS 102 reflects the 31 December 2020 price level value of a building in its envisaged physical condition at the end of 50 years. FRS 15 would have required the assessment to be made in terms of price levels at 1 January 2011.

The depreciation charge for 2020 would therefore be £6,780 (£428,000 – £150,000/41 years).

Choosing a method

12.25 The depreciation method selected should reflect the pattern in which the entity expects to consume the asset's future economic benefits.

The straight-line method is widely used, but other methods which might be appropriate in particular situations are:

- the diminishing (or reducing) balance method; and

- a method based on usage such as the unit of production method.

Example 12.6 – Straight-line depreciation method

A company purchases motor vehicles for company and private use by certain employees. The company's policy is to replace these cars every two years.

The company may decide that the straight-line method of depreciation, using a life of two years and taking account of estimated residual value at the end of this period, is an appropriate method in this situation.

Example 12.7 – Unit of production depreciation method

A company uses machinery in the process of producing hazardous chemicals. Government regulations on health and safety restrict the use of the machinery to a specific production output. (After this limit is exceeded, the machinery must be decommissioned, decontaminated and recycled.)

The company may decide that a method based on usage, such as the unit of production method, is appropriate.

Applying a depreciation method

12.26   Depreciation commences when the asset is available for use – meaning when it is in the location and condition necessary for it to be capable in the manner intended by management.

Depreciation ceases when the asset is derecognised (see **12.40**).

Where an asset becomes idle or retired from active use, depreciation should still be charged unless the asset is fully depreciated.

However, under a usage method of depreciation, a depreciation charge could be zero whilst there is no production.

Revalued assets

12.27   FRS 102, paragraph 17.18 requires that an entity shall allocate the *depreciable amount* of an asset on a systematic basis over its useful life. The

Glossary to FRS 102 defines the depreciable amount as the cost of an asset, or other amount substituted for cost (in the financial statements), less its residual value.

FRS 102 does not specify how the depreciation charge should be calculated when a revaluation has been incorporated into the accounts during the current year. The previous UK GAAP (FRS 15.79) stated that ideally 'the average value of the asset should be used to calculate the depreciation charge' but noted that 'in practice, however, either the opening or closing balance may be used instead provided that it is used consistently each period'.

At the present time, recommended practice has not been established, but until then, the above may provide a useful guide.

Example 12.8 – Revaluation of land and buildings

A company acquired freehold offices on 1 January 2014 at a cost of £150,000. The land element was estimated at £100,000, and the life of the buildings estimated at 50 years. The directors intend to adopt a policy of regular revaluation.

FRS 102 requires revaluations to be made with 'sufficient regularity to ensure that the carrying amount does not differ materially from that which would be determined using fair value at the end of the reporting period'.

In accordance with the company's policy to revalue items in this asset class, the directors obtain a revaluation at the end of 31 December 2015 which gives a total value of £173,000 split £120,000 for the land element and £53,000 for the building element. No change is made to the building's estimated useful life. For the purpose of this example, deferred tax has not been taken into account – under FRS 102, a deferred tax provision will be required (see **Chapter 25**).

The depreciation charge for 2014 will be based on historical cost.

There is no clear requirement under FRS 102 whether the depreciation charge for 2012 should be based on opening value, average value, or closing value (see comments above). The company has decided to base the charge on closing value, and will apply this policy consistently for future valuations.

The directors consider there has been no material change in value during 2016.

A valuation at 31 December 2017 is obtained, giving a total value of £210,000 split £150,000 for land and £60,000 for buildings. Again, useful life is not revised.

The surplus on revaluation is recognised in OCI and accumulated in equity under the heading of revaluation reserve.

	Land	*Buildings*	*Total*	*Reference to workings*
	£'000	*£'000*	*£'000*	
Net book value at 1 January 2014	–	–	–	
Additions 1 January 2014	100	50	150	
Depreciation charge 2014	–	(1)	(1)	W1
Net book value at 31 December 2014	100	49	149	
Net book value at 1 January 2015	100	49	149	
Depreciation charge 2015	–	(1.1)	(1.1)	W2
Surplus on revaluation	20	5.1	25.1	W3
Net book value at 1 January 2015	120	53	173	

Workings

W1

Charge for the year is based on cost (£50k/50 years = 1)

W2

Value of asset of £50k with a remaining life of 48 years as from 31 January 2015 gives a charge of 1.1 (£50k/48 years) based on closing value.

W3

Surplus on revaluation is a balancing figure. Had the depreciation charge been based on either opening value or average revaluation, the surplus would have been correspondingly different.

	Land	Buildings	Total	Reference to workings
	£'000	£'000	£'000	
Net book value at 1 January 2016	120	53	173	W4
Depreciation charge 2016	–	(1.1)	(1.1)	
Net book value at 31 December 2106	120	51.9	171.9	
Net book value at 1 January 2017	120	51.9	171.9	
Depreciation charge 2017	–	(1.3)	(1.3)	W5
Surplus on revaluation	30	9.4	39.4	W6
Net book value at 31 December 2017	150	60	210	

W4

Same amount as for 2015 as there has been no revaluation in 2016.

W5

Depreciation charge based on year-end value is £60k/46 years life remaining after year-end = 1.3.

W6

Surplus on revaluation is a balancing figure. Had the depreciation charge been based on either opening value or average revaluation, the surplus would have been correspondingly different.

Focus

Previous GAAP offered choices, and technical commentaries expressed their own preferences.

FRS 15 made no distinction between situations where assets recently acquired were being revalued for the first time and situations involving ongoing revaluations. In some of these latter situations, an adjustment may not have been required because no material change in value has been identified.

The example above illustrates one possible treatment where an asset was being revalued for the first time, and where a subsequent valuation was obtained.

Although companies have options as indicated above, it is essential that whatever policy is adopted, then that must be followed consistently on subsequent occasions (ie always use either opening value *or* always use average value *or* always use closing value).

Change of depreciation method

12.28 It is unusual to change a depreciation method for a particular asset or class of assets, but the situation is covered by FRS 102. A change may be appropriate where there is an indication that there has been a significant change since the last balance sheet date in the pattern by which an entity expects to consume an asset's future economic benefits.

In such a case, the entity should review the existing method and if appropriate, change the depreciation method to reflect the new pattern of consumption.

The change in depreciation method should be accounted for as a change in *accounting estimate* (see **Chapter 3**).

12.29 Previous UK GAAP (FRS 15, paragraph 82) contained more specific wording than that above and stated:

' ... the carrying amount of the tangible fixed asset is depreciated using the revised method over the remaining economic life, *beginning in the period in which the change is made* ...' (emphasis added).

So, if the change of method is adopted in the current period, the depreciation charge and the net book value for the current period will reflect this.

Focus

Note the disclosure implications where there is a change in estimate, FRS 102, paragraph 10.18 requires disclosure of both the nature of the change and its effect.

Example 12.9 – Change of depreciation method

In previous years, a company has adopted the reducing balance method of depreciation for a particular class of assets. During the year to 31 December 2016, the directors now consider that the straight-line method of depreciation is more appropriate and will be adopted in the future for that class of assets.

Determining useful life

12.30 The depreciable amount of an asset shall be allocated on a systematic basis over the asset's useful life. The following should be considered when determining the asset's useful life:

- the expected usage of the asset – determined by reference to the asset's expected capacity or physical output;

- expected physical wear and tear – dependent on operational factors such as the number of shifts for which the asset is to be used and the repair and maintenance programme, and the care and maintenance of the asset while idle;

- technical or commercial obsolescence arising from changes or improvements in production, or from a change in the market demand for the product or service output of the asset; and

- legal or similar limits on the use of the asset, such as the expiry dates of related leases.

Example 12.10 – Assessment of useful life

A vehicle hire company rents out motor cars and vans on short-term hire. The company's management policy is to replace vehicles after two years, irrespective of mileage.

The useful life of the cars and vans is two years. The depreciation charge will allocate the asset's cost less estimated residual value at the end of two years, over the useful life of two years.

Revision of useful life/residual value

12.31   Entities should be aware of factors which indicate that an asset's useful life or residual value or both, have changed.

Examples of factors that may have changed since the previous reporting date include:

- a change in how an asset is used;

- significant unexpected wear and tear;

- technological advancement; and

- changes in market prices.

12.32   Changes in residual value, useful lives and depreciation methods, should be accounted for as changes in accounting estimates (see **Chapter 3**).

Land and buildings

12.33   These are separable assets – they should be accounted for separately even though they are usually acquired together. The buildings element should be depreciated over its useful life whereas land will only be depreciated in rare circumstances, for example in the case of a quarry (see **Example 12.8** above).

IMPAIRMENT

Introduction

12.34   FRS 102, paragraph 27.9 refers to indicators of impairment. These may pinpoint situations where the carrying amount of an asset (or group of assets) exceeds its (or their) recoverable amount. Impairment is covered in **Chapter 18** so is referred to below only briefly.

For property, plant and equipment, impairment could result from damage to an asset, obsolescence, or a group of assets which are unlikely to be used in the foreseeable future as a result of extensive and long-standing operating losses.

Recognition and measurement of impairment

12.35   As indicated above, Section 27 of FRS 102 is crucial for applying this part of Section 17, Property, Plant and Equipment.

Paragraph 17.24 cross-refers to the following aspects of Section 27:

- how to recognise whether an asset (or assets) is (are) impaired – the indicators of impairment referred to above;

- when to recognise an impairment loss;

- how to determine recoverable amount;

- how to measure the impairment loss; and

- when to reverse an impairment loss.

Compensation for impairment

12.36   Compensation for impairment may be recoverable from a third party such as an insurance company, but in some cases the claim may be disputed. For example, an insurance company may argue that the impairment arose as a result of the company's negligence.

12.37   Compensation from third parties for items of property, plant and equipment that were impaired, lost or given up, should only be included in profit or loss when the compensation is *virtually certain*.

Property, plant and equipment held for sale

12.38   A plan to dispose of an asset before the previously expected date is an indicator of impairment. This should trigger the calculation of the asset's recoverable amount in order to determine whether the asset is impaired.

Focus

Note also the disclosure requirements of FRS 102, paragraph 4.14 regarding a binding sale agreement for a major disposal of assets (see **Chapter 33**).

DERECOGNITION

12.39   This rather inelegant technical term refers to the removal from the balance sheet of a previously recognised asset, either because the asset has been sold or because the asset no longer has value to the business.

When should an asset be derecognised?

12.40   An item of property, plant and equipment should be derecognised either on disposal or when no future economic benefits are expected from the asset's use in the business, or the asset's disposal (eg a company may have decided to scrap some items of plant and machinery where no significant value is expected to be received).

Recognising the gain or loss

12.41   The gain or loss should be recognised in profit or loss when the item of property, plant and equipment is derecognised.

The date of disposal should be determined by applying the criteria in the section of FRS 102 dealing with Revenue (see **Chapter 26**) but any such gains should not be classed as revenue.

The gain or loss is determined by comparing the sales proceeds with the carrying amount of the item of property, plant and equipment.

DISCLOSURE REQUIREMENTS

12.42   Disclosure requirements are set out in Schedule 1 paragraphs 51–53 and 63 of the Regulations to CA 2006 (see **7.4**).

Requirements for each class

12.43   The following must be disclosed for each class of property, plant and equipment:

● measurement bases used for determining the gross carrying amount;

● depreciation methods used;

● useful lives or depreciation rates used;

● gross carrying amount and accumulated depreciation (aggregated with accumulated impairment losses) at the beginning and end of the reporting period; and

● a reconciliation of the carrying amount at the beginning and end of the reporting period showing separately:

○   additions

○   disposals

○   acquisitions through business combinations

○   revaluations

○   transfers to investment property if a reliable measure becomes available

○ impairment losses recognised or reversed in profit or loss in accordance with Section 27

○ depreciation and

○ other changes.

The above reconciliation need not be presented for comparative periods.

Accounting policies

12.44 Section 3.17(e) of the FRS requires disclosure of 'a summary of significant accounting policies ...' (see **Chapter 3**).

Example 12.11

Note 1 – Property, plant and equipment

Items of property, plant and equipment are measured at cost less accumulated depreciation and accumulated impairment losses. Depreciation is charged so as to allocate the cost of assets less their residual values over their estimated useful lives, using the straight-line method.

Land has an indefinite useful life and is therefore not depreciated. The estimated useful lives of other items of property, plant and equipment are:

● Buildings: 60 years

● Machinery: 10 years

● Office equipment: 3 years.

Additional disclosures for revalued assets

12.45 The following disclosures are required where assets have been revalued:

● the effective date of the revaluation;

● whether an independent valuer was involved;

● the methods applied in estimating the fair value of the items; and

● for each revalued class of property, plant and equipment, the carrying amount that would have been recognised had the assets been carried under the cost model.

Example 12.12

Accounting policy note – revaluation of properties

Freehold and leasehold properties are revalued every five years. Any overall surplus over book value is credited to the revalution reserve and any overall deficit in excess of historic cost is charged to the profit and loss account in the year of revaluation. In subsequent years, transfers are made to retained profits to amortise surpluses over the remaining useful lives of the properties. On disposal, the profit or loss is calculated by reference to the net book value and any unamortised revaluation surplus is transferred from revaluation reserves to retained profits.

Other disclosures

12.46   The following must be disclosed:

- the existence and carrying amounts of property, plant and equipment to which the entity has restricted title or that is pledged as security for liabilities; and

- the amount of contractual commitments for the acquisition of property, plant and equipment.

SPECIFIC CONSIDERATIONS

Major spare parts, servicing and standby equipment

12.47   These are included as property, plant and equipment provided that the entity expects to use them during more than one period; or where they can be used only in connection with an item of property, plant and equipment (FRS 102, paragraph 17.6). Other than this, spare parts and servicing equipment will usually be carried as inventory and charged as an expense as they are consumed.

Replacement of components of assets

12.48   Some assets may include major components such as motors which require replacing at regular intervals. Where parts of an asset have significantly different lives, it may be necessary, from the outset, to allocate the initial cost of the asset over its major components and to depreciate each allocated component separately over its useful life.

Dismantling and restoration costs

12.49   On acquisition of an asset or as a result of using an asset during a period, an entity may incur an obligation which would require the entity to dismantle or remove the item at a future date and restore the site on which the asset is located.

In this situation, the cost of the item of property, plant and equipment should include the initial estimate of the dismantling, removing and site restoration costs.

At the same time, a corresponding provision would be required in accordance with FRS 102, Section 21 (see **Chapter 22**).

SUMMARY – WHAT IS DIFFERENT FROM THE
PREVIOUS UK GAAP?

- FRS 15 contained more detailed guidance on valuation methods.

- The definition of residual value in FRS 102 allows account to be taken of inflation arising after the acquisition of the asset and up to the current reporting date.

- The section of FRS 102 on property, plant and equipment includes investment properties whose fair value cannot be measured reliably without undue cost or effort. In practice, this may have little impact on UK companies who have previously been applying SSAP 19, where investment properties are likely to continue to be held at a current valuation in accordance with Section 16 of FRS 102 (see **Chapter 13**).

- FRS 102, Section 17, paragraph 17.4 (see **12.4** above) is explicit regarding recognition criteria whereas FRS 15 does not specifically address this (although existing UK GAAP FRS 5 gives general criteria regarding recognition of assets). FRS 102 explicitly makes the link between an item of property, plant and equipment, and the need for future economic benefits to flow to the entity.

- FRS 15 went into a lot of detail concerning the capitalisation criteria for *subsequent expenditure*. As a general rule, FRS 15 required subsequent expenditure to be written off to profit or loss unless the expenditure:

  o   provided an enhancement of the economic benefits of the asset in excess of the previously assessed standard of performance;

  o   related to a component of a tangible asset that had been treated

---

> separately for depreciation purposes which was replaced or restored; and
>
> ○ related to a major inspection or overhaul of the tangible fixed asset that restored the economic benefits of the asset(s) that had been used up by the entity and that have already been reflected in the depreciation charge.
>
> - Section 17, Property, Plant and Equipment deals with this issue at paragraph 17.15, but merely states that day-to-day servicing of property, plant and equipment must be recognised in profit or loss in the periods which the costs are incurred. Those preparing financial statements would therefore be directed to FRS 102, Section 2, Concepts and Pervasive Principles to determine whether any subsequent expenditure does, in fact, meet the definition and recognition criteria of an asset outlined in FRS 102, paragraphs 2.15(a) and 2.27(a) and (b).

Chapter 13

Investment property

SIGNPOSTS

- The accounting treatment of investment properties is set out in Section 16 of FRS 102.

- Interpreting the definition of what is an investment property requires particular care and in some cases judgement may be required to determine whether a particular property is an investment property or whether it falls within the definition of property, plant and equipment (see **Chapter 12**).

- Once an investment property has been recognised in the financial statements, its subsequent accounting treatment will be determined by circumstances and, unlike full IFRS, will not simply be an accounting policy choice between the cost and the revaluation models. If the fair value of the property can be measured reliably without undue cost or effort on an ongoing method, the entity *must* use the fair value model. This is likely to be the case for UK companies who have previously adopted SSAP 19 *Accounting for Investment Properties* and included investment properties in the balance sheet at open market value.

- However, FRS 102 requires investment properties whose fair value cannot be measured reliably without undue cost or effort to be accounted for in the same way as property, plant and equipment (see **Chapter 12**).

- Section 16 of FRS 102 does not go into much of the complexity of IAS 40 *Investment Properties* under full IFRS. For entities with relatively straightforward situations this will not be a problem. However, for entities where investment properties represent a significant part of their business, particularly those with complex situations, it may be necessary to refer to IAS 40 for authoritative guidance. Some of these situations are referred to below.

INTRODUCTION AND SCOPE

13.1 Section 16 of FRS 102 applies to accounting for investments in land or buildings that meet the definition of investment property (see **13.4**).

13.2 The section also applies to some property interests held by a lessee under an operating lease where the property interest is treated like an investment property (see **13.8–13.10**).

13.3 As indicated above, Section 16 strictly applies only to investment properties whose fair value can be measured reliably without undue cost or effort on an ongoing basis. All other investment property is accounted for as property, plant and equipment in accordance with Section 17 of FRS 102 (ie at cost less accumulated depreciation and accumulated impairment charges (see **Chapter 12**).

Focus

'Undue cost or effort' is not defined. However, it can be argued that UK companies who have previously adopted SSAP 19 and included the investment property in the balance sheet at open market value have demonstrated that they can obtain a reliable measurement of fair value without undue cost or effort and so fall within the scope of Section 16 of FRS 102, which is dealt with in this chapter.

WHAT IS AN INVESTMENT PROPERTY?

Definition

13.4 Investment property is defined as follows (FRS 102, paragraph 16.2):

'Property (land or a building, or part of a building, or both) held by the owner or by the lessee under a finance lease to earn rentals or for capital appreciation or both, rather than for:

(a) use in the production or supply of goods or services or for administrative purposes, or

(b) sale in the ordinary course of business.'

Example 13.1 – Building rented out to third parties

Company A owns a freehold building which it rents out to third parties under operating leases in return for rental payments.

Company A is a passive investor and holds the building for rental income and capital appreciation. The property is classified as an investment property.

Ancillary services

13.5   An entity may provide ancillary services such a cleaning, security, maintenance, secretarial and IT to the third-party occupants of a property owned by the entity.

If the services are assessed as insignificant to the arrangement as a whole, the property could be classed as an investment property. In some cases, the services may be of such significance that the overall arrangement is effectively the provision of services.

Judgement is required to assess the significance of the ancillary services, as this could be crucial in some cases in determining whether the property is an investment property, or an item of property plant and equipment. A key factor is to consider the entity's principal operations.

Example 13.2 – Rental agreement with additional services provided

Company B owns a freehold building which it rents out to third parties under operating leases in return for rental payments.

Company B provides cleaning, security and maintenance services for the lessees.

If the services provided are regarded as insignificant to the arrangement as a whole, the property would be classified as an investment property. The overall substance of the arrangement is that Company B holds the building for rental income and capital appreciation.

Example 13.3 – Building divided up and used to provide services to others

Company C owns a building which is divided into ten serviced offices. As part of the agreements with service users, the company provides significant other services including broadband internet access, telephone answering and cleaning. Secretarial assistance is available when required and terms are negotiated separately.

How should the building be classified in the balance sheet?

The building is held for the purpose of providing services to others and not as a passive investment. It should be classified under property, plant and equipment, not as an investment property (see **13.4**).

Mixed use property

13.6   Mixed use property should be separated between investment property and property, plant and equipment.

If the fair value of the investment property component cannot be measured reliably without undue cost or effort, the entire property should be accounted for as property plant and equipment.

Example 13.4 – Mixed use property with insignificant owner occupation

Company D owns a building which it rents out to independent third parties in return for rental payments. The company owns 5% of the building's floor area for the occupation of the company's administrative staff.

The portion of the building occupied by the company's staff is judged insignificant in relation to the overall arrangement. The overall substance of the arrangement is that Company D holds the building for rental income and capital appreciation. The property is classified as an investment property.

Example 13.5 – Mixed use property with significant owner occupation

The facts are the same as in the example above except that the floor area occupied by Company E's administrative staff is 40%. In this case, Company E clearly occupies a significant part of the property.

A question to ask is whether the 60% and 40% portions could be sold or leased out separately. If they could and if the fair value of the investment property portion could be measured reliably without undue cost or effort on an ongoing basis, the portions should be accounted for separately: the 60% portion as an investment property at fair value; the 40% portion as property, plant and equipment at cost less accumulated depreciation.

If the fair value of the investment property portion could not be reliably measured without undue cost or effort, the entire property should be accounted for as property, plant and equipment at cost less accumulated depreciation.

Example 13.6 – Mixed use property split between property, plant and equipment element and investment property element

Company E owns a three-storey block and uses the ground floor for its own administrative purposes. The first and second floors are rented out under operating leases.

The ground floor is classified as property, plant and equipment as it is a property held for use in the production or supply of goods or services or for administrative purposes (see **12.2**).

The second and third floors are held as passive investments – held for rentals and capital appreciation. These are classified as investment properties and provided reliable fair values can be established without undue cost or effort, accounted for at fair value at each reporting date.

If reliable fair values cannot be established, the entire block would be classified as property, plant and equipment.

Property held for the provision of social benefits

13.7   Such property should be accounted for as property, plant and equipment, *not* as investment property.

An example would be social housing held by a public benefit entity (FRS 102, paragraph 16.3A).

Property interest under an operating lease classified as an investment property

13.8   An entity holding a property interest under an operating lease may, in certain situations, classify and account for the property interest as an investment property.

13.9   The necessary condition is that the property would otherwise meet the definition of an investment property and the lessee can measure the fair value of the property interest without undue cost or effort on an ongoing basis.

13.10   Note that this is an accounting policy choice and the classification option is available on a property-by-property basis.

Example 13.7 – Property under an operating lease classified as an investment property

Company F, a lessee, rents a building under an operating lease from Company G, an independent third-party property company. Company F sublets portions of the building under operating leases to various third parties.

The aggregate of the rents charged to the various third parties is comfortably in excess of the rent paid to company G so the property is held to earn rentals and 'would otherwise meet the definition of an investment property'.

Provided Company F can reliably measure the fair value of its property interest, it may (but is not required – it is an option under paragraph 16.3 of FRS 102) classify its interest in the lease as an item of investment property. If it chooses to do this, the interest must be brought onto the balance sheet and accounted for (see **13.12**). If Company F could not measure its property interest reliably, it would not be allowed to treat its interest as an investment property. It would be accounted for as an operating lease.

Focus

The option is available on a property-by-property basis so a subsequent leasehold interest which would otherwise qualify as an investment property could be accounted for simply as an operating lease (ie off the balance sheet).

Land

13.11   Note that the definition of investment property in **13.4** includes 'land *or* a building ... or both...'.

A number of scenarios are possible, depending on the purpose for which the land is held. The two examples below are clear cut. FRS 102 does not indicate how land held for an indeterminate future use should be dealt with. In this and other complex situations it would be advisable to refer to IAS 40.

Example 13.8 – Land held as a long-term investment

Company H has purchased a piece of land as a long-term investment with the hope and expectation that, over time, the land will increase in value. Company H does not expect to generate any rental income from the land.

The land is held as a passive investment for capital appreciation. Assuming a reliable fair value can be obtained on an ongoing basis, the land will be classified as an investment property.

Example 13.9 – Land held for potential development

Company I has purchased a piece of land and intends to divide it up into a number of plots that the company hopes to sell to property developers and builders in the ordinary course of business.

The land is held for sale in the ordinary course of business and should be classed as inventory, not as investment property.

MEASUREMENT AT INITIAL RECOGNITION

General considerations

13.12 At initial recognition, an investment property should be measured at cost.

Cost comprises:

- purchase price;

- any directly attributable expenditure such as legal and brokerage fees;

- property transfer taxes; and

- other transaction costs.

13.13 Where payment is deferred beyond normal credit terms, cost is the present value of all future payments.

13.14 The cost of a self-constructed investment property should be determined in accordance with the requirements of Section 17, Property, Plant and Equipment (see **12.7**).

Leases

13.15 As indicated in **13.8** above, an entity may make an accounting policy choice to classify a property interest held under an operating lease as an investment property (see **13.8–13.10**).

13.16 In such situations, the initial cost of the property interest should be determined as though it were a finance lease (see **15.15–15.17**) even if the property interest would otherwise be classified as an operating lease.

The asset is recognised initially at the lower of the fair value of the property and the present value of the minimum lease payments. A corresponding liability should be recognised.

Any premium paid for a lease should be added to the minimum lease payments. The premium should be excluded from the liability figure.

SUBSEQUENT MEASUREMENT

General considerations

13.17 An investment property whose fair value can be measured reliably without undue cost or effort should be measured at fair value at each reporting date.

13.18 Changes in fair value should be recognised in profit or loss.

Focus

For UK companies, this will involve a significant change in presentation.

Under SSAP 19, changes in market value are taken to the statement of total recognised gains and losses and shown as a movement on an investment revaluation reserve.

Under FRS 102, the changes in fair value will be reflected in operating profit. How they will be presented will depend on the nature of the business (eg a non-property company might show these as part of other operating income). A property company would modify the format of the profit and loss account so as to reflect the special nature of its business.

Deferred tax

13.19   Section 29 of FRS 102 requires that deferred tax relating to investment property measured at fair value shall be measured using the tax rates and allowances that apply to the sale of the asset (see **Chapter 25**).

Investment property outside the scope of Section 16

13.20   This should be accounted for in the same way as property, plant and equipment (ie at cost less accumulated depreciation and accumulated impairment charges).

TRANSFERS TO OR FROM THE INVESTMENT PROPERTY CATEGORY

13.21   For an investment property measured using the fair value model, where a reliable measure of fair value is no longer available without undue cost or effort, the property should subsequently be accounted for as property, plant and equipment.

At the date of change of classification, the carrying amount of the investment property becomes its 'cost' for the purposes of accounting for it as property, plant and equipment.

13.22   Apart from the special situation above, property should only be transferred into the investment property classification when it first meets the definition of investment property and should only be transferred out when it ceases to meet the definition of investment property.

GROUP SITUATIONS

13.23   FRS 102 is silent on the treatment of investment properties let to and occupied by group companies, unlike previous UK GAAP SSAP 19 which specifically excluded 'a property let to and occupied by another group company' from the definition of investment property. This exclusion applied to both the company's own accounts, as well as the consolidated accounts.

13.24   However, interpretations based on IASB guidance suggest that FRS 102 does not exclude from investment properties those properties that are let to and occupied by group companies, which would be recognised in separate financial statements. However, in the group accounts, such properties would be part of property, plant and equipment.

Example 13.10 – Lease to a group company

Company J is a parent company which owns a property that it rents out to its subsidiary, Company K, under an operating lease in return for rentals to be paid at six-monthly intervals. Company K will use the property as a warehouse for storing goods to be despatched to its customers.

Company J is required to prepare consolidated accounts.

There are two separate considerations: treatment in individual company accounts and treatment in the consolidated accounts.

Separate accounts of J and K

In the separate accounts of J, the building would be classed as an investment property, assuming a reliable fair value could be determined.

In the separate accounts of K, the arrangement would be accounted for as an operating lease.

Consolidated accounts of J

The consolidated accounts present the position of the group as though it were a single entity, so the property should not be classified as an investment property. From the group perspective, the building is used in the group's operations. It is not held for investment potential.

MORE COMPLEX SITUATIONS

13.25   For guidance on more complex situations, reference should be made to IAS 40 and the training material modules on the IFRS website (see ifrs.org) in the section on IFRS for SMEs.

DISCLOSURE REQUIREMENTS

General disclosures

13.26   The following disclosures are required for all investment property accounted for at fair value through profit or loss:

●   methods and significant assumptions applied in determining fair value;

●   the extent to which the fair value is based on a valuation by an independent valuer who holds a recognised and relevant professional qualification and has recent experience in the location and class of the investment property being valued. If there has been no such valuation, that fact should be disclosed;

- the existence and amount of restrictions on the realisability of investment property or the remittance of income and proceeds of disposal; and

- contractual obligations to purchase, construct or develop investment property or for repairs, maintenance or enhancements.

Reconciliation of carrying amount

13.27   Disclosure is required of a reconciliation between the carrying amounts of investment properties at the beginning and end of the period showing separately:

- additions, showing separately those additions resulting from acquisitions through business combinations;

- net gains or losses from fair value adjustments;

- transfers to property, plant and equipment when a reliable measure of fair value is no longer available without undue cost or effort;

- transfers to and from inventories and owner-occupied property; and

- other changes.

The above reconciliation need not be presented for comparative periods.

Leases

13.28   An entity should provide all relevant disclosures about leases into which it has entered (see **15.47**).

SUMMARY – WHAT IS DIFFERENT FROM THE PREVIOUS UK GAAP?

13.29

- Under FRS 102, the classification of investment properties is determined by circumstances, whereas under SSAP 19, all investment properties are treated in the same way irrespective of circumstances.

- Under FRS 102, changes in fair are recognised in *profit or loss*, whereas under SSAP 19, changes in market value are taken to the statement of total recognised gains or losses, and shown as movements on investment revaluation reserve. This means that earnings will be more volatile under FRS 102 as compared with the existing UK GAAP.

- Under FRS 102, an investment property whose fair value cannot be measured reliably should be recognised initially at cost and depreciation subsequently provided. Under SSAP 19, investment properties should not be depreciated, except for properties held on lease which should be depreciated, at least over the period when the unexpired term is 20 years or less.

- Under FRS 102, where an entity adopts the accounting policy choice in FRS 102, paragraph 16.3 and classifies a property interest held under an operating lease as an investment property, the property is to be accounted for as a finance lease, regardless of the fact that the lease may have been accounted for under an operating lease if it was in the scope of Section 20, Leases. In this respect, the asset is recognised at the *lower* of the fair value of the property and the present value of the minimum lease payments with an equivalent amount being recognised as a liability.

- Under FRS 102, deferred tax must be recognised where the fair value model is used whereas no deferred tax is provided under FRS 19.

Chapter 14

Intangible assets other than goodwill

SIGNPOSTS

- The rules on recognition of internally generated intangibles are extremely restrictive and effectively limit recognition to certain development costs which satisfy strict criteria, similar to previous UK GAAP SSAP 13 (see **14.27**).

- Intangibles acquired as part of a business combination (as opposed to acquired separately) can be recognised provided stringent conditions are satisfied (see **14.7**, **14.8**).

- Revaluation of intangibles is possible in theory but likely to be extremely rare in practice due to conditions which are likely to be impossible to satisfy in most cases.

- Goodwill is covered in a separate section of FRS 102 (see **Chapter 30**).

INTRODUCTION AND SCOPE

Scope

14.1   Section 18 of FRS 102 applies to accounting for all intangible assets (see definition in **14.2** below), other than:

- Goodwill (covered in Section 19, Business Combinations and Goodwill – see **Chapter 30**);

- Intangible assets held by an entity for sale in the ordinary course of business (covered in Section 13, Inventories – see **Chapter 19**).

Example 14.1 – Licences treated as inventories

Company A trades in transferable fishing licences. It has recently acquired licences giving rights to fish in particular waters. Company A's operating activities do not include fishing.

The company has advertised the licences for sale. The licences are inventories and fall within the scope of Section 13.

14.2   This section does not apply to:

- financial assets (see **Chapter 35**);

- heritage assets (see **Chapter 40**); and

- mineral rights and mineral reserves, such as oil, natural gas and similar non-regenerative resources (see **Chapter 40**).

Definition

14.3   An intangible asset is an identifiable non-monetary asset without physical substance. Such an asset is 'identifiable' when:

- it is separable (ie capable of being separated or divided from the entity or sold, transferred, licensed, rented or exchanged, either individually or together with a related contract, asset or liability); or

- it arises from contractual or other legal rights, regardless of whether those rights are transferable or separable from the entity or from other rights and obligations.

(FRS 102, paragraph 18.2.)

Example 14.2 – Customer list intangible

Company A has a valuable customer list. This consists of a database which includes information about contact names, order histories, key suppliers etc.

The customer list is a non-monetary asset without physical substance, and is identifiable because it is separable (ie it could be sold to a third party). It is therefore an intangible.

Whether the intangible is recognised in the balance sheet will depend on whether it is internally generated, separately acquired or acquired as part of a business combination (see **14.10–14.12** below).

Example 14.3 – Franchise licence

Company B holds an exclusive licence to operate coffee shops in specified parts of the UK under a franchise agreement.

The licence is a non-monetary asset without physical substance. Although it is not separable – the terms of the franchise agreement would prevent Company B from selling its rights to a third party – it is identifiable because it arises from a contractual right. It is therefore an intangible.

Whether the intangible is recognised in the balance sheet will depend on whether the licence was separately acquired or acquired as part of a business combination (see **14.10–14.12** below).

Categories of intangibles

14.4 Intangibles cover a diverse range, and may be grouped into five broad categories:

- marketing-related intangibles (eg trademarks, internet domain names and non-competition agreements);

- customer-related intangibles (eg customer lists);

- artistic-related intangibles (eg example video and audio-visual material and musical works);

- contract-based intangibles (eg licensing and royalty agreements, franchise agreements and servicing contracts); and

- technology-based intangibles (eg computer software, patented technology, and databases).

Example 14.4 – Software licences

Company C owns ten software licences which are used by the company's finance, administrative, marketing and sales staff. The software licences are intangible assets.

Example 14.5 – Website

Company D owns and operates an interactive website which can be used by members of the public to post items of interest on a variety of topics. No charge is made to users. The website earns revenue from advertising sales.

The website is an intangible asset. The asset is identifiable because it has a contractual legal right of ownership, as its domain name has been properly registered (see **14.43** for the treatment of website costs).

INITIAL RECOGNITION OF INTANGIBLES

General principles – recognition criteria

14.5 An intangible should be recognised as an intangible asset if it satisfies all of the following criteria:

- it is *probable* that the expected future benefits that are attributable to the asset will flow to the entity; and

- the cost or value of the asset can be measured reliably.

Intangibles acquired separately

14.6   FRS 102 states that the 'probability' criteria, above, is always considered to be satisfied where an asset is separately acquired. Initial recognition is unlikely, therefore, to cause any problems.

> **Example 14.6 – Separately acquired intangibles**
>
> If the customer list in **Example 14.2** and the franchise licence in **Example 14.3** were separately acquired, they would automatically satisfy the recognition criteria.

Intangibles acquired as part of a business combination

14.7   An intangible asset acquired in a business combination is usually recognised as an asset because its fair value at acquisition date can normally be measured with sufficient reliability.

14.8   However, there is a restriction on the recognition of intangibles which arise from legal or other contractual rights, for example trademarks, internet domain names, licensing and royalty agreements, and franchise agreements.

Such intangibles should not be separately recognised in cases where there is no history or evidence of exchange transactions for the same or similar assets, and otherwise estimating fair value 'would be dependent on immeasurable variables' (FRS 102, paragraph 18.8).

> **Example 14.7 – Customer list acquired as part of a business combination**
>
> Suppose Company A in **Example 14.2** above obtained the customer list through the acquisition of another company. The customer list was created by the company and does not arise from legal or other contractual rights.
>
> The customer list would be recognised as a separate asset (distinct from goodwill) provided its fair value at acquisition date could be measured with sufficient reliability.
>
> Valuation techniques to establish fair values of customer lists are now well established under full IFRS, so it is likely that the recognition criteria would be satisfied.

Example 14.8 – Intangibles arising from legal or other contractual rights acquired in a business combination

Company D has acquired a number of marketing-related intangibles including several patents and trademarks as a result of acquiring Company E.

In this case, the intangibles were acquired in a business combination and arise from 'contractual or other legal requirements'.

In accordance with the requirements of paragraph 18.8 it is necessary to consider whether there is 'history or evidence of the same or similar assets'. If there is no such history or evidence, the intangibles would not be separately recognised but would, instead, be included as part of goodwill.

Focus

The criteria above may be difficult to satisfy, and may result in more intangibles being included as part of goodwill rather than separately.

Whether treated as a separate asset or as part of goodwill, the intangible would be subject to amortisation.

Expenditure which must be expensed as incurred

14.9   FRS 102 specifically refers to the following as examples of expenditure which must be expensed and not capitalised:

- internally generated brands, logos, publishing titles, customer lists and items similar in substance;
- start-up activities, including:
  - establishment costs such as legal and secretarial costs incurred in establishing a legal entity;
  - expenditure to open a new facility or business (pre-opening costs); and
  - expenditure for starting new operations or launching new products or processes (pre-operating costs);
- training activities;
- advertising and promotional activities (unless this meets the definition of inventories held for distribution at no or at nominal consideration (see **Chapter 19**);

- relocating or reorganising part or all of an entity; and

- internally generated goodwill.

INITIAL MEASUREMENT

General considerations

14.10   An intangible asset is initially recognised at cost, assuming it satisfies the recognition criteria above.

Intangibles acquired separately

14.11   The cost of a separately acquired intangible asset comprises:

- its purchase price, including import duties and non-refundable purchase taxes, after deducting trade discounts and rebates; and

- any directly attributable cost of preparing the asset for its intended use.

Intangibles acquired as part of a business combination

14.12   The cost of the intangible is its fair value at acquisition date. However, if its fair value cannot be measured with sufficient reliability and if it is caught by FRS 102, paragraph 18.8 (see **14.8** above), the intangible will not be separately recognised. It will effectively be subsumed within the goodwill figure.

Intangibles acquired by way of grant

14.13   The cost of the intangible asset is its fair value at the date the grant is received or receivable.

Exchanges of assets

14.14   An intangible asset may be acquired in exchange for a non-monetary asset or assets, or a combination of monetary and non-monetary assets.

14.15   The cost of the intangible should be measured at fair value, unless either:

14.16 *Intangible assets other than goodwill*

(a)   the exchange transaction lacks commercial substance; or

(b)   the fair value of neither the asset received nor the asset given up is reliably measurable.

In such cases the cost of the intangible is measured at the carrying amount of the asset(s) given up.

Internally generated assets

14.16   As indicated in **14.9** above, it will often be very difficult to justify recognising internally generated intangibles. Recognition will be restricted to specific situations relating to development expenditure where the entity chooses a policy of capitalisation and amortisation as opposed to a policy of expensing as incurred.

14.17   Subject to these constraints, the cost of an internally generated intangible is the sum of expenditure incurred from the date when the intangible first meets the recognition criteria in **14.5** above.

14.18   The cost comprises all directly attributable costs necessary to create, produce and prepare the asset to be capable of operating in the manner intended by management.

14.19   Examples of directly attributable costs are:

●   costs of materials and services used or consumed in generating the intangible asset;

●   costs of employee benefits arising from the generation of the intangible asset;

●   fees to register a legal right; and

●   amortisation of patents and licences that are used to generate the intangible asset.

14.20   Capitalisation of interest is covered in Section 25 of FRS 102 (see **Chapter 17**).

INTERNALLY GENERATED INTANGIBLES

General principles

14.21   General recognition criteria are referred to in **14.5** above.

To apply these criteria to this section of the FRS, it is necessary to classify the generation of the internally generated intangible into a research phase, and a development phase.

Focus

The distinction between research-phase expenditure and development-phase expenditure is crucial.

Research-phase expenditure is charged to profit or loss as incurred. Development-phase expenditure, provided it ticks all the boxes, may either be expensed as incurred, or alternatively capitalised and amortised.

14.22   If an entity cannot distinguish the research phase of an internal project from the development phase, the expenditure on the project will be treated as if it were incurred in the research phase only.

Research and development expenditure – research phase

14.23   As indicated above, expenditure on research, or the research phase of an internal project, must be expensed as incurred.

14.24   The following are examples of research activities:

- activities aimed at obtaining new knowledge;

- the search for, evaluation and final selection of applications of research findings and other knowledge;

- the search for alternatives for materials, devices, products, processes, systems or services; and

- the formulation, design, evaluation and final selection of possible alternatives for new or improved material, devices, projects, systems or services.

Research and development expenditure – development phase

14.25   An entity may recognise an intangible asset arising from development, or from the development phase of an internal project, *only* if it can demonstrate *all* of the following criteria:

- the technical feasibility of completing the intangible asset so that it will be available for use or sale;

- the entity's intention to complete the intangible asset and use or sell it;

- the entity's ability to use or sell the intangible asset;

- how the intangible asset will generate future economic benefits. Among other things, the entity can demonstrate the existence of a market for the output of the intangible asset or the intangible asset itself or, if it is to be used internally, the usefulness of the intangible asset;

- the availability of adequate technical, financial and other resources to complete the development and to use or sell the intangible asset; and

- the entity's ability to measure reliably the expenditure attributable to the intangible asset during its development.

The accounting policy adopted must be applied consistently to expenditure that meets all of these criteria.

Examples of development activities

14.26   These include:

- the design, construction and testing of pre-production or pre-use prototypes and models;

- the design of tools, jigs, moulds and dies involving new technology;

- the design, construction and operation of a pilot plant that is not of a scale economically feasible for commercial production; and

- the design, construction and testing of a chosen alternative for new or improved materials, devises, products, processes, systems or services.

Past expenses

14.27   The general rule is that expenditure on an intangible item that was initially recognised as an expense must not be recognised at a later date as part of the cost of the asset.

14.28   On transition to FRS 102, special considerations may apply (see **39.26**).

MEASUREMENT AFTER INITIAL RECOGNITION

Accounting policy choice

14.29   In principle, an entity may measure intangible assets after initial recognition using either the cost model or the revaluation model. In practice, this choice may be available only in very rare situations, given the stringent conditions which apply to the use of the revaluation model.

Cost model

14.30 After initial recognition under the cost model, an entity should measure the intangible at cost less any accumulated amortisation and any accumulated impairment losses.

14.31 The requirements for amortisation are set out in **14.36–14.38**. Requirements for recognition of impairment are dealt with in **Chapter 18**.

Revaluation model

14.32 Under the revaluation model, an intangible asset whose fair value can be measured reliably will be carried at a revalued amount, less any subsequent accumulated amortisation and accumulated impairment.

14.33 There a number of constraints to the use of the revaluation model:

- it can only be applied to assets that have previously been recognised as assets;

- such assets must have initially been recognised at cost (for an asset acquired as part of a business combination, 'cost' means fair value at acquisition date); and

- fair value 'shall be determined by reference to an active market'.

14.34 The term 'active market' is defined in the Glossary to FRS 102 as follows:

'A market in which all the following conditions exist:

(a) the items traded in the market are homogeneous;

(b) willing buyers and sellers can normally be found at any time; and

(c) prices are available to the public.'

In practice, very few intangibles would be able to get past this stringent definition.

Focus

The following extract from full IFRS (IAS 38, paragraph 78) may be helpful:

'It is uncommon for an active market to exist for an intangible asset, although this may happen. For example, in some jurisdictions, an active market may exist for freely transferable taxi licences, fishing licences or production quotas. However, an active market cannot exist for brands, newspaper mastheads, music and film publishing rights, patents or trademarks, because each such asset is unique. Also, although intangible assets are bought and sold, contracts are negotiated between individual buyers and sellers, and transactions are fairly infrequent. For these reasons, the price paid for one asset may not provide sufficient evidence of the fair value of another. Moreover, prices are not often available to the public.'

14.35   In view of the likely restricted application of this part of FRS 102, no further reference is made here. (For further information, the relevant paragraphs in FRS 102 are 18.18B–18.18H and 18.29A.)

AMORTISATION

General principles and method

14.36   The depreciable amount of an intangible should be allocated on a systematic basis over its useful life.

14.37   The method used should reflect the pattern in which the entity expects to consume the asset's future economic benefits. If that pattern cannot be determined reliably, the straight-line method should be used.

14.38   The depreciation charge should recognised as an expense except where another section of FRS 102 requires the depreciation cost to be recognised as part of the cost of an asset (eg inventory or property, plant and equipment).

Amortisation begins when the intangible is available for use (ie when it is in the location and condition necessary for it to be usable in the manner intended by management) and ceases when the asset is derecognised.

Useful life

14.39   All recognised intangible assets are considered to have a finite useful life. The useful life of an intangible asset that arises from contractual or other legal rights shall not exceed the period of contractual or other legal rights (but it may be shorter depending on the period over which the entity expects to use the asset).

14.40 Note that if an entity is unable to make a reliable estimate of the useful life of an intangible asset, the life shall be presumed to be *five years*.

Residual value

14.41 Residual value should be assumed to be zero unless there is a commitment by a third party to purchase the asset at the end of its useful life or there is an active market for the asset (likely to be rare).

DERECOGNITION

14.42 An intangible should be derecognised either on disposal or when no future economic benefits are expected from the use or disposal of the asset.

WEBSITE COSTS

14.43 FRS 102 does not make explicit reference to website costs. Under the previous UK GAAP, these were dealt with in UITF Abstract 29 *Website Development Costs*.

DISCLOSURE REQUIREMENTS

Requirements for each class

14.44 The following should be disclosed for each class of intangible assets:

- the useful lives or the amortisation rates used and the reasons for choosing those periods;
- the amortisation methods used;
- the gross carrying amount and any accumulated amortisation (aggregated with accumulated impairment losses) at the beginning and end of the reporting period;
- the line items in the statement of comprehensive income/income statement, in which any amortisation of intangibles is included; and
- a reconciliation of the carrying amount at the beginning and end of the reporting period showing separately:

    ○   additions (distinguishing between those from internal developments and those acquired separately)

    ○   disposals

    ○   acquisitions through business combinations

    ○   revaluations

    ○   amortisation

    ○   impairment losses

    ○   other changes.

The above reconciliation need not be presented for comparative periods.

Other disclosures

14.45   The following must be disclosed:

- a description, the carrying amount and remaining amortisation period of any intangible asset that is material to the entity's financial statements;

- for assets acquired by way of a grant and initially recognised at fair value – the fair value initially recognised and their carrying amounts;

- the existence and carrying amounts of intangible assets to which the entity has restricted title or that are pledged as security for liabilities;

- the amount of contractual commitments for the acquisition of intangible assets; and

- the aggregate amount of research and development expenditure recognised as an expense during the period.

Example 14.9 – Accounting policy note for intangibles

Accounting policy extracts – intangible assets

Intangibles acquired in a business combination

An intangible asset acquired in a business combination is deemed to have a cost to the group of its fair value as at the acquisition date. This fair value reflects market expectations about the probability that the future economic benefits related to the intangible asset will flow to the group.

Internally developed intangibles

Development costs incurred on software development are capitalised when all of the following conditions are satisfied:

- completion of the software module is technically feasible so that it will be available for use;

- the group intends to complete the development of the software module and use it;

- the software will be used to generate probable future economic benefits;

- there are adequate technical, financial and other resources to complete the development and to use the software; and

- the expenditure attributable to the software can be measured reliably.

Management applies judgement based on information available at each balance sheet date when deciding whether the recognition criteria have been met, as the economic success of any development is uncertain and may be subject to future technical problems at the time of recognition. All development activities are subject to continual monitoring by management.

The cost of internally generated intangibles comprises all directly attributable costs necessary to create, produce and prepare the intangible asset to be capable of operating in the manner intended by management. These costs include employee costs specifically incurred on software development.

Amortisation commences upon completion of the intangible asset and the charge is shown within administrative expenses. Development expenditure is amortised over the period expected to benefit.

Prior to completion of the intangible asset, costs capitalised are tested for impairment. After completion, the carrying amount is reviewed at each reporting date in accordance with the group's impairment review procedures.

Development costs not meeting the criteria for capitalisation are expensed as incurred.

SUMMARY – WHAT IS DIFFERENT FROM THE PREVIOUS UK GAAP?

- Under the previous UK GAAP, intangibles are dealt with in two separate standards:

  o   SSAP13 *Accounting for Research and Development*; and

  o   FRS 10 *Goodwill and Intangible Assets*.

- The criteria in FRS 102 for capitalisation of development costs are broadly consistent with those in SSAP 13.

- In business combinations, more intangibles are likely to be separately recognised under FRS 102 (as has often proved to be the situation under full IFRS) as opposed to being subsumed within the goodwill number in the case of UK GAAP.

- The amortisation period for goodwill and intangibles may turn out to be different as compared with existing UK GAAP:

  o   FRS 10 specifies a maximum period of 20 years, but this can be rebutted if a longer period can be justified (this would then require the use of the true and fair override).

  o   FRS 102, paragraphs 18.20 and 19.23(a) state that if an entity is unable to make a reliable estimate of the useful life of goodwill, the life shall not exceed five years (see **Chapter 30**).

- FRS 102 restricts revaluation of intangibles to situations where fair value can be determined by reference to an 'active market' (see **14.34** above) whereas FRS 10.43 states that 'where an intangible asset has a readily ascertainable market value, the asset may be revalued to its market value'. The difference in wording between the two sets of requirements is unlikely to have a significant effect (see also Focus box at **14.34**).

Chapter 15

Leases

SIGNPOSTS

- The classification criteria for determining whether a lease is an operating lease or a finance lease is slightly different from that in existing UK GAAP, although in practice the effect is likely to be the same in most cases (see **15.9**).

- The operation of lessee accounting is almost identical to existing UK GAAP.

- Some properties held under operating leases may be accounted for as investment properties in accordance with Section FRS 102, paragraphs 16.3 and 16.6 (see **15.43** and **13.8**).

- Sale and leaseback arrangements are dealt with in **Chapter 21**.

- Lease incentives are treated differently (see **15.25**).

- Note carefully requirements for disclosure of operating lease commitments (see **15.47**) – these are different from equivalent requirements in SSAP 21.

INTRODUCTION AND SCOPE

Definition

15.1   A lease is defined in the Glossary of Terms as: 'an agreement whereby the lessor conveys to the lessee in return for a payment or series of payments the right to use an asset for an agreed period of time.'

Example 15.1 – Property lease

Company A owns a freehold property that it holds to obtain rental income and capital appreciation. The property is let to Company B for an annual rent of £200,000 per annum, with rent reviews at five-yearly intervals. The agreement between the two companies gives Company B the right to use the building for 20 years.

The arrangement is a lease.

From the perspective of the lessee, Company B, the arrangement is an operating lease (see classification of leases, below). From the perspective of the lessor, Company A, the property is an investment property (see **Chapter 13**).

Example 15.2 – Lease of motor vehicles

Company A, a vehicle hire firm, owns cars and vans which are hired out to third parties for short periods, usually ranging from one day to up to four weeks.

The hire arrangement between the parties is a lease.

From the perspective of the hiree (the lessee), the arrangement is an operating lease (see below). From the perspective of Company B, the lessor, the vehicles are property, plant and equipment (see **Chapter 12**).

Scope exclusions

15.2   Section 20 covers accounting for all leases except for the following:

- leases to explore for or use minerals, oil, natural gas and similar non-regenerative resources;

- licensing agreements for such items as motion picture films, video recordings, plays, manuscripts, patents and copyrights – these should be accounted for as intangibles;

- measurement of property held by lessees that is accounted for as investment property, and measurement of investment property provided by lessors under operating leases (see **13.8**);

- measurement of biological assets held by lessees under finance leases and biological assets provided by lessors under operating leases; and

- leases that could lead to a loss to the lessor or the lessee as a result of non-typical contractual terms.

Substantial services provided by the lessor

15.3   Agreements that transfer the right to use assets fall within the scope of Section 20 even if such agreements call for the lessor to provide substantial services relating to the operation or maintenance of the assets.

15.4   Section 20 does not apply to agreements that are contracts for services that do not transfer the right to use assets from one party to the other.

Example 15.3 – Photocopier lease and maintenance services

Company D leases a photocopier from Company E under an operating lease. The agreement between the two companies states that Company E will provide maintenance services in respect of the photocopier.

The part of the agreement which gives Company D the right to use the photocopier is a lease. The provision of maintenance services is a separate provision of services.

From the perspective of Company D, the lessee, the part of the agreement that provides the right to use the asset falls within Section 20. The part of the payment to the lessor relating to maintenance services should be recognised as an expense in profit or loss in the period in which the expenses are incurred.

From the perspective of Company E, the lessor, the part of the agreement that provides Company D the right to use the photocopier should be accounted for in accordance with Section 20 (see **15.38–15.39** below). The maintenance services should be recognised as income in accordance with FRS 102, Section 22, Revenue (see **Chapter 26**).

Arrangements which are similar to legal leases

15.5   Certain types of arrangements which convey rights to use assets in return for payments are in substance leases even though they do not take the legal form of leases. These should be accounted for in accordance with Section 20.

15.6   Examples of such arrangements include the following:

●   outsourcing arrangements;

●   telecommunication contracts that provide rights to capacity; and

●   take-or-pay contracts.

CLASSIFICATION

Definitions

15.7   A finance lease is a lease which transfers substantially all the risks and rewards incidental to ownership.

15.8   An operating lease is a lease which does *not* transfer substantially all the risks and rewards incidental to ownership.

15.9   Whether a lease is classified as a finance lease or an operating lease depends on the substance of the transaction rather than the transaction's legal form. The assessment of the transaction's substance is referred to below.

Focus

The classification is broadly similar to that in UK GAAP SSAP 21 *Accounting for Leases and Hire Purchase Contracts* where an operating lease is defined as a lease that is not a finance lease.

There is no equivalent in FRS 102 to paragraph 15 of SSAP 21 – the presumption of a transfer of risks and rewards of ownership where the present value of the minimum lease payment is 90% or more of the fair value of the leased asset. As FRS 102 makes no reference to arithmetic calculation, more judgement will be required when compared with applying SSAP 21.

15.10   The lease classification should be made at the inception of the lease and should not be changed during the term of the lease. A simple renewal of a lease should not result in a change of lease classification.

However, if the lessor and lessee agree to *change the terms* of the lease, the lease classification should be reevaluated.

ACCOUNTING FOR THE SUBSTANCE OF THE TRANSACTION

Examples of situations which point towards finance lease classification

15.11   The following are examples, included in FRS 102, paragraph 20.5, of situations that either individually or in combination would normally lead to a lease being classified as a finance lease:

- the lease transfers ownership of the asset to the lessee by the end of the lease term;

- the lessee has the option to purchase the asset at a price that is expected to be sufficiently lower than the fair value of the asset at the date when the option becomes exercisable, in circumstances where it is reasonably certain at the start of the lease that the option will be exercised;

- the lease term is for the major part of the economic life of the asset even if title is not transferred;

- at the inception of the lease the present value of the minimum lease payments amounts to at least substantially all of the fair value of the leased asset; and

- the leased assets are of such a specialised nature that only the lessee can use them without major modifications.

Finance lease indicators

15.12   The following examples, taken from FRS 102, paragraph 20.6, are of indicators that either individually or in combination could also lead to a lease being classified as a finance lease:

- where the agreement allows the lessee to cancel the lease but the lessee would be required to bear the losses associated with the cancellation;

- gains or losses from the fluctuation of the leased asset's residual value accrue to the lessee (eg where the lessee will receive a rent rebate at the end of the lease equivalent to most of the sales proceeds of the leased asset); and

- the lessee has the ability to extend the lease term for a secondary period at a rent substantially lower than the market rate (eg a so-called 'peppercorn rent').

The importance of assessing risks and rewards incidental to ownership

15.13   All features of the lease arrangement should be considered. The pointers in **15.11** and **15.12** may not necessarily be conclusive for the purpose of determining lease classification.

15.14   If an overall assessment judges that the lease does not transfer substantially all risks and rewards incidental to ownership, the lease should be classified as an operating lease.

Example 15.4 – Lease where lessee does not have substantially all risks and rewards incidental to ownership

Under the terms of a lease, ownership of the asset at the end of the lease term is transferred to the lessee for a variable payment equal to the fair value of the asset at that date.

This is clearly not a situation where 'gains or losses from the fluctuation of the leased asset's residual value accrue to the lessee' (see **15.12** above). The lessee does not have substantially all risks and rewards incidental to ownership, and therefore the lease should be classified as an operating lease.

LESSEE ACCOUNTING – FINANCE LEASES

Initial recognition and measurement

15.15   The basic principle is that at the commencement of the lease term of the finance lease, the lessee should recognise rights of use under the lease as an asset and obligations under the lease as a liability.

15.16   The amount recognised should be the lower of:

- the fair value of the leased property; and

- the present value of the *minimum lease payments* (determined at the inception of the lease).

The term 'minimum lease payments' is defined in the Glossary to FRS 102 and, for a lessee, includes:

- the payments over the lease term that the lessee is or can be required to make (excluding contingent rent);

- costs for services and taxes to be paid by and reimbursed to the lessor; and

- any amounts guaranteed by the lessee or by a party related to the lessee.

The definition in the Glossary to FRS 102 also takes in the situation where the lessee has an option to purchase the asset at a price that is expected to be sufficiently lower than fair value at the date the option becomes exercisable for it to be reasonably certain, at the inception of the lease, that the option will be exercised.

In this situation, the minimum lease payments comprise the minimum payments payable over the lease term up to the expected date of exercise of the option and the payment required to exercise it.

15.17   Any initial direct costs of the lessee which are directly attributable to negotiating and arranging the lease, should be added to the amount recognised as an asset.

15.18   Where the amount recognised is based on the present value of the minimum lease payments, these should be calculated using the interest rate implicit in the lease. Where this rate cannot be determined, the rate used should be the lessee's incremental borrowing rate.

The interest rate implicit in the lease is defined in the Glossary to FRS 102 as:

'The discount rate that, at the inception of the lease, causes the aggregate present value of:

(a)   the minimum lease payments; and

(b)   the unguaranteed residual value, to be equal to the sum of:

(i)   the fair value of the leased asset; and

(ii)   any initial direct costs of the lessor.

The lessee's incremental borrowing rate of interest is defined as "the rate of interest the lessee would have to pay on a similar lease, or, if that is not determinable, the rate that, at the inception of the lease, the lessee would have to incur to borrow, over a similar term, and with a similar security, the funds necessary to purchase the asset".'

Subsequent remeasurement

15.19   Minimum lease payments should be apportioned between the finance charge and the reduction of the outstanding liability using the effective interest method (see **36.18–36.20** for a definition and illustration).

The finance charge should be allocated to each period so as to produce a constant periodic rate of interest on the remaining balance of the liability.

Example 15.5 – Lessee accounting calculations for lease liability

An item of plant and machinery with a useful life of ten years may be purchased outright for cash for £42,800. Alternatively, use of the asset may be obtained by means of a finance lease.

Under this arrangement, the lessee would be responsible for insurance and maintenance and would be required to make five annual payments of £11,600 all payable in advance. After the primary period of five years, the lessee would have the option to continue leasing the asset for an indefinite period for a nominal ('peppercorn') rental. The amount of the rental may be ignored.

It is assumed that the fair value of £42,800 provides an acceptable approximation to the present value of the minimum lease payments determined at the inception of the lease, discounted at the interest rate implicit in the lease.

Finance charge – effective interest method

The total finance charge to be allocated to periods equals the excess of rentals paid over the amount capitalised (ie £58,000 – £42,800 = £15,200). The finance charge is to be allocated using the effective interest method.

The interest rate is calculated as 18.0% (see table below for proof of the numbers).

The following table shows the movement on the liability account:

Year	Liability brought forward	Lease payments	Finance charge in profit or loss (at 18%)	Liability carried forward
	£	£	£	£
2011	42,800	(11,600)	5,616	36,816
2012	36,816	(11,600)	4,538	29,754
2013	29,754	(11,600)	3,268	21,422
2014	21,422	(11,600)	1,778	11,600
2015	11,600	(11,600)	–	
Totals		(58,000)	15,200	

15.20 An asset leased under a finance lease should be depreciated in accordance with Section 17 of FRS 102 (see **12.24** onwards).

Where there is no reasonable certainty that the lessee will obtain ownership by the end of the lease term, the leased asset should be depreciated over the shorter of:

- the lease term; and

- the useful life of the asset.

Example 15.6 – Lessee accounting calculations for fixed asset

Using the figure in **Example 15.5**, the fixed asset would be capitalised initially at £42,800. The asset should be depreciated over the shorter of the lease term and its useful life.

The lease term is effectively indefinite (as it can be extended by the payment of a peppercorn rental of an immaterial amount) and the asset's useful life is ten years.

If the straight-line method of depreciation is used, the asset will be depreciated over ten years giving an annual depreciation charge of £4,280.

15.21   At the end of each reporting date, the lessee should assess whether the asset leased under a finance lease is impaired (see **Chapter 18**).

LESSEE ACCOUNTING – OPERATING LEASES

Recognition and measurement

15.22   The requirements apply to lease payments under operating leases, excluding costs for services such as insurance and maintenance (see **Example 15.3** above).

15.23   Lease payments should be recognised as an expense on a straight-line basis, subject to two exceptions:

- where another systematic basis is representative of the time pattern of the user's benefit, even if the payments are not on that basis (eg see lease incentives below); or

- where the payments to the lessor are structured to increase in line with expected general inflation (based on published indexes or statistics) to compensate for the lessor's expected inflationary cost increases. If payments to the lessor vary because of factors other than general inflation, then this exception will not apply (Section 20, paragraph 20.15(b) includes a numerical example, this is not reproduced below).

Lease incentives

15.24   Lease incentives offered by lessors to lessees may arise when a new operating lease is being negotiated or when an existing lease is being renewed.

These incentives may take the form of a cash payment direct to the lessor, a rent-free period or the assumption of costs that would otherwise be borne by the lessee (eg relocation or fit-out costs).

The nature of incentives must be examined to establish if they are for the lessee's or the lessor's benefit. It is important that the accounts reflect the substance of the transaction.

15.25   Assuming the incentive is for the benefit of the lessee, the financial effect of the benefit, in whatever form it comes, should be spread over the period of the lease, normally on a straight-line basis (FRS 102, paragraph 20.15A).

Particular issues arising on transition to FRS 102 are dealt with in **Chapter 39** (see **39.27**).

Focus

Note that FRS 102 requires the lease incentive to be spread over the lease term, whereas existing UK GAAP UITF Abstract 28 requires the benefit to be spread over the 'shorter of the lease term and a period ending on a date from which it is expected the prevailing market rental will be payable'.

Example 15.7 – Lease incentive calculations

Lessor Ltd is negotiating a ten-year lease with Lessee Ltd. The annual rental will be £20,000 but it is agreed that the lessee will be entitled to an incentive of a rent-free period for the first six months.

The total payment to the lessor over the ten-year period will therefore be £190,000 and the annual lease expense will be £190,000/10 years = £19,000.

The balance sheet at the end of year 1 will show an accrual of £9,000 (the annual expense of £19,000 less the payment made in the first year of £10,000).

Example 15.8 – Lease incentive accounting policy

Accounting policies – leases (extract)

'... The rental cost of properties and other assets held under operating leases are charged to the profit and loss account on a straight-line basis. Benefits received as an incentive to sign a lease, whatever form they take, are credited to the profit and loss account on a straight-line basis over the lease term.'

LESSOR ACCOUNTING – FINANCE LEASES

Initial recognition and measurement

15.26   Assets held under finance leases should be presented in the balance sheet as a receivable and stated at an amount equal to the net investment in the lease.

15.27   The term 'net investment in a lease' is defined in the Glossary as the gross investment in a lease discounted at the interest rate implicit in the lease.

15.28   The term 'gross investment in a lease' is defined in the Glossary as the aggregate of:

- the minimum lease payments receivable by the lessor under a finance lease; and

- any unguaranteed residual value accruing to the lessor.

The term 'minimum lease payments' is defined in the Glossary to FRS 102, and for a lessor includes:

- the payments over the lease term that the lessee is or can be required to make (excluding contingent rent);

- costs for services and taxes to be paid by and reimbursed to the lessor; and

- any residual value guaranteed to the lessor by:

  ○ the lessee;

  ○ a party related to the lessee; or

  ○ a third party unrelated to the lessor that is financially capable of discharging the obligations under the guarantee.

The definition in the Glossary to FRS 102 also takes in the situation where the lessee has an option to purchase the asset at a price that is expected to be sufficiently lower than fair value at the date the option becomes exercisable for it to be reasonably certain, at the inception of the lease, that the option will be exercised.

In this situation, the minimum lease payments comprise the minimum payments payable over the lease term up to the expected date of exercise of the option and the payment required to exercise it.

Subsequent remeasurement

15.29   Finance income should be recognised in profit or loss based on a pattern which reflects a constant periodic rate of return on the lessor's net investment in the finance lease.

This is a potentially complex area which is dealt with in FRS 102, Section 20.19 – it is not further referred to here.

MANUFACTURERS AND DEALERS

Types of income of manufacturers or dealers

15.30   Manufacturers or dealers may offer customers a choice between buying or leasing an asset under a finance lease agreement.

15.31 *Leases*

15.31   A finance lease of an asset of a manufacturer gives rise to two types of income:

- a profit or loss equivalent to that which would be obtained from an outright sale, at normal selling prices and allowing for any applicable volume or trade discounts; and

- finance income over the lease term.

Recognition of income by a manufacturer or dealer lessor

15.32   The sales revenue recognised at the commencement of the lease term is the lower of:

- the fair value of the asset; and

- the present value of the minimum lease payments accruing to the lessor, computed at a market rate of interest.

15.33   The cost of sale recognised at the commencement of the lease term is:

- the cost (or carrying amount if different from cost) of the leased property; less

- the present value of the unguaranteed residual value.

15.34   The difference between the sales revenue and the cost of sale is the selling profit.

Selling profit is recognised in accordance with the entity's policy for outright sales (see **Chapter 26**).

Where artificially low rates are quoted

15.35   Where artificially low rates of interest are quoted, selling profit is restricted to that which would apply if market rates of interest were charged.

LESSOR ACCOUNTING – OPERATING LEASES

Assets

15.36   Assets subject to operating leases should be presented in the statement of financial position according to the nature of the asset.

> **Example 15.9 – Presentation of the leased asset**
>
> For example, a car-hire company would present its vehicle assets under 'property, plant and equipment', and present and disclose in accordance with Section 17 (see **Chapter 12**).

Lease income

15.37 Lease income recognised should exclude amounts for services such as insurance and maintenance (see **Example 15.3** above).

Income should be recognised in profit or loss on a straight-line basis subject to two exceptions:

- where another systematic basis is representative of the time pattern of the lessee's benefit from the leased asset, even if the receipt of payments is not on that basis; or

- where the payments to the lessor are structured to increase in line with expected general inflation (based on published indexes or statistics) to compensate for the lessor's expected inflationary cost increases. If payments to the lessor vary because of factors other than general inflation, then this exception will not apply.

Expenses

15.38 Expense costs, including depreciation, incurred in earning the income shall be recognised. The depreciation policy should be consistent with the normal policy for similar assets.

15.39 Initial direct costs incurred in negotiating and arranging an operating lease should be added to the carrying amount of the asset. The costs should be expensed over the lease term on the same basis as the lease income (ie normally straight-line unless one of the two exceptions above applies).

Impairment

15.40 The usual impairment requirements apply (see **Chapter 18**).

Manufacturer or dealer lessors (operating leases)

15.41 An operating lease is not the equivalent of a sale, so a manufacturer or dealer's lessor should not recognise any selling profit.

SALE AND LEASEBACK

15.42   Sale and leaseback transactions are dealt with in **Chapter 21**.

INVESTMENT PROPERTIES

15.43   Some properties held by lessees under operating leases may be accounted for as investment properties in accordance with FRS 102, Section 16, paragraph 16.3 (see **13.8** above). These are outside the scope of Section 15 (see **15.2** above).

DISCLOSURE REQUIREMENTS

Comparative information

15.44   Comparatives are required for all of the disclosure requirements below – the general rule in Section 3, paragraph 3.14 applies.

Financial statements of lessees – finance leases

15.45   The following disclosures are required:

- the net carrying amount by class of leased assets at the end of each reporting period;

- the total amount of future minimum lease payments at the end of each reporting period, for each of the following periods:

    ○   not later than one year;

    ○   later than one year and not later than five years; and

    ○   later than five years.

- a general description of the lessee's significant leasing arrangements including, for example, information about contingent rent, renewal or purchase options and escalation clauses, sub-leases, and restrictions imposed by lease arrangements.

15.46   Asset disclosures required by other sections of FRS 102 apply, in particular:

- Section 17, Property, Plant and Equipment (see **Chapter 12**); and

- Section 27, Impairment of Assets (see **Chapter 18**);

Example 15.10 – Accounting policy for leased assets

Where assets are financed by leasing agreements that give rights approximating to ownership ('finance leases') the assets are treated as if they had been purchased outright. The amount capitalised is the present value of the minimum lease payments payable over the term of the lease. The corresponding liability to the leasing company is included as an obligation under finance leases.

Depreciation on leased assets is charged to the profit and loss account on the same basis as shown above.

Leasing payments are treated as consisting of capital and interest elements, and interest is charged to profit or loss over the lease term using the effective interest method.

Financial statements of lessees – operating leases

15.47   The following disclosures are required:

- the total of future minimum lease payments under non-cancellable operating leases for each of the following periods:

  - not later than one year;

  - later than one year and not later than five years; and

  - later than five years.

- lease payments recognised as an expenses.

Focus

Contrast above requirement to disclose total of future minimum lease payments with equivalent in SSAP 21 which requires disclosure of payments in the next accounting period.

Example 15.11 – Note 30 – Operating lease commitments

At the balance sheet date, the company had outstanding commitments under non-cancellable operating leases, which fall due as follows:

	2015	2014
	£'000	*£'000*
Within one year	209	297
In the second to fifth years inclusive	1,320	1,339
After five years	592	830
	2,121	2,466

Operating lease payments represent rentals payable by the company for certain of its office properties. Leases are negotiated for an average term of seven years and rentals are fixed for an average of three years.

Financial statements of lessors – finance leases

15.48   The following disclosures are required:

- a reconciliation between the gross investment in the lease at the end of the reporting period, and the present value of minimum lease payments receivable at the end of the reporting period;

- the gross investment in the lease and the present value of minimum lease payments receivable at the end of the reporting period, for each of the following periods:

    o   not later than one year;

    o   later than one year and not later than five years; and

    o   later than five years.

- unearned finance income;

- the unguaranteed residual values accruing to the benefit of the lessor;

- the accumulated allowance for uncollectible minimum lease payments receivable;

- contingent rents recognised as income in the period; and

- a general description of the lessor's significant leasing arrangements, including for example, information about contingent rent, renewal or purchase options and escalation clauses, sub-leases, and restrictions imposed by lease arrangements.

Financial statements of lessors – operating leases

15.49   The following disclosures are required:

- the future minimum lease payments under non-cancellable operating leases for each of the following periods:

  ○   not later than one year;

  ○   later than one year and not later than five years; and

  ○   later than five years.

- total contingent rents recognised as income; and

- a general description of the lessor's significant leasing arrangements, including information about contingent rent, renewal or purchase options and escalation clauses and restrictions imposed by lease arrangements.

15.50   Asset disclosures required by other Sections of FRS 102 apply to lessors for assets provided under operating leases, in particular:

- Section 17, Property, Plant and Equipment (see **Chapter 12**); and

- Section 27, Impairment of Assets (see **Chapter 18**).

SUMMARY – WHAT IS DIFFERENT FROM THE
PREVIOUS UK GAAP?

- The guidance on determining whether a lease is a finance lease or an operating lease is less prescriptive than that in SSAP 21 but, in practice, may make little difference in the majority of cases.

- There is no equivalent in FRS 102 to paragraph 15 of SSAP 21 – the presumption of a transfer of risks and rewards of ownership where the present value of the minimum lease payment is 90% or more of the fair value of the leased asset. As FRS 102 makes no reference to arithmetic calculation, more judgement will be required as compared with applying SSAP 21.

- FRS 102 requires disclosure of total of future minimum lease payments compared with equivalent in SSAP 21 which requires disclose of payments in the next accounting period.

- The benefits of lease incentives are likely to be spread over a longer period as compared with existing UK GAAP.

Chapter 16

Agriculture

SIGNPOSTS

- The accounting treatment for agricultural activities is set out in Section 34 of FRS 102.

- There is no accounting standard in current UK GAAP which addresses this specific area although Schedule 1 of the Regulations to CA 2006 (see **7.4**) refers to 'living animals and plants' (these are referred to in Section 34 as 'biological assets').

- Agriculture covers a broad range of activities and businesses will need to be sure that their activities fall within the definition of 'agricultural activity' before applying Section 34 (see **16.7** below).

- An important issue in Section 34 is the accounting policy choice offered between two measurement models – the cost model and the fair value. This choice may be applied either to all of the entity's the agricultural activities or by class of its biological assets.

- Section 34 is likely to apply to a diverse range of UK entities, ranging from medium-sized standalone companies to large UK groups and UK subsidiaries of overseas parent companies who adopt IFRS for their consolidated accounts. This chapter includes a large number of examples covering this diverse range.

INTRODUCTION AND SCOPE

Background

16.1   Section 34 of FRS 102 *Specialised Activities*, includes detailed recognition, measurement, presentation and disclosure requirements for entities engaged in agricultural activity. Prior to the issuance of FRS 102, there were no specific accounting requirements dealing with this area.

16.2   The requirements in Section 34 are based on a modified version of the International Accounting Standards Board's IFRS for SMEs, following feedback to the Financial Reporting Council after the issuance of FRED 48.

Focus

Perhaps the most crucial difference between FRS 102 on the one hand and the IFRS for SMEs and IAS 41 *Agriculture* on the other hand, is that FRS 102 offers an accounting policy choice.

Under FRS 102, entities involved in agricultural activity will be able to choose between the cost model and the fair value model. Many UK entities already using the cost model may prefer to stay with this model under FRS 102.

IFRS for SMEs/IAS 41 require a fair value model except in special cases where a reliable fair value measurement cannot be obtained.

Scope

16.3   FRS 102 paragraphs 34.1 to 34.10A apply to entities involved in agricultural activity. This covers a diverse range of activities, including:

- dairy farming;

- wine growing;

- fruit growing;

- salmon farming; and

- forestry management.

16.4   Section 34 uses some industry-specific terms – these are defined below. It requires an entity engaged in *agricultural activity* to determine an accounting policy for:

- each class of *biological asset;* and

- its related *agricultural produce.*

16.5   Agricultural produce at the point of harvest falls within the scope of Section 34. Once harvested, agricultural produce falls within the scope of Section 13, Inventories (see **Chapter 19**).

KEY DEFINITIONS

Biological asset

16.6   This is defined as 'a living animal or plant'.

Agricultural activity

16.7   This is defined in the Glossary to FRS 102 as 'the management by an entity of the biological transformation of biological assets for sale, into agricultural products or into additional biological assets'.

Example 16.1 – Definition of biological asset

Exotic fish would fall within the definition of a biological asset. Consider three scenarios:

Company A breeds exotic fish and sells these to various retail outlets. Company A's activity falls within the definition of agricultural activity because it involves biological transformation of biological assets for sale. It therefore falls within the scope of Section 34.

Company B owns a number of retail outlets throughout the UK. The company buys exotic fish for sale within these outlets. Although the fish are biological assets, the company's business does not fit within the definition of agricultural activity. The fish are inventories and fall within the scope of Section 13, Inventories.

Company C operates several sea-life centres. Although the fish are biological assets, the business is not an agricultural activity, nor are the fish inventories as they are not held for sale in the ordinary course of business. The fish fall within the scope of Section 17, Property, Plant and Equipment.

Agricultural produce

16.8   This is defined in the Glossary to FRS 102 as 'the harvested product of the entity's biological assets'.

Example 16.2 – Examples of application of terminology

The following table provides some useful examples of the above terms:

Biological assets	*Agricultural produce*	*Products that are the result of processing after harvest*
Sheep	Wool	Yarn, carpet, pullovers
Trees in a plantation forest	Felled trees	Logs, lumber
Plants	Cotton	Thread, clothing
Plants	Harvested sugar cane	Sugar
Dairy cattle	Milk	Cheese, yoghurt
Pigs	Carcass	Sausages, cured ham
Bushes	Leaf	Tea
Vines	Grapes	Wine
Fruit trees	Picked fruit	Processed fruit, jam

Example 16.3 – Fruit-bearing tree up to point of harvest

A fruit-bearing tree before the fruit is harvested should be treated as a single biological asset.

After the point of harvest, the fruit harvested should be treated as a separate asset – agricultural produce – transferred to inventories, and accounted for in accordance with Section 13, Inventories.

The bare vine remains as a biological asset.

The accounting treatment will vary according to whether the cost model or the fair value model is adopted (see below).

RECOGNITION

16.9   A biological asset or an item of agricultural produce should be recognised only if all three of the following conditions are satisfied:

- the entity controls the asset as a result of past events;
- it is probable that future economic benefits associated with the asset will flow to the entity; and
- the fair value *or* cost of the asset can be measured reliably.

MEASUREMENT

16.10   Paragraph 34.3 is a crucial paragraph – it requires an entity to make an accounting policy choice for *each class* of biological asset and its related agricultural produce. The choice is between the:

- cost model; and

- fair value model.

16.11   The issue of choice of policy (or lack of choice) attracted a strong reaction from respondents to FRED 48. This is apparent from the comments published in March 2013 within the Accounting Council's Advice to the FRC to issue FRS 102:

'The IFRS for SMEs includes guidance for specialised activities including agriculture. The proposed requirements for agriculture are a predominantly fair value model and are based on IAS 41, Agriculture. Respondents questioned the proposed requirements noting that current FRSs do not set out accounting requirements [for agriculture] and although the proposals [in FRED 48] included an exemption from applying fair value where there is undue cost or effort, the fair value information is inconsistent with the way most agricultural businesses are managed and would not benefit the users of financial statements.

The Accounting Council evaluated the comments raised and advises that entities engaged in agricultural activities should be permitted an accounting policy choice for their biological assets, between the cost model and the fair value model set out in the IFRS for SMEs.'

(Paragraphs 94 and 95 of the Accounting Council's advice to FRC, page 245 of FRS 102.)

16.12   If an entity has chosen the fair value model for a particular class of biological asset and its related agricultural produce, it must not change back to the cost model.

16.13   The term 'class' is not defined, but the following examples taken from published accounts give some indication as to how the term might be applied:

- Company A which is a drinks manufacturer has a single class: grape vines and grape;

- Company B which is a fish farm has two classes: turbot and sturgeon; and

- Company C which grows apples for sale to cider manufacturers has two classes: mature apple trees (more than five years old) and immature apple trees (less than five years old).

16.14   An entity may choose to use the cost model for one class and the fair value model for another class.

COST MODEL

Measurement

16.15   Under the cost model, biological assets are measured at cost less any accumulated depreciation and any accumulated impairment losses.

16.16   FRS 102 has only two paragraphs dealing with the cost model, the same number as in the IFRS for SMEs. It is hardly surprising that the IFRS for SMEs gave little attention to this as it said the cost model should only be used for those biological assets whose fair value could not be 'readily determinable without undue cost or effort'.

Fortunately, the original paragraphs 34.8 and 34.9 in the IFRS for SMEs were completely redrafted, and FRS 102 gives a straight accounting policy choice.

Determining cost

16.17   Section 34 does not provide specific guidance on how to measure the cost of a biological asset.

16.18   Section 10 of FRS 102 *Accounting Policies, Estimates and Errors* requires management to use its judgement in developing and applying an accounting policy that results in information that is relevant to the needs of users (see FRS 102, paragraph 10.4 and **Chapter 3**).

FRS 102, paragraph 10.5 sets out a hierarchy which should be applied in making this judgement, which starts with 'the requirements and guidance in an FRS or Abstract dealing with similar and related issues'.

16.19   In relation to the cost model in Section 34, this could be applied to the relevant paragraphs of:

- Section 13, Inventories (where a biological asset is presented as 'current');

- Section 17, Property, Plant and Equipment (where a biological asset is presented as non-current); and

- Section 27, Impairment.

16.20   The cost of a biological asset may include all of the following:

● The purchase price, including legal and brokerage fees, import duties and non-refundable purchase taxes, after deducting trade discounts and rebates.

● Any costs directly attributable to bringing the asset to the location and condition necessary for it to be capable of operating in the manner intended by management.

(See **12.7** onwards and **19.5** onwards.)

Example 16.4 – Examples of costs to be included

In the case of dairy cows, costs could include delivery costs, feed, vaccines and other medicines provided the expenditure incurred is before the date when the cows are first capable of producing milk.

16.21   Borrowing costs would not be included in view of the restricted definition of qualifying assets in the Glossary to FRS 102 (see **Chapter 17**).

Depreciation

16.22   Again, the requirement to depreciate in Section 34 should be applied by reference to analogy with paragraphs 17.16 to 17.23 of Section 17, Property, Plant and Equipment (see **12.20** onwards).

The depreciation method should reflect the pattern in which the entity expects to consume the asset's future economic benefits. For example, the depreciation method applied to a fruit tree could allocate a greater charge to the periods in which the tree's fruit-yielding is greatest.

Agricultural produce harvested

16.23   In applying the cost model, FRS 102, paragraph 34.9 allows a choice for measuring at the point of harvest agricultural produce harvested, either at:

● the lower of cost and estimated selling price less costs to complete and sell; or

● its fair value less costs to sell (any gain or loss arising on initial recognition of agricultural produce at fair value less costs to sell shall be included in profit or loss for the period in which it arises).

Focus

Entities that adopt the cost model for biological assets may choose between the cost model and the fair value model for measuring agricultural produce (see Accounting Council Advice to FRC, paragraphs 96 and 97, p. 245).

The above measurement is the number used when the harvest produce is first transferred to inventories.

Disclosure requirements – cost model

16.24 The following disclosures should be given in respect of each class of biological assets for which the cost model has been adopted:

- a description of each class of biological asset;

- the depreciation method used;

- the useful lives or the depreciation rates used;

- a reconciliation of changes in the carrying amount of each biological asset between the beginning and end of the current period, including:

  o   increases resulting from purchases;

  o   decreases attributable to sales;

  o   decreases resulting from harvest;

  o   increases resulting from business combinations;

  o   impairment losses recognised or reversed in profit or loss; and

  o   other changes (eg exchange differences).

This reconciliation is required for the current period only.

Focus

The cost model option is available either for all biological assets, or alternatively, for particular classes of biological assets.

There is no disclosure requirement to justify the accounting policy choice of the cost model.

FAIR VALUE MODEL

Measurement

16.25 The fair value model requires the biological asset to be measured at fair value less costs to sell, both on initial recognition and subsequently at each reporting date. Changes in fair value less costs to sell must be recognised in profit or loss.

This could give rise to an immediate loss on initial recognition.

Example 16.5 – Initial recognition under the fair value model

A biological asset is purchased for its fair value of £50,000. If the asset were to be sold, it is estimated that costs to sell would amount to £3,000.

The asset would initially be recognised at £47,000 and a loss of £3,000 recognised in profit or loss.

16.26 As indicated above, agricultural produce up to the point when it is harvested falls with Section 34 and is classified in the balance sheet within the caption 'biological assets'. Once harvested, the agricultural produce is transferred to inventories and falls within Section 13. The amount at which it is transferred is fair value less costs to sell as measured at the point of harvest. This then becomes the cost figure for the purposes of Section 13.

Example 16.6 – Fair value measurement

At the end of 2016, a tomato grower's vines are just starting to bear fully developed ripened tomatoes which will soon be harvested. The accumulated cost of the vines is £18,000 and their fair value is £165,000. Anticipated costs to sell are £4,000. Once the tomatoes have been taken from the vine, and the vine harvested, the vine will have no value and will be abandoned.

The biological asset has a fair value of £165,000 less £4,000 = £161,000. The increase in fair value of £161,000 less £18,000 = £143,000 is recognised in profit or loss.

Example 16.7 – Fair value measurement

During 2016, a fruit grower with a year-end of 31 March bought vines at a cost of £45,000. At the end of the year the fruit was developed and the fair value of the vines was assessed at £65,000 and the costs to sell at £3,500 (ie net of £61,500). Expenses of planting and fertiliser etc, are expensed as incurred (this is the company's assumed policy as Section 34 does not set out specific requirements for such costs).

The increase in fair value of £16,500 (£61,500 less £45,000) was recognised in profit or loss for the year to 31 March 2017.

The fruit was harvested on 14 April 2017. Up to the point of harvest, the vine and the fruit are accounted for as a single asset. The fair value less costs to sell at the point of harvest is assessed at £69,000. After harvesting, the agricultural produce is transferred to inventories.

The change in fair value of £7,500 (£69,000 less £61,500) will be recognised in profit or loss.

The fruit vine after harvest is assumed to have come to the end of its useful life and therefore has a negligible fair value. Harvesting costs of £1,800 have been charged to profit or loss as incurred.

The amount transferred to inventory is £69,000. The above transactions may be summarised as follows:

Date	Details	Biological asset	Agricultural produce	Total	Comments
		£	£	£	
2016	Acquisition of vine and directly attributable costs	45,000		45,000	Dealt with as a single asset
31/3/17	Profit & loss	16,500		16,500	
31/3/17	Balance sheet	61,500		61,500	
14/4/17	Profit & loss	7,500		7,500	
14/4/17	Fair value less costs to sell	69,000		69,000	As measured at point of harvest
14/4/17	Transfer	(69,000)	69,000		Transfer to inventories
14/4/17	Assets after point of harvest	–	69,000	69,000	

Methods of determining fair value where an active market exists

16.27 Where an active market exists for a biological asset or agricultural produce in its present location and condition, the quoted price in that market is the appropriate basis for determining fair value.

16.28 In some cases, an entity may have access to different active markets. In these situations, the entity should use the prices existing in the market it expects to use.

Example 16.8 – Accounting policy example

Accounting policy extract

'Biological assets being cattle are carried at their fair value less estimated selling costs. Fair value has been determined based on independent valuations, on the basis of open market value, supported by market evidence ...'

Methods of determining fair value where an active market does not exist

16.29 In such cases, an entity should use one or more of the following methods of determining fair value, assuming these methods are appropriate and feasible:

- the most recent market transaction price – with the proviso that there has not been a significant change in economic circumstances between the date of that particular transaction, and the reporting date;

- market prices for similar assets – as adjusted to reflect differences;

- sector benchmarks – for example: the value of an orchard expressed per export tray, bushel or hectare; the value of cattle expressed per kilogram of meat; and

- present value of expected net cash flows from the asset discounted at a current market rate.

Where fair value cannot be measured reliably

16.30 Where the fair value of a biological asset cannot be measured reliably, the cost model should be applied. Note that it is assumed that this state of affairs is only temporary; once the fair value can be reliably measured, the fair value model will be resumed.

This is not an accounting policy choice it is driven by circumstances – namely an inability at a certain point to determine a reliable fair value. There are also disclosure implications in paragraph 34.7A (see **16.22**, below).

Example 16.9 – Determining fair value

An entity grows apples and classifies apple trees into two classes:

- mature trees – the entity identifies these as trees which are over five years old; and

- immature trees – less than five years old.

The entity's accounting policy is to use the fair value model for immature trees, for which quoted market prices are available, adjusted where necessary for differences.

The fair value of mature trees is measured at the present value of the expected net cash flows from the trees. The cash flows are based on financial budgets of the expected physical apple yield, based on historical yield information over the estimated remaining fruit-bearing life of each tree, and on the expected future prices of apples in the local market.

Example 16.10 – Accounting policy example under fair value measurement

Livestock is revalued to fair value at each reporting date based on an assessment of age.

Example 16.11 – Accounting policy example under fair value measurement

Biological assets comprise turbot which include fish with and without an active market ('mature' and 'juvenile' fish) which are farmed by the company.

Turbot is considered as 'mature' when it weighs more than 500 grams, whilst turbot is considered as 'juvenile' when it weighs less than 500 grams.

All mature turbot are held at fair value less costs to sell and costs related to packaging. Gains and losses from changes in fair value are recognised in the profit and loss account. Fair value is determined on the basis of market prices.

Juvenile turbot are carried at cost less provision for impairment as management do not believe that reliable fair values exist, for the following reasons:

- there is no active market for juvenile turbot; and

- a non-active market price based upon discounted cash flows requires a number of variables and assumptions which historically cannot be reliably determined.

After harvest, the produce from harvest is treated as inventory and the fair value at the point of harvest is treated as the cost of inventory.

Example 16.12 – Accounting policy example under fair value measurement

Biological assets comprise oil palm trees from initial preparation of land and planting of seedlings through to maturity and the entire productive life of the trees, as well as livestock and growing cane.

Oil palm trees

Oil palm trees are revalued to fair value at each reporting date on a discounted cash flow basis by reference to the fresh fruit bunches expected to be harvested over the full remaining productive life of the trees up to 22 years. Oil palms which are not yet mature at the accounting date and hence are not producing fresh fruit bunches, are valued at cost as an approximation of fair value.

All expenditure on the oil palms up to maturity is treated as an addition to the oil palms. Such costs include seedling costs, holing and planting, transport and field distribution, lining and pruning. The variation in the value of the oil palms in each accounting period, after allowing for additions to the oil palms in the period, is charged or credited in determining profit as appropriate, with no depreciation being provided on such assets.

Livestock

Livestock is revalued to fair value at each reporting date based on an assessment of age, average weights, and market value by the company's external beef manager.

Growing cane

Growing cane is revalued to fair value at each reporting date based on the estimated market value of fully grown cane adjusted for the age and condition of the cane at the reporting date.

Disclosure requirements – fair value model

16.31   The following disclosures should be given in respect of each class of biological assets for which the fair value model has been adopted:

- a description of each class of biological asset;

- the methods and significant assumptions applied in determining the fair value of each class of biological asset;

- a reconciliation of changes in the carrying amount of each biological asset between the beginning and end of the current period, including:

  o   the gain or loss arising from changes in fair value less costs to sell;

  o   increases resulting from purchases;

  o   decreases attributable to sales;

  o   decreases resulting from harvest;

  o   increases resulting from business combinations; and

  o   other changes (eg exchange differences).

  This reconciliation is required for the current period only.

- where fair value cannot be reliably measured (see **16.20** above), the notes should explain why. If circumstances have changed during the current period and it is now possible to obtain a reliable measurement, the notes should explain why and should disclose the effect of the change; and

- the methods and significant assumptions applied in determining the fair value at the point of harvest of each class of agricultural produce.

Note also the possible disclosure implications of paragraphs 8.6 and 8.7 of Section 8 dealing with information about judgements and key sources of estimation uncertainty (see **Chapter 3**).

Example 16.13 – Accounting policy example under fair value measurement

Grape cultivation by the company's wine business is accounted for as agricultural activity.

The company's biological assets, which comprise grape vines and grapes on the vine, are carried at fair value which, in the absence of third-party valuations, is computed on the basis of a discounted cash flow calculation.

Agricultural produce (harvested grapes) is valued at market value on transfer into inventory.

Example 16.14 – Accounting policy example under fair value measurement

Biological assets, being cattle, are carried at their fair value less estimated selling costs. Any changes in fair value, less estimated selling costs, are included in the income statement in the period in which they arise.

Note 18 (extract)

'Biological assets are stated at fair value less estimated selling costs, which has been determined based on independent valuations as at ..., on the basis of open market value, supported by market evidence ...'

Example 16.15 – Financial statements note on biological assets

Note 15 – Biological assets

	2017	2016
At 1 January	x	x
Change in fair value	x	x
Harvested fruit transferred to inventories	(x)	(x)
At 31 December	x	x

THE LARGE AND MEDIUM-SIZED COMPANIES AND GROUPS REGULATIONS TO CA 2006

16.32 Schedule 1 of the Regulations to CA 2006 (see **7.4**) which apply to the fair value model are:

- application of the fair value rules to agriculture (paragraph 39);

- accounting for changes in fair value (paragraph 40); and

- disclosure requirements (paragraph 58).

All of these requirements are compatible with the fair value accounting policy option and disclosure requirements in Section 34 and do not add any extra requirements.

TRANSITION TO FRS 102

16.33 Most companies adopting FRS 102 will previously have adopted the full UK GAAP which did not contain a specific accounting standard on agriculture. However, on the basis of responses to the FRC on previous draft FRED 48, it seems that most of these companies have, up to now, adopted some form of cost model.

16.34   It also seems likely that most of these companies will adopt the cost model in Section 34, in which case there will be little or no adjustment on transition (**Chapter 39** deals with transition issues on adopting FRS 102). However, if any of these companies elect to adopt the fair value model, significant adjustments are likely.

16.35   Any companies who adopted EU-endorsed IFRS on a voluntary basis may choose to take advantage of the provisions of *CA 2006* which allow a company to change its accounting framework without restriction. The impact of moving from the fair value model in IAS 41 to FRS 102 will depend on the company's accounting policy choice under Section 34, as referred to earlier in this chapter.

SUMMARY – WHAT IS DIFFERENT FROM THE PREVIOUS UK GAAP?

- Although there is no specific standard under existing GAAP which deals with agriculture, it appears that most business in this sector adopt some form of the cost model (see **16.11**), although the fair value model has been an alternative under *CA 2006* (see **16.32**).

- As indicated above, this contrasts with Section 34 which gives an accounting policy choice between the cost model and the fair value model.

Chapter 17

Borrowing costs

SIGNPOSTS

- Borrowing costs may be capitalised in the balance sheet as part of the cost of the asset to which the costs relate (see **17.3**).

- The amounts capitalised are calculated using a capitalisation rate (see **17.4**).

- Capitalisation rates are the weighted average of rates applicable to the entity's general borrowings which are outstanding during the period (see **17.4**).

- Reporting entities capitalising borrowing costs are required to make certain disclosures within their financial statements (see **17.5**).

INTRODUCTION

17.1   In contrast to the previous UK GAAP, Section 25 to FRS 102 deals specifically with the accounting treatment for borrowing costs. In the previous UK GAAP, such issues were dealt with within FRS 15 *Tangible Fixed Assets*. The capitalisation of borrowing costs has been the subject of many debates and the Accounting Standards Board's (now the Financial Reporting Council) discussion paper *Measurement of Tangible Fixed Assets* acknowledged that the capitalisation of such costs should either be mandatory or prohibited to achieve consistency. However, the ASB conceded that the arguments for each approach were finely balanced and thus allowed an optional policy of capitalisation.

There are many reporting entities that incur a significant amount of borrowing costs (eg Housing Associations who can build their own houses for rent to the general public and for whom such costs must be treated consistently from one accounting period to the next).

DEFINITIONS

17.2   Paragraph 25.1 to FRS 102 says that *borrowing costs* are interest and other costs that an entity incurs in connection with the borrowing of funds. It goes on to clarify that borrowing costs include:

- interest expense calculated using the effective interest method as described in Section 11, Basic Financial Instruments;

- finance charges in respect of finance leases recognised in accordance with Section 20, Leases; and

- exchange differences arising from foreign currency borrowings to the extent that they are regarded as an adjustment to interests costs.

It is also worth noting that paragraph 25.2A to FRS 102 clarifies that borrowing costs which are directly attributable to the acquisition, construction or production of a qualifying asset are those borrowing costs which would have been avoided if the expenditure on the qualifying asset had not been made.

RECOGNITION WITHIN THE FINANCIAL STATEMENTS

17.3   Section 25 permits an entity to capitalise any borrowing costs it incurs that are directly attributable to the acquisition, construction or production of a qualifying asset. Section 25 does not define a 'qualifying asset'; however, a definition is given in the Glossary to FRS 102 as follows:

'An *asset* that necessarily takes a substantial period of time to get ready for its intended use or sale. Depending on the circumstances any of the following may be qualifying assets:

(a)   inventories;

(b)   manufacturing plants;

(c)   power generation facilities;

(d)   intangible assets; and

(e)   investment properties.

Financial assets and inventories that are produced over a short period of time, are not qualifying assets.

Assets that are ready for their intended use or sale when acquired are not qualifying assets.'

The term *substantial period of time* is taken to generally mean longer than 12 months.

Where Section 25 applies, reporting entities can either capitalise directly attributable borrowing costs, or they can be recognised as an expense in profit or loss. Paragraph 25.2 to FRS 102 requires that where an entity chooses not to capitalise borrowing costs, it expenses such costs in the period in which the costs are incurred.

17.4 *Borrowing costs*

17.4 There are two situations which can give rise to borrowing costs:

- the borrowing of funds *specifically* for the purpose of obtaining a qualifying asset; or

- the use of an entity's general borrowings.

When an entity borrows funds specifically for the purpose of obtaining a qualifying asset, paragraph 25.2B requires the entity to determine the amount of borrowing costs that are eligible for capitalisation on the balance sheet. This is calculated as the actual borrowing costs incurred on that borrowing during the period less any investment income on the temporary investment of that borrowing.

Paragraph 25.2C requires that when a reporting entity uses general borrowings to fund the acquisition, construction or production of a qualifying asset, it determines the amount of borrowing costs eligible for capitalisation on the balance sheet by applying a capitalisation rate to the expenditure on that asset. The expenditure on the asset is the average carrying amount of the asset during the accounting period, including borrowing costs that have been previously capitalised. The capitalisation rate that an entity is required to use in an accounting period is calculated as the weighted average of rates that apply to the entity's general borrowings that are outstanding during that accounting period. It is important to emphasise that this *excludes* borrowings by the reporting entity which are specifically for the purpose of obtaining other qualifying assets. In addition, the amount of borrowing costs which a reporting entity capitalises during an accounting period must not exceed the amount of borrowing costs that it incurred during that period.

Example 17.1 – Calculation of capitalisation rate

Company A Limited has three sources of borrowing during an accounting period as follows:

	Outstanding liability £'000	Interest charge £'000
Five-year loan	9,000	1,500
30-year loan	14,000	2,000
Bank overdraft	6,000	750

If all of the above borrowings are used to finance the production of a qualifying asset, the capitalisation rate will be calculated as follows:

$$\frac{1,500,000 + 2,000,000 + 750,000}{9,000,000 + 14,000,000 + 6,000,000} \times 100 = 14.66\%$$

If the five-year loan is used to finance a specific qualifying asset, the capitalisation rate which should be used on the other qualifying assets will be:

$$\frac{2,000,000 + 750,000}{14,000,000 + 6,000,000} \times 100 = 13.75\%$$

Example 17.2 – Construction of an asset suspended

Company B Limited is in the process of constructing its new purpose-built headquarters and the company has a year-end of 31 December 2013. On 1 March 2013, construction was suspended and did not resume until 31 October 2013.

Paragraph 25.2D to FRS 102 requires that where active development of the asset has paused then capitalisation shall also be suspended.

In addition, once substantially all of the activities necessary to prepare the qualifying asset for its intended use or sale are complete, capitalisation must then cease.

Disclosure requirements

17.5 Entities that have capitalised borrowing costs during the accounting period must disclose the amount of borrowing costs capitalised in the period together with the capitalisation rate used.

Focus

Whilst Section 25 is flexible in its approach (it allows capitalisation of borrowing costs OR writing these costs off directly to profit or loss), the application must be consistent. Reporting entities cannot choose to capitalise borrowing costs in one year and then write them off to profit or loss in the next. If an entity chooses to write borrowing costs off rather than capitalise them in a year (or vice versa), this would represent a change in accounting policy and therefore the provisions contained in Section 10, Accounting Policies, Estimates and Errors would be triggered.

SUMMARY – WHAT IS DIFFERENT FROM THE PREVIOUS UK GAAP?

- A notable difference between FRS 102 and old UK GAAP is that FRS 102 differs in the way it describes how the borrowing cost to be capitalised is calculated.

- Previous UK GAAP did not have a separate standard relating to borrowing costs – users were generally directed to the provisions in FRS 15 *Tangible Fixed Assets.*

Chapter 18

Impairment of assets

SIGNPOSTS

- Reporting entities are required to consider whether assets (including inventory) are showing signs of impairment at the reporting date. This requirement has gathered more prominence in recent years, particularly due to the economic crisis. This is accentuated by the fact that assets cannot be carried in the statement of financial position (balance sheet) at any more than recoverable amount (see **18.1**).

- Specific requirements exist in Section 27, Impairment of Assets which relate to an entity's inventory values at the reporting date as well as any reversals of impairment relating to inventory values (see **18.2** and **18.3**).

- There are two components to *recoverable amount*: 'fair value less costs to sell' and 'value in use'. Recoverable amount is the *higher* of these two components (see **18.4** and **18.5**).

- Section 27 requires certain steps to be followed in the computation of 'value in use' and outlines certain items that must be considered and ignored for the purposes of cash flow calculation (see **18.6** and **18.7**).

- A reporting entity undertaking an impairment calculation is required to apply a discount rate(s) in order to discount cash flows included in the value in use calculation to present-day values. An assessment of time values of money and risks associated with the asset must be undertaken (see **18.8**).

- Impairment of assets included within a cash-generating unit are allocated in a certain pre-determined order in Section 27 (see **18.9**).

- The Section recognises that goodwill cannot be sold or generate cash flows that are independent of the entity (see **18.10**).

- There are specific requirements in Section 27 that relate to the testing of impairment of goodwill where goodwill cannot be allocated to specific cash-generating units (or groups of cash-generating units) on a non-arbitrary basis (see **18.11**).

- There are conditions that can give rise to impairment losses that have been recognised in previous accounting periods reversing in subsequent accounting periods. The allocation of such reversals will depend on whether the prior period impairment loss on the asset concerned was based on the recoverable amount of the individual asset or the recoverable amount of the cash-generating unit to which that asset belongs (see **18.12**).

- There are specific disclosures that are required in financial statements where impairments, and reversals of impairments, are concerned (see **18.13** and **18.14**).

INTRODUCTION

18.1   The issue concerning asset impairment has been given more prominence over recent years, primarily due to the economic crisis and the impact this has had on reporting entities and the assets that they carry in the balance sheet. The overarching principle in financial reporting where assets are concerned is that they should not be stated in the company's balance sheet at any more than their recoverable amount.

Section 27, Impairment of Assets deals specifically with such issues and, for the purposes of Section 27, *recoverable amount* is calculated as the *higher* of fair value less costs to sell and value in use. Section 27 does not, however, deal with the following issues:

- assets arising from construction contracts (**Chapter 20** and Section 23, Revenue);

- deferred tax assets (**Chapter 25** and Section 29, Income Tax);

- assets arising from employee benefits (**Chapter 23** and Section 28, Employee Benefits);

- financial assets within the scope of Section 11, Basic Financial Instruments or Section 12, Other Financial Instruments Issues; (**Chapters 35** to **38**);

- investment property measured at fair value (**Chapter 13** and Section 16, Investment Property);

- biological assets related to agricultural activity measured at fair value less estimated costs to sell (Section 34, Specialised Activities); and

- deferred acquisition costs and intangible assets arising from insurance contracts which are under the scope of FRS 103 *Insurance Contracts*.

IMPAIRMENT OF INVENTORY

18.2   The primary issue relating to inventory is the ease by which this figure can be manipulated to achieve a desired profit (or loss) or balance sheet position. This figure can also be manipulated for taxation reasons and it is therefore important that consideration is given to ensuring the valuation of closing inventory is calculated as accurately as possible. Inventory is clearly an asset in the balance sheet of a company and in accordance with **Chapter 19** and Section 13, Inventories, inventory should be carried in the balance sheet at the lower of cost and net realisable value.

Section 27 requires a reporting entity to make an assessment at each reporting date of their inventories and consider whether any items are impaired. If these items are impaired then they should be written down to net realisable value with the write-down being taken directly to profit or loss.

Focus

Inventory is a particularly sensitive area of the financial statements, impacting on both the profit and loss account and the balance sheet. This area of the financial statements has been known to be the subject of manipulation in financial reports as it can usually serve to arrive at a profit (or loss) amount that is desired rather than achieved through orthodox means. Notwithstanding this 'massaging' of the figures, inventory values particularly need to be considered for impairment, especially where the reporting entity has slow-moving items of inventory or where inventory quickly becomes obsolete.

Example 18.1 – Inventory valuation

A reporting entity has undertaken a stock count at 31 October 2013 and details of the following products have been extracted from the inventory system:

Item Ref:	Cost	Estimated selling	Valuation price
	£	£	£
VR4522	200.00	450.00	270.00 (note 1)
VT3125	150.00	340.00	150.00 (note 2)
VS4098	200.00	120.00	200.00 (note 3)

Notes

1. The finance director has included advertising costs of £70 as this is a new product and the director feels such costs should be included as they are directly attributable to this product.

2. This item of stock has been used for several years in the company's manufacturing process and there are no additional issues with the valuation of this product.

3. The company has just received notification from the supplier of this product that it is seriously defective and contains highly corrosive chemicals and they are advising us to destroy this product immediately.

Based on the above three issues, the revised inventory valuation should be as follows:

Item Ref:	Cost	Estimated selling	Valuation price
	£	£	£
VR4522	200.00	450.00	200.00 (note 1)
VT3125	150.00	340.00	150.00
VS4098	200.00	nil	nil (note 2)

Notes

1. Advertising expenditure should not be included within the inventory valuation as this would be considered a selling cost. Selling costs are prohibited to be recognised directly in inventory as per paragraph 13.13(d) in Section 13, Inventories. Such costs, therefore, should be removed from the valuation.

2. As this product is seriously defective and cannot be used in the production process, the net realisable is assumed to be nil and therefore the cost of this product has been written down accordingly.

18.3   Paragraph 27.4 recognises that there may be situations where the company recognises an impairment loss for its inventories but then carries out a subsequent assessment of selling price less costs to complete and sell that may give clear evidence that there has been an increase in selling price less costs to complete and sell because of changed economic circumstances. In such cases, the reporting entity will reverse the amount of the impairment.

Example 18.2 – Reversal of a previously recognised impairment

Jones Chemical Distribution Co Limited has carried out an impairment test on its inventories for the third quarter ended 30 September 2013. During that assessment there was evidence of impairment in a batch of chemicals where it was alleged that the mix of chemicals was unsuitable for the purposes for which it was originally intended. The company had written down this batch of chemicals by £2,000 in the third quarter ended 30 September 2013.

The company still had this batch of chemicals in inventory at its year-end of 31 December 2013. However, on 1 November 2013, the supplier's Quality Control director issued a statement confirming that investigations had taken place concerning the incorrect mix of chemicals. It had been concluded that there were, in fact, no issues at all with the chemicals and that they were still fit for their original intended purpose. Jones Chemical Distribution Co has also been informed that the same batch of chemicals has increased in price and will now cost £2,500.

Jones Chemical Distribution Co can still reverse its original impairment of £2,000. However, despite the increase in price, the amount of the reversal is limited to the amount of the original impairment loss; the fact that the supplier has increased its price by £500 for the same batch is irrelevant for the purposes of the impairment reversal.

IMPAIRMENT OF ASSETS OTHER THAN INVENTORIES

18.4   There is evidence of impairment when an asset's recoverable amount falls below its carrying value and, for the purposes of Section 27, recoverable amount is the *higher* of value in use and fair value less costs to sell and value in use.

Fair value less costs to sell

18.5   Section 27 defines fair value less costs to sell as:

'The amount obtainable from the sale of an asset in an arm's length transaction between knowledgeable, willing parties, less the costs of disposal.'

(Section 27, para 27.14.)

To arrive at a fair value less costs to sell figure, the standard recognises that the best evidence of such is in a binding sale agreement, where the price will be agreed upon by the parties in the sale, or *market price* in an *active market*.

An active market is one where such transactions are regularly traded and prices can be obtained reliably.

Value in use

18.6   Value in use requires more consideration to arrive at the figure for value in use. Essentially, value in use is the present value of the future cash flows that are expected to be derived from an asset. The following steps are required when computing value in use:

- estimate the future cash flows (inflows and outflows) which are likely to be received and incurred through continuing use of the asset and from its ultimate disposal; and

- apply the appropriate discount rate to those future cash flows.

It is important to emphasise that, to comply with paragraph 27.18, estimates of future cash flows should *not* include cash inflows or outflows that arise from financing activities, nor should they include cash inflows or outflows from income tax receipts or payments. Paragraph 27.16 also requires the following elements to be used in the calculation of an asset's value in use:

- an estimate of the future cash flows the entity expects to derive from the asset;

- expectations about possible variations in the amount or timing of those future cash flows;

- the time value of money, represented by the current market risk-free rate of interest;

- the price for bearing the uncertainty inherent in the asset; and

- other factors, such as illiquidity, that market participants would reflect in pricing the future cash flows the entity expects to derive from the asset.

(Section 18, para 27.16.)

18.7   Paragraph 27.17 requires estimates of future cash flows to include:

- projected cash inflows from the continuing use of the asset;

- projected cash outflows that are necessarily incurred to generate the cash inflows (which will also include those cash outflows incurred to prepare the asset for use) and which are directly attributable, or allocated on both a reasonable and consistent basis; and

- net cash flows that are expected to be received or paid on disposal of the asset.

Reporting entities should estimate future cash flows for the asset in its current condition. They must not include estimated future cash flows that are expected to arise from a future restructuring to which the entity is not yet committed; or cash flows for improving or enhancing the asset's performance.

18.8 When deciding on the discount rate(s) to be used to discount cash flows to present-day values, the company must use a pre-tax rate(s) which reflects current market assessments of:

● the time value of money; and

● the risks specific to the asset for which the future cash flow estimates have not been adjusted.

Example 18.3 – Calculation of recoverable amount

Zedcolour Manufacturing Limited is a large manufacturer of washing powder that has four brands: GleenClothes, Britewash, Ecowash and Kiddykind. Each manufacturing division is classed as a 'cash-generating unit' for the purposes of asset impairment testing. Zedcolour Manufacturing obtained the Ecowash brand through the acquisition of a small company several years ago and at the year-end 31 July 2013, the goodwill attributable to this brand was in the balance sheet at £140,000. Demand for the Ecowash brand of washing powder has seen a decrease in sales over the last 12 months, whereas demand for the other three brands has increased significantly.

In light of the fall in demand for Ecowash, the directors have undertaken an exercise relating to the expected cash inflows and outflows. The analysis is shown below:

Year	Cash inflows	Cash outflows
£	£	£
2014	70,000	27,000
2015	75,000	45,000
2016	85,000	65,000
2017	30,000	20,000

An exercise was recently undertaken by the external accountancy firm to value the goodwill using the 'whole company approach' and the goodwill specific to Ecowash was calculated by the external accountancy firm to be

£83,000. The external accountants have undertaken a further exercise to calculate value in use, using an assumed interest rate of 5% and this has been calculated as follows:

Year	Net Cash flows (£)	PV factor	Present value (£)
2014	43,000	0.952	40,936
2015	30,000	0.907	27,210
2016	20,000	0.864	17,280
2017	10,000	0.823	8,230
Value in use			**93,656**

Value in use exceeds the whole company approach valuation of £83,000 and therefore value in use becomes recoverable amount.

An impairment loss has arisen on the goodwill amounting to (£140,000 less £93,656) £46,344 and this impairment loss will be recognised directly in profit or loss as an operating expense within the amortisation charge or as a separate heading in the income statement (profit and loss account).

Other issues relating to cash-generating units

18.9   Components of an impairment loss relating to a single cash-generating unit should be recognised in order to reduce the carrying amount of the assets. The loss should be apportioned as follows:

- first, to reduce the carrying amount of any goodwill allocated to the cash-generating unit; and

- then, to the other assets of the unit pro-rata on the basis of the carrying amount of each asset in the cash-generating unit.

Focus

Under FRS 11, the impairment would have been allocated first to goodwill, then to any capitalised intangible asset in the unit and finally to the tangible assets in the unit on a pro-rata, or more appropriate basis.

Example 18.4 – Allocation of an impairment loss

Alexander Automotives Ltd has undertaken an impairment test on one of its groups of assets that is considered to be a cash-generating unit. Financial statement extracts for the year-ended 30 September 2013 are as follows:

30 September 2013

	£
Goodwill	130,000
Plant and machinery	200,000

The cash-generating unit has suffered an impairment loss of £150,000 during the year as the company has received widely publicised criticism about the safety of its vehicles and this has also had an impact on current orders.

The directors have undertaken an exercise in calculating fair value less costs to sell and value in use of the goodwill. They have determined that the fair value less costs to sell is £60,000 and the value in use is £50,000. The directors consider it not determinable to arrive at a figure for fair value less costs to sell or value in use for plant and machinery.

The impairment loss of £150,000 will be first allocated to goodwill, with the remainder being applied to the plant and machinery. However, neither the goodwill nor any asset in a cash-generating unit can be reduced below the *highest* of:

●   fair value less costs to sell (if determinable);

●   value in use (if determinable); and

●   zero.

As fair value less costs to sell is higher than value in use, goodwill is to be carried at £60,000, so of the £150,000 impairment, (£130,000 less £60,000) £70,000 will be allocated to goodwill, with the remaining £80,000 being charged against plant and machinery. Following the allocation of the impairment charge, the financial statement extracts will be as follows:

30 September 2013

	£
Goodwill	60,000
Plant and machinery	120,000

Other considerations for goodwill

18.10 The standard recognises that goodwill in isolation cannot be sold or generate cash flows which are independent of the cash flows of other assets, so it follows that the fair value of goodwill cannot be measured directly. As a consequence, the fair value of goodwill is derived from the measurement of fair value of the cash-generating unit(s) from which the goodwill belongs.

Focus

Goodwill has been the subject of much debate around the profession and has not been short of controversy. The primary issue with goodwill is its subjective nature and this was tested in the case of *Commissioners of Inland Revenue v Muller & Co Margarine* [1901] AC 217. In this case, Lord MacNaghten said:

> 'What is goodwill? It is a thing very easy to describe, very difficult to define. It is the benefit and advantage of the good name, reputation and connection of the business. It is the attractive force which brings in custom. It is the one thing which distinguishes an old established business from a new business at its first start. Goodwill is composed as a variety of elements. It differs in its composition in different trades and in different businesses in the same trade. One element may preponderate here, and another there.'

This statement by Lord MacNaghten merely sums up goodwill. The challenge for accountants is how such goodwill is to be valued.

Example 18.5 – Apportioning an impairment loss

Breary Brick Co Limited acquired 80% of the net assets of Byrne Breeze Blocks Limited on 1 January 2013 (the date of acquisition). The finance director is undertaking an impairment test on the goodwill acquired in Byrne Breeze Blocks but is unsure as to the starting point and how the apportionment of such an impairment loss would be split.

Goodwill that has been acquired in a business combination is impairment tested from the date of acquisition. Once this has been established and the impairment calculated, it is then allocated to each of the cash-generating units that are expected to benefit from the synergies of the combination, regardless of whether other associated assets or liabilities of the acquiree are assigned to those units.

Twenty per cent of the impairment loss will belong to the minority interests (non-controlling interests) as Breary Brick Co only obtained 80% of the value of Byrne Breeze Block's net assets. As a result, 20% of the recoverable amount of the cash-generating unit with the goodwill in it will belong to the minority interests. The finance director should notionally adjust the carrying amount of the cash-generating unit before comparing the unit to its recoverable amount. The finance director will do this by grossing up the carrying amount of goodwill so it includes the goodwill belonging to the minority interests. It is this 'grossed up' goodwill that is compared to the recoverable amount to determine whether the cash-generating unit is impaired.

18.11 If a company cannot allocate goodwill to specific cash-generating units (or groups of cash-generating units) on a non-arbitrary basis, paragraph 27.27 states that an entity will test goodwill for impairment by establishing the recoverable amount of either:

● the acquired entity in its entirety where goodwill relates to an acquired entity that has not been integrated (for the purposes of paragraph 27.27(a)), *integrated* means the business subject to the acquisition has been restructured or dissolved into the reporting entity or other subsidiary companies; or

● the entire group of entities (with the exception of entities that have not been integrated) if the goodwill relates to an entity that has been integrated.

These requirements will mean that such reporting entities will need to separate goodwill between goodwill that relates to entities that have been integrated and goodwill that relates to entities that have not been integrated. In addition, the provisions relating to cash-generating units insofar as calculating recoverable amount and the allocation of impairment losses and reversals will need to be followed.

REVERSALS OF IMPAIRMENT LOSSES

18.12 Impairment losses that have been charged to profit or loss in one accounting period can be reversed, but only where the reasons for the impairment loss no longer apply. This principle will mean, therefore, that a reporting entity not only needs to test assets for impairment at each reporting date, but should also assess whether previous impairment losses may no longer exist or have, in fact, decreased.

18.12 *Impairment of assets*

If circumstances suggest that impairment losses recognised in previous periods may no longer apply, the entity must consider whether all, or part, of the previously recognised impairment losses should be reversed in the current period. Section 27 at paragraph 27.29 (a) and (b) outline two situations that will determine the procedure for reversing the prior period impairment loss and it will depend on whether the prior period impairment loss on the asset concerned was based on:

- the recoverable amount of that individual asset; or

- the recoverable amount of the cash-generating unit to which that asset belongs.

Example 18.6 – Prior period impairment loss based on recoverable amount of the individual asset

On 31 December 2013, Byrne Enterprises Limited had an asset with a net book value of £70,000 that it considered had suffered impairment of £35,000, so duly wrote the asset down to have a carrying value of £35,000. Had the asset not suffered impairment in 2013, it would have had a carrying value of £60,000 (depreciation of the asset is being charged over a useful life of ten years on a straight-line basis). The directors have now obtained evidence that the impairment loss charged in 2013 is no longer appropriate on the grounds that significant changes that had an adverse effect on the market in 2013 have been turned around and the market is back to where it was originally. The finance director is now proposing to reverse the impairment loss in its entirety.

Had the asset not been impaired in 2013, the carrying value at the end of 2013 would have been £60,000 and in 2014 would have been £50,000. On the basis that the carrying amount of the asset is still £35,000, the maximum amount of impairment reversal in 2014 can only be (£50,000 less £35,000) £15,000. This is because paragraph 27.30(c) says that the reversal of an impairment loss should not increase the carrying amount of the asset above the carrying amount that would have been determined (net of amortisation or depreciation) had no impairment loss been recognised for the asset in prior years.

The finance director can, therefore, only debit the carrying amount of the asset with £15,000 and credit impairment in the profit and loss account. This will bring the asset up to its carrying amount of £50,000. Following the reversal of the impairment loss, Byrne Enterprises will adjust the depreciation charge for the asset in future periods to allocate the asset's depreciable amount over its remaining useful life.

However, if, at the end of 2014, the asset's recoverable amount was £40,000, Byrne Enterprises would increase the asset up to this recoverable amount (from £35,000 to £40,000) and recognise the credit of £5,000 in profit or loss (as part-reversal of the prior period impairment loss).

Example 18.7 – Prior period impairment loss based on recoverable amount of a cash-generating unit to which the asset belongs

On 31 December 2012, Byrne Enterprises accounted for an impairment loss of £360,000 on a division of its manufacturing plant that it considers to be a cash-generating unit. Extracts from the financial statements relating to the cash-generating unit are shown below:

	Post-Impairment 31 December 2012 £'000	Pre-Impairment 31 December 2012 £'000
Goodwill*	nil (Note 1)	220
Manufacturing plant	480 (Note 2)	500
Machinery	1,380 (Note 2)	1,500
	1,860	2,220**

A prominent dealer of the manufacturing plant had concluded that fair value less costs to sell of the plant was £480,000 and this amount was higher than value in use, so fair value less costs to sell was used as recoverable amount.

* Goodwill is tested annually for impairment, hence no amortisation as management deem the useful economic life to be more than five years.

** Net of depreciation charges (20% reducing balance).

Note 1

The impairment loss amounts to £360,000 and therefore £220,000 of the impairment is immediately written off against goodwill to reduce goodwill to zero.

Note 2

The manufacturing plant and machinery (pre-impairment) are in the ratio of 500:1,500 which means that manufacturing plant represents 25% of the remaining assets, thus 25% should be allocated to the manufacturing plant. However, if this were to be done it would reduce the manufacturing plant to (£500,000 less (25% × £140,000) £35,000) £465,000 (ie below the recoverable amount) which is not allowed. Therefore, the maximum impairment permitted is £20,000 so the remaining £15,000 is to be allocated against the manufacturing machinery.

The impairment loss attributed to manufacturing machinery has been calculated as follows:

(75% × £140,000) £105,000 + £15,000 = £120,000

On 31 December 2013, the draft financial statements of Byrne Enterprises Ltd show the following (after the depreciation charge has been calculated):

	31 December 2013	31 December 2012
	£'000	*£'000*
Goodwill	nil	nil
Manufacturing plant	384	480
Machinery	1,104	1,380
	1,488	1,860

The directors have received conclusive evidence that the original impairment charge in 2012 of £360,000 has reversed in the sum of £310,000. This reversal is allocated as follows:

- first to the assets (other than goodwill) of the unit pro-rata on the basis of the carrying amount of each asset in the cash-generating unit; and

- then to any goodwill allocated to the cash-generating unit.

Care must be taken here because the reversal of an impairment loss for a cash-generating unit cannot increase the carrying amount of any asset above the lower of:

- its recoverable amount; and

- the carrying amount that would have been determined had no impairment loss been recognised.

Had no impairment loss been recognised, the assets would have been carried (as at 31 December 2013) as follows:

31 December 2013   *£'000*

Goodwill   220
Manufacturing plant   400   Depreciation is being charged
Machinery   1,200   at 20% on a reducing balance basis
                                      ─────
                                       1,820

Manufacturing plant currently represents (£384 ÷ (£384 + £1,104) × 100) 26% of the total assets in the cash-generating unit. Allocating 26% of £310,000 would take the net book value of the plant higher than the carrying value of £400,000 if no impairment had originally been made, hence only £16,000 can be allocated.

The manufacturing machinery currently has a carrying amount of £1,104,000 and if the remaining 74% of the impairment is allocated against the machinery, this, too, will take the carrying amount (£1,104,000) over the carrying amount that would have been attributed to the machinery had no impairment been made of £1,200,000. Therefore only (£1,200,000 less £1,104,000) £96,000 of the remaining (£310,000 less £16,000) £294,000 can be allocated to the machinery.

The remaining reversal is taken to goodwill. Following the reversal, the financial statement extracts will be as follows:

	31 December 2013	*31 December 2012*
	£'000	*£'000*
Goodwill	198	nil
Manufacturing plant	400	480
Machinery	1,200	1,380
	1,798	1,860

DISCLOSURE REQUIREMENTS

18.13   Paragraphs 27.32 to 27.33A outline the disclosure requirements in respect of impairment and reversals of impairments. In respect of each class of assets, an entity must disclose:

18.14   *Impairment of assets*

- the amount of impairment losses recognised in profit or loss during the period and the line item(s) in the statement of comprehensive income (or in the income statement, where presented) in which those impairment losses are included; and

- the amount of reversals of impairment losses recognised in profit or loss during the period and the line item(s) in the statement of comprehensive income (or income statement, where presented) in which those impairment losses are reversed.

The information above is required in respect of each of the following classes of asset:

- inventories;

- property, plant and equipment (including investment property accounted for by the cost method);

- goodwill;

- intangible assets other than goodwill;

- investment in associates; and

- investments in joint ventures.

18.14   Where reversals of impairment losses are recognised in the accounting period, the reporting entity is also required to include a description of the events and circumstances that led to the recognition of the impairment loss.

SUMMARY – WHAT IS DIFFERENT FROM THE PREVIOUS UK GAAP?

- Components of an impairment loss relating to a single cash-generating unit are allocated first to goodwill and then to other assets of the unit pro-rata on the basis of the carrying amount of each asset in the cash-generating unit under FRS 102. This differs from FRS 11 which requires an impairment loss to be allocated first to goodwill, then against intangible assets and finally, to tangible assets pro-rata on the basis of the carrying amount.

- Recoverable amount in FRS 102 is the *higher* of 'fair value less costs to sell' and 'value in use'. In FRS 11, recoverable amount was the higher of 'net realisable value' and 'value in use'.

- Impairment losses relating to goodwill can only be reversed under FRS 102 if the reasons for the impairment loss have ceased to apply. Under FRS 11, an impairment loss relating to goodwill can only be recognised in the current period if, and only if:

  ○ an external event caused the recognition of the impairment loss in previous periods, and subsequent external events clearly and demonstrably reverse the effects of that event in a way that was not foreseen in the original impairment calculations; or

  ○ the impairment loss arose on an intangible asset with a readily ascertainable market value and the net realisable value based on that market value has increased to above the intangible asset's impaired carrying amount.

Chapter 19

Inventories

SIGNPOSTS

- Reporting entities are required to measure their inventories at the lower of cost and estimated selling price less costs to complete and sell (see **19.4**).

- There are a number of components that can be involved in the make-up of 'cost' (see **19.5**).

- Section 13 provides for two possible cost formulas: first-in first-out (FIFO) and weighted average cost (AVCO). Section 13 specifically outlaws the use of the last-in first-out (LIFO) method of cost formula (see **19.10**).

- Reporting entities must disclose certain information within their financial statements concerning their inventory valuations (see **19.14**).

INTRODUCTION

19.1   The valuation of an entity's inventories can have a significant impact on the financial statements and errors in the inventory valuation can have dramatic consequences. In addition, manipulation of the closing inventories valuation can seriously distort both the statement of comprehensive income (profit and loss account) and the statement of financial position (balance sheet).

Section 13 to FRS 102 deals with inventories and outlines the various cost methodologies permitted. A notable change between Section 13 and the previous UK GAAP (SSAP 9 *Stocks and Long-term Contracts*) is that FRS 102 specifically outlaws the use of the LIFO method of inventories valuation. This was not a surprising turn of events given that, despite SSAP 9 allowing the use of the LIFO method, it did not appear to favour the practice and contained a specific requirement for directors of companies that employ the use of the LIFO method to be assured that the circumstances of the company were such that the use of LIFO would result in the financial statements giving a true and fair view. Indeed SSAP 9 acknowledged that the use of LIFO can result in

238

the reporting of current assets that bear little relationship to recent costs. In addition, the international equivalent standard, IAS 2 *Inventories* also prohibits the use of the LIFO method.

DEFINITIONS

19.2 Paragraph 13.1 to FRS 102 confirms that inventories are assets:

- held for sale in the ordinary course of business;

- in the process of production for such sale; or

- in the form of materials or supplies to be consumed in the production process of in the rendering of services.

OUT OF SCOPE INVENTORIES

19.3 There are three types of inventories to which Section 13 will *not* apply. These are:

- work-in-progress arising under construction contracts, including directly related service contracts (Section 23, Revenue deals with these).

- financial instruments (Section 11, Basic Financial Instruments and Section 12, Other Financial Instruments Issues deal with these).

- biological assets related to agricultural activity and agricultural produce at the point of harvest (Section 34, Specialised Activities deals with these).

GENERAL PRINCIPLE

19.4 Reporting entities are required to measure their inventories at the *lower of cost or net realisable value*.

Cost

19.5 The term *cost* includes all costs of purchase, costs of conversion and other costs which are incurred in bringing the inventories to their present location and condition. Where an entity acquires inventories through a non-exchange transaction, paragraph 13.5A requires their cost to be measured at fair value at the date of acquisition. The paragraph also confirms that, for public benefit entities, such requirements will only apply to inventory that is recognised as a result of the incoming resources from non-exchange transactions as prescribed in Section 34, Specialised Activities.

19.5   *Inventories*

Costs of purchase include:

- purchase price;

- import duties;

- taxes (other than those recoverable by the entity);

- transport costs;

- handling costs; and

- any other costs directly attributable to the acquisition of finished goods, materials and services.

Cost should always be net of any trade discounts, rebates and other similar items.

If a reporting entity obtains inventories on deferred settlement terms, this may (in some cases) result in the arrangement containing an unstated financing element. Paragraph 13.7 to FRS 102 says that this is the difference between the purchase price for normal credit terms and the deferred settlement amount. When this situation arises, the difference is recognised as an interest expense in profit or loss over the period of the financing and is *not* added to the cost of the inventories.

Costs of conversion include all costs directly related to the units of production and paragraph 13.8 to FRS 102 suggests an example as direct labour. Reporting entities will also include a systematic allocation of fixed and variable production overheads which they incur in the manufacturing process from turning raw materials into finished goods. Paragraph 13.8 confirms that fixed production overheads are those indirect costs of production that remain relatively constant regardless of the volume of production, whilst variable production overheads are those indirect costs of production that do vary directly (or nearly directly) with the volume of production. The paragraph gives examples of indirect materials and indirect labour.

When a reporting entity is allocating production overheads it must do so on the basis of normal capacity of the production facilities. Paragraph 13.9 says that normal capacity is the production expected to be achieved, on average, over a number of periods or seasons under normal circumstances, taking into account the loss of capacity resulting from planned maintenance (sometimes referred to as 'down time'). Reporting entities should not increase the amount of fixed overhead it allocates to each unit of production because of low production or idle plant. Variable production overheads are to be allocated to each unit of production on the basis of the actual use of the production facilities to accord with paragraph 13.9 of FRS 102.

Any unallocated overheads must be recognised as an expense within profit or loss in the period in which the expense is incurred.

Example 19.1 – Allocation of overheads

Westhead Windows Limited manufactures windows for domestic and commercial buildings and has a year-end of 31 December 2013. Normally production is fairly static, however, in December 2013, an extremely large order was placed by a chemical company that had suffered an explosion at one of its depots and at the year-end the windows were still in production. The finance director has confirmed that this order will be a one off and has increased the amount of fixed overhead allocated to each unit of production.

Paragraph 13.9 to FRS 102 confirms that in periods of high production, the amount of fixed overhead allocated to each unit of production must be *decreased*. In this scenario, the finance director is therefore incorrect to increase the amount of fixed overhead allocated to each unit of production because this will result in inventories that are measured in the financial statement in excess of cost.

If a reporting entity is involved in the manufacture of products simultaneously and the costs of raw materials, or conversion of each product, are not separately identified, the reporting entity must allocate them between the products on a rational and consistent basis. Paragraph 13.10 gives an example of a rational and consistent basis by way of allocating the costs of raw materials or conversion costs on the relative sales value of each product either at the stage in the production process when the products become separately identifiable, or at the completion of production.

Where by-products are concerned these are generally immaterial and if this is the case the reporting entity must value them at selling price less costs to complete and sell and then deduct this amount from the cost of the main product. This valuation method achieves a carrying amount for the main product that is not materially different from its cost.

19.6   Paragraph 13.13 to FRS 102 outlines four types of cost that are excluded from the costs of inventories. These are:

- abnormal amounts of wasted materials, labour or other production costs;

- storage costs, unless those costs are necessary during the production process before a further production stage;

- administrative overheads that do not contribute to bringing inventories to their present location and condition; and

- selling costs.

Example 19.2 – Inclusion of employee costs in inventories

A firm of accountants is valuing its work-in-progress at the year-end and has estimated that the labour and other costs of personnel directly engaged in providing the uncompleted services at the year-end amounts to £43,000. The senior partner has asked if this amount includes the costs relating to the marketing and administrative personnel.

Paragraph 13.14 deals with the cost of inventories relating to service providers, such as a firm of accountants. It specifically states that labour and other costs relating to sales and general administrative personnel are not included in the cost of inventories, but are instead recognised as expenses in the periods in which the costs are incurred. In addition, the costs of inventories for a service provider will not include any profit margins or non-attributable overheads that may be included in the prices that are charged by a service provider.

Agricultural produce from biological assets

19.7   A biological asset is a living plant or animal. Agricultural produce is the harvested product of an entity's biological asset. Such activities are dealt with under Section 34, Specialised Activities. However, paragraph 13.15 interacts with Section 34 in that Section 34 requires that inventories which involve harvested produce from its biological asset should be measured on initial recognition at their fair value less estimated costs to sell at the point of harvest. This value then becomes the cost of the inventories at that date for the purposes of inventories valuation.

Focus

Agricultural and biological assets are dealt with in Section 34, Specialised Activities in FRS 102 and in this publication **Chapter 16**.

Net realisable value

19.8   Net realisable value is calculated as the estimated selling price less costs to complete and sell.

Where reporting entities have inventories which are held for distribution, paragraph 13.4A requires such inventories to be valued at current replacement cost. This is to be adjusted (where applicable) for any loss of service potential.

Cost measurement

19.9   There are several methods a reporting entity could employ in order to determine cost and paragraph 13.16 to FRS 102 outlines three possible examples:

- standard cost method;

- the retail method; and

- most recent purchase price.

The *standard cost method* takes into consideration normal levels of materials and supplies as well as labour, efficiency and capacity utilisation. Reporting entities using the standard cost method must ensure that they regularly review their standard costs and revise them where appropriate if current conditions dictate.

The *retail method* measures cost by taking the selling price of inventories and deducting the relevant gross margin from this selling price. This method of cost valuation is more commonly found in businesses with high volumes of inventory where similar mark-ups are applied to ranges of inventory items or groups of items. In these situations it is often disproportionately time-consuming to determine the cost of the closing inventories and thus the retail method works on a more practical basis by recording closing inventory on hand at selling price and converting this to cost by removing the normal mark-up.

There is a notable complication with the use of the retail method of inventory valuation in that it is often difficult to determine the margin to be applied to the inventory at selling price in order to convert it back to cost. The percentage must take into consideration the circumstances in which inventories have been marked down to below original selling price and adjustments will be needed to remove the effect of these markdowns to prevent any item of inventory being valued at less than both its cost and its net realisable value.

Cost formulas

19.10   There are two cost formulas recognised in paragraph 13.18 which are:

- first-in first-out (FIFO); and

- weighted average cost (AVCO).

Such methods are used when a cost-flow assumption is needed (in other words when there are large numbers of ordinarily interchangeable items).

The FIFO method works on the basis that the oldest items are sold or used first and because of the way this method works, it probably gives the closest approximation to cost.

Example 19.3 – FIFO cost methodology

During an accounting period a company records the following purchases and sales of products as follows:

Purchasing summary

	Qty/change	Total cost	Cost
Opening stock	100	£275	£27,500
Sale 1	(70)		
Purchase 1	140	£300	£42,000
Sale 2	(110)		
Purchase 2	60	£320	£19,200
	120		

The company's cost of sales is calculated in units as follows:

Opening stock	100
Purchases	200
Closing stock	(120)
	180 units

The figures for cost of sales in the profit and loss account are as follows:

	Units	Cost	Total cost
FIFO purchase 1	100	£275	£27,500
FIFO purchase 2	80	£300	£24,000
	180		£51,500

The closing inventories figure for the balance sheet is calculated as follows:

	Units	*Cost*	*Total cost*
FIFO purchase 1	60	£300	£18,000
FIFO purchase 2	60	£320	£19,200
	120		£37,200

Sale 1 sold 70 units which were used from the opening inventory which reduced opening inventory to 30 units. The company then bought an additional 140 units which totals 170 units. The company sold an additional 110 units of which 30 were still from opening inventory using all of the opening inventory; the remaining 80 units were sold out of purchase 1, meaning 60 units of purchase 1 are still in stock. The company then purchased an additional 60 units resulting in 120 units being held in inventory at the year-end.

If you add the cost of sales figure of £51,500 to the balance sheet closing inventories figure of £37,200, that totals £88,700 which agrees with the cost of the inventories in the purchasing summary above.

19.11   The weighted average cost method is suitable where inventory units are similar (or nearly similar). It involves the calculation of an average unit cost by dividing the total cost of units by the number of units. When a new batch of inventory is received, the average unit cost has to be revised.

Example 19.4 – Weighted average cost methodology

A company's purchasing schedule for the month of March 2013 is as follows:

1 March 2013	Opening stock	55 units at £16.00 per unit
4 March 2013	Purchase	150 units at £16.50 per unit
14 March 2013	Sale	200 units at £20.00 per unit
25 March 2013	Purchase	80 units at £16.00 per unit
30 March 2013	Sale	40 units at £19.50 per unit
Units available to sell:	55 + 150 + 80	= 285
Units actually sold:	200 + 40	= 240
Units in closing stock:		= 45

The weighted average cost is calculated as follows:

		Units	Cost (£)	Total (£)
1 March 2013	Opening stock	55	16.00	880
4 March 2013	Purchase	150	16.50	2,475
25 March 2013	Purchase	80	16.00	1,280
		285	16.26*	4,635
*£4,635 ÷ 285				
Cost of sales		240	16.26	3,902
Closing stock		45	16.26	732

Impairment of inventories

19.12   The general principle in financial reporting is that assets cannot be carried in the financial statements in excess of their recoverable amount. Section 27 to FRS 102 deals with impairment issues and interacts with Section 13 in this respect. Section 27 requires a reporting entity to assess whether any inventories are impaired at the end of the reporting period (in other words to assess whether the carrying amount of inventories is not fully recoverable). This can occur for various reasons including damaged goods, obsolescence or a fall in selling price.

Where it is evident that inventories (or a group of inventories) have suffered impairment, paragraphs 27.2 to 27.4 of FRS 102 require the reporting entity to measure the inventory at its selling price less costs to complete and to recognise an impairment loss, which is recognised immediately in the profit and loss account (income statement). The same paragraphs also require the reversal of previous impairment losses in certain situations.

Focus

The accuracy of a company's inventory is critical for the purposes of financial reporting. Companies in the past have had inventory valuations challenged by their own auditors and by HM Revenue and Customs because of the ease of manipulation of this figure and the desire to over- or under-state assets and profit. A key ratio of interest to auditors and accountants should be the gross profit margin which may indicate errors within a company's inventory calculation.

Recognising inventories in profit or loss

19.13   Inventories are recognised in profit or loss at the time they are sold and the related sale has also been recognised in the profit and loss account. This is to achieve the 'matching' principle.

For reporting entities that carry inventories which are held for distribution, the carrying value of such inventories are recognised in the profit and loss account at the time they are distributed.

Disclosure requirements

19.14   Paragraph 13.22 to FRS 102 outlines five disclosure requirements that should be disclosed within a reporting entity's financial statements concerning its inventories at the end of an accounting period. These disclosures are:

- The *accounting policies* adopted in measuring inventories, including the cost formula used.

- The total carrying amount of inventories and the carrying amount in classifications appropriate to the entity.

- The amount of inventories recognised as an expense during the period.

- Impairment losses recognised or reversed in profit or loss in accordance with Section 27.

- The total carrying amount of inventories pledged as security for liabilities.

SUMMARY – WHAT IS DIFFERENT FROM THE PREVIOUS UK GAAP?

The treatment of inventories in FRS 102 is similar to the requirements in the old UK GAAP at SSAP 9 *Stocks and Long-Term Contracts*. However, FRS 102 does outlaw the use of the LIFO method of stock valuation and potentially there will be increased disclosures.

Chapter 20

Construction contracts

SIGNPOSTS

- Revenue recognition in relation to construction contracts is also covered in **Chapter 26**. A separate chapter is needed because of the inherent complications in accounting for construction contracts (see **20.1**).

- The timing of revenue and subsequent profit is crucial in ensuring that the financial statements of a company dealing in construction contracts give a true and fair view (see **20.2**).

- Construction contracts are defined in the Glossary to FRS 102 (see **20.3**).

- The principal calculation involved in construction contracts is the percentage (or stage) of completion method (see **20.4**).

- Costs and income from a construction contract are generally accumulated in a contract account within the general ledger and income is not based on advances or progress billings received by the company (see **20.5**).

- There are various costs which can be attributed to a construction contract (see **20.6**).

- In practice, there are generally two types of contract: 'fixed-price' and 'cost plus' (see **20.7**).

- Different recognition criteria are used for both types of contract (see **20.8**).

- There are generally three outcomes of a contract: loss-making, uncertain outcomes and profit-making contracts (see **20.9**).

- Inappropriate accounting treatments for construction contract accounting can have implications on the truth and fairness of the financial statements of a company as well as taxation implications (see **20.10**).

- Various disclosure requirements exist in FRS 102 where construction contracts are concerned (see **20.11**).

INTRODUCTION

20.1   The method for recognising revenue on a construction contract is looked at in **Chapter 26**. Construction contracts, however, are not specifically dealt with in FRS 102 *The Financial Reporting Standard applicable in the United Kingdom and Republic of Ireland* in their entirety – although the revenue recognition policies are dealt with in Section 23, Revenue.

This publication deals with construction contracts as a separate chapter because many companies in the UK and Republic of Ireland handle construction contracts which may span several years and the accounting for such contracts can be complicated.

20.2   The principal concern of accounting for long-term construction contracts involves the timing of revenue and profit (revenue recognition for a construction contract is discussed in **Chapter 26**). As contracts can last for several years, it is important to address the principles involved in accounting for such contracts to ensure correct revenue and profit recognition for companies.

DEFINITION

20.3   As noted in **20.1**, FRS 102 does not contain a specific section devoted to accounting for a construction contract. However the term itself is defined in the Glossary to FRS 102 as:

'A contract specifically negotiated for the construction of an **asset** or a combination of assets that are closely interrelated or interdependent in terms of their design, technology and function or their ultimate purpose or use.'

ACCOUNTING METHODOLOGY

20.4   Construction contracts invariably span more than one accounting period and the generally accepted basis for accounting for construction contracts is by using the *percentage of completion* method (often referred to as the *stage of completion* method). The percentage of completion method is a method of accounting that recognises income on a contract as work progresses by matching contract revenue with contract costs incurred, based on the proportion of work completed.

The problem in dealing with the percentage of completion method lies in actually deciphering the extent to which the projects are being finished and to assess the ability of the entity to bill and collect for the work done.

FRS 102, paragraph 23.22 outlines possible methods which a reporting entity can use to determine the stage of completion of a transaction or contract as follows:

- the proportion that costs incurred for work performed to date bear to the estimated total costs. Costs incurred for work performed to date do not include costs relating to future activity, such as for materials or prepayments;

- surveys of work performed; and

- completion of a physical proportion of the contract work or the completion of a proportion of the service contract.

20.5   In practice, a construction company will use a 'contract account' to accumulate costs and recognise income. When using contract accounting, income is not based on advances (cash collections) or progress billings. Any advances and progress billings are based on contract terms which do not necessarily measure contract performance.

Where costs and estimated earnings in excess of billings occur, the excess is classified as an asset. If billings exceed costs and estimated earnings, the difference is essentially treated as a liability in the company's balance sheet (statement of financial position).

CONTRACT COSTS

20.6   All contract costs are costs that are identifiable with a specific contract, plus those costs that are directly attributable to contracting activity in general and which can be allocated to the contract and those that are contractually chargeable to a customer. Examples of such costs are:

- costs of material used in the construction contract;

- wages and other labour costs directly attributable to the contract;

- costs of design and technical assistance;

- costs of hiring plant and machinery to complete the contract; and

- depreciation charges in respect of plant and machinery used in the construction contract.

20.7   In practice, there can be two types of construction contract that are distinguished according to their contractual pricing arrangements:

- fixed-price contracts; and

- cost-plus contracts.

Fixed-price contracts are contracts for which the price is not usually adjusted due to costs incurred by the contractor. Where a contractor agrees a fixed-price contract, this essentially means that the contractor agrees to a fixed contract price or a fixed rate price per unit of output. These types of contracts are often subjected to escalation clauses.

Cost-plus contracts are where the contractor is reimbursed for costs plus a provision for a fee. The contract price is determined by the total amount of reimbursable expenses and a fee. The fee is the profit margin which is calculated as revenue less direct costs to be earned on the contract (essentially gross profit).

RECOGNITION CRITERIA

20.8   Where the contract is either fixed-price or cost-plus, the following criteria must be met to determine whether the outcome of the contract (ie whether it is profit-making, loss-making or uncertain) can be reliably estimated:

Fixed-price contract

●   Total contract revenue can be measured reliably and it is probable that future economic benefits associated with the contract will flow to the entity.

●   Both the contract costs to complete and the stage of completion can be measured reliably.

●   Contract costs attributable to the contract can be identified properly and measured reliably so that comparison of actual contract costs with estimates can be done.

Cost-plus contract

●   It is probable that economic benefits will flow to the entity.

●   The contract costs attributable to the contract, whether or not reimbursable, can be identified and measured reliably.

Focus

The importance of reviewing the actual contract terms cannot be over-emphasised. Certain contracts may contain specific terms that could affect the accounting treatment applied.

ESTIMATING THE OUTCOME OF A CONTRACT

20.9   Estimating the outcome of a contract with as much accuracy as possible cannot be over-emphasised. This is because the accounting treatment for a construction contract will depend on whether the outcome of the contract is unknown at the time, whether it is estimated to make a loss or whether the contract is estimated to be profitable. Generally most contracts are entered into by companies with a view to the contract being profitable. However, some contracts may contain provisions within the contract agreement that mean certain unexpected costs have to be borne by the sub-contractor (often referred to as 'rectification' or 'remedial' costs) which may result in a profitable contract becoming loss-making.

Outcome of the contract cannot be estimated reliably

20.10   Where the outcome of a contract cannot be estimated reliably, revenue should be recognised to the extent of contract costs incurred that it is probable will be recoverable and thus no profit will be recognised. Contract costs are recognised as an expense in the period in which they are incurred.

Example 20.1 – Uncertain outcome of a contract

A company enters into a two-year contract. The project accountant is unsure as to whether the contract will be profit- or loss-making. Costs incurred up to the year-end amount to £10,000.

As the outcome of the contract cannot be estimated reliably, the amount of revenue to be recognised in the year-end financial statements is the same as costs incurred resulting in no profit being taken, hence:

DR	Trade debtors	£10,000
CR	Turnover	£10,000

Outcome of the contract is loss-making

20.11   Where contracts are loss-making, revenue is recognised by reference to the percentage of completion and cost of sales is essentially a balancing figure which generates the required loss calculated on the contract.

Example 20.2 – Loss-making contract

Company B Ltd has entered into a two-year contract that is expected to make a loss of £1,000. The project accountant has taken instructions from the project surveyor who has assessed the percentage of completion and the accountant has calculated revenue to be recognised will be £800.

The profit and loss account (income statement) will include £800 worth of contract revenue. The loss is estimated to be £1,000 so cost of sales will be £1,800 to generate the required loss (ie cost of sales is a balancing figure).

Focus

In UK GAAP it is prudent to recognise losses in the financial statements as soon as they are foreseen, hence the treatment in the above example.

Outcome of the contract is profitable

20.12   Where the outcome of the contract is deemed to be profitable, the company must apply the percentage of completion method to determine revenue and profit to be recognised. There are various steps involved in a profit-making contract which are covered in the following example.

Example 20.3 – Profit-making contract

On 1 October 2012, Kai Construction commenced work on a construction contract. The price agreed for the contract was £50 million. Kai Construction purchased plant at a cost of £15 million exclusively for use on the contract and the directors have estimated that the plant will have no residual life at the end of the contract, which is due to finish on 30 September 2013. The company's year-end is 31 March 2013 and costs incurred on the contract, plus estimated costs to complete are as follows:

	Costs to date	Estimate of costs to complete
	£'000	*£'000*
Materials purchased	9,000	5,000
Labour and other overheads	7,000	8,000

All the costs which have been incurred to date have been debited to the contract account in the nominal (general) ledger. Kai Construction has appointed a surveyor to assess the progress of the contract and he has suggested that, at 31 March 2013, the contract was 40% complete at which point the customer made a progress payment to Kai Construction amounting to £15 million. The finance department has credited this progress payment to the contract account. There have been no other entries made in the books of Kai Construction in respect of this contract.

Step 1

Kai Construction will need to assess the outcome of the contract. This is calculated as follows:

	£'000	£'000
Contract revenue		50,000
Costs:		
Materials to date plus additional costs	14,000	
Labour and other overheads	15,000	
Plant purchased	15,000	44,000
Estimated profit		6,000

Step 2

The surveyor has confirmed that the contract is 40% complete, so 40% of the total costs are taken to cost of sales in the profit and loss account (income statement). In addition, 40% of the expected revenue is included in the profit and loss account (income statement). Extracts from the financial statements are shown below:

Kai Construction

Profit and Loss Account (extracts)

31 March 2013

		£
Turnover	(40% × £50 million)	20,000
Cost of sales	(40% × £44 million)	17,600
		2,400 (ie 40% × £6 million)

Step 3

Kai Construction then needs to work out how much should be included within the company's balance sheet (statement of financial position) as 'gross amount due from customer'. This is calculated as follows (this can be

254

shown as an 'other current asset' in the balance sheet (statement of financial position)):

	£	£
Costs to date:		
Purchase of materials	9,000	
Labour and other overheads	7,000	
Plant depreciation (£15,000 x 6/12)	7,500	
Total costs to date		23,500
Contract profit		6,000
		29,500
Less progress payment received		(15,000)
Gross amount due from customer		14,500

Focus

The Appendix to Section 23 contains comprehensive examples of revenue recognition under the principles in Section 23. **Example 12** gives a particularly good example of an agreement for the construction of real estate.

20.13 Estimating the outcome of a construction contract accurately is essential because this will have an effect on the overall accounting treatment and in turn will have an impact on a company's corporation tax liability if the methods employed by the company are inappropriate in the circumstances.

DISCLOSURE REQUIREMENTS

20.14 The disclosure requirements relating to revenue from construction contracts are dealt with specifically in FRS 102, Section 23, paragraph 23.31 which require reporting entities that enter into construction contracts to disclose:

- the amount of contract revenue recognised as revenue in the period;

- the methods used to determine the contract revenue recognised in the period; and

- the methods used to determine the stage of completion of contracts in progress.

In addition, reporting entities must also present:

- the gross amount due from customers for contract work, as an *asset*; and

- the gross amount due to customers for contract work, as a *liability*.

SUMMARY – WHAT IS DIFFERENT FROM THE PREVIOUS UK GAAP?

- The impact of FRS 102 on construction contracts is to bring the concepts more in line with the international equivalent (IAS 11 *Construction Contracts*).

- There are slight variations in the wording relating to the recognition of revenue in FRS 102 as opposed to SSAP 9, but the principles are still the same.

Chapter 21

Sale and leaseback transactions

SIGNPOSTS

- Sale and leaseback transactions have become increasingly common over recent years as a means of sourcing finance. They can also be extremely complicated to account for. Such transactions fall under the scope of Section 20 to FRS 102, Leases (see **21.1**).

- In a sale and leaseback transaction, the vendor transfers legal title to an asset to another party but retains use of the asset on a lease (see **21.2**).

- In a sale and *finance* leaseback there is no sale because no risks and rewards of ownership have been passed from the original lessee (see **21.3**).

- The asset is disposed of at net book value and is then brought back on to the balance sheet (statement of financial position) at its fair value (being the cash proceeds) (see **21.4**).

- Revaluation balances that are associated with sale and finance leaseback transactions are not crystallised because no sale has, in effect, occurred (see **21.5**).

- Lessees will recognise profit or loss on disposal of an asset that is subject to a sale and *operating* leaseback because the risks and rewards of ownership have been substantially transferred (see **21.6**).

- If proceeds are higher than fair value, the excess over fair value is deferred and amortised over the period for which the asset is expected to be used. If proceeds are lower than fair value, profits or losses are recognised immediately with an exception where the loss is compensated by future rentals at a price below market value (see **21.7** to **21.9**).

- The Section requires additional disclosures where sale and leaseback transactions have taken place to ensure the user of the financial statements can gain an understanding of the effect such transactions have had on the company's financial statements (see **21.10**).

INTRODUCTION

21.1   Sale and leaseback transactions have become increasingly common over recent years as a source of finance. They can, however, be quite complex to account for, hence the authors thought it appropriate to give such transactions their own chapter; however, such transactions also fall under the scope of Section 20, Leases (specifically paragraphs 20.32 to 20.35) and see **Chapter 15**.

21.2   In a sale and leaseback transaction a vendor sells an asset (such as a building) and immediately reacquires the use of that asset by entering into a lease with the buyer (often the bank). The way such transactions are accounted for under Section 20 depends on the type of lease entered into, as well as whether the sale and subsequent leaseback of the asset are on an arm's-length basis.

SALE AND LEASEBACK AS A FINANCE LEASE

21.3   **Chapter 15** covers finance leases in more detail but, in the broadest terms, a finance lease is a lease whereby the risks and rewards of ownership pass from the lessor to the lessee. When this type of transaction occurs, the substance of the transaction is that there is NO sale. The transaction is merely a financing operation and the risks and rewards of ownership of the asset have not passed from the original owner (now the lessee). In recognition of this, the seller/lessee will not recognise a profit or loss on the sale of the asset.

Paragraph 20.33 says that where the sale and leaseback transaction results in a finance lease, then the excess of sales proceeds over carrying values (net book values) are to be deferred and amortised over the term of the lease.

Example 21.1 – Disposal of an asset by way of a finance lease

Lucas Lighting Limited disposes of an asset by way of a finance lease. The carrying value of the asset is £80,000 and the sales proceeds received amount to £130,000. The directors of Lucas Lighting Limited have estimated the useful economic life of the asset to be five years and there are five annual rentals remaining of £27,000.

The journal entries required on disposal of the asset are as follows:

		£
DR	Cash	130,000
CR	Property, plant and equipment (NBV)	80,000
CR	Deferred profit (£130,000 – £80,000)	50,000

Being sale of asset in a sale/leaseback transaction

		£
DR	Non-current asset	130,000
CR	Lease creditor	130,000

Being restatement of asset at fair value

The entries in the profit and loss account (income statement) over the lease term will be as follows:

	£
Depreciation (£130,000/5)	26,000
Finance charge $\frac{[(5 \times £27,000) - £130,000)]}{5}$	1,000
Release of deferred profit (£50,000/5)	(10,000)
	17,000

21.4   In the above example, the net book value of the asset is disposed of and the resulting profit on disposal is recognised as deferred profit. The asset is then brought back on to the balance sheet (statement of financial position) at fair value (the sale proceeds that have been debited to bank) and credited to a liability account to represent the present value of the obligation under the finance lease. In the authors' opinion; this treatment better reflects the commercial substance of the transaction because it is only the legal form of the transaction that represents a disposal and subsequent reacquisition of the underlying asset.

21.5   Some assets may be subject to a sale and finance leaseback arrangement, which are carried under the revaluation model, as permitted in Section 17, Property, Plant and Equipment and for which a revaluation surplus may be shown within the reserves section of the balance sheet. The question here is whether or not the revaluation surplus on the asset becomes realised on completion of a sale and leaseback transaction.

In a sale and leaseback transaction the risks and rewards of ownership of the asset are not transferred to the lessee as the transaction merely represents a financing arrangement, therefore these principles would argue that the seller/lessee does not dispose of the risks and rewards of ownership under a sale and finance leaseback arrangement. Furthermore, *section 853(4)* to *Companies Act 2006* states that whether or not profits are realised depends on *principles generally accepted, at the time when the accounts are prepared, with respect to the determination, for accounting purposes, of realised profits or losses.*

In view of the fact that there is no genuine disposal of the asset by the seller/lessee, the view here is that the revaluation surplus is not realised and should remain on the balance sheet.

SALE AND LEASEBACK AS AN OPERATING LEASE

21.6   When an asset is sold in a sale and leaseback arrangement that results in an operating lease (a lease whereby the risks and rewards remain with the lessor), the seller/lessee must recognise any profit or loss immediately. This is because in the sale and operating leaseback, the seller disposes of substantially all the risks and rewards of owning the asset in the sale transaction. The lessee may reacquire some of the risks and rewards in the leaseback, but will not acquire substantially all of them.

21.7   Where the sale price is above fair value, the excess shall be deferred and amortised over the period for which the asset is expected to be used. Conversely, if the sale price is below fair value, any profit or loss is immediately recognised *except* that if the loss is compensated by future rentals at a price below market value, it shall be deferred and amortised in proportion to the rental payments over the period for which the asset is expected to be used.

Example 21.2 – Effects on profit or loss under different arrangements

Gabriella Gardening Equipment Limited (Gabriella) has an asset with a net book value of £70,000 and a fair value of £100,000. Gabriella has approached three different finance houses who have offered the following arrangements:

Arrangement 1

Sale price of £100,000 with an annual rental for five years of £28,000.

Arrangement 2

Sale price of £120,000 (more than fair value) with an annual rental for five years of £28,000.

Arrangement 3

Sale price of £80,000 (less than fair value) with an annual rental for five years of £20,000.

The effect on the profit and loss account in each of these arrangements would be as follows:

	£
Arrangement 1	
Profit on disposal	30,000
Rental	(28,000)
	2,000
Arrangement 2	
Profit on disposal	30,000
Deferred profit (£20,000/5 years)	4,000
Rental	(28,000)
	6,000
Arrangement 3	
Profit on disposal	10,000
Rental	(20,000)
	(10,000)

21.8   Where the sales price is higher than fair value, the excess does not represent a genuine profit as the rentals that the lessee has to pay in future years will undoubtedly be higher than market value. It follows, therefore, that the excess of the sale proceeds over the fair value should be deferred and amortised over the period for which the asset is expected to be used.

21.9   Where the sales price is below the fair value, profits or losses should be recognised immediately. The reasoning here is that the company may have been motivated to raise cash very quickly and thus negotiated a poor deal. The Section provides an exception where losses are compensated by future rentals which are below market levels. In this situation the lessee requires the loss (to the extent that it is compensated by future rentals below market levels) to be deferred and amortised in proportion to the lease payments over the period for which the asset is expected to be used. At first glance it may seem that this practice goes against the prudence principles, but what it does is merely reverse the effect of artificial losses created by artificially establishing sales prices and subsequent rentals.

DISCLOSURE REQUIREMENTS

21.10   Paragraph 20.35 requires the same disclosure requirements for lessees and lessors and such disclosure requirements apply equally to sale and leaseback transactions (see **Chapter 15**). In addition, the Section also requires

21.10 *Sale and leaseback transactions*

a description of a significant leasing arrangement which must also include a description of unique or unusual provisions of the agreement or terms of the sale and leaseback transactions.

SUMMARY – WHAT IS DIFFERENT FROM THE PREVIOUS UK GAAP?

There are no significant differences between FRS 102 and SSAP 21, although the Guidance Notes on SSAP 21 do give fairly comprehensive guidance on gain deferral.

Chapter 22

Provisions and contingencies

SIGNPOSTS

- The issue surrounding provisions has been extremely controversial over the years with the act of 'big bath accounting' being prevalent prior to the issuance of standards governing the recognition of provisions (see **22.1**).

- A provision is a 'liability of uncertain timing or amount' whilst a contingent liability is defined as 'either a possible but uncertain obligation or a present obligation that is not recognised because it fails to meet one or both of the conditions (b) and (c) in paragraph 21.4' (see **22.2**).

- A contingent asset is defined as 'a possible asset that arises from past events and whose existence will be confirmed only by the occurrence or non-occurrence of one or more uncertain future events not wholly within the control of the reporting entity' (see **22.3**).

- There are three strict criteria that have to be met before a provision can be made in the financial statements (see **22.3**).

- Provisions are often subjected to a degree of estimation and careful consideration must be given to the way the estimate is calculated in order to arrive at a 'best estimate' for the provision (see **22.4**).

- Third parties such as HM Revenue and Customs (HMRC) are very interested when it comes to provisions to ensure that they are not excessive and companies must therefore be prepared to justify their methodologies where provisions are concerned in the event of any enquiries (see **22.5**).

- Where the time value of money is material, FRS 102 requires provisions to be discounted accordingly (see **22.6**).

- Contingent assets cannot be recognised within the financial statements unless it is virtually certain that they will be received (see **22.7**).

- Provisions previously recognised must be reviewed at each reporting date and adjusted so they reflect the current best estimate of the amount that would be required to settle the obligation (see **22.8**).

- If a contract becomes onerous, the provision for future rentals will be recognised and measured in the same way as any other sort of provision (see **22.9**).

- Future operating losses must not be recognised as there is no obligating event (see **22.10**).

- Extensive disclosures are required in the financial statements where provisions and contingencies are concerned (see **22.11**).

INTRODUCTION

22.1   Provisions and contingencies have long since been a controversial subject in the world of financial reporting and over the years have lent themselves to a whole host of accounting manipulations. Prior to the issuance of accounting standards in the area of provisioning, there was no guidance which dealt with the definition, recognition, measurement, use and presentation of provisions and hence reporting entities were frequently exploiting this loophole by creating provisions, under the guise of prudence, in one accounting period, only to release them in the next accounting period primarily for the purposes of profit manipulation. Such an act was fairly common prior to the issuance of FRS 12 *Provisions, Contingent Liabilities and Contingent Assets.*

In years when profits were high, management would create a provision to reduce profit to an acceptable level as invariably shareholders would expect profits to go in an upward direction (ie if profit was very high in one year, shareholders' would expect an even higher profit in the succeeding years). This attitude put pressure on management to deliver even better results. Conversely, when profitability came in lower than shareholder expectations, management would simply reverse prior year provisions to enable profitability to increase.

The creation and reversal of artificial provisions became known as 'big bath accounting' or 'big bath provisions' and it was this practice that eventually led to the issuance of FRS 12.

Provisions and contingencies are dealt with in FRS 102, Section 21. Section 21 also deals with financial guarantee contracts, except where:

- an entity has chosen to apply IAS 39 *Financial Instruments: Recognition and Measurement* and/or IFRS 9 *Financial Instruments* to its financial instruments; or

- an entity has elected under FRS 103 *Insurance Contracts* to continue the application of insurance contract accounting.

In addition, Section 21 does not apply to those financial instruments that will fall under the scope of Section 11, Basic Financial Instruments and Section 12, Other Financial Instruments as well as insurance contracts that will fall under the scope of FRS 103 *Insurance Contracts*.

Executory contracts will also not fall under the scope of Section 21 unless they are onerous contracts. Paragraph 21.2 explains that executory contracts are contracts under which neither party has performed any of its obligations or both parties have partially performed their obligations to an equal extent.

There has been a long-standing principle in financial reporting that in exercising *prudence* any uncertain liabilities should be recognised forthwith, whereas, in contrast, any uncertain assets should not be recognised. FRS 12 aimed to address the boundaries of such recognition and this principle has followed through into Section 21 of FRS 102. The Section itself determines the criteria that have to be met before a provision is recognised in the balance sheet (statement of financial position) as a liability and also when an asset can be recognised. Failure to meet the required criteria in Section 21 results in no recognition within the financial statements, but disclosure as a contingency (if the issue is, of course, material).

DEFINITIONS

22.2 Paragraph 21.1 refers to *provisions* as being *'liabilities of uncertain timing or amount'*. The term 'provision' is often used in the context of depreciation, impairment and bad debt provisions. It is important to distinguish the term 'provision' in the context of Section 21 rather than a 'provision for bad debts' because the latter is essentially an adjustment to carrying amounts of assets rather than the recognition of a liability.

A *contingent liability* is defined in FRS 102, paragraph 21.12 as 'either a possible but uncertain obligation or a present obligation that is not recognised because it fails to meet one or both of the conditions (b) and (c) in paragraph 21.4'.

A *contingent asset* is defined in the Glossary as 'a possible asset that arises from past events and whose existence will be confirmed only by the occurrence or non-occurrence of one or more uncertain future events not wholly within the control of the reporting entity'.

RECOGNITION WITHIN THE FINANCIAL STATEMENTS

22.3 Section 21 permits a provision to be recognised as a liability only when three criteria are met as follows:

- the entity has an obligation at the reporting date as a result of a past event;

- it is probable (ie more likely than not) that the entity will be required to transfer economic benefits in settlement; and

- the amount of the obligation can be estimated reliably.

Should any *one* of the above three criteria not be met than an entity must not recognise a provision. If all three criteria are met, the reporting entity must recognise the provision as a liability in the balance sheet (statement of financial position) and as an expense in the profit and loss account except in situations where another Section of FRS 102 would require recognition as part of the cost of an asset, such as inventories or property, plant and equipment.

The Section itself recognises two types of 'obligation' – a *legal* obligation and a *constructive* obligation. A legal obligation is fairly self-explanatory – it is one in which the reporting entity is legally obliged to discharge its obligations by transferring economic benefits in settlement. A *constructive* obligation is a little more subjective. Such an obligation can be defined as:

> 'An obligation arising from an entity's actions such that the entity, by an established pattern of past practice, published policies or a sufficiently specific current statement, has indicated to third parties that it will accept certain responsibilities and as a result has created a valid expectation in the minds of third parties that it will discharge those responsibilities.'

Constructive obligations are, therefore, established processes that have created an expectation in the mindsets of individuals within the organisation.

Example 22.1 – Uncertain obligation

Westhead Trading Ltd has been defending itself in legal proceedings brought against it by one of its customers, Mark Breary. Westhead Trading supplies plant and machinery to the building industry. Mr Breary purchased an angle grinder from Westhead Trading on 2 July 2013 and suffered a serious electrical shock which was found to be as a result of a power surge in the machine. Westhead Trading are disputing the claim as they believe that Mr Breary used the machine without following the instructions and they have evidence from their supplier that if the machine had been used in accordance with the instructions, such a power surge would not have occurred.

Westhead Trading's year-end is 31 October 2013 and the case is due to be heard on 1 December 2013. To date, Westhead Trading has incurred legal costs of £5,000 in defending the case and it is possible that further costs, estimated in the region of £10,000, could be incurred after the trial. The finance director is proposing to make a provision in the company's financial statements for £10,000 in the event that Westhead Trading lose the case. The company's legal advisers are unable to confirm whether Mr Breary will be successful in his claim; the barrister stating that, in his experience, the claim could go either way.

Section 21 to FRS 102 requires three criteria to be met *before* a provision can be made within the financial statements. One of those criteria is that it is *probable* (ie more likely than not) that the entity will be required to transfer economic benefits in settlement. Westhead Trading's legal advisers have confirmed that they cannot be certain regarding the outcome of this case, therefore a provision should not be made as all three criteria cannot be met. As a result, disclosure as a contingent liability should be made within the financial statements.

Example 22.2 – Constructive obligation

Scanlon's Scanning Ltd is a very successful document management bureau. They offer a range of products and services to handle customers' document management in the modern age of becoming 'paperless'. They supply scanning equipment to customers and associated software onsite so that their customer can scan paperwork into electronic client files and then send the paper files to their storage department where these files are held in secure units. In addition, Scanlon's Scanning offers routine upgrades to its customers and onsite maintenance and support for both software and scanning equipment.

The company has been operating successfully for over 30 years and was originally set up by husband and wife, Les and Lisa. As the company grew, Les and Lisa remain on the board of directors but have taken a more 'back seat' role in the company allowing their three co-directors to deal with the day-to-day running of the company.

In the mid-1990s, the company experienced rapid expansion and a bonus system was put in place for the directors. An annual bonus is paid if pre-tax profit reaches a certain benchmark and anything over and above the benchmark is taken into consideration. The benchmark has been reached each year.

The Annual General Meeting was held on 27 March 2013 and initial indications suggested that the pre-tax profit target had been hit and there was going to be a large excess over this target. However, the directors agreed that a bonus would be provided once the actual figures were confirmed, which the accountants have indicated will be around the middle of May 2013.

The final figures were agreed on 15 May 2013 for the year ended 31 March 2013 and a bonus was accrued in the year-end financial statements.

The question here relates to whether the bonus *should* have been accrued in the 31 March 2013 year-end financial statements, or if it should be provided for in the 31 March 2014 financial statements when it is paid.

Since the scheme was introduced, the directors have 'expected' this bonus to be paid because the benchmark has been reached. This has created a 'constructive' obligation on the part of the company. Paragraph 21.6 to FRS 102 confirms that such an obligation means that the entity has no realistic alternative to settling the obligation, therefore such a constructive obligation can be recognised as a provision within the financial statements as at 31 March 2013.

ESTIMATING PROVISIONS

22.4   There are many industries where provisions are frequently included within the financial statements simply because of the business in which the company operates (eg a clothing retailer will have a provision for returns included, or a domestic appliance retailer will more than likely have a provision included in the financial statements to cover issues such as repairs under warranty). Such provisions will often require the use of estimation techniques, based on past practice, to arrive at an informed amount for the provision.

In situations when a provision involves a large population of items, paragraph 21.7 to FRS 102 requires that the estimate reflects the weighting of all possible outcomes by their associated probabilities. As a consequence, it may well be that the amount of the provision will differ depending on whether the probability of financial loss to the company is, say, 60% or 90%. In companies where there are a range of possible outcomes, a mid-point will be selected. However, if the provision arises from a single obligation, the provision will be based on the best estimate required to settle the obligation (eg a best estimate of legal costs required to settle a litigation claim) – although paragraph 21.7(b) does require the reporting entity to consider other possible outcomes and if such possible outcomes are mostly higher or mostly lower than the most likely outcome, a best estimate will be a higher or lower amount.

Example 22.3 – Estimating a warranty provision

Appliances R Us sells domestic appliances with a standard warranty under which its customers are covered in the event of any manufacturing defects that occur within six months of the customer purchasing the appliance. It has a year-end of 31 October 2013 and the directors have made assessments, based on past experience as follows:

- If minor defects are detected in all products sold, the cost of the repairs will be £800,000.

- If major defects were detected in all products sold, the cost of the repairs will be £3,000,000.

- 70% of the goods sold are expected to have no defects, whilst 25% will have minor defects and the remaining 5% will have major defects.

The financial statements for the year ended 31 October 2013 will have a provision in respect of the expected warranty repairs based on the following calculation:

	£
70% × nil	Nil
25% × £800,000	200,000
5% × £3,000,000	150,000
	350,000

22.5   When using estimation techniques as a means of arriving at a provision, it is important that the reporting entity keeps in mind that Section 21 requires the estimate to be a 'best estimate' of the amount that a reporting entity would rationally pay to settle the obligation at the end of the reporting period or to transfer it to a third party at that time.

This is important, not only from a financial reporting perspective, but also from the perspective of HMRC. It is not uncommon for HMRC to open enquiries into a company's financial statements where they suspect that a provision for a liability has been over-stated in the financial statements and hence tax relief granted on the excess. HMRC has been known to disallow a certain proportion of provision when challenging companies on the grounds of overstatement. This can also result in penalties and interest being levied by HMRC for such actions. Conversely, it is also important from a financial reporting perspective that provisions are not disproportionately understated so as not to mislead the users of the financial statements.

DISCOUNTING

22.6   When an entity has arrived at the cash flows required to settle the obligation, the company is required to consider whether the time value of money will have a material impact on the sums to be paid. Paragraph 21.7 goes on to say that when the time value of money is material, the amount of the provision is the present value of the amount expected to settle the obligation. The company will use pre-tax discount rate(s) that reflect(s) current market assessments of the time value of money and risks specific to the liability.

Focus

Paragraph 21.7 makes it clear that it is only in instances where the time value of money is **material** that the provision should be discounted to present-day values. The reality is that most provisions will reverse in the short term (often within the succeeding financial year) and therefore the effects of discounting will be, in the vast majority of cases, immaterial; thus a reporting entity will not need to adjust the provision for the time value of money.

CONTINGENT ASSETS

22.7   Care must be taken when dealing with contingent assets and the recognition of such in the financial statements. These assets usually arise when the amount required to settle a provision will be reimbursed by a third party (usually an insurance company). However, paragraph 21.9 to FRS 102 states that a company can only recognise the reimbursement as a separate asset (ie a receivable/debtor) when it is *virtually certain* that the entity will receive the reimbursement on settlement of the obligation. The standard does not define *virtually certain* but there must be evidence from the third party that they will be willing to reimburse the obligation before the contingent asset is recognised in the financial statements. This is to avoid reporting entities disproportionately inflating assets and increasing profit (or reducing losses) and therefore misleading the users of the financial statements.

Focus

The amount of the receivable/debtor in respect of the reimbursement cannot exceed the amount of the provision.

Example 22.4 – Example of INCORRECT treatment

A firm of accountants has been sued by one of its clients for negligently preparing a corporation tax return. The firm has received confirmation from its Professional Indemnity Insurers that the insurance company will refund part of the obligation and has provided this confirmation in writing on 30 September 2013. The firm's year-end is 31 October 2013. The accountant preparing the firm's financial statements for the year ended 31 October 2013 has made the following journal entries to incorporate the receivable into the firm's financial statements:

Debit	Provisions for liabilities	£X
Credit	Claims account	£X

The original provision was sent to the claims account in the profit and loss account (income statement) and hence the claims account is presented net, as is the liability account (representing the provision) in the balance sheet (statement of financial position).

The treatment by the accountant preparing the financial statements is in contravention of paragraph 21.9 to FRS 102. The reimbursement receivable/debtor should be presented in the balance sheet (statement of financial position) as an asset and must not be offset against the provision. However, in the profit and loss account (income statement), the expense relating to a provision may be presented net of the amount recognised for a reimbursement.

SUBSEQUENT MEASUREMENT

22.8   The Section makes it clear that reporting entities that have recognised a provision that complies with the recognition criteria in Section 21 can only charge against a provision those expenditures for which the provision was originally recognised and therefore offsetting other such costs against the provision would be inappropriate.

Provisions must also be recognised at each reporting date and be adjusted so they reflect the current best estimate of the amount that would essentially be required to settle the obligation at that reporting date. This is important because information may come to light after the provision was initially recognised that may require the provision to be written down or increased depending on the information obtained. Any adjustments made to provisions will be recognised in profit or loss.

Example 22.5 – Increasing a provision after the balance sheet date

Dodgy Building Co Ltd (Dodgy) has a 31 July year-end and has been involved in a long, arduous legal case with one of its customers. On 31 July 2012, the company's legal advisers confirmed that the chances of Dodgy successfully defending itself in this case were slim to non-existent and they have advised that, in their opinion, a provision amounting to £100,000 (including £30,000 costs) should be provided for in the 2012 financial statements. This provision was duly made and, despite the lawyers advising that the chances of a successful defence for Dodgy were slim, it nonetheless decided to fight the claim.

On 1 September 2013 the company received confirmation from the courts that the Judge had found in favour of the claimant and awarded costs and damages to the claimant of £150,000. This was duly paid on 15 September 2013.

In this example, information has come to light which suggests that the provision as at 31 July 2013 needs to be increased further. The company had previously recognised a provision in the sum of £100,000, although once judgment was passed, the amount awarded to the claimant was £50,000 more, therefore the entries in the company's financial statements as at 31 July 2013 need to be:

DR	Income statement	£50,000
CR	Provisions for liabilities	£50,000

Being uplift in the provision for costs and damages.

ONEROUS CONTRACTS

22.9   An onerous contract is defined in the Glossary as:

'A contract in which the unavoidable costs of meeting the obligations under the contract exceed the economic benefits expected to be received under it.'

Example 22.6 – An onerous contract

A company has recently started to trade selling soft furnishings such as curtains and cushions. It entered into a lease with an unconnected third party to rent premises for a five-year period with no break or early cancellation clause. In year three, due to unprecedented demand for the company's products and services, sales have reached a level whereby the company has outgrown its current premises. The owner has sourced larger premises which can house seamstresses to make the products as well as two sales consultants who will help with the design of the products which are all tailor-made to customers' requirements.

The landlord of the property which is being vacated has refused to allow the property to be sub-let and is refusing to allow the company to come out of the lease early. This is representative of an onerous contract – a property lease which has been abandoned by the company which cannot be sub-let and from which the company expects to receive no further benefit, but to which it is still committed to conform with the terms of the original lease.

The provision for future rentals will be recognised and measured in the same way as any other sort of provision.

FUTURE OPERATING LOSSES

22.10 The Section is clear where future operating losses are concerned – they must not be recognised and directs users to Example 1 of the Appendix to Section 21 of FRS 102. This particular example concerns a company that concludes that a segment of its operations will incur future operating losses for several years. On the grounds that there is no past event that *obliges* the entity to pay out resources (note there has to be an *obligating event* to recognise a provision) and hence expected future losses do not meet the definition of future operating losses. Indeed the expectation of future losses is more an indicator of asset impairment and therefore the Appendix directs users to Section 27, Impairment of Assets.

Focus

The Appendix to Section 21 contains some comprehensive examples of when, and, importantly, when not to, recognise a provision.

DISCLOSURES

22.11 Disclosures are required for both provisions and contingencies which are detailed in paragraphs 21.15 to 21.17A as follows:

Disclosures about provisions

22.12   For each class of provision, an entity shall disclose the following:

- a reconciliation showing:
  - ○   the carrying amount at the beginning and end of the period;
  - ○   additions during the period, including adjustments that result from changes in measuring the discounted amount;
  - ○   amounts charged against the provision during the period; and
  - ○   unused amounts reversed during the period.
- a brief description of the nature of the obligation and the expected amount and timing of any resulting payments;
- an indication of the uncertainties about the amount or timing of those outflows; and
- the amount of any expected reimbursement, stating the amount of any asset that has been recognised for that expected reimbursement.

It is to be noted that the Section does not require comparative information for prior periods.

Disclosures about contingent liabilities

22.13   Unless the possibility of any outflow of resources is remote, when practicable the entity must give a brief description of the nature of the contingent liability and, when practicable:

- an estimate of its financial effect, measured in accordance with paragraphs 21.7 to 21.11;
- an indication off the uncertainties relating to the amount or timing of any outflow; and
- the possibility of any reimbursement.

If it is impracticable to make one, or more, of these disclosures, that fact shall be stated.

Disclosures about contingent assets

22.14   Where an inflow of economic benefits is probable (but not virtually certain), the reporting entity must disclose a description of the nature of the contingent assets at the end of the reporting period, and, when practicable, an estimate of their financial effect, measured using the principles set out in paragraphs 21.7 to 21.11. That fact shall be stated where the entity deems it impracticable to make these disclosures.

Prejudicial disclosures

22.15   The Section recognises that only in *extremely rare cases* can the disclosures required in paragraphs 21.14 to 21.16 be expected to prejudice seriously the position of an entity in a dispute with other parties on the subject matter of the provision, contingent liability or contingent asset. In such situations, the entity is not required to disclose the information, but instead is expected to disclose the general nature of the dispute, together with the fact that, and the reason why, the information has not been disclosed.

Disclosures about financial guarantee contracts

22.16   Where a reporting entity has issued financial guarantee contracts, it must disclose the nature and business purpose of the financial guarantee contracts, together with the disclosures required by paragraphs 21.14 and 21.15 to Section 21.

SUMMARY – WHAT IS DIFFERENT FROM THE PREVIOUS UK GAAP?

The principles contained in Section 21 are closely aligned to the principles that were contained in FRS 12 *Provisions, Contingent Liabilities and Contingent Assets* and there are no major changes as to how such issues are dealt with in FRS 102.

Chapter 23

Employee benefits

SIGNPOSTS

- Employee benefits are dealt with in Section 28 to FRS 102 and there are four types of employee benefits which this Section covers (see **23.1**).

- A liability is recognised once a reporting entity has deducted amounts that have been paid (see **23.2** and **23.3**).

- Section 28 provides examples of four types of short-term employee benefits (see **23.4**).

- Profit-sharing arrangements and bonus plans are also covered by Section 28 and these interact with Section 21, Provisions and Contingencies (see **23.5**).

- Post-employment benefits include defined contribution pension plans and defined benefit pension plans (see **23.6**).

- Defined contribution plans are the simplest form of pension plan to account for, with defined benefit pension plans being the most complicated (see **23.7** and **23.8**).

- There may be occasions when a defined benefit pension plan is accounted for as a defined contribution plan (see **23.9**).

- A liability has to be recognised where agreement is made between a multi-employer pension plan and the employer as to how the entity will fund a deficit arising in a defined benefit pension plan that is a multi-employer plan and accounted for as if it were a defined contribution plan (see **23.10**).

- Care must be taken to correctly account for insured benefits where an entity will pay insurance premiums in order to fund a post-employment benefit plan (see **23.11**).

- Defined benefit contributions are accounted for in profit or loss and a liability is recognised after deducting amounts already paid (see **23.12**).

- Actuarial information will be needed to correctly account, and make the necessary disclosures, for a defined benefit pension plan (see **23.13**).

- The defined benefit pension obligation is measured using the projected unit credit method (see **23.14**).

- A qualified actuary need not necessarily be used, nor will annual valuations be needed where principal actuarial assumptions have not significantly changed in the periods between the comprehensive actuarial valuations (see **23.15**).

- Various components of the defined benefit pension plan will be reported in the profit and loss account (income statement), balance sheet (statement of financial position) and other comprehensive income (statement of total recognised gains and losses) (see **23.16**).

- There are additional accounting considerations in respect of introductions of new defined benefit pension plans, changes to existing plans, curtailments and settlements (see **23.17**).

- Defined benefit plan surpluses (assets) can only be recognised to the extent that the entity is expected to be able to recover the asset, either through reduced contributions or by way of refund from the plan (see **23.18**).

- Reimbursements should be treated as separate assets and in the same way as plan assets (see **23.19**).

- Other long-term employee benefits are subjected to recognition in the financial statements by way of a formula (see **23.20**).

- Termination benefits are recognised in profit or loss as soon as they are incurred (see **23.21** and **23.22**).

- Careful consideration of contractual provisions needs to be made where group plans are concerned to ensure correct recognition in the financial statements (see **23.23**).

- Extensive disclosures are required in the financial statements where pension plans are concerned (see **23.24**).

INTRODUCTION

23.1   Employee benefits are dealt with in Section 28, Employee Benefits and are defined as 'all forms of consideration given by an entity in exchange for services rendered by employees, including directors and management'. Section 28 does not, however, deal with issues relating to share-based payment transactions which are covered in Section 26, Share-based Payment and in **Chapter 28**.

23.2   *Employee benefits*

There are four types of employee benefits which are covered by Section 28(a) to (d) as follows:

- short-term employee benefits, which are employee benefits (other than termination benefits) that are expected to be settled wholly before 12 months after the end of the reporting period in which employees render the related service;

- post-employment benefits, which are employee benefits (other than termination benefits and short-term employee benefits) that are payable after the completion of employment;

- other long-term employee benefits, which are all employee benefits, other than short-term employee benefits, post-employment benefits and termination benefits; or

- termination benefits, which are employee benefits provided in exchange for the termination of an employee's employment as a result of either:

  - an entity's decision to terminate an employee's employment before the normal retirement date; or

  - an employee's decision to accept voluntary redundancy in exchange for those benefits.

RECOGNITION AND MEASUREMENT

23.2   Generally, reporting entities must recognise a liability once they have deducted amounts that have been paid to employees or as a contribution to a pension fund. Where amounts paid exceed the obligation arising before the retirement date, the entity will recognise a prepayment.

A company has a year-end of 30 November 2013 and, on that date, calculated that an amount of £20,000 was owed by the company in respect of employee holiday entitlement which it expects to be paid over to employees in the following financial year.

In order to comply with the provisions in paragraph 28.4, the company should make a provision for a liability in respect of this unpaid holiday entitlement as a current liability at the year-end.

23.3   After recognising a liability, the opposite side of the entry will be to the relevant expense account in the profit and loss account (income statement). However, there may be situations where another Section of FRS 102 might require the cost to be recognised as part of the cost of an asset (such as inventories or property, plant and equipment). If this is the case, the debit side of the entry will go to the relevant asset section in the balance sheet (statement of financial position).

EXAMPLES OF SHORT-TERM EMPLOYEE BENEFITS

23.4   Paragraph 28.4 gives four types of examples relating to short-term employee benefits which are expected to be settled within 12 months from the reporting date:

- wages, salaries and social security contributions;

- paid annual leave and paid sick leave;

- profit-sharing and bonuses; and

- non-monetary benefits (such as medical care, housing, cars and free or subsidised goods or services) for current employees.

Focus

Prior to the issuance of FRS 102, it was relatively uncommon for reporting entities to make accruals for unpaid annual leave and sick leave. In the majority of cases these amounts may be immaterial but, technically, reporting entities were incorrect not to make accruals for such because such short-term employee benefits do meet the definition of a provision at the reporting date in accordance with Section 21, Provisions and Contingencies.

Example 23.1 – Interaction of Section 21, provisions and contingencies

The Bury Corporation has been established for many years and has always paid annual bonuses, based on a pre-determined formula, to its staff and management. The company's year-end is 31 December and, on this date, it recognised a provision for a bonus payable to its staff and management amounting to £30,000 plus £4,140 representing 13.8% employer's social security costs. This amount was incorporated within the financial statements on 12 February. On 4 April, HM Revenue and Customs opened an enquiry into the company's corporation tax return disputing the inclusion of the bonus and relevant social security costs on the grounds that it was paid in the succeeding financial year and therefore should be included in the next year's financial statements and associated tax computation on the grounds that there was no legal obligation on the part of the company to pay the bonus to staff and management.

This example shows where two sections of FRS 102 will interact. Section 21, Provisions and Contingencies can also apply in this situation because, whilst a legal obligation has not arisen to pay the staff and management a bonus, a constructive obligation has arisen because of the bonus scheme in place. It is this expectation that has been created in the minds of the employees that gives rise to an obligating event, therefore a provision in respect of the bonus will be required. Had the Bury Corporation been, say, a new start-up, then it may well be inappropriate to recognise such a provision if the resolution to pay a bonus had been made by the board of directors after the year-end date.

23.5   Profit-sharing arrangements and bonus plans are dealt with in paragraph 28.8 which says that an entity shall recognise the expected cost of profit-sharing and bonus payments only when:

- it has a present legal or *constructive obligation* to make such payments as a result of past events (this means that the entity has no realistic alternative but to make the payments); and

- a reliable estimate of the obligation can be made.

POST-EMPLOYMENT BENEFITS

23.6   There are two specific types of examples relating to post-employment benefits that Section 28 in FRS 102 deals with:

- retirement benefits, such as pensions; and

- other post-employment benefits, such as post-employment life insurance and post-employment medical care.

Where pensions are concerned, there are two specific types of pension plan, both of which vary considerably in terms of how they are accounted for:

- defined contribution pension plans; and

- defined benefit pension plans.

Defined contribution pension plans

23.7   These are the simplest types of pension plans to account for. A defined contribution pension plan is a plan in which the company pays fixed contributions into a pension fund and once these amounts are paid, the reporting entity has no further legal or constructive obligation to pay further benefits, even if the pension fund has insufficient assets available to pay all employee benefits which relate to employee service in the current and previous periods.

Employees will receive post-employment benefits based on the amount of contributions paid by the entity (and in many cases by the employee also), hence the term 'defined contribution' essentially means the amount of post-employment benefits the employee will receive will be defined by the amount of contributions the fund has received in respect of that employee.

Defined benefit pension plans

23.8   These are the most complicated plans to account for. Defined benefit pension plans are also referred to in the UK as 'final salary pension schemes' and are post-employment benefit plans other than defined contribution plans. Under such plans, a reporting entity does have an obligation to pay further contributions if the defined benefit pension plan has insufficient assets available to pay employee benefits relating to employee service in the current and prior periods. As a consequence, actuarial risk (the risk that benefits will cost more or less than expected) and investment risk (the risk that returns on assets set aside to fund the benefits will differ from expectations) are borne, in substance, by the reporting entity.

Example 23.2 – Intervention by the Pensions Regulator

Lockland Chemicals Limited has a defined benefit pension plan in operation for employees and has a year-end of 31 December. On 31 December 2013, the company received a valuation for the purposes of Section 28 showing that its defined benefit pension plan had a deficit amounting to £1.1 million. In 2012, the pension plan had a deficit of £900,000 and the plan's actuary has recommended that the company increases its pension contributions by 20% in an attempt to reduce the deficit. However, the directors have refused.

As actuarial and investment risk are borne by the employer, the company should increase its contributions accordingly. The Pensions Regulator in the UK has the power to mandate the company to increase its contributions if it deems it necessary in order to meet its obligations in law to pay post-employment benefits to employees in the current and previous periods.

Defined benefit plans accounted for as defined contribution plans

23.9   There are occasions when a defined benefit plan requires to be accounted for as a defined contribution plan and this is usually the case with *multi-employer plans* and *state plans*. A multi-employer plan is defined in the Glossary as:

23.10 *Employee benefits*

'Defined contributions plans (other than state plans) or defined benefit plans (other than state plans) that:

(a)   pool the assets contributed by various entities that are not under common control, and

(b)   use those assets to provide benefits to employees of more than one entity, on the basis that contribution and benefit levels are determined without regard to the identity of the entity that employs the employees concerned.'

A state plan is defined in the Glossary as:

'Employee benefit plans established by legislation to cover all entities (or all entities in a particular category, for example a specific industry) and operated by national or local government or by another body (for example an autonomous agency created specifically for this purpose) which is not subject to control or influence by the reporting entity.'

Example 23.3 – Multi-employer pension plan accounted for as a defined contribution plan

The Briary School for Girls has decided to convert to Academy status and 'opt-out' of Local Authority control. The conversion to Academy status was approved and completed in August 2012 and it is required to prepare financial statements to 31 August each year (to coincide with the academic year).

The Academy has two pension plans in operation: the Teachers' Pension Scheme and a Local Government Pension Scheme. The Local Government Pension Scheme is a defined benefit pension scheme and actuarial information is provided to the Academy each year in order that the relevant accounting input and disclosures can be made in the Academy's financial statements.

The Teachers' Pension Scheme is a multi-employer pension scheme. The Academy is unable to identify its share of the underlying assets and liabilities of the scheme and therefore will account for the scheme in accordance with paragraphs 28.13 and 28.13A to FRS 102 (in other words as if it were a defined contribution plan) and make the necessary disclosures required in paragraphs 28.40 and 28.40A).

23.10   Where a reporting entity has a defined benefit plan which is a multi-employer plan that is accounted for as if it were a defined contribution scheme, there may be an agreement between the entity and the multi-employer plan which stipulates how the entity will fund a deficit arising on the pension plan.

Where such an agreement exists, paragraph 28.11A requires that the entity recognises a liability on the balance sheet (statement of financial position) which represents the contributions payable that arise from the agreement and to the extent that they relate to the deficit with the resulting expense being reported in profit or loss for the accounting period.

Focus

In contrast to paragraph 28.11A to FRS 102, reporting entities were not required under FRS 17 *Retirement Benefits* to provide for a liability in respect of contributions payable under such agreements. This paragraph was one of the final amendments made to FRS 102 immediately prior to its final publication.

Insured benefits

23.11   Care must be taken where an entity pays insurance premiums in order to fund a post-employment benefit plan. This is because such plans will only be accounted for as a defined benefit pension plan where there is a legal or constructive obligation either:

- to pay the employee benefits directly when they become due; or

- to pay further amounts if the insurer does not pay all future employee benefits relating to employee service in the current and prior periods.

Example 23.4 – Company paying insurance premiums to fund a pension plan

A company pays insurance premiums to fund a pension plan. The company has no legal or constructive obligation to pay employee benefits directly when they become due, nor do they have a legal or constructive obligation to pay further amounts if the insurer does not pay all future employee benefits that relate to employee service in both the current and previous periods.

In this instance, the 'default' accounting treatment is the same as accounting for a defined contribution pension plan.

Focus

There are various ways in which a constructive obligation could arise where insured benefits are concerned and paragraph 28.12 cites the mechanism by which future premiums are set or through a related party relationship with the insurer.

RECOGNITION AND MEASUREMENT

Defined contribution pension plans

23.12   The recognition and measurement for a defined contribution pension plan is relatively simple. They are merely reported as liabilities after deducting any amounts already paid to the plan. Where contribution payments exceed the contributions due for the accounting period, the excess is recognised as a prepayment.

The corresponding debit (that is not recognised as a prepayment) is recognised in profit or loss provided that another Section of FRS 102 does not require the cost to be recognised as part of the cost of an asset (such as inventories or property, plant and equipment).

Example 23.5 – Recognition of a liability taking into account the time value of money

A company has made contributions into a defined contribution pension plan which are not expected to be settled within 12 months after the end of the company's accounting period in which the employees have rendered the related service.

In this instance, the company will recognise the liability taking into account the time value of money – in other words, it will recognise the *present value* of the contributions payable (having reference to market yields at the reporting date on high quality corporate bonds). The unwinding of the discount will be recognised as a finance cost (interest charge) in profit or loss in the period to which it relates.

Defined benefit pension plans

23.13   Accounting for a defined benefit pension plan is inherently more complicated than a defined contribution plan. Actuarial information will be needed to allow for the accounting input and relevant disclosures to be made in the entity's financial statements. Without this information, the defined benefit pension plan will be impossible to account for.

Paragraph 28.15 to FRS 102 outlines the measurement of the net defined benefit liability. This particular paragraph requires an entity to measure the net defined benefit liability for its obligations under a defined benefit pension plan at the net of the following amounts:

- the present value of its obligations under defined benefit plans (its *defined benefit obligation*) at the reporting date (paragraphs 28.16 and 28.21A to FRS 102 provide guidance for measuring this obligation); *minus*

- the *fair value* at the reporting date of plan assets (if any) out of which the obligations are to be settled. Paragraphs 11.27 to 11.32 to FRS 102 establish requirements for determining the fair values of those plan assets, except that, if the asset is an insurance policy that exactly matches the amount and timing of some or all of the benefits payable under the plan, the fair value of the asset is deemed to be the present value of the related obligation.

Paragraph 28.17 requires the present value of an entity's obligations in point 1 above to be the discounted present value. This particular paragraph requires the entity to discount the future payments to the pension plan by reference to market yields at the reporting date on high quality corporate bonds and this paragraph also requires the currency and term of the corporate bonds or government bonds to be consistent with the currency and estimated period of the future payments.

23.14 As mentioned earlier, in order to account for a defined benefit pension plan, the reporting entity will need to obtain actuarial information in order for this to be undertaken. The defined benefit obligation (together with the related expense) is to be measured using the *projected unit credit method*. The Glossary defines the *projected unit credit method* as follows:

'An actuarial valuation method that sees each period of service as giving rise to an additional unit of benefit entitlement and measures each unit separately to build up the final obligation (sometimes known as the accrued benefit method pro-rated on service or as the benefit/years of service method).'

Example 23.6 – Defined benefit plan based on future salaries payable to employees

A company provides post-employment benefits under a defined benefit pension plan and has a year-end of 31 December. The defined benefits in the pension plan are based on future salaries payable to the employees.

Where defined benefits are based on future salaries, paragraph 28.18 to FRS 102 requires the projected unit credit method to measure its defined benefit obligations on a basis that reflects estimated future salary increases.

Focus

The projected unit credit method also requires an entity to make assumptions (referred to as *actuarial assumptions*) in respect of discount rates, employee turnover, and mortality and (for defined benefit medical plans) medical cost trend rates, in arriving at the defined benefit obligation.

23.15 Unlike in the previous UK GAAP at FRS 17, Section 28 in FRS 102 does not explicitly require a reporting entity to utilise the services of a qualified actuary to arrive at an actuarial valuation for the defined benefit pension plan – however, the reality is that unless the reporting entity has the ability to arrive at its own actuarial valuation for its defined benefit pension plan, it will need to utilise the services of an experienced actuary. Section 28 also does not require a comprehensive actuarial valuation to be undertaken on an annual basis if the principal actuarial assumptions have not changed significantly in the periods between the comprehensive actuarial valuations and where the defined benefit pension obligation can be measured merely by adjusting the prior period measurement to reflect changes in employees and salary levels.

23.16 A summary of the accounting input is shown below:

Profit and loss account (income statement)	*Profit and loss account (income statement) finance costs section*	*Other comprehensive income*
Current service cost	Interest cost; *less*	Differences between actual and expected return on plan assets
Past service cost	Expected return on plan assets	Experience adjustments affecting the plan's liabilities
Gains and losses on curtailments and settlements		Effects of changes in actuarial assumptions

Remeasurement of the net defined benefit liability comprises:

- actuarial gains and losses; and

- return on plan assets, excluding amounts included in net interest on the net defined benefit liability.

Focus

Remeasurement of a plan's net defined benefit liability that is recognised within other comprehensive cannot be reclassified to profit or loss in a subsequent accounting period.

Example 23.7 – Impact of a defined benefit pension plan on the financial statements

Hill Haulage Limited operates a defined benefit pension scheme for its employees and has an accounting year-end date of 31 December each year and is currently preparing financial statements for the year ended 31 December 2013. The actuaries have provided the following information relevant to the defined benefit pension plan:

	31 December 2013	31 December 2012
	£'000	£'000
Plan assets		
Opening plan assets	4,197	4,021
Expected return on plan assets	218	216
Actuarial gain (loss)	230	(321)
Employer contributions	310	458
Employee contributions	31	33
Benefits paid	(141)	(210)
Plan assets at end of period	4,845	4,197
Plan liabilities		
Opening plan liabilities	5,208	4,597
Current service cost	69	67
Past service cost	Nil	Nil
Interest on scheme liabilities	248	259
Actuarial (gain) loss	318	462
Employee contributions	31	33
Benefits paid	(141)	(210)
Plan liabilities at end of period	5,733	5,208

23.16 *Employee benefits*

Impact on profit and loss

The amounts charged to profit or loss in both periods will be as follows:

	31 December 2013	31 December 2012
	£'000	£'000
Current service cost	69	67
Past service cost	0	0
Total operating charge	69	67

Amounts recognised in respect of finance costs in the profit and loss account (income statement) will be as follows:

	31 December 2013	31 December 2012
	£'000	£'000
Expected return on plan assets	218	216
Interest on scheme liabilities	(248)	(259)
Net interest charge	(30)	(43)

Impact on other comprehensive income

Actuarial gains and losses are reported in other comprehensive income (previously referred to as the statement of total recognised gains and losses).

	31 December 2013	31 December 2012
	£'000	£'000
Actuarial gain (loss)	(88)	(783)

Balance sheet position

	31 December 2013	31 December 2012
	£'000	£'000
Value of plan liabilities	5,733	5,208
Value of plan assets	4,845	4,197
Surplus (deficit)	(888)	(1,011)

Focus

Readers familiar with the requirements of the old UK GAAP at FRS 17 *Retirement Benefits* will be familiar with the accounting requirements for the expected return on plan assets and interest cost. However, FRS 102 requirements are essentially based on the revisions to IAS 19 *Employee Benefits* in 2011. Under the revisions, the annual expense for a defined benefit plan includes the net interest expense or income, calculated by applying the discount rate to the net defined benefit asset or liability. This replaces the finance charge and expected return on plan assets, where income is credited with the expected long-term yield on the assets in the fund. This revised treatment may increase the annual benefit expense and could, in turn, have a potential impact on earnings.

INTRODUCTIONS, CHANGES, CURTAILMENTS AND SETTLEMENTS

23.17   For the purposes of Section 28, *curtailments* and *settlements* are not defined in the Glossary to FRS 102, but are events which significantly change the liabilities relating to a defined benefit pension plan and which are not covered by normal actuarial assumptions. In the previous UK GAAP, FRS 17 defined a *curtailment* as 'an irrevocable action that relieve the employer (or the defined benefit scheme) of the primary responsibility for a pension obligation and eliminates significant risks relating to the obligation and the assets used to effect the settlement'. Settlements essentially eliminate a portion of the plan's liabilities by transferring scheme assets, such as when a subsidiary is sold.

A *curtailment* was defined in FRS 17 as 'an event that reduces the expected years of future service of present employees or reduces for a number of employees the actual of defined benefits for some or all of their future service'. As a result, a curtailment reduces the obligations that relate to future service and usually arises because of a significant reduction in the number of employees (eg due to redundancy through termination of an operation). A curtailment could also arise by way of a change to the plan's rules.

Example 23.8 – Changes in the plan's terms

A company operates a defined benefit pension plan that had a deficit amounting to £2,500,000 as at 31 October 2012. On 31 October 2013 (the company's year-end date) the terms of the scheme have changed which has had an effect on the benefits in the current period. The value of the deficit following the change is £3,000,000 but would have been £3,015,000 (as per the actuarial valuation) had the change not been implemented. The financial controller has included the defined benefit pension plan in the year-end financial statements at the actuarial valuation of £3,015,000.

Paragraph 28.21 says that when a defined benefit plan is introduced, or the benefits have changed in the current period (as in the example above), the company must increase, or decrease, its net defined benefit liability to reflect the change, and shall recognise the increase (decrease) as an expense (income) in measuring profit or loss in the current reporting period. The company will therefore reduce its net defined benefit liability from £3,015,000 to £300,000,000 and recognise the £15,000 credit in profit or loss.

Example 23.9 – Transfer of obligations

A company has a year-end of 30 November 2013 and is preparing its financial statements for the year then ended. The net defined pension plan liability as at 30 November 2012 was £4 million. During the year to 30 November 2013, the company successfully transferred all obligations to an insurance company who agreed to take over the deficit in exchange for a cash sum from the company.

This transfer would represent a settlement and the company would extinguish its defined benefit pension liability and recognise the resulting gain in profit or loss in the current period. Had the value of the pension scheme been a surplus (ie plan assets were in excess of plan obligations), the company would instead recognise a loss in the current period.

DEFINED BENEFIT PENSION PLAN ASSETS

23.18   The reality is that most defined benefit pension plans are in deficit and have been for some time, and are likely to remain in deficit for some time into the future. However, there are some (rare) occasions when a defined benefit pension plan is actually in surplus (in other words, the defined benefit plan's assets are in excess of its liabilities). The primary objective of financial reporting where assets are concerned is that they should not be carried in the balance sheet (statement of financial position) at any more than their *recoverable* amount. For the purposes of a defined benefit pension plan, any surplus (asset) can only be recognised to the extent that the entity is expected to be able to recover the asset, either by way of reduced contributions in the future or through refunds from the plan.

REIMBURSEMENTS

23.19   Any reimbursement in respect of a defined benefit pension plan should be recognised as a separate asset in the balance sheet (statement of financial position) if it is virtually certain that another party will reimburse some, or all, of the expenditure required to settle a defined benefit obligation. In addition, the reporting entity must also treat that asset in the same way as plan assets.

OTHER LONG-TERM EMPLOYEE BENEFITS

23.20   In addition to defined benefit pension plans, Section 28 outlines five additional examples of other long-term employee benefits that may not be expected to be settled in full within 12 months after the end of the accounting period. These are:

- long-term paid absences such as long-service or sabbatical leave;
- other long-service benefits;
- long-term disability benefits;
- profit-sharing and bonuses; and
- deferred remuneration.

Paragraph 28.30 to FRS 102 gives a formula for measuring these long-term employee benefits in the current accounting period which is as follows:

- present value of the benefit obligation at the reporting date (calculated using a discount rate based on market yields at the reporting date on high quality corporate bonds) *less*
- the fair value at the reporting date of plan assets (if any) out of which the obligations are to be settled directly.

Changes in liabilities for long-term employee benefits will be recognised within profit or loss unless another Section in FRS 102 requires such changes to be recognised in the cost of an asset (such as property, plant and equipment or inventories).

TERMINATION BENEFITS

23.21   When a company decides to terminate the employment of a staff member (whether it be a member of staff, management or a director), legislation in the UK and Republic of Ireland protects the employee against any disadvantage the employee may suffer as a result of their termination. Invariably, contracts of employment will also make provision for such termination benefits. Paragraph

28.32 to FRS 102 recognises that such termination benefits do not provide a reporting entity with future economic benefits (ie an asset) and therefore all benefits that are representative of termination benefits are recognised in profit or loss immediately as they are incurred.

Example 23.10 – Termination of staff in a defined benefit plan

A company operates in the construction industry and over the last couple of years has witnessed a sharp decline in activity due to the economic recession. The company also operates a defined benefit pension plan which it has operated for several years.

The company's management accounts show that it is going to sustain a heavy loss for the year ended 31 January 2014 with the cash flow forecast showing negative cash outflow for the next 12 months. The directors have instigated a recovery plan but this involves making around 70 of the staff redundant. Before making compulsory redundancies, the company has decided to offer a package to 70 employees to encourage voluntary redundancies and has set these funds aside in order to meet the full cost of all 70 employees.

On 1 December 2013, the company announced its redundancy programme to all employees and confirmed this announcement in writing. It also communicated its package available to employees to encourage voluntary redundancy. The financial controller is unsure whether or not to recognise the costs of the termination benefits as a liability in the financial statements to 31 January 2014.

Paragraph 28.34 says that an entity shall recognise termination benefits as a liability and as an expense only when the entity is demonstrably committed either:

- to terminate the employment of an employee or group of employees before the normal retirement date; or

- to provide termination benefits as a result of an offer made in order to encourage voluntary redundancy.

As the company has committed itself to the redundancy programme (by way of announcing to the staff members and confirming details of the package available to encourage voluntary redundancy), the financial controller should make provision in the financial statements by way of a liability and an associated expense for the costs of the termination. For clarity, paragraph 28.35 to FRS 102 says:

'An entity is demonstrably committed to a termination only when the entity has a detailed formal plan for the termination and is without realistic possibility of withdrawal from the plan.'

In addition, the company may also have to account for a curtailment of retirement benefits, or other employee benefits in accordance with paragraph 28.33.

Termination benefits: measurement in the financial statements

23.22   When it is evident that termination benefits meet the recognition criteria in the financial statements, the company is required to measure the value of the termination benefits using a 'best estimate' of the expenditure required in order to settle the obligation at the reporting date. In the example above, where the company had made an offer to encourage voluntary redundancy, the measurement of retirement benefits would be based on the number of employees that are expected to take up the offer.

Focus

In situations where termination benefits will fall due after more than 12 months from the reporting date, the termination benefits will be measured at the present value using a discount rate that is based on market yields on high quality corporate bonds.

GROUP PLANS

23.23   There may be situations when a group structure may participate in a defined benefit pension plan that shares risks between entities that are under common control. Careful scrutiny of the contractual agreement relating to this plan is needed.

Example 23.11 – Group companies: Contractual agreement in place

A group of companies are under common control and participate in a defined benefit pension plan for which there is a contractual agreement in place. The terms of the agreement provide for a method of charging the net defined benefit cost, measured in accordance with Section 28 in FRS 102, to each individual subsidiary company.

In this scenario, as there is a contractual agreement in place, each individual subsidiary company shall, in its own individual financial statements, recognise the net defined benefit cost of a defined benefit plan.

Example 23.12 – Group companies: No contractual agreement in place

A group of companies are under common control and participate in a defined benefit pension plan for which there is no contractual agreement in place.

In this instance, the net defined benefit cost of the defined benefit pension plan shall be recognised in the individual financial statements of the group entity that is legally responsible for the plan. The other members of the group shall, in their individual financial statements, recognise a cost which is equal to their contribution payable for the period.

Focus

For group entities, it is worthwhile considering whether the group would want to introduce contractual agreements or a stated policy relating to the defined benefit pension plan's charge before the transition date. A key point to consider will be the distributable reserves in each member of the group.

DISCLOSURES

23.24   Paragraphs 28.39 to 28.44 deal with the disclosures issues relating to employee benefits which are as follows:

Defined contribution plans

23.25   An entity shall disclose the amount recognised in profit or loss as an expense for defined contribution plans.

If an entity treats a defined benefit multi-employer plan as a defined contribution plan because sufficient information is not available to use defined benefit accounting (see paragraph 28.11 to FRS 102), it shall:

- disclose the fact that it is a defined benefit plan and the reason why it is being accounted for as a defined contribution plan, along with any available information about the plan's surplus or deficit and the implications, if any, for the entity;

- include a description of the extent to which the entity can be liable to the plan for other entities' obligations under the terms and conditions of the multi-employer plan; and

- disclose how any liability recognised in accordance with paragraph 28.11A to FRS 102 has been determined.

Defined benefit plans

23.26   The following information is to be disclosed about defined benefit plans (except for any defined multi-employer benefit plans that are accounted for as a defined contribution plan for which the disclosures under defined contributions plans above apply). If an entity has more than one defined benefit plan, these disclosures may be made in aggregate, separately for each plan, or in such groupings as are considered to be the most useful:

- A general description of the type of plan, including *funding* policy.

- The date of the most recent comprehensive actuarial valuation and, if it was not as of the reporting date, a description of the adjustments that were made to measure the defined benefit obligation at the reporting date.

- A reconciliation of opening and closing balances for each of the following:*

  o   the defined benefit obligation;

  o   the fair value of plan assets; and

  o   any reimbursement right recognised as an asset.

- Each of the reconciliations above shall show each of the following, if applicable:*

  o   the change in the defined benefit liability arising from employee service rendered during the reporting period in profit or loss;

  o   interest income or expense;

  o   remeasurement of the defined benefit liability, showing separately actuarial gains and losses and the return on plan assets less amounts included in interest income or expense; and

  o   plan introductions, changes, curtailments and settlements.

- The total cost relating to defined benefit plans for the period, disclosing separately the amounts:

  o   recognised in profit or loss as an expense; and

  o   included in the cost of an asset.

- For each major class of plan assets, which shall include, but is not limited to, equity instruments, debt instruments, property, and all other assets, the percentage or amount that each major class constitutes of the fair value of the total plan assets at the reporting date.

- The amounts included in the fair value of plan assets for:

  o   each class of the entity's own *financial instruments*; and

  o   any property occupied by, or other assets used by, the entity.

- The return on plan assets.

- The principal actuarial assumptions used, including, when applicable:

  o   the discount rates;

  o   the expected rates of salary increases;

  o   medical cost trend rates; and

  o   any other *material* actuarial assumptions used.

* *Reconciliations need not be presented for prior periods.*

Focus

FRS 102 does not include the same requirement to present the surplus or deficit in a defined benefit pension plan on the face of the balance sheet after other net assets as the previous FRS 17 did. A deficit in a defined benefit pension plan can therefore be included within 'provisions' and a surplus could go into 'other assets'.

In addition, FRS 17 required entities to state the defined benefit pension plan net of related deferred tax. There is no requirement to do this in FRS 102 and therefore deferred tax in relation to a defined benefit pension plan can be included within other deferred tax.

23.27   If an entity participates in a defined benefit plan that shares risks between entities under common control it shall disclose the following:

- The contractual agreement or stated policy for charging the cost of a defined benefit plan or the fact that there is no policy.

- The policy for determining the contributions to be paid by the entity.

- If the entity accounts for an allocation of the net defined benefit cost, all the information required in the disclosure requirements above for the defined benefit pension plan.

- If the entity accounts for the contributions payable for the period, the following must be disclosed:

○   a general description of the type of plan, including *funding* policy;

○   the date of the most recent comprehensive actuarial valuation and, if it was not as of the reporting date, a description of the adjustments that were made to measure the defined benefit obligation at the reporting date;

○   for each major class of plan assets, which shall include, but is not limited to, equity instruments, debt instruments, property, and all other assets, the percentage or amount that each major class constitutes of the fair value of the total plan assets at the reporting date; and

○   the amounts included in the fair value of plan assets for:

–   each class of the entity's own *financial instruments*; and

–   any property occupied by, or other assets used by, the entity.

This information can be disclosed by cross-reference to disclosures in another group entity's *financial statements* if:

● that group entity's financial statements separately identify and disclose the information required about the plan; and

● that group entity's financial statements are available to users of the financial statements on the same terms as the financial statements of the entity and at the same time as, or earlier than, the financial statements of the entity.

Long-term benefits

23.28   For each category of other long-term benefits that an entity provides to its employees, the entity shall disclose the nature of the benefit, the amount of its obligation and the extent of funding at the reporting date.

Termination benefits

23.29   For each category of termination benefits that an entity provides to its employees, the entity shall disclose the nature of the benefit, its *accounting policy*, and the amount of its obligation and the extent of funding at the reporting date.

When there is uncertainty about the number of employee who will accept an offer of termination benefits, a *contingent liability* exists. Section 21, Provisions and Contingencies requires an entity to disclose information about its contingent liabilities unless the possibility of an outflow in settlement is remote.

SUMMARY – WHAT IS DIFFERENT FROM THE PREVIOUS UK GAAP?

- There is a requirement in FRS 102 for reporting entities to make accruals for unpaid annual leave and sick leave. Previous UK GAAP did not make an explicit requirement for these sorts of accruals, however, FRS 12 at paragraph 11(b) did cite accrued holiday pay as an example of a liability that had been received but not yet paid.

- Under FRS 17, reporting entities that had an agreement with a multi-employer pension plan to fund a deficit arising on a pension plan did not need to provide for a liability in respect of the contributions payable under such an agreement. FRS 102 makes provision for this requirement at paragraph 28.11A.

- FRS 102 does not include the requirement to present the surplus or deficit in a defined benefit pension plan on the face of the balance sheet after other net assets as the previous FRS 17 did. A deficit in a defined benefit pension plan can therefore be included within 'provisions' and a surplus could go into 'other assets'.

- FRS 17 required entities to disclose the defined benefit pension plan net of the related deferred tax. There is no requirement to do this in FRS 102, therefore deferred tax in respect of a defined benefit pension plan can be included within other deferred tax amounts.

- With regards to the accounting requirements for the expected return on plan assets and the interest cost, FRS 102 requirements are based on the revisions made to IAS 19 in 2011. Under these revisions, the annual expense for a defined benefit plan includes the net interest expense or income which is arrived at by applying the discount rate to the net defined benefit asset or liability. This revised treatment may increase the annual benefit expense and could, in turn, have a potential impact on earnings.

- There is no distinction in FRS 17 between a group plan and other multi-employer plans.

Chapter 24

Grants

SIGNPOSTS

- Grants (which also include non-monetary grants) are recognised in the financial statements when two conditions have been satisfied (see **24.3**).

- There are two models in FRS 102 under which grants are recognised: the performance model or the accrual model (this will generally reflect the same treatment as under the previous SSAP 4 *Accounting for Government Grants* (see **24.4** and **24.5**).

- Grants must be recognised in the entity's financial statements at the fair value of the asset received or receivable (see **24.3**).

- There are restrictions on the way in which grants related to items of fixed assets can be treated in both FRS 102 and under the *Companies Act 2006* (see **24.5**).

- Various disclosure requirements exist where grants are concerned, together with additional disclosure requirements where a reporting entity receives government assistance (see **24.6**).

INTRODUCTION

24.1   Many companies receive government grants in some form or another (eg companies can receive grants for setting up operations in a deprived area of the country to encourage employment opportunities). New start-up companies can receive grants to assist them with the initial day-to-day running expenses or to fund certain items of fixed assets.

The way in which grants are accounted for has become the subject of some debate. The Financial Reporting Council has intimated that this area will be revisited in the future with a view to overhauling the ways in which grants are accounted for within a reporting entity's financial statements (but at the time of writing there was no indication as to when this was going to happen).

Section 24 of FRS 102 deals specifically with government grants and the disclosure of government assistance provided to an entity. However, it does not deal with government assistance that is provided to an entity in the form of benefits which are available in computing taxable profit or loss, or are determined or limited on the basis of income tax liability. Paragraph 24.3 to FRS 102 gives various examples of such assistance including income tax holidays, investment tax credits, accelerated depreciation allowances and reduced income tax rates. Section 29 to FRS 102 deals with issues relating to income tax.

DEFINITIONS

24.2   Paragraph 24.1 defines a government grant as 'assistance by government in the form of a transfer of resources to an entity in return for past or future compliance with specified conditions relating to the operating activities of the entity'.

Paragraph 24.7 defines government assistance as 'action by government designed to provide an economic benefit specific to an entity or range of entities qualifying under specified criteria'. The paragraph then goes on to give some examples of government assistance including free technical or marketing advice, provision of guarantees and loans at nil or low interest rates.

RECOGNITION AND MEASUREMENT IN THE FINANCIAL STATEMENTS

24.3   There are two conditions that must be met before a grant (including a non-monetary grant) can be recognised in an entity's financial statements. There must be reasonable assurance that:

- the entity will comply with the conditions attaching to the grant; and
- the grants will be received.

FRS 102 does not define *reasonable assurance* and this raises the question as to whether it means the same as *probable*. In the authors' opinion, this is taken to mean that it is more likely than not that the above conditions will be met and one would not expect a reporting entity to recognise government grants in the financial statements until it was at least probable that the entity would comply with the conditions attached to them.

Reporting entities must measure grants at the fair value of the asset received or receivable in order to comply with paragraph 24.5 of FRS 102. In addition, if any of the grant becomes repayable it must be recognised as a liability at the point in time the repayments meets the definition of a liability.

Once those conditions have been met, the next consideration is the method by which the grants will be recognised in the financial statements. Section 24 contains two possible models:

● the performance model; or

● the accrual model.

Note: this is an accounting policy choice which should be applied consistently on a class-by-class basis in accordance with FRS 102, paragraph 24.40.

The performance model

24.4 The performance model is a model which imposes three specific methods of recognising grants within the entity's financial statements:

● A grant that does not impose specified future performance-related conditions on the recipient is recognised in income when the grant proceeds are receivable.

● A grant that imposes specified future performance conditions on the recipient is recognised in income only when the performance-related conditions are met.

● Grants received before the revenue recognition criteria are satisfied are recognised as a liability.

Example 24.1 – Recognition of a grant

A company has decided to set up operations in a UK city where unemployment is significantly higher than other areas in the UK. They have purchased a commercial building to house their operations for a purchase price of £400,000. The government has agreed to provide a grant to the company amounting to £100,000 which will be used purely for the purchase of the building. No other performance conditions are contained in the grant terms.

The company will recognise the £100,000 grant in income on receipt because the conditions of the grant (the purchase of the building) have been fulfilled. Under the previous accounting standard governing grants, SSAP 4 *Accounting for Government Grants*, the grant would have been deferred and released to the profit and loss account over the life of the asset to which it relates (in other words to match the grant income against the depreciation charge). In this scenario, the company is using the performance model and there are no other conditions requiring deferral of the grant.

In applying the performance model, a reporting entity must have due regard to the terms and conditions attached to the grant as this would ordinarily dictate the required accounting treatment. The fact that the building may be depreciated over several years (eg over a 50-year straight-line basis) thus recognition of the grant in the profit and loss account over this 50-year period would not necessarily be the case under the performance model.

24.5 *Grants*

The accrual model

24.5 When a reporting entity adopts the use of the accrual model, paragraph 24.5C requires management to distinguish between a revenue grant and a grant relating to assets. This follows the similar treatment under the previous SSAP 4.

There are four methods of accounting for grants under the accrual model depending on whether they are revenue-based grants or capital-based grants:

- Grants relating to revenue shall be recognised in income on a systematic basis over the periods in which the entity recognises the related costs for which the grant is intended to compensate.

- A grant that becomes receivable as compensation for expenses or losses already incurred or for the purpose of giving immediate financial support to the entity with no future related costs shall be recognised in income in the period in which it becomes receivable.

- Grants relating to assets shall be recognised in income on a systematic basis over the expected useful life of the asset.

- Where part of a grant relating to an asset is deferred it shall be recognised as deferred income and not deducted from the carrying value of the asset.

Example 24.2 – Matching a grant against previously recognised costs

A newly formed company has incurred costs of £100,000, all of which have been correctly treated as profit and loss account items during the accounting period ended 31 August 2013. It has been successful in applying for a government grant, which it duly received on 20 July 2013 for £35,000. There are no additional future related costs attached to the grant.

In this scenario, the company will recognise the grant in profit or loss during the period to 31 August 2013, by:

Debit bank	£10,000
Credit grants received	£10,000

This being the grant received for reimbursement of expenses previously incurred.

Example 24.3 – Offsetting a grant against the cost of an asset

Company A Limited has decided to replace a large vessel used in the production of raw materials. The vessel has a purchase price (including freight costs and installation costs) of £175,000 (funded out of cash). The machine is expected to last for ten years with nil residual value at the end of its useful economic life. The company's year-end is 30 September 2013 and the machine was fully installed on 1 September 2013 and is now in operation. The company's accounting policy is to charge a full year's depreciation in the year of acquisition of all fixed assets, and nil depreciation in the year of disposal. The company received a government grant amounting to £35,000 for the purpose of purchasing this machine. This grant has been recorded in the books of Company A Ltd as follows:

Debit bank	£35,000
Credit plant and machinery additions	£35,000

The first issue relates to the initial accounting treatment of the grant – being the offset of the grant against the cost of the machine. This would be in contravention of paragraph 2.52 of FRS 102 which specifically prohibits the offsetting of assets and liabilities, or income and expenses, unless required or permitted by the FRS. It is not possible to offset the grant against the cost of an asset under FRS 102 (and this is also prohibited under the *Companies Act 2006*). The accounting treatment should be as follows:

DR plant and machinery additions	£175,000
CR cash at bank	£175,000

This being the initial recognition of the new machine.

DR cash at bank	£35,000
CR deferred income	£35,000

This being the initial recognition of the government grant.

DR depreciation charge P&L account	£17,500
CR plant and machinery depreciation	£17,500

This being the depreciation charge for the year (£175,000 × 1/10).

DR deferred income	£3,500
CR grant received	£3,500

This being one-tenth of grant received.

The above treatment is the same as that which originally occurred under the previous SSAP 4 guidelines. The remaining deferred income of £31,500 (£35,000 less £3,500) would be split between the portion that falls due within one year from the balance sheet date and the portion that would fall due after more than one year from the balance sheet date.

Disclosure requirements

24.6   Paragraphs 24.6 and 24.7 outline the various disclosure requirements that entities which have received government grants, or have been provided with government assistance, should disclose within their financial statements. In respect of government grants, an entity should make the following disclosures:

- the accounting policy adopted for grants in accordance with paragraph 24.4 to Section 24;

- the nature and amounts of grants recognised within the financial statements;

- unfulfilled conditions and other contingencies attaching to grants that have not been recognised in income; and

- an indication of other forms of government assistance from which the entity has directly benefited.

Paragraph 24.2 above offers the definition of *government assistance* which will assist preparers to comply with the requirements of the disclosure at point 4 above.

Focus

SSAP 4 permitted the netting off of a grant against the cost of an asset. However, companies and Limited Liability Partnerships are prevented from doing so by legislation. However, for some other entities (eg public benefit entities) who report under FRS 102, there will now be a change in accounting practice as a result of FRS 102's explicit prohibition in netting grants off against the cost of an asset.

SUMMARY – WHAT IS DIFFERENT FROM THE PREVIOUS UK GAAP?

FRS 102 introduces the 'performance' model which was not recognised in SSAP 4.

Chapter 25

Taxation

SIGNPOSTS

- Section 29 to FRS 102 covers the issue of income tax and the scope of this is wide, including all domestic and foreign taxes which are based on a reporting entity's taxable profits (see **25.1**).

- Companies are required to account for both current tax (based on the amount of tax payable or refundable in respect of the taxable profit (loss) for the current periods) and deferred tax which relates to the future tax consequences of transactions and other events that have been recognised within the financial statements (see **25.2**).

- Current tax is much easier to deal with than deferred tax and once the company's liability to corporation tax has been calculated the figure can be incorporated within the financial statements by debiting (crediting) tax expense in the profit and loss account (income statement) and crediting (debiting) income tax liability in the balance sheet (statement of financial position) (see **25.3**).

- In the vast majority of cases, a company's taxable profit will be different than the profit reported in the financial statements (accounting profit) (see **25.4**).

- Deferred taxation relates to past transactions and events which will only have a future consequence for the purposes of tax if they can be classified as timing differences that have originated, but not reversed, by the balance sheet date (see **25.5**).

- Timing differences are said to originate when a transaction is reflected in the financial statements but not yet in the tax computation or vice versa (see **25.6**).

- Companies in the UK and Republic of Ireland reporting under FRS 102 are required to calculate deferred tax using the timing difference plus approach (see **25.7**).

- This approach gives rise to three additional instances where deferred tax must be considered (that the previous FRS 19 *Deferred Tax* standard did not require) (see **25.8**).

25.1 *Taxation*

- Deferred tax is never provided on 'permanent' differences (see **25.10**).

- The timing difference plus approach uses the income statement liability method to recognise liabilities for tax payable in the future or tax assets that are recoverable in the future (see **25.11**).

- A company which purchases assets that are subjected to grants will also need to consider deferred tax issues (see **25.12**).

- Grants cannot be deducted from the cost of an asset due to restrictions imposed in the *Companies Act 2006* (see **25.13**).

- Assets subjected to the revaluation model (including investment properties) will also trigger deferred tax considerations as well as assets acquired in business combinations (see **25.14** and **25.15**).

- All companies in a group structure must follow uniform accounting policies when preparing consolidated financial statements. In many cases this will trigger various adjustments at consolidation level which, in turn, will also trigger deferred tax considerations (see **25.16**).

- Leasing transactions also fall under the scope of deferred tax considerations (see **25.17**).

- HMRC may stipulate that capital allowances relating to assets acquired in a finance lease are to be claimed by the lessor (not the lessee) and this will have deferred tax considerations attached (see **25.18** and **25.19**).

- Deferred tax assets are not generally as common as deferred tax liabilities but can arise, although extreme care should be taken in appropriately recognising deferred tax assets (see **25.20**).

- Where a company operates a defined benefit pension scheme tax relief will generally only be available on contributions paid, therefore timing differences will arise between the charges in the profit and loss account (income statement) and the tax relief granted by HMRC (see **25.21** and **25.22**).

- Companies that operate share-based payment arrangements will need to consider deferred tax issues carefully because HMRC will only grant tax relief on the intrinsic value of the shares at the exercise date (see **25.23**).

INTRODUCTION

25.1 This chapter deals with the issues surrounding taxation. Unlike the previous UK GAAP, FRS 102 *The Financial Reporting Standard applicable in the United Kingdom and Republic of Ireland* brings together issues relating to current taxation and deferred taxation into one Section (as opposed to the two standards that the old UK GAAP used to have: namely FRS 16 *Current Tax* and FRS 19 *Deferred Tax*) which is Section 29, Income Tax. Section 29 is a relatively short section (spanning just over four pages in total), however the concepts that it deals with in relation to taxes can be extremely complex. Section 29 also brings in the issues relating to Value Added Tax (VAT) which, again, was dealt with in a very old standard in the previous UK GAAP, namely SSAP 5 *Accounting for Value Added Tax*.

Section 29 is called 'Income Tax'. Its scope is wide and, for the purpose of this FRS, income tax covers all domestic and foreign taxes which are based on an entity's *taxable profit*. The Glossary defines *taxable profit (tax loss)* as:

> 'The profit (loss) for a *reporting period* upon which income taxes are payable or recoverable, determined in accordance with the rules established by the taxation authorities. Taxable profit equals taxable income less amounts deductible from taxable income.'

As well as dealing with domestic and foreign taxes based on taxable profit or loss, the Section also includes taxes such as withholding taxes payable by a subsidiary, associate or joint venture on distributions to the reporting entity.

25.2 Accounting for income taxes is a twofold exercise; reporting entities are required to account for *current tax* which is the amount of income tax payable (refundable) in respect of the taxable profit (tax loss) for the current period or past reporting periods (in the UK such taxes usually represent *corporation tax*). In addition, Section 29 requires a reporting entity to recognise the future tax consequences of transactions and other events that have been recognised within the financial statements, referred to as *deferred tax*.

Focus

Deferred tax is the most complex accounting concept where income taxes are concerned and there are some notable additions to the requirements of deferred tax in FRS 102 as opposed to the previous regime in FRS 19 which are discussed later in this chapter.

CURRENT TAX

25.3   Current tax is, by far, the most straightforward aspect of Section 29 in FRS 102 and relates to the income tax charge (or credit) and the associated liability or asset depending on whether the company has a liability to income tax (as defined) based on taxable profit or is due a refund from HM Revenue and Customs (HMRC) because of taxable losses that have, perhaps, been carried back and offset against the previous year's taxable profit.

Paragraph 29.3 to Section 29 in FRS 102 requires a reporting entity to recognise a current tax liability for tax payable on taxable profit for the current and past periods. This will, in almost all cases, be based on the company's taxable profit for the financial year which is often not the same amount as accounting profit. This is because of items that are recognised within the entity's financial statements but which are not recognised for taxation purposes.

Example 25.1 – Calculation of taxable profit

Weaver's Windows Limited (Weaver) is a manufacturer of double-glazed products (such as windows and doors). As well as the manufacturing process, Weaver also installs the products to domestic and commercial buildings. The company has been established for several years and is considered one of the leading double-glazing window companies in the United Kingdom and Republic of Ireland.

The company's year-end is 31 March 2014 and the draft financial statements have been finalised prior to the audit. The company pays tax at the main rate of corporation tax which is 23%. Details of the information contained in the company's financial statements are shown below:

	£
Profit before taxation	2,175,000
Items making up the above profit:	
Allowable staff entertaining expenditure	8,000
Customer entertaining	23,500
Wine given to major customers at Christmas	1,700
Fine for illegal dumping of waste	11,000
Depreciation charges	230,000
Loss on sale of a motor vehicle	1,675
General bad debt provision movement	65,400

On 6 June 2013, the company spent £20,000 on a new item of plant that qualifies for 100% First Year Allowances from HMRC in accordance with the *Capital Allowances Act 2001, section 45A* (ie energy-saving plant or machinery). Weaver also had brought forward capital allowances amounting to £82,250 which are being written down at a rate of 18%. The vehicle (a low-emission car) which was sold at a loss of £1,675 was sold for sales proceeds of £6,000.

Here is how the company's *taxable* profit will be calculated:

	Note	£	£
Profit before tax			2,175,000
Addback:			
Depreciation charges	1	230,000	
Loss on disposal of motor vehicle	2	1,675	
Customer entertaining	3	23,500	
Christmas gifts	4	1,700	
Fine for dumping of waste	5	11,000	
General bad debt provision	6	65,400	
			333,275
			2,508,275
Less:			
Capital allowances	7		(33,725)
Profit chargeable to corporation tax (taxable profit)			2,474,550

Note 1

Depreciation is not allowable for the purposes of tax but is required to be charged under Companies Act 2006 and UK GAAP. HMRC will grant their own version of depreciation instead which are 'capital allowances' (often referred to as 'tax allowable depreciation').

Note 2

The loss on disposal of the motor vehicle is also added back for tax purposes as the sales proceeds received on the vehicle will form part of the capital allowances computation (see note 7).

Note 3

Customer entertaining is not allowable for tax purposes (although certain staff entertaining is allowable).

Note 4

The Christmas gifts to customers including wine and such gifts (including tobacco) are not allowable for tax purposes.

Note 5

Fines for illegal acts are not permissible for the purposes of tax.

Note 6

General bad trade debt provisions (ie a blanket percentage of total trade debtors) are not permissible for tax purposes but *specific* bad debt provisions (ie those which can be attributed to specific customers) are generally allowable.

Note 7

Capital allowances computation:

Written down value b/f	Capital additions	Written down disposals	Allowances	Value c/f
£82,250	£20,000	(£6,000)	(£33,725)*	£62,525

*(£82,250 – £6,000) × 18% = £13,725

£20,000 × 100% FYA = £20,000

£33,725

25.4   As illustrated above, a company's *taxable* profit may be higher or lower than *accounting* profit because of disparities between UK GAAP and tax legislation and vice versa.

Assuming that the company in the above example pays tax at the rate of 23%, the tax liability would be £569,147 (£2,474,550 × 23%) and the journals to get the corporation tax liability into the books of the company would be:

DR corporation tax charge (profit and loss)	£569,147
CR corporation tax liability (current liability)	£569,147

DEFERRED TAXATION

25.5   Deferred taxation has long since been a topical issue within the accountancy profession. The objectives of deferred taxation are essentially twofold:

- to ensure that the future tax consequences of past transactions and events are recognised as assets or liabilities within a reporting entity's financial statements; and

- to disclose any additional special circumstance that may have an effect on future tax charges.

The overarching principle relating to deferred tax is that past transactions and events will only have a future consequence for the purposes of tax if they can be classified as timing differences that have originated, but not reversed, at the balance sheet date. The premise here is that timing differences will arise in one period and reverse in another period and hence the tax that is charged in the later period will be affected by transactions or events that have arisen in the previous period. Paragraph 29.6 to FRS 102 defines a timing difference as follows:

'Timing differences are differences between taxable profits and *total comprehensive income* as stated in the financial statements that arise from the inclusion of *income* and *expenses* in tax assessments in periods different from those in which they are recognised in the financial statements.'

Example 25.2 – Timing difference

A company purchases an item of machinery for use in its production line for £10,000. This item of machinery qualifies for HMRC's *Annual Investment Allowance* whereby the company can write off the entire cost of the new machine, for the purposes of tax, by way of enhanced capital allowances. The company's accounting policy in respect of the machine is to charge a full year's depreciation in the year of acquisition with no depreciation charge in the year of disposal. The directors have assessed the machine to have a useful economic life of five years with zero residual value at the end of this economic life.

Financial statement extracts for the year-end 31 December 2013 will show the following in relation to the new machine:

	£
Cost	10,000
Depreciation charge (£10,000/5 years)	(2,000)
Net book value	8,000

> The directors have taken advantage of HMRC's *Annual Investment Allowance* and the same machine will have a tax written down (tax base) value at the year-end 31 December 2013 of zero. A disparity arises between the net book value per the financial statements and the tax base of the same machine amounting to £8,000. This difference will trigger a deferred tax liability. Assuming the company pays tax at the rate of 20% the deferred tax liability will be £1,600.

25.6   The deferred tax liability in the example above arises because there will be a future tax consequence for the company. The company has made a cash flow saving in the year of acquisition by claiming HMRC's *Annual Investment Allowance* – this allowance will not be available in the next accounting period and therefore the tax liability will essentially be higher.

Timing differences are said to originate when a transaction is first reflected in the financial statements, but not yet in the tax computation, or vice versa. Timing differences subsequently reverse when over time the transaction is reflected in the financial statements or in the tax computation either wholly, or in part.

Focus

The theory so far will be familiar with those operating under old UK GAAP, however FRS 102 brings with it some additional deferred tax requirements that need consideration.

TIMING DIFFERENCE PLUS

25.7   Section 29 requires a reporting entity to calculate deferred tax under the timing difference plus approach. The intention by the Financial Reporting Council (FRC) was to have a deferred tax methodology similar to the international equivalent, IAS 12 *Income Taxes*. The notable difference between Section 29 and IAS 12 is the fact that IAS 12 uses a 'temporary difference' approach rather than a timing difference approach. As a result, IAS 12 is more focused on the balance sheet and the values at which assets and liabilities are crystallised rather than the timing difference approach which is focussed on the inclusion of income and expenditure in the profit and loss account (income statement).

In order to bridge the gap between Section 29 and IAS 12, the FRC introduced the timing difference plus approach. The plus part builds on the existing timing difference approach that many accountants and tax advisers are familiar with and also has the objective that the calculation of deferred tax would be the same in almost all cases (except in rare circumstances) as if the deferred tax had been calculated under the temporary difference approach, essentially bringing the method of calculating deferred tax in the UK and Republic of Ireland more in line with the international methods.

25.8 There are three additional considerations for reporting entities where deferred tax is concerned and the timing difference plus approach that were not considered in the previous UK GAAP. Reporting entities are required to calculate deferred tax provisions in respect of:

• non-monetary assets that have been subjected to the revaluation model (or carried at fair value at each reporting date);

• fair values on business combinations; and

• unremitted earnings on overseas subsidiaries or associates.

Focus

Care will be needed in the detailed application of Section 29 to ensure that these additional requirements are dealt with appropriately.

PERMANENT AND TIMING DIFFERENCES

25.9 A company's 'profit' for the purposes of accounting and tax are often different and these differences can be analysed into two categories: permanent differences and timing differences. The term 'permanent difference' means that certain types of income in the financial statements are not taxable and certain types of expenditure are not tax deductible. Timing differences, however, arise from items that are either taxable or tax deductible but in periods different from those in which they are dealt with in the financial statements.

There may be occasions when timing differences arise and then reverse but are never actually reflected in the tax computation (eg a provision for bad debts could be included in the financial statements in one year and then written back in the next as the provision has been deemed unnecessary). Other examples of timing differences are:

• accelerated capital allowances in respect of fixed (non-current) assets;

• accrued pension liabilities in the financial statements which are subsequently granted tax relief when they are paid at a later date; and

• intra-group profits in stock which are unrealised at group level and reversed on consolidation.

25.10 Timing differences originate in one accounting period and then reverse in subsequent accounting periods, hence the tax charge in the later periods will be affected by transactions or events that have arisen in a previous accounting period. This has a direct impact on a reporting entity because future tax assessments will be higher or lower than they would have been if those timing differences had not occurred (similar to the worked example above when a company purchases an item of machinery that qualifies for HMRC's *Annual Investment Allowance*). The overarching objective of deferred tax, therefore, is to 'balance out' the effects of future tax consequences by recognising the tax effects of all income and expenditure, gains and losses, assets and liabilities in the same period in which they are recognised as opposed to the period in which they form part of a company's taxable profit – in other words to achieve the matching concept.

Focus

Deferred tax is not provided for on permanent differences.

25.11   The timing difference plus approach uses the income statement (profit and loss account) liability method to recognise the expected tax effects of timing differences as either liabilities for tax payable in the future or as assets that are recoverable in the future. Deferred tax on timing differences that have arisen in the period is calculated using the rate of tax expected to apply when the asset is recovered or the liability is settled. This rate of tax is the tax rate that has been enacted or substantively enacted at the balance sheet date.

Example 25.3 – Calculation of deferred tax

Aidan Limited (Aidan) prepares financial statements to 31 March each year and makes an annual profit of £90,000. Facts associated with this scenario are outlined below:

Fact 1

On 1 April 2012 an item of plant was purchased at a cost of £80,000 and for the purposes of this example does not qualify for HMRC's *Annual Investment Allowance*. The directors have estimated that the machine will have zero residual value after its useful economic life of eight years. Aidan's accounting policy in respect of this machine is to depreciate it on a straight-line basis over its estimated useful life.

Fact 2

On 1 April 2014, Aidan purchased an additional machine to cope with the increase in demand for its goods (again, for the purposes of this example this machine does not qualify for HMRC's *Annual Investment Allowance*). This new machine cost £150,000 and the directors have estimated that at the end of this machine's useful economic life of seven years, it will have a residual

---

value of £10,000. Aidan's accounting policy in respect of this machine is to depreciate it on a straight-line basis over its estimated useful life.

The rate of capital allowances is 18% on a reducing balance basis and Aidan pays tax at the rate of 20%.

Deferred tax is calculated as follows:

	2012	2013	2014	2015	2016
Per financial statements					
Carrying value b/f	–	70,000	60,000	180,000	150,000
Addition	80,000	–	150,000	–	–
Depreciation	(10,000)	(10,000)	(30,000)	(30,000)	(30,000)
Carrying value c/f	70,000	60,000	180,000	150,000	120,000
Per tax computation					
Pool b/f	–	65,600	53,792	167,109	137,029
Additions	80,000	–	150,000	–	–
Capital allowances	(14,400)	(11,808)	(36,683)	(30,080)	(24,665)
Pool c/f	65,600	53,792	167,109	137,029	112,364
Timing differences					
Capital allowances	14,400	11,808	36,683	30,080	24,665
Depreciation	(10,000)	(10,000)	(30,000)	(30,000)	(30,000)
Originating (reversing)	4,400	1,808	6,683	80	(5,335)
Cumulative timing differences	4,400	6,208	12,891	12,971	7,636

	2012	2013	2014	2015	2016
Deferred tax balances					
Tax on opening cumulative difference	–	880	1,242	2,578	2,594
Tax on closing cumulative difference	880	1,242	2,578	2,594	1,527
Tax provided (released)	880	362	1,336	16	(1,067)

FIXED ASSETS SUBJECTED TO GRANTS

25.12   When a reporting entity receives a grant (such as a government grant) for the purchase of a qualifying fixed asset, Section 24, Government Grants will require an entity to recognise the grant as deferred income and write this off to profit or loss over the life of the asset to which the grant relates. Grants that are received by a reporting entity may not be subject to corporation tax (non-taxable), although essentially some are basically taxed by reducing the cost of the fixed asset for the purposes of capital allowances.

When a capital-based grant is non-taxable, this will not give rise to a deferred tax adjustment. However, any accelerated capital allowances (such as the *Annual Investment Allowance*) will need to be calculated. This is the difference between the net book value of the asset in the financial statements and the tax base of the same asset (the tax base is calculated as gross cost less capital allowances).

25.13   Grants that are taxable will give rise to a timing difference between the accounting profit and the taxable profit. The deferred tax adjustment for companies will not depend on whether the grant is deducted from the cost of the asset because the *Companies Act 2006* will prohibit this treatment. However, if the grant was deducted from the cost of the asset, for both financial reporting and tax purposes, the deferred tax calculation would be relatively straightforward because accelerated capital allowances would be based on a reduced cost. However, as the requirements of *Companies Act 2006* do not allow incorporated entities to deduct such grants from the cost of the asset, in practice the grant will be treated as a deferred credit in the balance sheet (statement of financial position) but deducted against the cost of the asset for capital allowances purposes; here, the deferred tax calculation will consist of two components:

- A debit balance on the deferred tax account will arise on the unamortised balance of the grant.

- A credit balance on the deferred tax account will arise on the accelerated capital allowances.

In practice, the deferred tax debit and credit will be offset against each other.

REVALUATIONS OF NON-MONETARY ASSETS

25.14 A notable difference between Section 29 and the previous FRS 19 *Deferred Tax* is the requirement to provide for deferred taxation on non-monetary assets (such as buildings) that have been subjected to revaluation. A typical asset that is subject to regular revaluation is a property held for investment purposes and classified as an investment property in accordance with Section 16, Investment Property.

Example 25.4 – Deferred tax on a revaluation of a non-monetary asset

Paul's Properties Limited (Paul) has a portfolio of investment properties that it uses to generate rental income for a number of years and then sells them at a profit. On 1 January 2013, Paul acquired an investment property that satisfied the classification of such under Section 16, Investment Property for £100,000.

Paul is preparing the company's financial statements for the year ended 31 December 2013 and on this date commissioned a chartered surveyor to carry out a valuation of this property (along with the rest of the other investment properties). Because of an increase in house prices during 2013, the chartered surveyor has confirmed that the property has benefited from a £10,000 increase in fair value to £110,000. The company pays tax at the UK's small companies' rate of 20% and this rate of corporation tax is due to stay in force for the foreseeable future.

The accounting entries for this fair value gain will be:

DR	Investment properties	£10,000
CR	Profit and loss account	£10,000

Being fair value gain in investment property

In addition to the journals above, Paul must also provide for deferred tax on the investment property. Paragraph 29.16 says that deferred tax relating to investment property that is measured at fair value is to be measured using the

---

tax rates and allowances that apply to the sale of the asset. Rates of tax in the UK are announced each year in the Chancellor's Budget and therefore Paul may not necessarily know what the tax rate will be when the company sells the investment property. As a consequence, Paul should calculate deferred tax using the rates of tax that have been enacted (or substantively enacted) by the reporting date. In this case, it would be 20%. Therefore, deferred tax would be accounted for as follows:

| DR | Income tax expense | £2,000 |
| CR | Deferred tax | £2,000 |

Being provision for deferred tax on investment property

If the rate of corporation tax for small companies were to be reduced in, say, four years' time to 18%, then on the assumption that Paul will still have the investment property in four years, he should charge deferred tax at 18%.

BUSINESS COMBINATIONS

25.15 Business combinations are dealt with in **Chapter 30**. They interact where deferred tax is concerned because paragraph 29.11 to FRS 102 says:

'When the amount that can be deducted for tax for an asset (other than goodwill) that is recognised in a business combination is less (more) than the value at which it is recognised, a deferred tax liability (asset) shall be recognised for the additional tax that will be paid (avoided) in respect of that difference. Similarly, a deferred tax asset (liability) shall be recognised for the additional tax that will be avoided (paid) because of a difference between the value at which a liability is recognised and the amount that will be assessed for tax. The amount attributed to goodwill shall be adjusted by the amount of deferred tax recognised.'

Focus

Chapter 30 contains a comprehensive example at **30.23** dealing with such issues.

25.16 In group situations, it is a requirement that the group must follow uniform accounting policies when preparing its consolidated financial statements. This will more than likely trigger various adjustments to be made at consolidation level (eg if a reporting entity has an overseas subsidiary which has not followed group accounting policies because of local legislation or local GAAP requirements). These adjustments may result in additional timing differences in the consolidated financial statements for which deferred tax should be recognised.

Focus

In a group acquisition situation, deferred tax is provided for when the amount that will be charged or deductible for tax differs from the fair value of the assets acquired with the other side of the entry going to goodwill.

LEASES

25.17 Many companies in the UK and Republic of Ireland will acquire assets under a leasing arrangement with a lessor. Such leasing arrangements give rise to timing differences between the amounts that are recorded in an entity's profit and loss account (income statement) and the amount recorded in the tax computation.

In a group acquisition situation, deferred tax is provided for when the amount that will be charged or deductible for tax differs from the fair value of the assets acquired with the other side of the entry going to goodwill.

Focus

It is to be noted that where a leasing arrangement is one that gives rise to an operating, not a finance, lease, no deferred tax issues will arise. This is because the amount that is charged in the profit and loss account will generally be the same amount that has been charged in arriving at taxable profit (though this will not be the case where there are accrued rentals that may give rise to a potential short-term timing difference). The leasing costs of cars with high emissions are subject to a disallowance for tax purposes.

25.18 Timing differences normally arise when a lessee enters into a finance lease (as defined in Section 20, Leases and **Chapter 15**) and HMRC legislation may require that capital allowances are to be claimed by the lessor (not the lessee). Under a finance lease, the lessee will record an asset in its balance sheet (statement of financial position) and a corresponding liability to represent the obligations to pay the lessor rentals. The lessee will then depreciate the asset over the shorter of the lease term or the useful economic life of the asset. Periodic rental payments will then be apportioned between the capital element of the lease and the interest charges.

25.19 In practice, HMRC usually accepts the accounting treatment under Section 20 and therefore there may not be any deferred tax issues to consider.

However, in principle, timing differences in leasing transactions will exist and this can be illustrated in an example where the finance lessee cannot claim capital allowances, but can claim deduction for tax purposes of the total rents paid to the lessor.

Example 25.5 – Deferred tax in a lease arrangement

Reese Limited enters into a finance lease with Byrne Limited for a machine that does not qualify for capital allowances under UK tax legislation. The lease term is for a period of five years and Byrne will make payments amounting to £12,000 to Reese Limited annually.

In the first year, Byrne's financial statements will show the asset in the balance sheet (statement of financial position) at an amount of £48,000 which is the present value of the minimum lease payments. Depreciation will be charged at £9,600 per annum.

Deferred tax is calculated as follows:

	Year 1	*Year 2*	*Year 3*	*Year 4*	*Year 5*
Rental	12,000	12,000	12,000	12,000	12,000
Finance cost (7.93%)	(3,806)	(3,158)	(2,455)	(1,699)	(882)
Capital element	8,194	8,842	9,545	10,301	11,118
Timing differences					
Interest	3,806	3,158	2,455	1,699	882
Depreciation	9,600	9,600	9,600	9,600	9,600
	13,406	12,758	12,055	11,299	10,482
Rentals per tax comp	12,000	12,000	12,000	12,000	12,000
Timing difference	(1,406)	(758)	(55)	701	1,518
Net book value	38,400	28,800	19,200	9,600	–
Capital outstanding	39,806	30,964	21,419	11,118	–
Cumulative timing difference	(1,406)	(2,164)	(2,219)	(1,518)	–

DEFERRED TAX ASSETS

25.20   Deferred tax liabilities are very common in companies' financial statements. However, deferred tax assets can also be recognised, but extreme care should be taken where deferred tax assets are concerned. The most common instance giving rise to a deferred tax asset is when a company has unutilised tax losses because these losses can be offset against any future profits that the company may generate. However, for the purposes of Section 29, a prudent approach needs to be adopted in order to comply with the provisions in paragraph 29.7 which says:

'Unrelieved tax losses and other *deferred tax assets* shall be recognised only to the extent that it is **probable** that they will be recovered against the reversal of *deferred tax liabilities* or other future taxable profits (the very existence of unrelieved tax losses is strong evidence that there may not be other future taxable profits against which the losses will be relieved).'

Example 25.6 – Recognition of a deferred tax asset

Cahill Conservatories Ltd has been established for many years. However, during the recent recession, the company has sustained a loss (both for financial reporting and for tax purposes) amounting to £65,000. The company's year-end is 31 October and the financial statements have been completed to draft stage, but are awaiting signature. The financial statements are expected to be approved on 10 January 2014.

On 4 January 2014, the company was awarded a contract with a well-known builder to fit conservatories on each of its sites for a period of five years. The company is expected to make a healthy level of profit from this contract which commences in the summer of 2014.

In this instance a deferred tax asset could be recognised in the financial statements for the year ended 31 October 2013 because there is evidence that the company *will* generate suitable taxable profits in the future for which the deferred tax asset can be utilised.

DEFINED BENEFIT PENSION SCHEMES

25.21   In the UK, tax legislation states that a company is granted tax relief on pension contributions usually in the period in which contributions are paid as opposed to when the contributions are recognised in profit or loss. As a result, if there is a disparity between the pension contributions accounted for in accordance with Section 29 and the pension contributions actually paid this will result in a timing difference for the purposes of deferred taxation.

25.22   A defined benefit pension scheme will comprise of various costs that are reported in profit or loss, such as:

● current service cost;

● past service cost;

● gains or losses on curtailments and settlements;

● interest cost; and

● expected return on the scheme's assets.

Actuarial gains and losses (remeasurements), however, are reported in other comprehensive income.

Because certain components of a defined benefit pension scheme are reported in both profit and loss and in other comprehensive income, the accounting for such costs may result in tax relief for the actual contributions paid by the company as well as deferred tax on the timing differences between contributions and costs. Deferred tax, therefore, needs to be split between the amounts relating to items reported in profit or loss and the amounts reported via other comprehensive income.

Example 25.7 – Calculation of a deferred tax asset for a defined benefit pension plan

Bury Corporation Ltd has obtained the actuarial information to enable the accounting input to be completed for its defined benefit pension scheme. The scheme is currently in deficit and details are as follows:

Opening scheme liability	(£200,000)
Contributions paid into the scheme	£80,000
Past service cost	(£20,000)
Interest cost	(£70,000)
Expected return on plan assets	£20,000
Actuarial loss	(£20,000)
Closing scheme liability	(£210,000)

Bury Corporation Ltd pays tax at the rate of 20%. As the company has a scheme that is in deficit, a deferred tax asset will be calculated as follows:

	Deficit	*Tax Relief*	*Deferred Tax Asset*
	£	£	£
Opening deficit	(200,000)		40,000
Contributions paid	80,000	(16,000)	
Profit and loss account charge	(70,000)	14,000	
Actuarial loss (OCI)	(20,000)	2,000	2,000
Balance carried forward	(210,000)	–	42,000

The profit and loss account charge comprises the past service cost of £20,000, interest cost of £70,000 less the expected return on plan assets (essentially finance income) of £20,000.

Tax relief will be granted by HMRC on the actual contributions paid and this is allocated first to the profit and loss account charge of £70,000. The difference between the contributions paid and the profit and loss account charge of £10,000 is allocated against the actuarial loss which will be reported in other comprehensive income.

SHARE-BASED PAYMENT

25.23 **Chapter 28** deals with the issues surrounding share-based payment transactions and are dealt with in Section 26, Share-based Payment in FRS 102. Section 26 requires organisations operating share-based payment arrangements to recognise the cost of equity-settled share-based transactions on the basis of the fair value of the award at the date of the grant and this is spread over the vesting period. For the purposes of taxation, the amount of the tax relief granted by HMRC will often not be the same as the amount charged in profit or loss; this is because under the UK's tax legislation, tax relief is given under a share option scheme at the date the options are exercised and is measured on the basis of the share option's *intrinsic* value at that date. The term *intrinsic* value is the difference between the share's market price at the date of the exercise and the option's exercise price.

A timing difference will arise for the purposes of deferred taxation when the charge (based on the share option's fair value at the grant date) is recognised in profit or loss. This timing difference is the difference between the cumulative charge and the related deduction for the purposes of tax that will be received in the future and will give rise to a deferred tax asset, provided it meets the recognition criteria in Section 29 (ie that there will be suitable taxable profits generated in the future against which the deferred tax asset can be utilised).

Example 25.8 – Intrinsic value of a share option falls below fair value

Alicia Enterprises PLC grants share options to all its employees on 31 March 2013 and a deferred tax asset was recognised at this date as the directors were satisfied that the deferred tax asset met the recognition criteria in Section 29. On 31 March 2014 it was found that the share option's intrinsic value had fallen below the option's fair value at the grant date.

Where the share option's intrinsic value falls below the option's fair value at the grant date, then the carrying value of the deferred tax asset may not be recoverable and therefore the directors should consider the need to write this deferred tax asset down to its recoverable amount.

25.24   Reporting entities will need to recognise both current and deferred taxation in the profit and loss account relating to share-based payment transactions, except to the extent that the tax is attributable to a gain or loss that has been recognised in other comprehensive income, in which case the tax is also recognised in other comprehensive income.

Example 25.9 – Deferred tax calculation on share options

On 1 April 2011, Byrne Enterprises Ltd issues 100,000 share options with a fair value of £300,000 which are expected to vest in three years' time and on this date it is expected that all shares will be exercised and all share options are exercised in year four. Byrne Enterprises pays tax at 21% and the intrinsic value of the all the share options at the ends of each year and the year they are exercised are as follows:

Year 1	£270,000
Year 2	£240,000
Year 3	£320,000
Year 4	£340,000

In each financial year, Byrne Enterprises Ltd will recognise £100,000 (£300,000/3) as a charge in the profit and loss account (income statement). In the UK, HMRC will not grant tax relief until the share options are actually exercised and therefore a timing difference for deferred tax purposes arises.

The timing difference for the purposes of deferred tax can be based on two policy choices:

- the cumulative share-based payment charge which will be based on the fair value at the grant date and capped at the total intrinsic value; or

- a pro-rata share of the intrinsic value at the balance sheet date capped at the cumulative share-based payment charge which will mean that any permanent difference is not recognised.

Option 1 – Deferred tax based on cumulative share-based payment charge

In year 1, the company will charge £100,000 to the income statement in respect of the share-based payment arrangement and as the intrinsic value is £270,000 in year 1, this covers the expected tax relief HMRC will grant and as it is deemed acceptable for the timing difference to be based on the cumulative share-based payment charge up to the extent of the option's intrinsic value, the deferred tax asset can be calculated as £100,000 × 21% = £21,000.

In year 2, the cumulative charge will be £200,000 and this is also covered by the intrinsic value of £240,000, hence the deferred tax asset will be £200,000 × 21% = £42,000.

In year 3, the cumulative charge becomes £300,000 and this is covered by the intrinsic value of £320,000 and the deferred tax asset will be £300,000 × 21% = £63,000.

Extracts from the financial statements of Byrne Enterprises Ltd for years one to three are as follows:

	Income statement		*Balance sheet*
	Charge	Deferred tax	Deferred tax asset
Year 1	£100,000	(£21,000)	£21,000
Year 2	£100,000	(£21,000)	£42,000
Year 3	£100,000	(£21,000)	£63,000
	£300,000	(£63,000)	

Option 2 – Deferred tax based on intrinsic value at the balance sheet date

Where deferred tax is based on the intrinsic value of the options at the balance sheet date, the tax deductions relating to the cumulative share-based payment charge is pro rata of the total intrinsic value of the share options at the balance sheet date and this is capped at the cumulative share-based payment charge.

In year 1, the timing difference is £270,000 × 1/3 = £90,000 and the deferred tax asset is therefore £90,000 × 21% = £18,900.

In year 2, the timing difference is £240,000 × 2/3 = £160,000 and the deferred tax asset is therefore £160,000 × 21% = £33,600.

In year 3, the deferred tax asset is £300,000 × 21% = £63,000 and a deferred tax asset is not recognised in respect of the excess of the options' intrinsic value (£320,000) over the cumulative share-based payment charge amounting to £300,000.

Extracts from the financial statements of Byrne Enterprises Ltd will be as follows:

	Income statement		Balance sheet
	Charge	*Deferred tax*	*Deferred tax asset*
Year 1	£100,000	(£18,900)	£18,900
Year 2	£100,000	(£14,700)	£33,600
Year 3	£100,000	(£29,400)	£63,000
	£300,000	(£63,000)	

The share options are exercised, as expected, in year four and HMRC will grant tax relief based on the intrinsic value in the year the shares are exercised. The intrinsic value of the shares in year four is £340,000 and therefore tax relief of £340,000 × 21% = £71,400 will be granted by HMRC in this year. In year four, the deferred tax asset of £63,000 is reversed through the profit and loss account (income statement) and the profit and loss account in year four will receive a credit of £8,400 being the tax relief granted on the share options by HMRC of £71,400 less the reversal of the deferred tax asset of £63,000. Extracts from the financial statements of Byrne Enterprises Ltd illustrating the impact of this journal are shown below:

	Income statement			Balance sheet	
	Expense	*Corporation tax*	*Deferred tax*	*Tax debtor*	*Deferred tax*
At end of Year 3	£300,000		£63,000		£63,000
Year 4 movement	–	(£71,400)	(£63,000)	£71,400	(£63,000)
	£300,000	(£71,400)	–	£71,400	–

Discounting deferred tax balances

25.25 FRS 102 prohibits reporting entities from discounting deferred tax balances to present day values. In reality, very few entities discount deferred tax balances so this prohibition will largely go unnoticed.

DISCLOSURE REQUIREMENTS

25.26 Paragraphs 29.25 to 29.27 outline the disclosure requirements relating to income tax as follows:

An entity shall disclose information that enables users of its financial statements to evaluate the nature and financial effect of the current and deferred tax consequences of recognised transactions and other events.

An entity shall disclose separately the major components of tax expense (income). Such components of tax expense (income) may include:

- current tax expense (income);
- any adjustments recognised in the period for current tax of prior periods;
- the amount of deferred tax expense (income) relating to the origination and reversal of timing differences;
- the amount of deferred tax expense (income) relating to changes in tax rates or the imposition of new taxes;
- adjustments to deferred tax expense (income) arising from a change in the tax status of the entity or its shareholders; and
- the amount of tax expense (income) relating to changes in *accounting policies* and *material errors* (see Section 10, Accounting Policies, Estimates and Errors) (see **Chapter 3**).

An entity shall disclose the following separately:

- the aggregate current and deferred tax relating to items that are recognised as items of other comprehensive income or equity;
- a reconciliation between:
  - ○ the tax expense (income) included in profit or loss; and
  - ○ the profit or loss on ordinary activities before tax multiplied by the applicable tax rate.
- the amount of the net reversal of deferred tax assets and deferred tax liabilities expected to occur during the year beginning after the *reporting period* together with a brief explanation for the expected reversal;

- an explanation of changes in the applicable tax rate(s) compared with the previous reporting period;

- the amount of deferred tax liabilities and deferred tax assets at the end of the reporting period for each type of timing difference and the amount of unused tax losses and tax credits;

- the expiry date, if any, of timing differences, unused tax losses and unused tax credits; and

- in the circumstances described in FRS 102, paragraph 29.14, an explanation of the nature of the potential income tax consequences that would result from the payment of dividends to its shareholders.

SUMMARY – WHAT IS DIFFERENT FROM THE PREVIOUS UK GAAP?

There are some notable differences between Section 29 and FRS 19 which preparers need to be aware of:

- Deferred tax is to be provided when accounting for a business combination and where amounts that are assessable or deductible for the purposes of tax differ from the value of items acquired in the acquisition.

- Deferred tax will need to be recognised on revaluations of assets.

- Discounting of deferred tax balances is prohibited.

Chapter 26

Revenue recognition

SIGNPOSTS

- The timing of revenue recognition is extremely important and financial statements should not be manipulated by inappropriately delaying or accelerating revenue. Section 23 to FRS 102 deals with this by addressing the methods in which companies should recognise the sale of goods, rendering of services (including construction contracts) and revenue from interest, royalties and dividends (see **26.1**).

- Section 23 does not apply to certain transactions and events (see **26.2**).

- Revenue is recognised at the fair value of the consideration received or receivable (see **26.3**).

- Sales under deferred payment terms that give rise to a financing transaction need careful consideration as such sales may also give rise to interest income on the part of the seller (see **26.4**).

- Care must be taken when goods or services are exchanged for similar or dissimilar goods or services because there has to be commercial substance to the transaction in order for revenue to be recognised (see **26.5**).

- There are requirements that need to be considered where a reporting entity offers 'loyalty awards' or a 'points system' to its customers (see **26.6**).

- HM Revenue and Customs (HMRC) is very keen to ensure that companies recognise an appropriate level of revenue in their financial statements (see **26.7**).

- It is advisable to document judgements made on the timing of revenue recognition (see **26.8**).

- For the sale of goods, five conditions must be met before revenue can be recognised (see **26.9** and **26.10**).

- Four conditions must be met for revenue to be recognised in respect of the rendering of service (see **26.11**).

- Reference is made to 'specific' and 'significant' acts in FRS 102 and when a 'specific' act is more significant than any other act, revenue recognition is postponed until the significant act is executed (see **26.12**).

- Nil profit is recognised when a reporting entity is unable to reliably estimate the outcome of a transaction that involves the rendering of services (see **26.13**).

- Revenue in respect of construction contracts is recognised using the stage of completion method (see **26.14**).

- Construction contracts can cover single asset construction projects or one contract may cover the construction of a number of assets (see **26.15**).

- Progress payments received do not reflect the work performed on construction contracts (see **26.16**).

- Where the outcome of a construction contract is uncertain, nil profit is recognised. Where the outcome is estimated to be a loss, the loss is recognised immediately (see **26.17**).

- There are specific requirements relating to revenue in respect of interest, royalties and dividends (see **26.18**).

INTRODUCTION

26.1   Revenue recognition has been the subject of much controversy in both the United Kingdom and the Republic of Ireland over recent years. This controversy is largely due to the acts by some companies to delay revenue recognition or accelerate revenue recognition purely for the purposes of financial statement manipulation. Of course, such acts clearly detract from the relevance and reliability of the financial statements and such acts are clearly unethical, both from a professional perspective as well as a legal perspective.

Section 23, Revenue, deals with the way in which a reporting entity must recognise revenue in its financial statements. The Section itself is very comprehensive, with an Appendix that gives useful examples of the methods in which revenue is recognised in an entity's financial statements. Section 23 deals with revenue arising from:

- sales of goods (whether produced by the entity for the purpose of sale or whether such goods have been purchased exclusively for resale);

- rendering of services;

- construction contracts in which the entity is the contractor; and

- the use by others of entity assets yielding interest, royalties and dividends.

26.2   Paragraph 23.2 outlines certain transactions and events which are not covered by Section 23 and also goes to inform preparers which relevant standard is applicable in these situations which are outlined below:

Section 23 does NOT apply to:	Relevant applicable Section of FRS 102:
Lease agreements	Section 20, Leases
Dividends/other income from investments accounted for under the equity method	Section 14, Investments in Associates and Section 15, Investments in Joint Ventures
Fair value changes of financial assets and financial liabilities or their disposal	Section 11, Basic Financial Instruments and Section 12, Other Financial Instruments Issues
Fair value changes in investment property	Section 16, Investment Property
Initial recognition and changes in the fair value of biological assets related to agricultural activity	Section 34, Specialised Activities
Initial recognition of agricultural produce	Section 34, Specialised Activities

Section 23 also does not deal with revenues or other income that arise from transactions or events that fall under the scope of FRS 103 *Insurance Contracts* (once issued).

BASIC MEASUREMENT PRINCIPLES

26.3   The main measurement principle that Section 23 is based on is the fact that a reporting entity will recognise revenue at the *fair value* of the consideration 'received' or 'receivable'. The Glossary in FRS 102 defines fair value as:

> 'The amount for which an *asset* could be exchanged, a *liability* settled, or an equity instrument granted could be exchanged, between knowledgeable, willing parties in an arm's length transaction. In the absence of any specific guidance provided in the relevant section of this FRS, the guidance in paragraphs 11.27 to 11.32 shall be used in determining fair value.'

Focus

See **36.31** for guidance through the fair value hierarchy as covered in these sections of FRS 102.

Example 26.1 – Revenue recognition

Heaton Enterprises Limited (Heaton), a UK-based company, manufactures and sells office furniture to its customers. Most customers have a credit account on Heaton's sales ledger with the vast majority having payment terms of 30 days from date of invoice. Some larger and more established customers have payment terms of between 60 and 90 days and most customers pay in accordance with these terms. Newer customers pay cash on delivery until they become established.

On 30 September 2013, Heaton made a sale to one of its major customers for £10,000 before trade discount and VAT. The terms of the sale make provision for a 1% discount to the customer for goods purchased to the value of £11,000 and 2% between £11,000 and £15,000 with additional discounts at the company's discretion being applied for sales of over £15,000 on a monthly basis.

This particular sale will attract a discount of £100 (£10,000 at 1%). To comply with the requirements in Section 23, the fair value of the consideration receivable must take into account amounts of trade discounts, prompt payment discounts and volume rebates allowed by the entity. Assuming the whole value of the goods are subject to VAT at the standard rate of 20%, Heaton will recognise revenue as follows:

Revenue before discount	£10,000
Discounts allowed	(£100)
Revenue after discount	£9,900
VAT at 20%	£1,980
Trade debtor	£11,880

Example 26.2 – Agent and principal

Whitaker Enterprises Limited (Whitaker) acts as an agent on behalf of Westhead Enterprises Limited (Westhead) in the travel and tourism industry. Westhead sells tailormade holidays to the general public. Certain countries (such as the United States and India) require travellers to carry a visa and Westhead organises such visas through Whitaker. Westhead charges its customers for the cost of the visa, plus Whitaker's commission. Westhead then sends the funds to Whitaker so Whitaker can organise the visa for their customer's travel.

In this scenario, Whitaker is acting as an agent to Westhead and paragraph 23.4 covers the agent/principal scenario. The paragraph requires the agent to include in its revenue only the commission amount – not the amounts collected on behalf of the principal.

Example 26.3 – payment received in advance

Norah's Nightwear Limited operates in the clothing industry. Customers can purchase goods from one of their retail outlets located across the country, or they can order online via the company's website. Ordering online has seen a significant increase in recent years and the company has recognised that more of their sales will be made online. As a result, the company has introduced a feature on their website where customers can order their goods and, if they are not in stock, they can be given an accurate date as to when delivery of the goods will take place. This feature has proved popular and the company's reputation has been further enhanced.

One of Norah's Nightwear's new customers has placed an order for 200 of its own brand of dressing gowns on 30 October 2013 – new customers must pay in full and are not offered credit until they have been a customer for a period of two months. Norah's Nightwear has a financial year-end of 31 October 2013. The dressing gowns are currently out of stock with an estimated delivery date to the customer of 8 November 2013. The customer is happy with this delivery date and has paid the balance in full.

As the goods have yet to be delivered to the customer, Norah's Nightwear must not recognise revenue in respect of this sale, despite the fact that the transaction has taken place before the year-end. This is because Norah's Nightwear still owes the goods to the customer, hence a liability is owed. As a result, Norah's Nightwear will recognise the sale in creditors less than one year (as 'deferred income') and will recognise the balance as revenue in the next financial year when the goods have been shipped to its customer.

26.4   There may be occasions when a reporting entity will sell goods to its customer on *deferred payment terms* – which will give rise to a financing transaction. A common example of this is an interest-free credit period to the buyer. In such cases, the fair value of the consideration is the present value of all future receipts determined using an imputed interest rate. Paragraph 23.5 confirms that the imputed rate of interest is the more clearly determinable of either:

● the prevailing rate for a similar instrument of an issuer with a similar credit rating; or

● a rate of interest that discounts the nominal amount of the instrument to the current cash sales price of the goods or services.

Interest income must be accounted for under the provisions in paragraph 23.29(a) which states that an entity must recognise revenue on the following bases:

26.5 *Revenue recognition*

'Interest shall be recognised using the *effective interest method* as described in paragraphs 11.15 to 11.20. When calculating the *effective interest rate*, an entity shall include any related fees, finance charges paid or received (such as 'points'), *transaction costs* and other premiums or discounts.'

Example 26.4 – Calculation of interest income

On 1 January 2013, Aidan Audios Ltd sold audio equipment amounting to £4,000 to a customer with three years' interest-free credit. The accountant has worked out that the rate of interest that discounts the nominal amount of the instrument to the current cash sales price of the goods is 8% and Aidan Audios has a year-end of 31 December each year.

For the year ended 31 December 2013, revenue will be £3,175 (£4,000 × $1/(1.08)^3$. Interest income will be recognised amounting to £254 (£3,175 × 8%).

In the 2014 financial statements, interest income will be £274 ((£3,175 + £254) × 8%) and in 2015, the remaining interest income will be £297.

This treatment enables the full £4,000 transaction to be recognised as revenue in Aidan Audios profit and loss account (income statement) over the three years.

EXCHANGES OF GOODS OR SERVICES – COMMERCIAL SUBSTANCE

26.5 It is important that revenue is only recognised in transactions that possess *commercial substance*. Financial reporting often uses the term *substance over form* which is essentially the same; in other words a reporting entity must only recognise revenue where the reality is that a transaction giving rise to revenue has taken place.

Paragraph 23.6 to FRS 102 recognises two instances where a reporting entity must *not* report revenue:

- when goods or services are exchanged for similar goods or services; or

- when goods or services are exchanges for dissimilar goods or services, but the transaction lacks commercial substance.

When either one (or both) of these characteristics are present, a reporting entity cannot recognise revenue.

Example 26.5 – Exchange of dissimilar goods

Humphries Limited sells a range of clothing aimed at both male and female teenagers and young adults. It has entered into negotiations with a company called Fallon Limited that sells homeware products such as bedding, furniture, cookware and lighting. Fallon Limited is exploring the possibility of adding clothing into its range and has approached Humphries with a view to placing a small initial order of clothing to sell in a couple of its stores located in the South-West of the country where such clothing is in demand. If the sales are successful, Fallon will look to place a larger order.

During the negotiations, the director of Humphries expressed a desire to try a similar strategy and see if their store could sell homeware products. The purchasing director of Fallon Limited has agreed to exchange some homeware produce to the same value of the value of goods that Humphries will supply, hence no additional assets (such as cash) will need to be transferred by/to either party.

Section 23.7 to FRS 102 says that an entity shall recognise revenue when goods are sold or services are exchanged for dissimilar goods or services in a transaction that has commercial substance. In this case, the transactions will be measured:

- at the fair value of the goods or services received adjusted by the amount of any cash or cash equivalents transferred (in this case no additional cash or cash equivalents have been transferred as both sets of goods are at equivalent fair values);

- if the amount above cannot be measured reliably, then at the fair value of the goods or services given up adjusted by the amount of any cash or cash equivalents transferred; or

- if the fair value of neither the goods or services received nor the goods or services given up can be measured reliably, then at the carrying amount of the goods or services given up adjusted by the amount of any cash or cash equivalents transferred.

As fair values can be easily obtained in the scenario, the transactions will be measured under point 1.

CUSTOMER LOYALTY AWARDS

26.6   Many outlets in the United Kingdom and the Republic of Ireland offer their customers 'loyalty awards'. These awards generally work by the customer obtaining a certain number of 'points' which can be redeemed at a future point in exchange for free or discounted goods or services.

When such schemes are in place, the entity offering the award must account for the credits given to their customers as a separately identifiable component of the initial sales transaction. It achieves this by splitting the fair value of the consideration received or receivable in respect of the initial sale between the award credits and the other components of the sale. The monetary value attributed to the award credits will be measured by reference to their fair value, which will be the amount for which the award credits could be sold separately. See also FRS 102, Appendix to Section 23, Example 13.

SPECIFIC ISSUES RELATING TO REVENUE RECOGNITION

26.7   Section 23 deals with four main aspects to revenue recognition:

- sale of goods;
- rendering of services;
- construction contracts; and
- interest, royalties and dividends.

The timing of revenue is critical for each of the above revenue types to ensure that the financial statements give a true and fair view. Disproportionately delaying revenue could clearly have implications where HM Revenue and Customs (HMRC) is concerned, as companies could end up seriously underpaying corporation tax, which would in turn incur penalties and interest charges if HMRC is satisfied that revenue had been inappropriately delayed to mitigate tax liabilities. In addition, disproportionately accelerating revenue recognition (eg to achieve a desired level of profit for bank covenant purposes or to make the figures look impressive to secure additional finance) would also have tax implications as the tax treatment for such transactions would often follow the accounting treatment; hence revenue recognised too soon would be taxed in the year or period that it is recognised in the financial statements.

26.8   Section 23 is quite specific on the timing of revenue and it is important in order to achieve a true and fair view, that revenue is appropriately recognised at the right point. In some cases it may not be absolutely certain when and at what point revenue should be recognised and professional judgement may have to be exercised. In such ambiguous circumstances, it is advisable to document any judgements in case these are challenged by HMRC or other third parties.

Sale of goods

26.9   *Five* conditions must be satisfied before a reporting entity can recognise revenue in respect of the sale of goods:

- the entity has transferred to the buyer the significant risks and rewards of ownership of the goods;

- the entity retains neither continuing managerial involvement to the degree usually associated with ownership nor effective control over the goods sold;

- the amount of revenue can be measured reliably;

- it is *probable* that the economic benefits associated with the transaction will flow to the entity; and

- the costs incurred or to be incurred in respect of the transaction can be measured reliably.

Example 26.6 – Recognition of revenue and ongoing obligations

Bury Corporation Limited enters into a contract to sell 20 items of machinery to Cahill Corporation (Overseas) Inc – a company located in Spain. The terms of the contract are that Bury Corporation will ship the machines to Cahill Corporation, install the machines and ensure that the machines are in full working capacity prior to Cahill Corporation signing to say that they are satisfied with them. The financial director of Bury Corporation Limited is keen to recognise the sale in the 31 October 2013 year-end financial statements, but the engineers have said they cannot install the machines until at least 1 December 2013 due to their present workload. The finance director has, nevertheless, recognised the sale because the machines were despatched on 29 October 2013.

The finance director cannot recognise the sale in the year-end 31 October 2013 financial statements because Bury Corporation Ltd has an ongoing obligation to install the machines after dispatch and to ensure that they are at full working capacity, at which point Cahill Corporation will sign to say that they are satisfied with the machines. Bury Corporation Ltd can only recognise revenue on those machines at the point Cahill Corporation signs the contract to say they are satisfied because, at this point, Cahill Corporation is acknowledging that all contractual obligations owed to them have been fulfilled by Bury Corporation Ltd.

This situation is confirmed in paragraph 23.12 to FRS 102. That paragraph says that an entity will not recognise revenue if it retains significant risks and rewards of ownership and gives examples of these situations as follows:

- when the entity retains an obligation for unsatisfactory performance not covered by normal warranties;

- when the receipt of the revenue from a particular sale is contingent on the buyer selling the goods;

- when the goods are shipped subject to installation and the installation is a significant part of the contract that has not yet been completed; and

- when the buyer has the right to rescind the purchase for a reason specified in the sales contract, or at the buyer's sole discretion without any reason, and the entity is uncertain about the probability of return.

26.10   The key to ensuring revenue is correctly recognised in the financial statements is to ensure that ALL of the conditions in paragraph 26.9 are met. If any one of those conditions are not met, revenue cannot be recognised.

Focus

Many might argue that a sale can be recognised when legal title to the goods passes to the buyer. However, the main bedrock principle in financial reporting is to report the substance of a transaction and not its legal form. Where the sale of goods is concerned, a sale would normally be recognised when the risks and rewards of ownership of the goods passes from seller to buyer, which is at the point that all the five conditions in paragraph 26.9 are met. However, in some entities both the legal title and the risks and rewards of ownership could be passed at the same time (eg in a retail outlet).

Example 26.7 – Return of goods

Scanlon Electricals Ltd is a retailer of domestic appliances and has been trading successfully for over 30 years. All products come with a three-year warranty which covers the item for manufacturer faults. In addition, the store also offers a 14-day return period where a customer can have a full refund if a non-faulty item is returned within the 14-day window.

The question arises as to whether revenue can be recognised in respect of such goods. In situations where an entity can estimate the returns reliably, then revenue in respect of the sale of the goods can be recognised. However, the company must also recognise a provision for returns in accordance with Section 21, Provisions and Contingencies.

If Scanlon Electricals were also to sell goods to a customer, but a condition of the sale contract is that Scanlon Electricals retains the legal title to the goods in order that they can be taken back in the event of non-payment, a sale can still be recognised on the grounds that Scanlon Electricals have retained an *insignificant* risk of ownership.

Rendering of services

26.11 In contrast to the sale of goods, the rendering of services can be much more subjective. In order to qualify for recognition as revenue, there is often the need to estimate the value and the way this is done is by reference to the stage of completion of the transaction (often referred to as the *percentage of completion* method). There are four conditions that must be satisfied where the rendering of services is concerned to qualify for recognition of revenue:

- the amount of revenue can be measured reliably;

- it is probable that the economic benefits associated with the transaction will flow to the entity;

- the stage of completion of the transaction at the end of the reporting period can be measured reliably; and

- the costs incurred for the transaction and the costs to complete the transaction can be measured reliably.

Example 26.8 – Revenue for services where payments received in advance

Crazy Christmas Parties Ltd organises Christmas parties for companies around the UK. These events are usually held over a period of one week during the week immediately prior to Christmas Eve at specific venues across the country.

Brochures will be sent to companies that are listed on the company's database. These brochures are usually sent out around the first week of July each year in order that companies can book early as spaces are limited. A deposit is taken at the time of booking and the balance is due to be paid by the customer one month before the Christmas party.

The finance director is unsure at what point revenue in respect of these parties can be recognised. He acknowledges that the deposit should be recognised as a liability at the point of receipt, but he has queried with the auditor as to whether both the deposit and the balance can be recognised as revenue at the time the final balance is due to be paid on the grounds that the customer is unlikely to cancel the booking.

Revenue in respect of these types of events should be recognised when the event takes place. In addition, Crazy Christmas Parties should also allocate each fee received to each event on the basis that correctly reflects the extent to which services are performed at each event.

This treatment is necessary because revenue cannot be recognised until the company has discharged all its contractual obligations to the customer, which will be when the event has taken place.

Example 26.9 – Services spanning more than one accounting period

Sue's Software Co Limited (Sue) sells computer software to domestic and commercial customers and has been trading successfully for approximately ten years. The company has a year-end of 31 March.

Many commercial customers purchase software, including updates, but also require telephone support which generally relates to technical queries to resolve difficulties. Sue invoices these customers for a calendar year (1 January to 31 December) and the cost of the support service is £200 plus VAT per year.

On 1 January 2013, Sue invoiced 100 commercial customers for support services for the calendar year 1 January 2013 to 31 December 2013. The total value of these sales amounted to £20,000 (200 customers × £200). The bookkeeper has recognised the full value of these sales within turnover for the year ended 31 March 2013.

As nine months of the support contract relates to the 2013/2014 financial year (1 April 2013 to 31 December 2013), this period cannot be included in the 31 March 2013 turnover. It is therefore reallocated to 'deferred income' within the current liabilities section of the balance sheet (statement of financial position).

26.12   Paragraph 23.15 to FRS 102 refers to 'specific' and 'significant' acts. When contractual obligations contain a 'specific' act that is much more significant than any other act, this particular paragraph requires revenue recognition to be postponed until the significant act is executed.

26.13   In situations when a reporting entity cannot estimate the outcome of a transaction that involves the rendering of services reliably, nil profit is recognised. This is achieved by recognising revenue only to the extent of the expenses recognised which are recoverable.

Percentage of completion method

26.14   Revenue in respect of transactions involving the rendering of services is recognised by reference to the percentage of completion method (or at the 'stage of completion'). This particular method also applies to revenue in respect of construction contracts (see the next section in this chapter). Paragraph 23.22 to FRS 102 outlines three possible methods of determining the stage of completion of a transaction (or construction contract) as follows:

- the proportion that costs incurred for work performed to date bear to the estimated total costs. Costs incurred for work performed to date do not include costs relating to future activity, such as for materials or prepayments;

- surveys of work performed; and

- completion of a physical proportion of the contract work or the completion of a proportion of the service contract.

Example 26.10 – Recognition of deferred income

Computers R Us Limited sells a batch of new computers to a commercial customer on 1 January 2013 for £15,000. The terms of the sales contract include a servicing element for three years from the date of sale and Computers R Us estimates that the cost of service will be approximately £1,500 per year. They have estimated a profit margin of 25% on the servicing work. Computers R Us Ltd has a year-end of 31 December.

How much revenue should be recognised in this transaction in the 2013 financial statements?

£4,000 (£1,500/0.75) × 2 years will be removed from the value of the sale and presented as deferred income in the company's balance sheet (statement of financial position). £11,000 will be recognised in the profit and loss account (income statement) as a sale. This is comprised of the £9,000 sale of the computer equipment plus one year's servicing contract of £2,000.

Construction contracts

26.15 Construction contract accounting can become extremely complicated and often involves a large degree of estimation and exercising professional judgement. The details relating to construction contract accounting are covered in **Chapter 20**. However, because construction contract accounting and revenue recognition are closely interrelated, the issues relating to revenue recognition in relation to construction contracts are looked at in this section.

Contracts can cover single asset construction projects, or one contract may cover the construction of a number of assets.

Example 26.11 – Construction contracts covering a number of assets

Claire Construction Limited is undertaking the construction of a retail park in the South of the UK as one contract. The retail park will comprise a number of retail outlets which will include clothing retailers, a catalogue company, a coffee shop, a gardening and 'do-it-yourself' outlet and a supermarket.

Each outlet that will be operating from the retail park has been subjected to separate proposals by their individual Head Offices. In addition, each asset has been subjected to a detailed negotiation process. A number of offers were rejected by the contractor for each outlet until, eventually, a satisfactory price was agreed. As details have now been finalised, each outlet has been assigned costs and revenues by the contractor.

When a contract covers a number of assets, such as in the example above, the construction of each asset is treated as a separate construction contract.

If, on the other hand, Claire Construction Ltd undertook a group of contracts, it could class the group of contracts as a *single* contract if:

- the group of contracts is negotiated as a single package;

- the contracts are so closely interrelated that they are essentially a part of a single project with an overall profit margin; and

- the contracts are performed concurrently or in a continuous sequence.

26.16   Construction contracts will often include amounts received from customers that are referred to as 'progress payments' or 'advances'. The FRS recognises that such amounts do not reflect the work performed and these will therefore be credited to a 'contract account' in the nominal ledger. In addition, where the contractor has incurred costs for items such as materials or services which span more than one accounting period (and hence result in a prepayment) these can be recognised as an asset but only if it is probable that such costs will be recovered. If it is not probable that such costs will be recovered, the entity will recognise them immediately as an expense.

Example 26.12 – Rectification costs

A contractor is undertaking a building project on a new housing development for Holmes' Homes Limited – a well-established house builder that has been trading for many years.

On 31 October 2013, a problem occurred on the site which resulted in remedial costs (sometimes referred to as 'rectification costs') to the houses amounting to £120,000. The finance director is almost certain that Holmes' Homes will have to cover these costs. However, the contractor's legal advisers have subsequently informed the finance director that there is a clause within the contract that such remedial costs are to be borne by the contractor and are therefore deemed to be irrecoverable.

In such situations, as the costs will not be recovered, they must be written off against profit or loss as an expense of the contractor.

Other revenue recognition aspects for construction contracts

26.17   Accounting for construction contracts involves a large degree of estimation and the overall outcome of the construction contract has to be ascertained in order to gain an understanding of how to recognise revenue and expenses. There are two situations that Section 23 covers where revenue recognition aspects and construction contracts are concerned:

- where the outcome of the contract is uncertain; and

- where the contract is loss-making.

When the outcome of the contract is *uncertain*, the entity cannot recognise profit. It will recognise revenue to the extent of the contract costs incurred that it is probable to be recovered and contract costs are recognised as an expense in the period in which they are incurred.

Example 26.13 – outcome of the contract is uncertain

A contractor is unable to ascertain whether a contract it is working on will be loss- or profit-making. Contract costs (which are deemed to be recoverable on the contract) amount to £35,000 which have been recognised as an expense in the period to which they relate.

In this scenario, the amount of revenue recognised will be £35,000 to match with the expenses deemed to be recoverable, hence no profit element is recognised.

When the contract is *loss-making*, the entity recognises such losses immediately. This is achieved by recognising revenue to the stage of completion and cost of sales will be a balancing figure to generate the required loss.

Example 26.14 – loss-making contract

A contractor has estimated that total contract revenue on Project A will be £5 million. Costs will be £6 million resulting in a loss of £1 million. The contract has been assessed as being 75% complete at the year-end 31 October 2013. The financial statement extracts will be as follows:

		£'000
Revenue	(75% × £5 million)	3,750
Cost of sales	(balancing figure)	(4,750)
Loss		1,000

Interest, royalties and dividends

26.18   There are common instances where a company will use another company's assets for use in their premises which will give rise to interest, royalties and dividend payments being received by the reporting entity. Such circumstances are dealt with in Section 23 at paragraphs 23.28 and 23.29. Paragraph 23.28 outlines the point at which revenue is recognised by the receiving entity and this is when:

- it is probable that the economic benefits associated with the transaction will flow to the entity; and

- the amount of revenue can be measured reliably.

When these conditions are met, the reporting entity measures interest, royalty and dividend revenue on the following basis (paragraph 23.29):

- interest is recognised using the effective interest method. An entity calculates the effective interest method by including any related fees, finance charges paid or received, transaction costs and other premiums or discounts;

- royalties are recognised on an accruals basis in accordance with the substance of the relevant agreement; and

- dividends are recognised when the shareholder's right to receive payment is established.

Example 26.15 – Interest calculated using the effective interest method

The effective interest method discounts the expected future cash inflows and outflows expected over the life of an underlying asset (such as a financial instrument). It is essentially the effective interest rate multiplied by the carrying amount of the financial instrument.

Assume a company sells a financial instrument to another company that has a nominal value of £1,000 but sells it at a discount for £900. The instrument has a coupon interest rate amounting to 5% that is paid at the end of each year. Based on the nominal value, the interest payments will be three instalments of £50 each and a principal payment of £1,000 on maturity. The effective interest rate is 8.95% and the value of the interest income can be calculated using the following amortisation table:

Year	Opening amortised cost (A)	Interest and principal payments (B)	Interest income [A × 8.95%] (C)	Debt discount amortisation [C–B] (D)	Closing amortised cost [A+D]
1	900	50	81	31	931
2	931	50	83	33	964
3	964	1,050	86	36	1,000

Example 26.16 – Royalties

A software developer grants exclusive rights to a customer to use its software. The terms of the agreement are that the customer will use the software for a period of three years and the total amount of royalties paid to the software developer will be £12,000 over the three-year period.

Paragraph 23.29(b) requires royalties to be recognised on an accrual basis in accordance with the substance of the relevant agreement. Therefore the software developer will recognise £4,000 (£12,000/3 years) in years one, two and three of the agreement.

Example 26.17 – Dividends

Company A Limited owns a 40% stake in Company B Limited (hence an associated company). Both companies have a 31 December 2013 year-end. On 30 November 2013, the board of Company B declared a dividend to shareholders which would be paid on 20 January 2014. Company A's dividend amounts to £20,000 and the finance director is proposing to recognise the dividend in the 2014 financial statements.

Paragraph 23.29(c) to FRS 102 states that dividends shall be recognised when the shareholder's right to receive payment is established. This is the date on which the shareholders approve the dividend in the general meeting or by the members passing a written resolution and therefore the finance director should recognise the dividend in the financial statements to 31 December 2013 even though the money will not physically appear in the bank account until 20 January 2014.

Disclosure requirements

26.19 Paragraph 23.30 outlines the disclosure requirements where revenue recognition is concerned. The paragraph requires a reporting entity to disclose:

- the *accounting policies* adopted for the recognition of revenue, including the methods adopted to determine the stage of completion of transactions involving the rendering of services; and

- the amount of each category of revenue recognised during the period, showing separately, at a minimum, revenue arising from:

    o   the sale of goods;

    o   the rendering of services;

    o   interest;

    o   royalties;

    o   dividends;

    o   commissions;

    o   grants; and

    o   any other significant types of revenue.

26.20 The disclosure requirements relating to revenue from construction contracts is dealt with at the end of **Chapter 20**.

SUMMARY – WHAT IS DIFFERENT FROM THE PREVIOUS UK GAAP?

- For exchanges of goods or services which are dissimilar, revenue is recognised only when the transaction has commercial substance and is measured at the fair value of the goods or services received which is adjusted for any cash transferred. There are not directly comparable sections to UITF 26 *Barter Transactions for Advertising* but the general principles will need to be applied – in other words, revenue is only recognised where there is evidence of what the cash prices of the advertising would have been and hence this cash equivalent would be recognised as revenue.

- There are subtle differences in the wording in FRS 102 and UITF 40 *Revenue Recognition and Service Contracts*. UITF 40 refers to a 'right to consideration', whereas Section 23 requires revenue to be recognised when:

  - ○ the amount of revenue can be measured reliably;

  - ○ it is probable that the economic benefits associated with the transaction will flow to the entity;

  - ○ the stage of completion of the transactions at the end of the reporting period can be measured reliably; and

  - ○ the costs incurred for the transaction and the costs to complete the transaction can be measured reliably.

Chapter 27

Share capital and equity

SIGNPOSTS

- The concept of share capital is dealt with in both Section 22 to FRS 102 and in the *Companies Act 2006* (see **27.1**).

- Equity is the residual interest in the net assets of an entity after deducting all its liabilities (see **27.1**).

- Shares can be treated as both equity and debt, depending on the characteristics of the shares themselves (see **27.2** and **27.3**).

- Puttable instruments are classified as equity, provided certain characteristics are present, even though they might meet the definition of a liability (see **27.4**).

- Some instruments can be liabilities (debt) OR equity and paragraph 22.5 to FRS 102 gives some examples of such instruments (see **27.5**).

- The timing of the consideration received in exchange for equity instruments and the timing of the issuance of such equity instruments is critical in order for the transaction to be recognised within the financial statements (see **27.6**).

- Any transaction costs are treated as a deduction from equity and net of any related income tax benefit (see **27.7**).

- The *Companies Act 2006* specifies that shares issued at a premium are accounted for by sending the excess of the premium over par value to a share premium account in equity (see **27.8**).

- A bonus issue takes place when a company issues further shares to shareholders in proportion to their existing holding. Such issues do not change total equity (see **27.9** and **27.10**).

- A share split divides an entity's existing shares into multiple shares (see **27.11**).

- Rights issues are a means of raising finance and are usually offered to shareholders in proportion to their existing shareholders and at a discounted price (see **27.12**).

- Convertible debt and compound financial instruments need to be 'split accounted' to arrive first at the liability component of the instrument and then at the equity component (see **27.13**).

- The debt component of convertible debt or a compound financial instrument is subsequently accounted for as a financial instrument (see **27.14**).

- Section 22 deals with the concept of treasury shares which are shares that have been issued and then subsequently reacquired by the entity (see **27.15**).

- The acquisition of a company's own shares is dealt with in the *Companies Act 2006* (see **27.16**).

- The accounting for redeemable shares can be complicated and the *Companies Act 2006* only allows redeemable shares to be redeemed if they are fully paid (see **27.17**).

- Companies can repurchase shares at a premium which will trigger a capital redemption reserve to be maintained (see **27.18**).

- For shares purchased out of a fresh issue of shares, the general rule is that any premium paid on the shares must be made out of distributable profits in accordance with *Companies Act 2006* (see **27.19**).

- The 'permissible capital payment' is the amount by which the purchase or redemption costs exceeds the amount of profits available for distribution plus the proceeds of any new share issue and is calculated using a simple equation (see **27.20**).

- Distributions to shareholders are accounted for by reducing the value of the entity's equity by the amount of the distribution (see **27.21**).

- Consolidated financial statements where the parent does not wholly-own a subsidiary will contain the non-controlling interests (minority interests) equity in the equity section of the consolidated balance sheet (statement of financial position). Changes in a parent's controlling interest where the parent still retains control following the change in ownership interest is accounted for as a transaction between equity holders. The main reporting requirements, as a result of both, are dealt with in this chapter (see **27.22**).

INTRODUCTION

27.1   The concept of share capital is dealt with in both the *Companies Act 2006* and in Section 22 to FRS 102. Shares can take two forms: debt or equity, depending on the characteristics of the shares involved. Traditionally preference shares have been recognised as debt because such shares entitle the holder to receive cash, either by way of dividend or redemption and hence the substance of such shares is of a debt nature rather than equity.

Section 22 refers to 'equity' and is defined in paragraph 22.3 to FRS 102 as follows:

> 'Equity is the residual interest in the *assets* of an entity after deducting all its liabilities. Equity includes investments by the owners of the entity, plus additions to those investments earned through profitable operations and retained for use in the entity's operations, minus reductions to owners' investments as a result of unprofitable operations and distributions to owners.'

27.2   Ordinary shares are normally treated as equity and referred to as 'equity shares' on the grounds that the issuer has discretion over future dividend payments and the shares are non-redeemable. In addition, ordinary shares do not contain a contractual obligation to deliver cash or another financial asset, unlike preference shares may. This is because Section 22 is largely based on IAS 32 *Financial Instruments: Presentation* and the governing principle involved in this Section is if the issuer has no discretion over the payment, the instrument (or a component of the instrument) is to be recognised as a liability.

Section 22 defines a 'financial liability' as any liability that is:

(a)   a contractual obligation:

    (i)   to deliver *cash* or another *financial asset* to another entity; or

    (ii)   to exchange financial assets or financial liabilities with another entity under conditions that are potentially unfavourable to the entity; or

(b)   a contract that will or may be settled in the entity's own equity instruments and:

    (i)   under which the entity is or may be obliged to deliver a variable number of the entity's own equity instruments; or

    (ii)   which will or may be settled other than by the exchange of a fixed amount of cash or another financial asset for a fixed number of the entity's own equity instruments. For this purpose the entity's own equity instruments do not include instruments that are themselves contracts for the future receipt or delivery of the entity's own equity instruments.

27.3   It follows therefore, that where the issuer has no choice but to avoid settling in cash or by way of transferring another financial asset and where settlement depends on the occurrence or non-occurrence of uncertain future events which are beyond the control of the issuer and the holder, the entity recognises a liability.

Example 27.1 – Preference shares

A company issues 10,000 £1 preference shares in order to raise finance. The terms of the issue are that the holders of the shares will be able to redeem those shares in five years' time at their fair value on the date of redemption.

The issue of the preference shares contains a right for the holders of those preference shares to receive cash on redemption. As the redemption will be in cash, the reporting entity will recognise the issue of the preference shares in liabilities as opposed to equity.

Paragraph 22.3A contains three instances where a financial liability will not be recognised, which are as follows:

- the part of the contingent settlement provision that could require settlement in cash or another financial asset (or otherwise in such a way that it would be a financial liability) is not genuine;

- the issuer can be required to settle the obligation in cash or another financial asset (or otherwise to settle it in such a way that it would be a financial liability) only in the event of liquidation of the issuer; or

- the instrument has all the features and meets the conditions in paragraph 22.4 to FRS 102.

Focus

Paragraph 22.4 to FRS 102 acknowledges that some financial instruments that meet the definition of a liability are classified as equity because they represent the residual interest in the net assets of the entity.

Classification of instruments as liabilities or equity

27.4   Paragraph 22.4 to FRS 102 acknowledges that a puttable instrument containing all of the following characteristics will be classified as equity:

- It entitles the holder to a pro-rata share of the entity's net assets in the event of the entity's liquidation. The entity's net assets are those assets that remain after deducting all other claims on its assets.

- The instrument is in the class of instruments that is subordinate to all other classes of instruments.

- All financial instruments in the class of instruments that is subordinate to all other classes of instruments have identical features.

27.4 *Share capital and equity*

- Apart from the contractual obligation for the issuer to repurchase or redeem the instrument for cash or another financial asset, the instrument does not include any contractual obligation to deliver cash or another financial asset to another entity, or to exchange financial assets or financial liabilities with another entity under conditions that are potentially unfavourable to the entity, and it is not a contract that will or may be settled in the entity's own equity instruments as set out in paragraph 22.3(b) of the definition of a financial liability.

- The total expected *cash flows* attributable to the instrument over the life of the instrument are based substantially on the *profit or loss*, the change in the recognised net assets or the change in the *fair value* of the recognised and unrecognised net assets of the entity over the life of the instrument (excluding any effects of the instrument).

Paragraph 22.4 goes on at (b) to say that instruments, or components of instruments, that are subordinate to all other classes of instruments are classified as equity if they impose on the entity an obligation to deliver to another party a pro-rata share of the net assets of the entity only on liquidation.

Example 27.2 – Instrument classified as EITHER liabilities or equity

Company A issues preference shares to raise finance. The terms of the issue are that annual dividends will be paid amounting to 8% of the holding per annum until redemption.

Company B undertakes a rights issue in order to raise finance. The shares in the rights issue are ordinary shares that do not contain any form of redemption feature and dividends on ordinary shares are payable at the sole discretion of the entity.

The preference shares issued by Company A contain a right, on the part of the holder, to receive cash (the 8% dividends per annum). There is also a redemption feature present in the preference shares. As the preference shares entitle the holder to receive cash (in addition to the redemption feature), these shares will be classified as liabilities. Payments in respect of the dividends will be classified as finance costs in the company's income statement (profit and loss account).

In Company B's scenario, the rights issue relates to ordinary shares and dividends on such shares are payable at the sole discretion of the company. The ordinary shares do not contain any sort of redemption feature. Such shares will be classified as equity as they do not entitle the holder to receive cash (either by way of dividend or redemption).

27.5   Paragraph 22.5 to FRS 102 contains examples of instruments that are classified as liabilities OR equity as follows:

- An instrument of the type described in paragraph 22.4(b) (see above) is classified as a liability if the distribution of net assets on liquidation is subject to a maximum amount (a ceiling). For example, if on liquidation the holders of the instrument receive a pro-rata share of the net assets, but this amount is limited to a ceiling and the excess net assets are distributed to a charity organisation or the government, the instrument is not classified as equity.

- A puttable instrument is classified as equity if, when the put option is exercised, the holder receives a pro-rata share of the net assets of the entity determined by:

  - ○   dividing the entity's net assets on liquidation into units of equal amounts; and

  - ○   multiplying that amount by the number of the units held by the financial instrument holder.

  However, if the holder is entitled to an amount measured on some other basis the instrument is classified as a liability.

- An instrument is classified as a liability if it obliges the entity to make payments to the holder before liquidation, such as a mandatory dividend.

- A puttable instrument that is classified as equity in a subsidiary's *financial statements* is classified as a liability in the consolidated financial statements.

- A preference share that provides for mandatory redemption by the issuer for a fixed or determinable amount at a fixed or determinable future date, or gives the holder the right to require the issuer to redeem the instrument at or after a particular date for a fixed or determinable amount, is a financial liability.

Example 27.3 – Shares in co-operative entities

Alex has subscribed to shares in his local credit union (a credit union is a financial institution which is owned and controlled by its members). The terms of the subscription say that the credit union has an unconditional right to refuse redemption of members' shares. On subscription of the shares, the question arises as to whether these shares are to be classified as equity or as a liability.

Paragraph 22.6 to FRS 102 deals with such issues and that paragraph says that members' shares in co-operative entities and similar instruments are equity if:

- the entity has an unconditional right to refuse redemption of the members' shares; or

- redemption is unconditionally prohibited by local law, regulation or the entity's governing charter.

The shares to which Alex has subscribed will, therefore, be classified as equity in the credit union's balance sheet (statement of financial position).

Issuance of shares and other equity instruments

27.6   When a reporting entity issues shares (and providing they do not contain an obligation to pay the holder of those shares cash, or contain any redemption features at a later date), the entity will classify those shares (or other equity instruments) as equity in its balance sheet (statement of financial position) at the time it issues those instruments and the third party subscribing to those instruments becomes obliged to settle the transaction in cash or other forms of consideration. However, there are situations that may arise which may restrict the reporting entity from recognising a full subscription of shares which can be illustrated in the following example.

Example 27.4 – Increasing equity to the extent of consideration received

A company has made a board resolution to issue additional ordinary shares to three of its shareholders. The shareholders give the company cash BEFORE the shares have been issued and the company is not required to repay any of the cash received.

In this example, the entity shall debit the bank/cash account with the value of the monies received from the shareholders and credit equity. The credit to equity will ONLY be to the extent of the monies received by the shareholders.

Example 27.5 – Share subscription not yet settled

A company has agreed to issue additional ordinary shares as a means to raise finance. The additional share subscription involves a fresh issue of 10,000 £1 ordinary shares and these were issued on 30 December 2013. As at this date the company had not yet received the cash from the new shareholders for the fresh issue of shares.

Paragraph 22(c) to FRS 102 says that to the extent that the equity instruments have been subscribed for but not issued (or called up), and the entity has not received the cash or other resources, the entity shall not recognise an increase in equity.

As a consequence, the entity can only recognise a corresponding increase in equity when the shareholders pay for the additional shares.

Focus

Where a company issues equity instruments, the issue shall be measured at fair value of the cash (or other resources) received or receivable. The transaction is also measured *net* of any costs that are directly attributable to the issuance of the equity instruments and where payment is deferred and the time value of money is material, the initial measurement of the transaction must be the present value of the transaction.

Transaction costs

27.7   Transaction costs in relation to financial instruments are defined in the Glossary to FRS 102 as:

'Incremental costs that are directly attributable to the acquisition, issue or disposal of a *financial asset* or *financial liability*, or the issue or reacquisition of an entity's *own equity instrument*. An incremental cost is one that would not have been incurred if the entity had not acquired, issued or disposed of the financial asset or financial liability, or had not issued or reacquired its own equity instrument.'

Focus

Transaction costs for an issue of equity instruments are treated as a deduction from equity, net of any related income tax benefit.

Share premium

27.8   It is not uncommon for businesses to raise capital by issuing shares in excess of their par value. Moreover, in today's modern business climate, banks and finance houses often want companies to approach their shareholders to pay more for shares as this offers the financiers an element of comfort that shareholders have confidence in the business. Companies that issue ordinary shares for more than par value issue such shares at a premium and in the UK and the Republic of Ireland, the treatment of such transactions is determined by the *Companies Act 2006*.

Focus

In the UK and Republic of Ireland, the excess of the price paid for the shares over the par value of the shares is taken to a *share premium account* in the balance sheet (statement of financial position).

Example 27.6 – Shares issued at a premium

On 1 July 2013, the issued share capital of Gabriella Gardening Equipment Ltd was £5,000 ordinary £1 shares. The company has seen rapid expansion over the last year and has recognised the need to raise additional finance to cope with the expansion programme. In order to meet part of the costs, the company decides to issue a further 3,000 ordinary shares at £2 each and receives the cash for these shares on 1 August 2013.

On receipt of the cash, Gabriella Gardening Equipment Ltd will account for the share issue as follows:

DR Cash at bank	£6,000
CR Ordinary shares	£3,000
CR Share premium	£3,000

Being issue of additional ordinary shares

Bonus issue of shares

27.9   Bonus issues (sometimes referred to as *scrip issues* or *capitalisation issues*) take place when a company issues further shares to shareholders in proportion to their existing holding (eg an additional one share for every five shares held).

Focus

There is an inherent advantage in a company making a bonus issue of shares in that shareholders receive additional shares at no extra cost to them. From the company's perspective, such bonus issues are made as an alternative to paying dividends to existing shareholders and thus the company preserves cash. It's also advantageous for a company that is under-capitalised to make bonus issues because when under-capitalisation occurs, the rates of dividends paid to existing shareholders are much higher.

27.10   When a company makes a bonus issue of shares, the transaction itself does not change total equity as can be seen from the following example.

Example 27.7 – Bonus issue of shares

A company makes a bonus issue of shares, at par value, for one share for every five held by existing shareholders and all shareholders take up the bonus issue. The value of the bonus issue is £10,000.

The journals required to increase the issued ordinary share capital of the company are:

DR Profit and loss account reserves (retained earnings)	£10,000
CR Issued share capital	£10,000

Being bonus issue of shares (one for five)

Share splits

27.11   A share split (sometimes referred to as a *stock split*) is the dividing of an entity's existing shares into multiple shares. Although the number of issued shares increases by a specific multiple, the total value of the shares remains the same because no real value has been added as a result of the split.

Example 27.8 – Share split

A company has seen its share price rapidly increase over the last year because of new products that have entered the marketplace which have boosted its reputation. In order to attract new investors the company has decided to undertake a share split on the grounds that the shares are too expensive to buy in round lots.

The share split will be a two-for-one. In this situation each shareholder will receive an additional share for each share he or she holds. This is advantageous because if the company's shares are each worth £1,000 before the share split, investors would need to purchase £100,000 in order to own 100 shares. If the shares were split and each share was then worth only £10, investors would only need to pay £1,000 to own 100 shares.

Rights issue

27.12   A rights issue is another alternative way in which a company can raise finance and works by the company selling shares to existing shareholders in proportion to their current shareholding. A primary incentive of existing shareholders taking up a rights issue is that the price at which the shares are offered in a rights issue is usually set at a discount to the current share price, although companies can offer a rights issue to existing shareholders at market value if it so chooses.

Focus

In a rights issue where the price of the shares is set at below par value, the 'discount' element is essentially a bonus issue of shares because existing shareholders are receiving additional shares for free. This will have an impact on earnings per share, but as this book concerns unlisted companies, the area of earnings per share is beyond the scope of this publication.

Example 27.9 – Simple calculation of a rights issue

On 1 January 2014, a company had 800,000 ordinary £1 shares in issue. On 1 April 2014 it offered existing shareholders a rights issue in the proportion of one share for every five shares held.

The rights issue is one share for every five, therefore 800,000 shares already in issue multiplied by one share and divided by five shares gives additional shares in the rights issue of 160,000.

Convertible debt and compound financial instruments

27.13   Convertible debt and compound instruments are financial instruments that contain a mixture of both debt and equity. The most common instrument that is classed as a compound financial instrument is a convertible loan where the loan note holders have an option when the loan notes mature to either convert the capital amount into shares of the company, or to receive cash in redemption. In these situations part of the instrument will be recognised as debt (a liability) with the remainder being recognised as equity.

Focus

To make the allocation, the entity shall first determine the amount of the liability component as the fair value of a similar liability that does not have a conversion feature or similar associated equity component. The entity shall allocate the residual amount as the equity component.

Example 27.10 – Convertible loan

On 1 April 2012 an 8% convertible loan note with a nominal value of £600,000 was issued at par. It is redeemable on 31 March 2016 also at par. Alternatively it may be converted into equity shares of the entity on the basis of 100 new shares for each £200 of loan note.

An equivalent loan note without the conversion option would carry interest at 10%. Interest of £48,000 has already been paid to the loan note holders and has been included within interest payable and similar charges in the profit and loss account.

Present value rates are as follows:

| End of year | Present value | |
	8%	10%
1	0.93	0.91
2	0.86	0.83
3	0.79	0.75
4	0.73	0.68

As there is an option to convert the shares into equity there is clearly an obligation to transfer economic benefits. There is the issue of both 'debt' and 'equity' and there is an obligation to pay cash (the interest at 8% per annum) and a redemption amount which is the debt component of the instrument. The equity component of the instrument is the loan note holders' option to convert.

The calculation of the debt and equity portion is shown as follows:

	8% interest *(£600,000 × 8%)* *£*	*Factor at a rate* *of 10%*	*Present* *value* *£*
Year 1 – 2013	48,000	0.91	43,600
Year 2 – 2014	48,000	0.83	39,800
Year 3 – 2015	48,000	0.75	36,000
			119,400
Year 4 – 2016	648,000	0.68	440,600
Amount recognised as a liability			560,000
Initial proceeds			(600,000)
Amount recognised as equity			40,000

359

The next step is to consider the interest charge that has been recognised as a finance cost. The example shows that £48,000 worth of interest has already been paid to the loan note holders which have been debited to loan interest in the profit and loss account. This represents 8% of the loan. However, the entity has to recognise the fact that an equivalent loan without the option to convert the capital element into shares would carry interest at a rate of 10% and therefore it is necessary to reflect this.

The present value of the debt component is £560,000 and therefore this would be charged interest of (£560,000 × 10%) £56,000. £48,000 has already been charged to the profit and loss account so the difference of £8,000 (£56,000 less £48,000) is also charged to finance costs as this essentially represents the 'rolled up' interest in the loan.

Focus

Where convertible debt or a compound financial instrument is concerned, any associated transaction costs are to be allocated between the debt component and the equity component on the basis of their relative fair values.

27.14 After initial recognition of convertible debt or a compound financial instrument, paragraph 22.15 to FRS 102 requires the entity to account for the *liability* component as a financial instrument in accordance with Section 11, Basic Financial Instruments or Section 12, Other Financial Instruments Issues as appropriate.

There is an example in the Appendix to Section 22 which deals with the issuer's accounting for convertible debt.

Treasury shares

27.15 Treasury shares are shares in a company that have been issued and then subsequently reacquired by the entity. Any consideration given for the treasury shares is deducted from equity and no gain or loss in profit or loss on the purchase, sale, transfer, or cancellation of treasury shares is recognised.

Focus

Illustrative examples showing the acquisition of a company's own shares is dealt with in the next section.

ACQUISITION OF A COMPANY'S OWN SHARES

27.16 *Companies Act 2006 (CA 2006)* deals with the acquisition by a company of its own shares in *Part 18* in *sections 658* to *737. Section 658* places a restriction on companies acquiring their own shares (whether by purchase, subscription or otherwise) unless the exceptions in *section 659* apply. The exceptions are summarised as follows:

1   A limited company may acquire any of its own fully paid shares otherwise than for valuable consideration.

2   *Section 658* does not prohibit:

- the acquisition of shares in a reduction of capital duly made;

- the purchase of shares in pursuance of an order of the court under:

    ○   *section 98* (application to court to cancel resolution for re-registration as a private company);

    ○   *section 721(6)* (powers of court on objection to redemption or purchase of shares out of capital);

    ○   *section 759* (remedial order in case of breach of prohibition of public offers by private company); or

    ○   *Part 30* (protection of members against unfair prejudice).

- the forfeiture of shares, or the acceptance of shares surrendered in lieu, in pursuance of the company's articles, for failure to pay any sum payable in respect of the shares.

Accounting issues

27.17 *Section 686(1)* of *CA 2006* only allows redeemable shares to be redeemed if they are fully paid. The similar principle is contained in *section 691(1)* which prohibits companies from purchasing their own shares if the shares are not fully paid. Section 691(2) also requires companies that purchase their own shares to pay for those shares on purchase.

Section 733 under *Chapter 7* of *CA 2006 Supplementary Provisions* makes reference to the 'capital redemption reserve'. *Section 733(2)* requires a company whose shares are redeemed or purchased wholly out of the company's profits to transfer a sum equivalent to the amount by which the company's share capital is diminished on cancellation of the shares. This transfer is required to maintain the company's capital and also to protect creditors.

In addition, *section 733* also requires:

- a transfer to the capital redemption reserve where shares are redeemed or purchased wholly or partly out of the proceeds of a fresh issue;

- the aggregate amount of the proceeds is less than the aggregate nominal value of the shares redeemed or purchased (*s 733(3)(a)* and *(b)*); and

- the amount by which a company's share capital is diminished in accordance with *section 729(4)* (on the cancellation of shares held as treasury shares) must be transferred to the capital redemption reserve.

The company can only then use the capital redemption reserve to make a bonus issue of shares.

Example 27.11 – Redemption out of capital redemption reserve

The balance sheet of Company A Ltd is as follows:

	£
	£
Cash at bank	40,000
Ordinary share capital (£1 shares)	18,000
Profit and loss account	22,000
	40,000

A resolution was passed for the company to repurchase 4,000 shares at par value. The accounting for such would be as follows:

DR ordinary share capital	4,000
CR cash at bank	(4,000)

Redemption of share capital

DR profit and loss account	4,000
CR capital redemption reserve	(4,000)

Share capital redeemed - maintain share capital

Company A's balance sheet will now look like this:

	£
Cash at bank	36,000
Ordinary share capital (£1 shares)	14,000
Capital redemption reserve	4,000
Profit and loss account	18,000
	36,000

Share buy-back at a premium

27.18 There may be occasions when a company may decide to repurchase some shares at a premium. Using the same example as the one above, if we assume that the company repurchased the shares at a 50p premium, the journals would be:

DR ordinary share capital	4,000
DR profit and loss account (4,000 shares × 0.50p)	2,000
CR cash at bank	(6,000)

Redemption of share capital at a premium of £2,000

A further journal would then be required in order that the capital of the company is maintained as follows:

DR profit and loss account	4,000
CR capital redemption reserve	(4,000)

To maintain the capital of the company

Company A's balance sheet would now look like this:

	£
Cash at bank	34,000
Ordinary share capital (£1 shares)	14,000
Capital redemption reserve	4,000
Profit and loss account	16,000
	34,000

The above is the step-by-step process, whereas *CA 2006* expresses the accounting treatment as follows (which ends up with the same result):

CR cash at bank	(6,000)
DR profit and loss account	6,000
DR ordinary share capital	4,000
CR capital redemption reserve	(4,000)

The company has still maintained capital at £18,000 and the company has made the purchase out of distributable profits (because the total debited to profit and loss account reserves is the £6,000, which is equivalent to the consideration for the share buy-back).

Shares purchased out of a fresh issue of shares

27.19 The general rule is that any premium that is paid on the shares that a company acquires must be made out of distributable profits. However, *CA 2006, section 687(4)* says that if the redeemable shares were issued at a premium, any premium payable on their redemption may be funded from the proceeds of the new share issue. The amount of the premium that can be funded in this way is equal to the lower of:

- the aggregate of the premiums the company received on issuance of the shares that it is now redeeming; or

- the amount of the company's share premium account after crediting the premium (if any) on the new issue of shares it makes to fund the purchase or redemption.

Example 27.12 – Shares purchased out of a fresh issue

On 1 January 2008, Company B Limited issued 100,000 ordinary £1 shares. Included in this share issue are a shareholder's 10,000 ordinary shares which were issued to him at a premium of 0.10p per share. Following this issue the balance on Company B's share premium account was £3,500. On 1 January 2010, Company B made a bonus issue of shares to its shareholders and used the entire balance on the share premium account on the issuance of the bonus shares.

In 2012, the shareholder announced that he would like to retire and has asked the company to purchase his shares. The company has agreed to purchase his shares for £2.50 per share (hence at a premium of £1.50 per share) and in order to do this has made a further issue of 10,000 ordinary shares with a par value of £1 at a premium of 0.75p (hence issued at £1.75). The balance to purchase the shareholder's shares of £7,500 has been made out of the bank account.

The premium on the purchase is the lower of the initial premiums the company received on the original issuance of the shares and the balance on the share premium account after the issue as follows:

	£	£
Par value of the shares purchased		10,000
Lower of:		
– initial premium on share issue (10,000 shares at 0.10p premium)	1,000	
– balance on share premium account including premium on new issue of shares	7,500	
		1,000
Total (which cannot exceed proceeds of new issue)		11,000
Balance funded from distributable profit		14,000
Cost of purchase of shareholder's shares		25,000 (or 10,000 shares @ £2.50)

To record the above in the accounts, the journals will be:

DR cash at bank	17,500	
CR share capital	(10,000)	
CR share premium account	(7,500)	

Being new share issue of 10,000 £1 shares at £0.75 premium

DR share capital	10,000
DR share premium	1,000*
DR profit and loss account reserves	14,000 (see reconciliation above)
CR cash at bank	(25,000)

Being purchase of 10,000 ordinary £1 shares at a premium of £1.50

*Section 692(4) of CA 2006 allows the share premium account to be reduced by part of the premium payable on the purchase/redemption that is allowed to be funded out of the proceeds of the new share issue rather than it being made out of profit and loss account reserves.

You will note that in the above scenario there have been no amounts credited to the capital redemption reserve. This is because the par value of the shares purchased (£10,000) is less than the total proceeds of the new issue of (10,000 shares@£1.75) £17,500 and therefore the company's capital has been maintained, so there is no need for a transfer to the capital redemption reserve.

Permissible capital payments

27.20   *CA 2006, section 710* deals with the concept of the *permissible capital payment* (PCP). The PCP is the amount by which the purchase or redemption costs exceeds the amount of profits available for distribution plus the proceeds of any new share issue, hence is calculated as:

> purchase price of shares less (distributable profit + proceeds from new share issue) = PCP

The objective of the PCP is to make sure that a company makes use of its available profits and any proceeds arising from new share issues before it makes any payments out capital.

Section 734(2) states that, where the PCP is less than the nominal value of the shares redeemed or purchased, the difference is transferred to the capital redemption reserve. Conversely, where the PCP is greater than the nominal value of the shares redeemed/purchased, *section 734(3)* says the excess can be used to reduce any of the following:

- capital redemption reserve;
- share premium;
- fully paid up share capital; and
- revaluation reserve

Example 27.13 – Payment out of insufficient reserves

The balance sheet of Company C Ltd is as follows:

	£
Cash at bank	20,000
Ordinary share capital (£1 shares)	16,000
Profit and loss account	4,000
	20,000

One of the shareholders has expressed his disagreement with the way the company is being run and it has been agreed that the company should purchase 6,000 shares at par from the shareholder on the grounds that the relationship has become irretrievable. Clearly, the company has insufficient reserves available to make the purchase and therefore a payment out of capital will be required. Company C Ltd is required to follow the rules in *CA 2006 sections 709* to *723* and, once these procedures have been carried out, the journals will be as follows:

DR ordinary share capital	6,000
CR cash at bank	(6,000)

Payment to redeem shares

Profit and loss account	4,000
Capital redemption reserve	(4,000)

Maintenance of capital and protection of creditors

Company A's balance sheet will now look like this:

	£
Cash at bank	14,000
Ordinary share capital (£1 shares)	10,000
Capital redemption reserve	4,000
	14,000

In this example the PCP would be 6,000 £1 shares requiring redemption less profit and loss reserves of £4,000 equals £2,000 (or the shortfall on the profit and loss account reserves balance immediately before the purchase).

In the example above, the scenario indicated that the company would just be making an outright purchase of shares at par with no additional shares being issued. This is not always the case and it might be that the company issues new shares but still needs a PCP.

Example 27.14 – Effect of buyback at a premium and subsequent issue

Company D Ltd has the following balance sheet:

	£
Cash at bank	14,000
Ordinary share capital (£1 shares)	10,000
Share premium account	2,500
Profit and loss account	1,500
	14,000

Company D wishes to buy 4,000 shares which were originally issued at par value to a shareholder that is retiring. The company has agreed to buy these shares back at a premium of 0.30p. The company has also agreed to issue a further 1,000 ordinary £1 shares at a premium of £2.00.

	£
Purchase cost (4,000 × £1.30)	5,200
Profit and loss account reserves	(1,500)
Proceeds from new share issue (1,000 × £3.00)	(3,000)
Permissible capital payment	700
Value of purchase at par value	4,000
Proceeds from new share issue	(3,000)
Permissible capital payment	(700)
Transfer to capital redemption reserve	300

In order to get the above transaction into the accounts, the company will make the following journal entries:

DR cash at bank	3,000
CR ordinary share capital	(1,000)
CR share premium account	(2,000)
Being issue of new shares at £2 premium	
DR ordinary share capital	4,000
DR profit and loss account reserves	1,200
CR cash at bank	(5,200)

Effect of buy-back of 4,000 shares at a 30p premium

DR profit and loss account	300
CR capital redemption reserve	(300)

To maintain the company's capital

Company D's balance sheet will now look like this:

	£
Cash at bank and in hand	11,800
Ordinary share capital (£1 shares)	7,000
Share premium	4,500
Capital redemption reserve	300
Profit and loss account	nil
	11,800

Distributions

27.21 If an entity makes any distributions to its shareholders, then it must reduce the value of its equity for the amount of the distribution to comply with FRS 102, paragraph 22.17. The entity is also required to comply with FRS 102, paragraph 22.18 and disclose the fair value of any non-cash assets that have been transferred to owners during the reporting period. An exception to this requirement is where the non-cash assets are ultimately controlled by the same parties both before and after the distribution.

Group issues

27.22 In a set of consolidated financial statements where a parent does not wholly own a subsidiary company, the equity section of the consolidated balance sheet (statement of financial position) will comprise of the non-controlling interest (minority interest) share of net assets. FRS 102, paragraph 22.19 says that where changes in a parent's controlling interest in a subsidiary does not result in the parent losing control, the transaction is treated as one between equity holders and therefore does not have any impact on profit or loss. FRS 102 is different to previous UK GAAP in that a gain or loss relating to a partial disposal where the parent still retains control following the transaction, would have been recognised in the consolidated profit and loss account (income statement).

Example 27.15 – Retention of control

Company A owns 90% of Company B. Company B has net assets amounting to £4,000 and Company A sells a 10% interest for £500 to the non-controlling interests.

In this scenario, Company A still has a controlling interest as ownership has reduced from 90% to 80%. The entries in the equity section of the consolidated balance sheet are as follows:

DR	Cash at bank	£500
CR	Non-controlling interest	£50 (ie 10% × £500)
CR	Equity	£450

Focus

There is no change in the carrying amount of assets (including goodwill) or liabilities as a result of such transactions.

SUMMARY – WHAT IS DIFFERENT FROM THE PREVIOUS UK GAAP?

- There are few changes to the way in which share capital and equity are accounted for in FRS 102. Users may notice some terminology changes (profit and loss reserves = retained earnings, minority interests = non-controlling interests and capital and reserves = equity).

- Previous UK GAAP did not contain any specific requirements on accounting for the distribution of non-cash assets, which is now covered in FRS 102, paragraph 22.18.

- In a step acquisition, or partial disposal, where there is a change in the parent's controlling interest in a subsidiary (and where the parent still retains control of the subsidiary following the transaction), the transaction is treated as one between equity holders and therefore there is no impact on profit or loss. However, under the previous UK GAAP, in the case of a disposal, any gain or loss that arose on the transaction would have been recognised in the consolidated profit and loss account.

Chapter 28

Share-based payment

SIGNPOSTS

- Previous accounting treatments did not recognise an expense in profit or loss in respect of share-based payment arrangements, therefore standards were introduced to address such issues accordingly and to make adequate disclosures so that users can obtain an understanding of the effect share-based payment arrangements have on an entity's financial statements (see **28.1** and **28.2**).

- Section 28 deals with all share-based payment transactions including equity-settled share-based payment transactions and cash-settled share-based payment transactions. In addition, the Section also deals with share-based payment transactions where the terms of the grant provide for a choice of receiving goods or services or settling the transaction in cash, other assets or issuing equity instruments (see **28.3**).

- Goods or services acquired or received in a share-based payment transactions are recognised when the company obtains the goods or receives the services (see **28.4**).

- Vesting dates are not relevant where goods are concerned because the date on which the goods are received is effectively the vesting date. However, the vesting date is particularly relevant where employee services are concerned (see **28.5**).

- For equity-settled share-based payment transactions, the entity measures the goods or services received, and the corresponding uplift in equity, at the fair value of the goods or services received (see **28.6**).

- For transactions with employees, the entity measures the fair value of the equity instruments at the grant date and for transactions with other third parties, the measurement date is the date on which the entity obtains the goods or the third party renders the services (see **28.7**).

- The measurement of shares and the related goods or services rendered follows the fair value hierarchy approach (see **28.8** and **28.9**).

- An entity could modify the terms and conditions on which equity instruments were originally granted and if this is done to the benefit of the employee, the entity must take into account the modified vesting conditions in accounting for the share-based payment transaction (see **28.10**).

- Cancellations of an equity-settled share-based payment award are accounted for as an acceleration of vesting (see **28.11**).

- Liabilities in respect of cash-settled share-based payment transactions are measured at the fair value of the liability and any changes in fair value are recognised in profit or loss for the period (see **28.12**).

- For share-based payment transactions with cash alternatives, these will be accounted for as cash-settled share-based payment transactions; although there are two exceptions (see **28.13**).

- The expense in a group share-based payment arrangement can be recognised and measured on the basis of a reasonable allocation of the expense for the group (see **28.14**).

- In more complex group situations, there are additional factors that must be considered when recognising the expense relating to a share-based payment transaction (see **28.15**).

- Equity investors obtaining equity without providing goods or services, or where the goods or services supplied or rendered are clearly less than the fair value of the equity instruments granted gives an indication that other consideration has been, or will be, received (see **28.16**).

- Disclosures are required in the financial statements of an entity participating in a share-based payment arrangement (see **28.17**).

INTRODUCTION

28.1   The granting of share options to employees has become increasingly common over the years with many companies now operating such plans as part of efforts by the company to motivate employees to help the company increase profitability. Previous accounting concepts did not recognise an expense in respect of the share-based payment arrangement because there is no associated cash flow and, as such, accounting standards governing the accounting for share-based payment arrangements brought a new approach. Often the shares are awarded to employees at nominal value or at zero cost but share-based payment arrangements are also used as a method by which entities can procure other goods or services.

28.2 Section 26, Share-based Payment deals with the accounting for such arrangements as well as outlining the required disclosures a reporting entity participating in such a scheme is required to make in their financial statements.

SCOPE

28.3 Section 26 applies to all share-based payment transactions including:

- *Equity-settled share-based payment transactions* in which an entity receives goods or services (but has no obligation to settle the transaction with the supplier). Such arrangements also includes employees' services, as consideration for its own equity instruments. Such transactions include employee share option and share incentive plans.

- *Cash-settled share-based payment transactions* in which an entity acquires goods or services by incurring liabilities (usually to be settled in cash), but where the amount paid is based on the price (or value) of the entity's shares or other equity instruments.

- Transactions in which the entity receives or acquires goods or services and the terms of the arrangement provide either the entity or the supplier of those goods or services with a choice of whether the entity settles the transaction in cash (or other assets) or by issuing equity instruments (eg shares).

Section 26 recognises that some share-based payment transactions may be settled by another group entity, or shareholder of a group entity, on behalf of the company that receives or acquires the goods or services as well as applying to an entity that:

- receives goods or services when another entity in the same group (or shareholder of any group entity) has the obligation to settle the share-based payment transaction; or

- has an obligation to settle a share-based payment transaction when another entity in the same group receives the goods or services.

The overarching objective of Section 26 is to provide the accounting treatment to require an entity to reflect the effect of share-based payment arrangements in the profit and loss account (income statement).

RECOGNITION

28.4 Goods or services which are received or acquired in a share-based payment transaction are recognised when the company obtains the goods or receives the services. The corresponding credit entry will either be to equity or to liabilities.

Example 28.1 – Accounting for an equity-settled share-based payment transaction

A company receives goods that are subjected to a share-based payment transaction as agreed with the supplier. The terms of the agreement confirm that the share-based payment arrangement is that of an equity-settled share-based payment transaction. The bookkeeper has correctly debited the cost of the goods to the appropriate profit and loss expense account but is unsure where the credit entry should be posted to.

As the arrangement is that of an *equity-settled* share-based payment transaction, the credit entry will be to equity.

Example 28.2 – Accounting for a cash-settled share-based payment transaction

A company receives goods that are again subjected to a share-based payment transaction as agreed with the supplier. The terms of the agreement provide for the transaction to be cash-settled. Again the bookkeeper has correctly debited the cost of the goods to the appropriate profit and loss expense account but is unsure where the credit side should be posted to.

As this arrangement is that of a *cash-settled* share-based payment transaction, the credit entry will be to a liability account.

Focus

If the goods or services that have been received or acquired by the company in a share-based payment arrangement do not qualify for recognition as assets (eg fixed assets), the company must recognise them as an expense in the profit and loss account.

VESTING CONDITIONS

28.5   The term *vesting conditions* refers to conditions that the third party must satisfy in order to become entitled to receive cash, other assets or shares in a share-based payment arrangement at the *vesting date* which is the date on which the shares become exercisable.

Where goods are involved in a share-based payment the vesting date is not relevant because the date on which the goods are received becomes the vesting date. However, in respect of employee services, the vesting date is particularly relevant. When a company issues shares that immediately vest, the presumption is that these shares are a form of consideration of past employee service, hence the company must immediately recognise the expense for the employee services as they have been received in full on the date on which the shares (or share options) have been granted. This is in accordance with paragraph 26.5 to FRS 102.

For the purposes of this Section, the Glossary defines the term 'grant date' as follows:

'The date at which the entity and another party (including an employee) agree to a share-based payment arrangement, being when the entity and the counterparty have a shared understanding of the terms of the arrangement. At grant date the entity confers on the party the right to *cash*, other *assets*, or equity instruments of the entity, provided the specified vesting conditions, if any, are met. If that agreement is subject to an approval process (for example, by shareholders), grant date is the date when that approval is obtained.'

Example 28.3 – Ascertaining the grant date

On 5 July 2013, the directors of Alex Automobiles PLC sent letters to its employees offering options to subscribe to shares in the entity of 10,000 shares at the market price of £9.50 per share. This letter was agreed at a board meeting, where all directors voted unanimously in favour of the offer. The awards were approved by the shareholders on 29 July 2013 by which time the market price of the shares had risen to £11.25 per share and the fair value of the options had also increased. The question arises as to the grant date. Is it:

- the date on which the original offers were made (5 July 2013); or

- the date on which the awards were approved by shareholders (29 July 2013)?

The allotment of shares or rights to shares in general must be approved by the shareholders in a general meeting, or by the entity's articles. The award was subject to shareholder approval and thus, in this case, the grant date is 29 July 2013.

However, in situations when the share-based payment does *not* vest until the employee completes a specific period of service, the company will presume the services to be rendered by the employee as consideration for those share-based payments will be receivable in the future, during the vesting period. As a consequence, the entity shall account for such services as they are rendered by the employee during the vesting period with a corresponding increase in equity or liabilities.

Example 28.4 – Simple share-based payment transaction

Alicia's Interiors Limited grants 2,000 share options to each of its three directors on 1 January 2014. The terms of the options are that the directors must still be in the employment of the company on 31 December 2016 when the options vest. The fair value of each option as at 1 January 2014 is £10 and all of the options are expected to vest. The options will only vest if Alicia's Interiors share price reaches £16 per share. As at 31 December 2014, the share price was only £7 and it is not expected to rise in the next two years. Further, it is expected that only two directors will be employed as at 31 December 2016.

The increase in the share price should be ignored for the purposes of calculating the value of the share options as at 31 December 2014. Market conditions are ignored for the purposes of estimating the number of shares that will vest (the idea behind this is that these conditions have already been taken into consideration when fair valuing the shares). However, the fact that only two directors will be employed as at 31 December 2016 must be taken into account, hence the calculation will be:

2,000 options × 2 directors × £10 × 1 year/3 years = £13,333

The journals will be:

DR profit and loss account

CR equity

Focus

It is acceptable to present the credit entry in profit and loss reserves and this is where it is commonly seen. It would be permissible in the UK and Republic of Ireland to present the credit entry within a separate 'Share-based payment reserve' but it is important that any credit is *not* taken to the share premium account.

MEASUREMENT PRINCIPLES

Equity-settled share-based payment arrangements

28.6   Clearly there are situations where a large degree of uncertainty will be present in share-based payment transactions such as market conditions, share prices and stability of employee numbers. However, Section 26 outlines the measurement principles of share-based payment arrangements in quite some detail.

For *equity-settled* share-based payment transactions, a reporting entity must measure the goods or services received (together with the corresponding uplift in equity) at the fair value of the goods or services received. Where this is not possible, the reporting entity must measure the fair value by reference to the fair value of the equity instruments granted. There is an inherent difficulty in measuring these values where employees' services are concerned and this issue is addressed in paragraph 26.7. For transactions with employees and others that provide similar services, a reporting entity must measure the fair value of the services received by reference to the fair value of the equity instruments granted. Typically, it is not possible to reliably estimate the fair value of the services received.

28.7   For transactions with employees, a reporting entity must measure the fair value of the equity instruments at the grant date. For transactions with third parties (other than employees) the measurement date becomes the date on which the entity obtains the goods, or the third party renders the service.

Focus

All vesting conditions that relate purely to employee service or to a non-market performance condition (such as a company achieving a pre-determined growth in profit) must be taken into account when estimating the number of equity instruments that are expected to vest. A reporting entity must revise that if new information emerges that indicates the number of instruments expected to vest differs from previous estimates. This has the effect that on the vesting date the company will revise the estimate to equal the number of equity instruments that ultimately vested. Paragraph 26.9 confirms that all market conditions and non-vesting conditions are taken into consideration when estimating the fair value of the shares or share options at the measurement date, with no subsequent adjustment regardless of the outcome of the market or non-vesting condition (provided that all other vesting conditions are satisfied).

28.8   *Share-based payment*

Example 28.5 – Settling of fees by way of a share-based payment

Sarmonia Enterprises PLC (Sarmonia) has hired the services of a management consultant to liaise with its major customers to identify any areas of concern its customers have with the services that Sarmonia provide to them. The management consultant will interview the major customers and put a comprehensive report together for the board of directors of Sarmonia who will then instigate a process to implement any recommendations. It is estimated that this process will take six months to complete.

The company and the management consultant have agreed that the fees for this service can be settled by way of 100 shares to the consultant which have been independently valued at £30,000 at the date the contract was signed by both parties. The value of the service has been calculated at £27,000 – an average of the other bids received from similar management consultants. In addition, the company has also received confirmation that for the purposes of this exercise, the management consultant is to be classed as employee in the eyes of HM Revenue and Customs.

As the management consultant is to be considered as an employee, management should recognise the service at the fair value of the granted equity instruments, which is £30,000.

28.8   The measurement of shares (together with the related goods or services received) follows the fair value hierarchy approach and paragraph 26.10 requires reporting entities to do as follows:

- If an observable market price is available for the equity instruments granted, use that price.

- If an observable market price is not available, measure the fair value of equity instruments granted using the entity-specific observable market data such as:

  o   a recent transaction in the entity's shares; or

  o   a recent independent fair valuation of the entity or its principal assets.

- If an observable market price is not available and obtaining a reliable measurement of fair value is impracticable, indirectly measure the fair value of the shares using a valuation technique that uses market data to the greatest extent practicable to estimate what the price of those equity instruments would be on the grant date in an arm's-length transaction between knowledgeable, willing parties. Paragraph 26.10(c) requires the directors to apply their judgement in applying an accepted valuation methodology for valuing equity instruments that is appropriate in the entity's circumstances.

28.9   For share options and equity-settled share appreciation rights, an entity must measure the fair value of share options and equity-settled share appreciation rights (together with the related goods or services received) using the three-tier fair value hierarchy in paragraph 26.11 as follows:

*   If an observable market price is available for the equity instruments granted, use that price.

*   If an observable market price is not available, measure the fair value of share options and share appreciation rights granted using entity-specific observable market data as for a recent transaction in the share options.

*   If an observable market price is not available and obtaining a reliable measurement of fair value is impracticable, indirectly measure the fair value of share options or share appreciation rights using an alternative valuation methodology such as an option pricing model (eg the Black-Scholes Model). The inputs for an option pricing model (such as the weighted average share price, exercise price, expected volatility, option life, expected dividends and the risk-free interest rate) will use market data to the greatest extent possible. Paragraph 28.8 above gives further guidance on determining the fair value of the shares used in determining the weighted-average share price. The entity shall derive an estimate of expected volatility consistent with the valuation methodology used to determine the fair value of the shares.

MODIFYING THE TERMS AND CONDITIONS

28.10   An entity could modify the terms and conditions on which equity instruments were originally granted. If an entity does modify the vesting conditions in a manner that is beneficial to the employee, the entity must take the modified vesting conditions into consideration in accounting for the share-based payment transaction. Paragraph 26.12 to FRS 102 outlines the ways in which this is undertaken as follows:

*   If the modification increases the fair value of the equity instruments granted (or increases the number of equity instruments granted) measured immediately before and after the modification, the entity shall include the incremental fair value granted in the measurement of the amount recognised for services received as consideration for the equity instruments granted. The incremental fair value granted is the difference between the fair value of the modified equity instrument and that of the original equity instrument, both estimated as at the date of the modification. If the modification occurs during the vesting period, the incremental fair value granted is included in the measurement of the amount recognised for services received over the period from the modification date until the date when the modified equity instruments vest, in addition to the amount based on the grant date fair value of the

original equity instruments, which is recognised over the remainder of the original vesting period.

- If the modification reduces the total fair value of the share-based payment arrangement, or apparently is not otherwise beneficial to the employee, the entity shall nevertheless continue to account for the services received as consideration for the equity instruments granted as if that modification had not occurred.

Example 28.6 – Modifications to the terms and conditions

Zedcolour Trading PLC (Zedcolour) operated a share option award with an option exercise price of £20 (this price is equivalent to the market price of the shares at the grant date). At the Annual General Meeting, the directors voted to roll these options into a new award. As a consequence, Zedcolour cancelled the original options and issues new share options under the new award. The new options are granted at a price of £17 because the market price of the shares had fallen to £16 since the date of the grant of the old award; the original exercise price was below the market price of the shares at the date of the grant of the new options. In all other respects, the terms of the grant are the same.

The fact that Zedcolour has cancelled one award and replaced it with another would not constitute a 'cancellation' and a subsequent new award. This would be classed as a modification because Zedcolour has indicated that this new award replaces a cancelled award, therefore it is treated as if it has been modified. Zedcolour would have to account for the incremental fair value of the new award (compared with the existing award) at the date of modification and spread this over the vesting period of the new award. Zedcolour would continue to charge for the original award over the original vesting period.

28.11   If an entity cancels an equity-settled share-based payment award, it will account for such a cancellation as an acceleration of vesting, and will immediately recognise the amount that would otherwise have been recognised for services received over the remainder of the vesting period.

Example 28.7 – Cancellation

On 1 January 2012, Breary Corporation PLC (Breary) made an award of 100 ordinary shares to one of its employees on the condition that the employee must remain in the employment of Breary for a period of three years. At the grant date, the fair value of the award was £1,200 and, as the employee was a long-standing employee of Breary, it was considered the award was expected to vest. The company has a 31 December year-end.

On 1 January 2013, it was agreed that Breary would cancel the award. The company duly settled, in cash, based on a pro-rata basis, hence the employee received £400 (£1,200 × 1/3). In the 2013 financial statements, Breary recognised £400 as an expense (£1,200 × 1/3). However, paragraph 26.14 to FRS 102 requires the entity to account for the cancellation or settlement of an equity-settled share-based payment award as an acceleration of vesting and recognise immediately the amount that it would have otherwise recognised for services received over the remainder of the vesting period. Therefore, on the basis of the number of awards outstanding at the cancellation date, Breary should recognise £800 as an expense (£1,200 less £400) with the associated credit entry to equity.

Cash-settled share-based payment arrangements

28.12 For cash-settled share-based payment transactions, reporting entities are required to follow the requirements in paragraph 26.14 which requires entities to measure the goods or services acquired and the liability incurred at the fair value of the liability. Until the liability is settled, the entity must remeasure the fair value of the liability at each reporting date and at the date of settlement. Any changes in fair value must be recognised in profit or loss for the period.

Example 28.8 – Cash-settled share-based payment with remeasurement

Byrne Enterprises PLC grants 1,000 share options to 50 members of management on 1 January 2010. The terms of the arrangement are that on the exercise date, the employees will receive cash which will be equivalent to the increase in the company's share price since the grant date. All of the options vest on 31 December 2011 and can be exercised during 2012 and 2013. The directors of Byrne Enterprises estimate that, at the date of the grant, the fair value of each share option will be £10 and that 10% of the management team will leave evenly during the two-year period. Details of the fair values of the options at each year-end are shown below:

31 December 2010	£13
31 December 2011	£ 9
31 December 2012	£12
31 December 2013	£11

The director's estimate that 10% of management would leave before the end of 2011. The intrinsic value of each option as at 31 December 2012 was £10 and six employees exercised their options, whilst the remaining 39 exercised their options at the end of 2013 when the intrinsic value was equal to the fair value of £11. The amount recognised as an expense and as a liability each year is as follows:

Year		Expense £	Liability £
2010	45 × 1,000 × 13 × ½	292,500	292,500
2011	45 × 1,000 × 9	112,500	405,000
2012	39 × 1,000 × 12	123,000	468,000*
2013	39 × 1,000 × 11	(39,000)	0**

* = the expense includes an additional £60,000 being the cash paid to those exercising their options (six employees × 1,000 × £10).

** = the liability is extinguished and the previous cost reversed as cash paid to those that have exercised their options of (39 × 1,000 × £11) was less than the opening liability of £468,000.

SHARE-BASED PAYMENT TRANSACTIONS WITH CASH ALTERNATIVES

28.13   In some situations, an entity that has entered into a share-based payment arrangement with a third party, or the third party themselves, can have the choice of settling the transaction either in cash, by way of other assets, or by a transfer of equity instruments. In such instances the reporting entity will account for the transaction as a cash-settled share-based payment transaction. However, there are two exceptions to this requirement:

- the entity has a past practice of settling by issuing equity instruments; or

- the option has no commercial substance because the cash settlement amount bears no relationship to, and is likely to be lower in value than, the fair value of the equity instrument.

In the above two cases, the reporting entity will account for the transaction as an equity-settled share-based payment.

GROUP PLANS

28.14　　Paragraph 26.16 to FRS 102 deals with the issue of share-based payment transactions in a group situation. The paragraph confirms that where a share-based payment award is granted to the employees of one or more members in a group, the expense can be recognised and measured on the basis of a reasonable allocation of the expense for the group.

The issue here is that sometimes it may be uncertain which entity, or entities, within a group of companies should reflect the share-based payment charge within the individual financial statements.

Example 28.9 – Identification of the share-based payment charge

The Heaton Group of Companies has a parent company and 35 subsidiary companies and the group employs several hundred employees, 175 of whom have share options which can be exercised in four years' time. These employees also perform services for other members of the group.

In such a situation, the reporting entity that is essentially the staff member's employer should bear the charge within its individual financial statements.

28.15　　Where group plans are concerned there is often confusion as to where to allocate the share-based payment expense. A number of additional factors should be considered, as not all instances will be as simplistic as the example above. Such factors include:

- Has a service company arrangement been established? In these situations it is more than likely that a staff member will be seconded to other entities within the group, but the 'principal' employer will be the service company, hence the service company will take the share-based payment charge in its financial statements.

- Which member company in the group receives the rewards associated with the employee? This is often the case with directors that act as a director at both parent level and at an individual subsidiary level. Consideration should be given to whether the director receives the reward for the group as a whole, or whether the director receives the reward in respect of the subsidiary. If it is the latter, then the subsidiary would be deemed the 'employer', hence the subsidiary should take the share-based payment charge.

- Which entity within the group bears the cost of the employment? In many group situations there are inter-group recharges to the subsidiary receiving the employee services and, in this respect, the share-based payment charge would follow the costs of the employee (ie the subsidiary receiving the recharge).

- What are the terms of the employee's contract? If the employee's contract stipulates that they may be temporarily seconded to another entity within the group, the entity receiving the employee on secondment would be deemed the employer for the period of the secondment.

- Which entity is responsible for issuing the employee's contract and appraising the employee as well as sanctioning overtime and bonuses? Share-based payment charges would normally be included within the entity having responsibility for performing such functions.

GOVERNMENT-MANDATED PLANS

28.16   There are programmes in some jurisdictions (though these are rarely seen in practice) whereby equity investors can obtain equity in an entity without providing goods or performing services which can be specifically identified. Alternatively, equity investors can provide goods and perform services which are clearly less than the fair value of the equity instruments granted and in such situations the indication is that other consideration has been, or will be, received.

Such arrangements are to be accounted for as equity-settled share-based payment arrangements. The portion of the unidentifiable goods or services (to be) received will be measured as the difference between the fair value of the share-based payment and the fair value of any identifiable goods or services (to be) received measured at the grant date.

DISCLOSURES

28.17   Paragraphs 26.18 to 26.23 outline the disclosures required in a reporting entity's financial statements that has entered into share-based payment transactions. The following information concerning the nature and extent of share-based payment arrangements that existed during the period shall be disclosed as follows:

- A description of each type of share-based payment arrangement that existed at any time during the period, including the general terms and conditions of each arrangement, such as vesting requirements, the maximum terms of options granted, and the method of settlement (eg whether in cash or equity). An entity with substantially similar types of share-based payment arrangements may aggregate this information.

- The number and weighted average exercise prices of share options for each of the following groups of options:

    o   outstanding at the beginning of the period;

    o   granted during the period;

    o   forfeited during the period;

    o   exercised during the period;

    o   expired during the period;

    o   outstanding at the end of the period; and

    o   exercisable at the end of the period.

For equity-settled share-based payment arrangements, an entity shall disclose information about how it measured the fair value of goods or services received or the value of the equity instruments granted. If a valuation methodology was used, the entity shall disclose the method and its reason for choosing it.

For cash-settled share-based payment arrangements, an entity shall disclose information about how the liability was measured.

For share-based payment arrangements modified during the period, an entity shall disclose an explanation of those modifications.

If the entity is part of a group share-based payment plan, and it recognises and measures its share-based payment expense on the basis of a reasonable allocation of the expense recognised for the group, it shall disclose that fact and the basis for the allocation (see **28.14** above).

An entity shall disclose the following information about the effect of share-based payment transactions on the entity's profit or loss for the period and on its financial position:

- the total expense recognised in profit or loss for the period; and

- the total carrying amount at the end of the period for liabilities arising from share-based payment transactions.

SUMMARY – WHAT IS DIFFERENT FROM THE PREVIOUS UK GAAP?

- FRS 20 *Share-based Payment* specifically required the use of an option pricing model where fair values were not available. In FRS 102, the use of an option pricing model is not mandatory.

- There is no option in FRS 20 to recognise a charge that is based on an allocation of the group expense, whereas in FRS 102 a charge based on a reasonable allocation of the group expense is required.

- Potentially, more judgement is needed on the part of the directors under FRS 102.

Chapter 29

Consolidated and separate financial statements

SIGNPOSTS

- This chapter deals mainly with basic consolidation procedures, including share disposals and purchases – note that discontinued operations are dealt with in **Chapter 33**.

- The crucial concept of control – which triggers the need to consolidate on a line-by-line basis, is dealt with in **29.4** below.

- Business combinations and goodwill are dealt with in **Chapter 30**.

- Section 9 of FRS 102 requires special purpose entities (SPEs) to be consolidated on a line-by-line basis (see **29.10** onwards).

- Section 9 permits merger accounting to be used in restricted circumstances relating to internal group reconstructions (see **29.32** and **30.42**).

- Issues specific to foreign operations are dealt with in **Chapter 32**, whilst those relating to joint ventures and associates are dealt with in **Chapter 31**.

- Reduced disclosure exemptions for individual financial statements of parents companies and subsidiaries are dealt with in **Chapter 34**.

INTRODUCTION AND SCOPE

29.1   This chapter deals with issues in Section 9 of FRS 102 including:

- the circumstances in which an entity should prepare consolidated financial statements including scope exemptions;

- the procedures for preparing consolidated financial statements; and

- guidance on separate financial statements.

Scope

29.2   Section 9 of FRS 102 applies to all parents that prepare consolidated financial statements. *CA 2006* uses the term 'group accounts'. Paragraph 9.1 requires that parents which do not report under *CA 2006* should comply with the requirements of Section 9 (and the requirements of *CA 2006* where referred to in Section 9) except to the extent that these requirements are not permitted by any statutory framework under which such parent entities report.

DEFINITIONS

Parent and subsidiary

29.3   A parent is defined as an entity that has one or more subsidiaries.

A subsidiary is defined as an entity, including an unincorporated entity such as a partnership, that is controlled by another entity (known as the parent).

This definition is slightly different, and considerably shorter, than that in existing UK GAAP (*CA 2006, s 1162*), but the differences are unlikely to have practical implications in most circumstances.

Control

29.4   Control is referred to in paragraphs 9.4 to 9.6A. The key points in these paragraphs are as follows:

- control is the power to govern the financial and operating policies of an entity so as to obtain benefits from its activities;

- control is presumed to exist when the parent owns, directly or indirectly through subsidiaries, more than half of the voting power of an entity (in exceptional circumstances, it potentially could be demonstrated that such ownership does not constitute control);

- paragraph 9.5 sets out circumstances where control exists when the parent owns half or less of the entity's voting power;

- control can also be achieved by having options or convertible instruments that are currently exercisable; and

- control can also exist when the parent has the power to exercise, or actually exercises, dominant influence or control over the undertaking, or it and the undertaking are managed on a unified basis.

REQUIREMENT TO PRESENT CONSOLIDATED FINANCIAL STATEMENTS

29.5   Subject to the exemptions referred to immediately below, a parent entity which is a parent at the year-end is required to present consolidated financial statements which include all of its subsidiaries.

29.6   Paragraph 9.3 exempts a parent from preparing consolidated financial statements on *any* one of the following grounds:

- the parent is a wholly owned subsidiary and its immediate parent is established under the law of an EEA State (exemption is conditional on compliance with *CA 2006, s 400(2)*);

- the parent is a majority-owned subsidiary and meets all the conditions for exemption in *section 400(2)* as well as the additional conditions in *section 400(1)(b)*;

- the parent is a wholly owned subsidiary of another entity and that parent is not established under the law of an EEA State – exemption is conditional on compliance with *section 401(2)*;

- the parent is a majority-owned subsidiary and meets all the conditions for exemption as a wholly owned subsidiary set out in *section 401(2)*, as well as the conditions set out in *section 401(1)(b)*;

- the parent, and group headed by it, qualify as small as set out in *section 383*, and the group is not ineligible as set out in *section 384*;

- all of the parent's subsidiaries are required to be excluded from consolidation (see **29.7** below); and

- for parents not reporting under *CA 2006*, if the parent's statutory framework does not require the preparation of consolidated financial statements.

EXCLUSION FROM CONSOLIDATION

29.7   A subsidiary *should* be excluded from consolidation in either of the following circumstances:

- severe long-term restrictions substantially hinder the exercise of the rights of the parent over the assets or management of the subsidiary; or

- the interest in the subsidiary is held exclusively with a view to subsequent resale and the subsidiary has not previously been consolidated within the consolidated financial prepared in accordance with FRS 102.

29.8   If a subsidiary is excluded on the grounds of 'held exclusively with a view to subsequent resale' and it is held as part of an investment portfolio, it should be measured at fair value with changes in fair value recognised in profit or loss.

Example 29.1 – Investments held exclusively with a view to resale

Holdings Limited holds a controlling interest in several companies. Two of these holdings are held purely for capital appreciation and investment income. These should be consolidated on a line-by-line basis, but instead are presented as one-line items in the consolidated financial statements.

The two investments should be presented in the consolidated balance sheet as one-line items and measured at fair value. Changes in fair value should be dealt with in the consolidated income statement/profit and loss account in arriving at profit for the year.

These should not be consolidated on a line-by-line basis. For further and more detailed guidance in complex cases, it may be helpful to refer to the amendment to IFRS 10 *Consolidated Financial Statements* dealing with investment entities.

29.9   If it is *not* held as part of an investment portfolio, it should be measured in accordance with FRS 102, paragraph 9.26, which is dealt with in **29.13** below.

SPECIAL PURPOSE ENTITIES

29.10   The standard requires consolidated financial statements to include, on a usual line-by-line basis, any special purpose entities (SPE) that are controlled by the entity.

29.11   An entity may be created to accomplish a narrow objective such as undertaking research and development activities or facilitating employee shareholdings. Such an SPE may take the form of a corporation, trust, partnership or unincorporated entity.

This is a complex area and is dealt with only briefly in FRS 102. Paragraph 9.11 lists the following as circumstances which may indicate that an entity controls an SPE, including:

* the activities of the SPE are being conducted on behalf of the entity according to its specific business needs;

* the entity has the ultimate decision-making powers over the activities of the SPE, even if the day-to-day decisions have been delegated;

389

- the entity has rights to obtain the majority of the benefits of the SPE and therefore may be exposed to risks incidental to the activities of the SPE; and

- the entity retains the majority of the residual or ownership risks related to the SPE or its assets.

29.12   SPEs are not defined in the Glossary, but features of SPEs (including those above) are described in FRS 102, paragraphs 9.10–9.12.

CONSOLIDATION PROCEDURES

Basic elements

29.13   The consolidated financial statements should present financial information about the group as a single economic entity. The following key procedures should be followed (FRS 102, paragraph 9.13):

- combine the financial statements of the parent and subsidiaries line-by-line by adding together like items of assets, liabilities, equity, income and expenses;

- eliminate the carrying amount of the parent's investment in each subsidiary and the parent's portion of equity of each subsidiary;

- measure and present non-controlling interest in the profit or loss of subsidiaries separately from the interest of the owners of the parent (see **29.23**); and

- measure and present non-controlling interests in the net assets of the subsidiaries separately from the parent shareholders' equity in them (see **29.23**).

Intra-group balances and transactions

29.14   Intra-group balances and transactions and profits and losses arising from intra-group transactions recognised in assets such as inventory and property, plant and equipment should be eliminated in full.

29.15   Intra-group losses may indicate an impairment that requires recognition in the consolidated financial statements.

29.16   Paragraph 9.15 refers to the deferred tax implications arising from eliminations of profits and losses resulting from intra-group transactions.

Uniform reporting date

29.17   The financial statements of the parent and its subsidiaries should be prepared to the same reporting date unless it is impracticable to do so.

29.18   Where the reporting date and reporting period of a subsidiary are not the same as those of the parent, the consolidated financial statements are made up in one of two ways:

- by combining the financial statements of the subsidiary made up to an earlier date than that of the parent and adjusting for the effect of significant transactions or events between the two reporting dates – provided that the reporting date of the subsidiary is no more than three months before that of the parent; or

- using interim statements prepared by the subsidiary and made up to the parent's reporting date.

Example 29.2 – Non-coterminous year-ends

A group is preparing consolidated financial statements for the year to 31 December 2015. One subsidiary makes up its accounts to 30 September.

The group has two options:

The preferred option is to include nine months of the results of the subsidiary for the period from 1 January 2015 to 30 September and three months of the unaudited results based on interim management accounts for the period from 1 October 2015 to 31 December 2015; or

The less ideal option would be to consolidate the full year accounts for the year to 30 September 2015 and make adjustments for any significant transactions of the subsidiary between 1 October 2015 and 31 December 2015.

Uniform accounting policies

29.19   Uniform accounting policies should be used for like transactions and other events and conditions in similar circumstances.

29.20   Where a member of the group uses accounting policies other than those adopted in the consolidated financial statements for like transactions, appropriate adjustments should be made when preparing the consolidated financial statements. This might apply, for example, in the case of a UK Group adopting the FRS 102, which has French and German subsidiaries who use their local GAAP for tax reasons.

MINORITY INTERESTS (NON-CONTROLLING INTERESTS)

Terminology

29.21   Although FRS 102 refers to the term 'non-controlling interest', the term 'minority interest' may continue to be used, if preferred, as it is referred to as such in Schedule 6, paragraph 17 of the Regulations.

MEASUREMENT

29.22   The non-controlling interest (or minority interest) in the profit or loss and of the net assets of consolidated subsidiaries for the reporting period should be measured in accordance with Section 9, paragraph 9.13(d):

- in the consolidated balance sheet, the non-controlling interest (NCI) should consist of the amount of the NCI's interest in the net amount of the identifiable assets, liabilities and contingent liabilities measured in accordance with Section 19, as at the date of the original combination *plus* the NCI's share of changes in equity since that date; and

- in the consolidated statement of comprehensive income, the NCI should be based on its share of profit or loss plus its share of other comprehensive income in the subsidiary.

Subsequent changes in ownership of a subsidiary

29.23   Where a parent, which already has control, acquires further shares in a subsidiary, the transaction should be accounted for as a transaction between equity holders.

Any difference between the amount by which the non-controlling interest is reduced and the fair value of the consideration paid, must be recognised directly in equity. No gain or loss should be recognised in profit or loss and the carrying amount of consolidation goodwill must not be adjusted as a result of the transaction (FRS 102, paragraph 22.19).

Example 29.3 – Subsequent changes in ownership

Minority interest at 1 January 2015 relating to a 30% holding stands at £30,000. The parent company acquires a further 10%, so the minority interest is reduced to 20% or £20,000. Cash paid for the holding is £11,500.

The loss of £1,500 (£30,000 – £20,000 + £11,500) is not recognised in either profit or loss, or other comprehensive income. Instead, it is treated as a movement on profit and loss reserves and dealt with in the statement of changes in equity.

Presentation

29.24   Schedule 6, paragraph 17 of the Regulations requires the minority interest to be presented separately in both the consolidated balance sheet and the consolidated profit and loss account.

29.25   FRS 102, paragraph 5.6 requires the consolidated statement of comprehensive income to present separately the two following amounts:

- NCI share in profit or loss for the period; and

- NCI share of total comprehensive income.

ACQUISITION OF SUBSIDIARIES AND SHARES IN SUBSIDIARIES

General considerations

29.26   Under the method of consolidation normally used, referred to in Section 19.6 as the purchase method (previously referred to as 'acquisition accounting'), income and expenses of subsidiaries are included in the consolidated financial statements from the acquisition date until the date on which the parent ceases to control the subsidiary. Accounting for business combinations is dealt with in **Chapter 30**.

29.27   The special circumstances where the merger accounting method may be used are referred to in **Chapter 30**.

Control achieved in stages

29.28   Where control is acquired in stages (piecemeal acquisition), the entity should apply the following requirements of Sections 9 and 19 of FRS 102:

- FRS 102, paragraph 9.19A refers to control achieved in stages:

   'Where a parent acquires control of a subsidiary in stages, the transaction shall be accounted for in accordance with paragraphs 19.11A and 19.14 applied at the date control is achieved.'

- FRS 102, paragraph 19.11A states:

   'Where control is achieved following a series of transactions, the cost of the business combination is the aggregate of the fair values of the assets given, liabilities assumed and equity instruments issued by the acquirer at the date of each transaction in the series.'

- FRS 102, paragraph 19.22 refers to the difference between the cost of the business combination and the acquirer's interest in the net amount of the identifiable assets, liabilities and contingent liabilities, recognised and measured in accordance with the requirements of FRS 102, paragraphs 19.15, 19.15A–19.15C (see **30.14** and **30.23**).

Example 29.4 – Control achieved in stages

H Limited acquired a controlling interest in S Limited in two transactions as follows:

30 June 2015: 15% holding at a cost of £33,000 when the fair value of the assets of S Limited amounted to £180,000.

31 March 2016: 45% holding at a cost of £162,000 when the fair value of the assets of S Limited amounted to £290,000.

The cost of the business combination is £195,000. The group share of the fair value of the assets at the date control is achieved is 60% × £290,000 = £174,000. Goodwill is therefore £21,000.

29.29   Appendix IV, Note on Legal Requirements, paragraphs A4.19–A4.21 discusses special situations where the above treatment may not be appropriate.

DISPOSAL OF SHARES IN SUBSIDIARIES

Loss of control

29.30   Where a parent ceases to control a subsidiary, a gain or loss on disposal is recognised in the consolidated statement of comprehensive income in arriving at profit or loss for the year.

The gain or loss is measured as the difference between the proceeds of disposal, and the carrying amount of the subsidiary's net assets (including any related goodwill) as at the date of disposal.

FRS 102, paragraph 9.19 sets out specific requirements when the entity ceases to be a subsidiary, but the former parent company subsequently continues to hold an investment in an associate, a jointly controlled entity, or an investment which is neither of these.

In the case of the disposal of a foreign subsidiary, the cumulative amount of any exchange differences relating to that subsidiary which have been recognised in equity, should not be recognised in profit or loss as part of the gain or loss on disposal.

Any amounts relating to that subsidiary and held on voluntary basis in a separate foreign currency reserve should be transferred to retained earnings. Note, however, that paragraph 30.25(a) does not require such amounts to be classified in a separate component of equity as they arose but simply requires the entity to disclose the amount of exchange differences arising during the period and classified in equity at the end of the period.

Disposal where control is retained

29.31 Where a parent reduces its holding in a subsidiary but where control is still retained, the transaction should be accounted for as one between the equity shareholders. The consequent change in non-controlling interest (minority interest) should be recognised directly in equity. Any gain or loss should not be recognised in other comprehensive income (FRS 102, paras 9.19A, 22.19). This contrasts with the requirements in previous UK GAAP to recognise the gain or loss in the profit and loss account (FRS 2.52).

GROUP RECONSTRUCTIONS

29.32 Merger accounting is permitted for internal group reconstructions (business combinations under common control) – basically following the well-established principles of UK GAAP, FRS 6 *Acquisitions and Mergers*. The details of this are contained in paragraphs 19.29–19.33 of Section 19, Business Combinations and Goodwill (see **Chapter 30**).

29.33 Public Benefit Entity Combinations are dealt with in paragraphs PBE34.75–PBE34.86 of Section 34, Specialised Activities.

OTHER ISSUES

Exchanges of businesses or other non-monetary assets for an interest in a subsidiary, joint venture or associate

29.34 This specialised topic (dealt with in paragraphs 9.31–9.32) is not further referred to here. It was included in FRS 102 to maintain the relevant requirements of existing UK GAAP (UITF Abstract 31 with the same title).

Intermediate payment arrangements

29.35 Likewise, this element of previous UK GAAP is taken from UITF Abstract 32 *Employee Benefit Trusts* and other intermediate payment arrangements. Again, this specialised topic is not further referred to here – further reference should be made to paragraphs 9.33–9.38.

DISCLOSURE REQUIREMENTS

29.36   The following disclosures are required:

- the fact that the statements are consolidated statements;

- the basis for concluding that control exists when the parent does not own (directly or indirectly) more than half of the voting power;

- any differences in the respective reporting dates for the financial statements of the parent and its subsidiaries used in the preparation of the consolidated financial statements;

- the nature and extent of any significant restrictions on the ability of subsidiaries to transfer funds to the parent in the form of cash dividends or to repay loans (para 9.23(d), but see also para 7.21 referring to statement of cash flows disclosures); and

- the name of any subsidiary excluded from consolidation and the reason for exclusion.

SEPARATE FINANCIAL STATEMENTS

29.37   When a parent presents separate financial statements, it must adopt a policy of accounting for its investments in subsidiaries, associates and jointly controlled entities, either:

- at cost less impairment; or

- at fair value with changes in fair value recognised in other comprehensive income; or

- at fair value with changes in fair value recognised in profit or loss.

The policy must be applied consistently for all investments in a single class (subsidiaries, associates and jointly controlled entities would each be regarded as a single class).

In practice, it is likely that the cost method will be used in the majority of cases.

29.38   Where a parent prepares separate financial statements, these should disclose that the statements are separate financial statements, together with a description of the methods used to account for the investments in subsidiaries, associates and jointly controlled entities.

29.39   Where a parent uses one of the exemptions from presenting consolidated financial statements (see **29.6** above), it should disclose the grounds on which the parent is exempt.

396

29.40   Special considerations apply where investments are accounted for at fair value, with changes in fair value recognised in profit or loss (paragraph 29.27B refers to *CA 2006* and FRS 102, Section 11 requirements). This is not likely to be a common situation.

SUMMARY – WHAT IS DIFFERENT FROM THE PREVIOUS UK GAAP?

- The requirements of FRS 102 are broadly consistent with existing UK GAAP.

- Section 9, Consolidated and Separate Financial Statements, deals with the preparation of consolidated financial statements. There are some important changes from old UK GAAP.

- Where subsidiaries are held for resale, FRS 102, paragraph 9.9B distinguishes between:

    ○   subsidiaries which are held as part of an investment portfolio – these should be measured at fair value, with changes in fair value recognised in profit or loss; and

    ○   subsidiaries which are not held as part of an investment portfolio – FRS 102 offers an accounting policy choice in accordance with FRS 102, paragraph 9.26 between measurement at cost less impairment provisions and measurement at fair value (with further accounting policy choices between changes in fair value through profit or loss, and changes in fair value through other comprehensive income).

- Where a change in non-controlling interests (minority interests) occurs, but does not result in the parent losing control of the subsidiary, this is treated as a transaction with equity holders and hence has no impact on profit or loss (see **29.31** above).

- As regards the separate financial statements of the parent company, the accounting policy choices for accounting for investments in subsidiaries, associates and jointly controlled entities are set out in **29.37** above.

- Previous UK GAAP did not contain a separate accounting standard for accounting for investments, so companies could only refer to Schedule 1 of the Regulations to CA 2006 (see **7.4**), as they must continue to do now.

- In the few cases where the parent company chose to account for its investments at fair value and followed the alternative accounting rules in Schedule 1, FRS 3 *Reporting Financial Performance* required any revaluations gains or losses to be recognised in the statement of total recognised gains and losses whereas, under FRS 102, these will be included within other comprehensive income.

Chapter 30

Business combinations and goodwill

SIGNPOSTS

- FRS 102 defines a business combination (see **30.2**).

- The purchase method should be used for all business combinations except group reconstructions and specified public benefit entity combinations (see **30.8**).

- The detailed requirements of the purchase method cover: identifying an acquirer; measuring, and if necessary adjusting, the cost of the business combination; allocating the purchase consideration to the assets acquired and liabilities assumed, including hindsight adjustments (see **30.9–30.31**).

- Section 19 deals with control achieved by a series of transactions (see **30.32**).

- Section 19 deals with accounting for goodwill – both positive and negative (see **30.33–30.41**).

- As regards positive goodwill, FRS 102 states that if the entity is unable to make a reliable estimate of the goodwill's useful life, the life shall not exceed five years (see **30.35**).

- Internal group reconstructions are referred to in **30.42** below.

- Disclosure requirements are extensive (see **30.48–30.53**).

SCOPE

30.1   Section 19 applies to all business combinations except for:

- the formation of a joint venture; and

- the acquisition of a group of assets that do not constitute a business (see **30.2**).

The implications of Section 19 for public benefit entities are referred to briefly in paragraphs PBE 19.2A and 19.6(b).

BUSINESS COMBINATIONS

30.2 FRS 102 adds clarification to existing UK GAAP in the light of increasingly complex group and ownership structures.

A business combination is defined as the bringing together of separate entities or businesses into one reporting entity. The term 'business' is defined in the Glossary to FRS 102 as an integrated set of activities and assets conducted and managed for the purpose of providing:

- a return to investors; or

- lower costs or other economic benefits directly and proportionately to policyholders or participants.

A business generally consists of inputs, processes applied to those inputs, and resulting outputs that are, or will be, used to generate revenues. If goodwill is present in a transferred set of activities and assets, the transferred set shall be presumed to be a business.

30.3 Business combinations may be structured in a number of different ways, for legal, taxation or other reasons, including:

- the purchase by an entity of the equity of another entity;

- the purchase of all the net assets of another entity;

- the assumption of the liabilities of another entity; and

- the purchase of some of the net assets of another entity that together form one or more businesses.

Example 30.1 – Share purchase

A Limited acquired the business of a competitor, B Limited, by buying all B's shares for cash. A does not own any other businesses.

In its separate financial statements, A chooses to account for its investment in B at cost (the cost model in paragraph 9.26(a) of Section 9).

Consolidated financial statements will be required, combining the individual assets and liabilities of B with those of A on a line-by-line basis. The excess of the purchase consideration over the fair value of the net assets acquired is accounted for as goodwill.

Example 30.2 – Asset purchase

C Limited acquired the business of a competitor, D Limited. In this case the business combination is effected by the transfer of D's assets and liabilities to C. C does not own any other businesses.

The fair value of the individual assets less liabilities of D will be combined with those of C in C's financial statements. Goodwill representing the excess of the purchase consideration over the fair value of D's net assets will be included in C's balance sheet. As the business combination is a net asset purchase, consolidated financial statements are not applicable.

Focus

The transaction which brings about the business combination may be between the shareholders of the combining entities, or between one entity and the shareholders of another entity.

It may involve the establishment of a new entity to control the combining entities or net assets transferred, or the restructuring of one or more of the combining entities.

30.4 Finance for the possible structures may be provided in a number of ways, including:

- the issue of equity instruments;

- the transfer of cash, cash equivalents, or other assets; or

- a mixture of the above.

30.5 In most business combinations, the acquirer obtains control of one or more other businesses (the acquiree or acquirees).

Control is the power to govern the financial and operating policies of an entity so as to obtain benefits from its activities (see also **29.4** above).

30.6 The acquisition date which is particularly relevant to the purchase method below, is the date on which the acquirer obtains control of the acquiree and from which the application of the purchase method starts (note FRS 102, paragraph 19.17 and **30.30** below).

THE PURCHASE METHOD

Introduction

30.7   The term 'purchase method' used in Section 19 has not previously been used in UK GAAP, but it has the same meaning as the more familiar UK GAAP term, 'acquisition accounting'.

Scope of the purchase method

30.8   FRS 102 requires all business combinations to be accounted for by applying the purchase method with two exceptions:

- group reconstructions which *may* be accounted for using merger accounting (see **30.42**); and

- public benefit entity combinations that are in substance a gift or that are a merger to be accounted for in accordance with Section 34, Specialised Activities (see **40.28**).

Applying the purchase method

30.9   This involves the following three steps, each of which is further referred to below:

- identifying an acquirer;

- measuring the cost of the business combination; and

- allocating the cost of the business combination to assets acquired, and liabilities and provisions assumed.

Identifying an acquirer

30.10   The acquirer is the entity that obtains control of the other combining entities or businesses.

Where it is difficult to identify an acquirer, the following indicators may be helpful:

- if the fair value of one of the combining entities is significantly greater than that of the other combining entity, the one with the greater fair value is likely to be the acquirer;

- if the business combination is effected through an exchange of voting ordinary equity instruments for cash or other assets, the entity giving up cash or other asset is likely to be the acquirer; or

- if the business combination results in the management of one of the combining entities being able to dominate the selection of the management team of the resulting combined entity, the entity whose management is able so to dominate is likely to be the acquirer.

Measuring the cost of the business combination

30.11   The cost of a business combination should be the aggregate of:

- the fair values at acquisition date of the consideration given in the form of assets given, liabilities incurred or assumed, and equity instruments issued by the acquirer, in exchange for control of the acquired; plus

- any costs attributable to the business combination.

Example 30.3 – Determining the cost of a business combination

E Limited acquired all the share capital of F Limited on 30 June 2019 for consideration of 500,000 shares in E (which at acquisition date had a fair value of £6 per share) and £2,750,000 in cash. E Limited has no other investments. The company's reporting date is 30 June 2019 and its first set of consolidated financial statements will be made up to this date.

E incurred the following costs in connection with the acquisition:

- £120,000 expenses for issuing the shares; and

- £150,000 for legal and other advisor fees.

The cost of the business combination should include the £150,000 as these are 'attributable to the business combination' (paragraph 19.11(b)).

The costs of £120,000 should not be capitalised, but should be accounted for as a deduction from equity (Section 22, paragraph 22.9).

The cost of the acquisition is £5.9 million made up of fair value of shares £3 million, cash £2.75 million and expenses £0.15 million. Note that paragraph 19.25(d) requires disclosure of the components of the cost of the combination.

This example is continued further in Examples **30.5** and **30.13**.

Adjustments to the cost of a business combination

30.12   A business combination may provide for an adjustment to the cost of the combination contingent on future events, for example the purchase contract may include an earn-out clause.

In such cases, the acquirer is required to include the estimated amount of that adjustment in calculating the cost of the combination at acquisition date, *provided that the adjustment is probable and can be measured reliably.*

30.13   If the potential adjustment is *not* recognised at acquisition date, it may become probable and capable of reliable measurement at a subsequent date. In this case, the cost of the consideration should be adjusted, with a consequent effect on the amount of goodwill.

Example 30.4 – Contingent purchase consideration

The group acquired the entire issued share capital of Worle Limited for an initial consideration of £1.9 million, satisfied by the issue of 1 million ordinary shares of 50p valued at £1.5 million (ie £1.50 per share) and the payment of £400,000 in cash.

Further consideration may be payable if specified profit targets are achieved. The acquisition agreement provides for contingent consideration of up to £300,000 payable in cash. This is the maximum payable but the actual amount will be determined once the results of Worle Limited for the year ended 31 December 2020 have been finalised.

The calculation of contingent consideration is based upon the application of a series of formulae to the adjusted net profits of Worle Limited for the 12-month period ended 31 December 2018; for each of the two financial years ending 31 December 2019 and 31 December 2020; and to the average adjusted net profits of Worle Limited for the three years ending 31 December 2020.

On the basis of current projections, the company had estimated that the probable amount of contingent consideration will amount to £120,000.

Provided there is reasonable evidence to support the estimate of £120,000, this should be capitalised, with a corresponding entry in provisions. The creditor note should disclose the amount accrued, and state the basis on which further consideration may need to be provided. This may require a brief explanation of the formula for determining the purchase consideration.

The situation will need to be reviewed annually on the basis of the latest available information and the cost of consideration adjusted if appropriate, until the 2020 profits have been finalised and agreed. Further consideration should be provided if the amount payable is probable and can be measured reliably.

ALLOCATING THE PURCHASE CONSIDERATION TO THE ASSETS ACQUIRED AND LIABILITIES ASSUMED

30.14 At acquisition date, the acquirer should allocate the cost of the business combination by recognising the following at fair values at that date:

- the acquiree's identifiable assets and liabilities; or

- a provision for those contingent liabilities that satisfy the recognition criteria in paragraph 19.20 (see **30.27** below).

This is subject to the exceptions referred to in **30.25** below.

30.15 Any difference between:

- the cost of the business combination; *and*

- the acquirer's interest in the net amount of the identifiable assets, liabilities and contingent liabilities satisfying the recognition criteria, should be accounted for as either positive or negative *goodwill* (see **30.35** and **30.40**).

Goodwill is defined in the Glossary to FRS 102 as 'future economic benefits arising from assets that are not capable of being individually identified and separately recognised'.

30.16 The respective assets and liabilities should be recognised separately only if they satisfy the following three conditions:

- in the case of an asset other than an intangible asset, it is probable that any associated future benefits will flow to the acquirer and the asset's fair value can be measured reliably;

- in the case of a liability other than a contingent liability, it is probable that an outflow of resources will be required to settle the obligation and its fair value can be measured reliably; and

- in the case of an intangible asset or a contingent liability, its fair value can be measured reliably.

Example 30.5 – Acquisition and fair value adjustments

Basic information

E Limited acquired 100% of the share capital of F Limited on 30 June 2019. The cost of the acquisition was £5.9 million made up of fair value of shares £3 million, cash £2.75 million and expenses £0.15 million (see **Example 30.3** above).

The following fair value adjustments were made to the carrying amounts of F's assets for the purpose of measuring consolidation goodwill at acquisition date:

- the fair value of F's property, plant and equipment was assessed as £2.9 million as compared with a book value of £2.8 million;

- F's customer list (not previously recognised in its own separate financial statements) has been assessed as £440,000 (see **30.19** below); and

- the fair value of F's inventories has been assessed at £390,000 compared with a book value of £370,000.

Both companies have identical accounting policies, so no adjustment is required for accounting policy alignments.

The individual balance sheets and the consolidated balance sheet at 30 June 2019 are as follows. The relevant disclosures for this example are shown in **Example 30.13** below.

Balance sheets and consolidation adjustments:

	H £'000	S £'000	Consolidation adjustments £'000	Explanatory notes	Consolidated balance sheet £'000
Fixed assets					
Goodwill	–	–	5,900	1	2,563
			(500)		
			(2,445)		
			(560)		
			168		
Intangible asset	–	–	440		440
Property, plant and equipment	5,000	2,800	100		7,900
Investment in F	5,900		(5,900)		–
Total	10,900	2,800			10,903
Current assets					
Stocks	2,700	370	20		3,090
Debtors	300	125			425
Cash	1,600	65			1,665
Total	4,600	560			5,180

	H £'000	S £'000	Consolidation adjustments £'000	Explanatory notes	Consolidated balance sheet £'000
Creditors	(500)	(135)			(635)
Loans	(800)	(100)			(900)
Deferred tax	(1,200)	(180)	(168)	2	(1,548)
Total	(2,500)	(415)			(3,083)
Net assets	13,000	2,945			13,000
Share capital	(3,500)	(500)	500		(3,500)
Profit and loss reserves	(9,500)	(2,445)	2,445		(9,500)
Shareholders funds	(13,000)	(2,945)			(13,000)

Explanatory note to consolidation adjustments

1.   Goodwill is calculated as the excess of the cost of the business combination over the fair value of the net assets acquired, allowing for the deferred tax adjustment (see note 2 below).

2.   Deferred tax must be provided on the fair value adjustments (see **30.23** below) – for illustration a tax rate of 30% is used and adjustment of 30% × (£440 + £100 + £20) = £168 (see **30.23** below).

The impact of fair value adjustments at acquisition date on the statement of comprehensive income

30.17   The acquiree's income and expenses arising after acquisition date should be included in the acquirer's statement of comprehensive income.

30.18   The acquiree's income and expenses should reflect the effect of fair value adjustments made at acquisition date in order to allocate the purchase consideration over asset and liability categories, and to determine goodwill. For example, the post-acquisition depreciation expense relating to the acquiree's depreciable assets, should be based on the fair values of those depreciable assets at acquisition date.

Example 30.6

In **Example 30.5** above, the consolidated profit or loss in the periods after acquisition should reflect the amortisation of the customer list and depreciation based on the fair value of £2.9 million.

Intangibles acquired as part of a business combination

30.19   Section 18 of FRS 102 deals with intangible assets other than goodwill:

- paragraph 18.8 dealing with recognition states that an intangible asset acquired in a business combination is usually recognised as an asset because its fair value at acquisition date can normally be measured with sufficient reliability; and

- paragraph 18.11 dealing with measurement states that if an intangible asset is acquired in a business combination, the cost of that intangible asset is its fair value at the balance sheet date.

Example 30.7 – Intangibles acquired in a business combination

R Limited acquired the business of a rival taxi firm S Limited for cash consideration amounting to £400,000. The net assets of S amounted to £290,000 including taxi licences with a carrying amount of £25,000. S also has a registered trade name but this has not been recognised in the balance sheet under existing UK GAAP as it was internally generated and had no readily ascertainable market value (FRS 10 *Goodwill and Intangible Assets*, paragraph 14).

30.20   Paragraph 18.11 is very brief (simply two lines) but crucial. For example, the intangible asset referred to may be a customer list. From the acquiree's perspective, the asset was internally generated and therefore was not recognised in the acquiree's balance sheet. For the acquirer, the intangible is an acquired asset and will therefore be recognised in the acquirer's consolidated balance sheet.

However, the intangible is not acquired as an individual asset and therefore has no identifiable cost. Paragraph 18.11 says that the intangible's fair value must be used as the 'cost' going forward. This raises measurement issues.

30.21   These are referred to in Section 11, Basic Financial Instruments. Paragraph 11.27 refers to a number of sections including Section 18 dealing with intangibles. Paragraph 11.28 refers to valuation techniques (see **36.1** and **36.2**).

30.22   Paragraph 11.28 refers to discounted cash flow analysis. In practice, under IFRS, some companies refer to 'excess earnings method' and 'relief from royalty' method.

Example 30.8 – Accounting policy for valuing intangibles

Accounting policy extract – Intangible assets

Intellectual property has been valued using the relief from royalties basis which reflects the discounted future cash flows saved from not incurring royalty payments following the acquisition of X Limited.

Customer lists are valued using discounted cash flows expected to be generated by the customer bases.

Focus

Guidance on fair value in Section 11 is very limited. In more complex cases, IFRS 13 *Fair Value Measurement* gives further guidance (see IFRS 13, para 62 and Application Guidance, paras B5–B12).

Business combinations and deferred tax

30.23   Paragraph 19.15A requires the acquirer to recognise and measure a deferred tax asset or liability arising from the assets acquired and liabilities assumed in accordance with Section 29, Income Tax.

Paragraph 29.11 states:

'When the amount that can be deducted for tax for an asset (other than goodwill) that is recognised in a business combination is less (more) than the value at which it is recognised, a deferred tax liability (asset) shall be recognised for the additional tax that will be paid (avoided) in respect of that difference. Similarly, a deferred tax asset (liability) shall be recognised for the additional tax that will be avoided (paid) because of a difference between the value at which a *liability* is recognised and the amount that will be assessed for tax. *The amount attributed to goodwill shall be adjusted by the amount of deferred tax recognised'* (emphasis added).

Example 30.9 – Deferred tax liability

Entity A Limited acquires Entity B Limited for purchase consideration of £1 million paid in cash. B Limited has built up a valuable customer list, but this was never recognised in its balance sheet as it is an internally generated intangible that does not satisfy the recognition rules. B Limited has obtained tax relief during the period in which the expenditure was incurred in creating this asset.

The fair value of the intangible has been assessed at £140,000 (see **30.19** above) and the fair value of the other net assets is £500,000.

The applicable tax rate is assumed to be 30%.

The difference between the amount that can be deducted for tax (nil, because tax relief has already been claimed) and the value at which the asset is recognised (£140,000) (ie £140,000 gives rise to a deferred tax liability in the consolidated financial statements amounting to £42,000 (30% of £140,000)).

The amount attributed to goodwill is adjusted by the amount of deferred tax recognised and is calculated as follows:

	£
Cost of acquisition	1,000,000
Fair value of intangible	(140,000)
Fair value of other net assets	(500,000)
Deferred tax	42,000
Goodwill	402,000

Suppose the useful life of the intangible is assessed as four years, then, in the consolidated financial statements, the intangible will be amortised at an annual rate of £35,000. The deferred tax liability will be released to the consolidated income statement (credited against the consolidated tax charge) at the annual rate of £10,500 (£42,000/4 years).

Two issues concerning recognition of liabilities

30.24   Two particular issues to take care over when applying the allocation rules in **30.19** and **30.20** above:

● liabilities for terminating or reducing the activities of the acquiree should *only* be recognised as liabilities to the extent that the acquiree has an existing liability in accordance with Section 21 on provisions; and

- liabilities recognised at acquisition date should *not* include liabilities for future losses or other costs expected to be incurred as a result of the business combination.

Exceptions to the recognition criteria

30.25 The three exceptions referred to in **30.14** above are:

- Business combinations – a deferred tax asset arising from the assets acquired and the liabilities assumed in accordance with the requirements of Section 29, Income Tax, should be measured in accordance with the requirements of that section (see **25.20**).

- Employee benefits – a liability (or asset, if any) related to the acquiree's employee benefit arrangements, should be recognised and measured in accordance with Section 28, Employee Benefits (see **Chapter 23**).

- Share-based payment – the acquirer should recognise a share-based payment in accordance with Section 26, Share-based Payment (see **Chapter 28**).

Contingent liabilities

30.26 A provision for contingent liabilities in a business combination should only be recognised at acquisition if its fair value can be measured reliably.

30.27 After being separately recognised in accordance with the requirements of **30.14** above, contingent liabilities should be measured at the higher of:

- the amount that would be recognised in accordance with Section 21, Provisions and Contingencies; and

- the amount initially recognised less amounts previously recognised as revenue in accordance with Section 23, Revenue.

Hindsight adjustments to the fair values of assets and liabilities

30.28 In some cases, the initial accounting for a business combination may not have been completed by the end of the reporting period. FRS 102 requires the acquirer to recognise provisional amounts for the relevant items.

30.29 These provisional amounts can subsequently be revised and retrospectively adjusted in the light of new information obtained, provided the revision is made with 12 months of the acquisition date.

Note that the revision to fair values of assets acquired and liabilities assumed will have a consequential effect on the previously calculated goodwill figure.

The relevant financial statement items should be accounted for as if they were made at acquisition date. This will impact on the amortisation of goodwill and depreciation of fixed assets in both the year of the acquisition and the year in which the hindsight adjustment is made.

Any adjustments to the initial accounting more than 12 months after the acquisition date will only be recognised if required to correct a material error (FRS 102, paragraph 19.19).

Example 30.10 – Adjustment to provisional fair values of assets acquired

K Limited acquired 100% of the share capital of M Limited on 30 September 2019 for cash consideration of £500,000. Both companies have a 31 December year-end. Certain valuations of property, plant and equipment were incomplete at the year-end, and provisional valuations were used to determine the goodwill arising on acquisition.

Year ended 31 December 2019

For the year ended 31 December 2019, goodwill is determined at £50,000 (acquisition cost of £500,000 less net assets of £450,000).

The net assets include £100,000 in respect of the assets for which provisional fair values have been used. For 2019, a depreciation charge of £20,000 × 3/12 = £5,000 has been put through for these assets based on a useful life of five years and a residual value of nil so the net book value at the year-end is £100,000 – £5,000 = £95,000.

Goodwill is being amortised over a period of 10 years as the directors have been able to obtain a reliable estimate of its useful life. The annual charge on a straight-line basis is £5,000 so for three months, the charge is £1,250. Net book value of goodwill at 31 December 2019 is £50,000 – £1,250 = £48,750.

Year ended 31 December 2020

The provisional fair value of £100,000 is revised to a fair value of £130,000 following an independent valuation. The provisional goodwill figure is

411

therefore recalculated as £20,000. As a result, prior year information for 2019 must be adjusted retrospectively.

The impact of this on the consolidated balance sheet is as follows:

	2020	*2019 (restated)*
Goodwill	£20,000 less 15 months accumulated amortisation of £2,500 = £17,500	£20,000 less 3 months accumulated amortisation of £500 = £19,500
Plant and machinery	£130,000 less 15 months accumulated depreciation of £32,500 = £97,500	£130,000 less 3 months accumulated depreciation of £6,500 = £123,500

The carrying amount of plant and machinery at 31 December 2020 has been increased by £28,500 (£123,500 – £95,000) and goodwill reduced by £29,250 (£48,750 – £19,500). The net decrease in assets of £750 (£29,250 – £28,500) will be adjusted against profit and loss reserves.

The impact of this on the consolidated profit and loss account is as follows:

	2020	*2019 (restated)*
Goodwill	Amortisation of £2,000	Amortisation of £500
Plant and machinery	Depreciation of £26,000	Depreciation of £6,500

The date from which the purchase method is applied

30.30   The purchase method is applied from acquisition date, the date when the acquirer obtains control of the acquiree.

30.31   Control is the power to govern the financial and operating policies of the acquiree or business so as to obtain benefit from its activities. Paragraph 19.17 makes clear that it is not necessary for a transaction to be closed or finalised at law before the acquirer obtains control. All pertinent facts and circumstances should be considered in assessing whether control has been obtained.

Control achieved by a series of transactions

30.32   This is dealt with in **Chapter 29** (see **29.28**).

GOODWILL

Introduction

30.33 Purchased goodwill may arise on the acquisition of a body corporate, giving rise to goodwill only in the consolidated balance sheet. However, purchased goodwill may also arise on the purchase of an unincorporated body such a sole trader or partnership, in which case it will appear in the individual balance sheet of the acquiring company (see **Examples 30.1** and **30.2** above).

Measurement – positive goodwill

30.34 Goodwill is initially recognised at acquisition date and is measured at cost. Cost is measured as the excess of the cost of the business combination over the acquirer's interest in the net amount of the identifiable assets, liabilities and contingent liabilities.

30.35 Goodwill is considered to have a finite useful life, and should be amortised on a systematic basis over that useful life. *If the entity is unable to make a reliable estimate of that useful life, it shall be considered to be five years.*

Focus

Companies and groups may have to think hard about this. Good justifications will be required to overturn this presumption – paragraph 19.25(g) requires disclosure of the useful life of goodwill, if this exceeds five years, and supporting reasons for this. This applies to business combinations both before and after the transition date (see **39.21–39.23**).

30.36 Goodwill is subsequently measured at cost less accumulated amortisation and accumulated impairment losses. As regards impairment, principles of Section 27, Impairment of Assets apply (see **Chapter 18**).

Measurement – Negative goodwill

30.37 'Negative goodwill' is not a defined term referred to in FRS 102, although it is often referred to as such in practice (it is sometimes referred to as a 'bargain purchase').

It refers to the situation where the acquirer's interest in the net amount of the identifiable assets, liabilities and recognised contingent liabilities exceeds the cost of the business combination.

30.38 Negative goodwill is usually regarded as arising from one of the following:

- a genuine bargain purchase – for example where a seller is forced to sell a business at a low price in order to generate cash; or

- where the purchase price is low because of expected or future losses or costs, for example where the acquirer expects to incur significant reorganisation costs before the business is restored to profitability.

30.39 Where it initially appears that negative goodwill has arisen, the acquirer should reassess:

- the identification and measurement of the acquiree's assets, liabilities and contingent liabilities; and

- the measurement of the cost of the business combination.

As with previous UK GAAP, FRS 10, paragraph 48, FRS 102 aims to ensure that negative goodwill is not overstated and so it requires a careful re-assessment of fair values.

Focus

Particular care should be taken where negative goodwill appears to arise in situations referred to above where losses and/or reorganisation costs are expected.

Some commentators have previously expressed the view that negative goodwill is most likely to arise in bargain purchase situations.

30.40 The negative goodwill (referred to in Section 19, paragraph 19.24(c) as 'the excess') should be dealt with as follows:

- the amount of negative goodwill up to the fair value of non-monetary assets acquired (eg property, plant and equipment or inventories) should be recognised in profit or loss over the periods in which non-monetary assets are recovered; or

- if the amount of negative goodwill exceeds the fair value of non-monetary assets acquired, the difference should be recognised in profit or loss over the periods expected to be benefitted.

This is consistent with current UK GAAP FRS 10, paragraphs 49 and 50.

Example 30.11 – Negative goodwill calculation

R Limited acquired all of the share capital of S Limited on 1 July 2020 for cash consideration of £500,000. The fair value of S's identifiable assets and liabilities was as follows:

	£'000
Property, plant and equipment	400,000
Inventories	200,000
Trade debtors	140,000
Intangibles	160,000
Assets acquired at fair value	900,000
Liabilities	(360,000)
Net assets acquired at fair value	540,000

The initial calculation indicates 'negative goodwill' amounting to £40,000 (£500,000 – £540,000).

The reassessment referred to in **30.39** above is applied to all the identifiable assets and liabilities. All the amounts above are confirmed except for property, plant and equipment where the fair value is reassessed as £370,000. The revised number for negative goodwill is adjusted by £30,000.

This amount does not exceed the fair value of the non-monetary assets acquired, so the negative goodwill should be recognised in profit or loss over the periods in which non-monetary assets are recovered.

The property, plant and equipment is expected to have a useful life of five years and the inventories are expected to be sold within one year.

The FRS does not specify how the recovery period should be calculated. One approach would be to use a five-year recovery period, although an alternative approach based on a weighted average of, say, four years could be argued.

Example 30.12 – Negative goodwill accounting policy

Accounting policy extract

Negative goodwill on the monetary net assets is amortised through the profit and loss account on the following basis:

- Tangible fixed assets – as recovered, based on the depreciation or disposal of the relevant assets of the acquired subsidiaries.
- Stock – as recovered based on the disposal of the stock of the acquired subsidiaries.

30.41   Negative goodwill should be shown as a separate line item on the face of the balance sheet (statement of total financial position), immediately below positive goodwill.

The subtotal of the net amount of positive and negative goodwill should be separately presented.

GROUP RECONSTRUCTIONS

Introduction

30.42   Group reconstructions *may* be accounted for using the merger accounting method provided:

- the use of the method is not prohibited by company law or other relevant legislation;

- the ultimate equity owners remain the same, and the rights of each equity holder relative to the others are unchanged; and

- no non-controlling interest in the net assets of the group is altered by the transfer.

Focus

For group reconstructions, merger accounting is an accounting policy choice – paragraph 19.33(b) requires disclosure of whether the business combination has been accounted for as an aquisition or as a merger.

The relevant legislation referred to above is the Regulations to CA 2006, Schedule 6, paragraph 10.

Merger accounting

30.43   Merger accounting aggregates the financial statements of the parties to the business combination as though these parties had always been part of the same reporting entity.

Even though a merger may have taken place part-way through the year, the full year results of the combining entities for both current and previous year are included in the consolidated financial statements. No fair value adjustments are made and no goodwill is recognised.

Merger accounting method

30.44   The key features of the method are as follows:

- The carrying values of the assets and liabilities of the parties to the combination are not required to be adjusted to fair value.

- The results and cash flows of all the combining entities should be brought into the financial statements of the combined entity as from the beginning of the financial year in which the combination occurred.

- Comparatives in the financial statements of the combined entity should be restated by combining the following in respect of the individual entities which have combined during the current reporting period:

    o   the total of their comprehensive income for the previous reporting period; and

    o   their statements of financial position at the previous reporting date.

- Appropriate adjustments should be made where required to achieve conformity of accounting policies – this relates to both carrying values and results of the combining entities.

- The difference (if any) between (a) the nominal value of the shares issued plus the fair value of any consideration given, and (b) the nominal value of the shares received in exchange, should be shown as a movement on *other reserves*, in the consolidated financial statements.

    o   any existing balances on the share premium account or capital redemption reserve of the new subsidiary should be brought in by being shown as a movement on *other reserves*; and

    o   the movements on 'other reserves' should be shown in the *statement of changes in equity* (see **Chapter 10**).

- Merger expenses are excluded from the above adjustment, and should be charged to the statement of comprehensive income as part of the combined profit or loss of the combined entity, at the effective date of the group reconstruction.

30.45   The above requirements are consistent with the Regulations to CA 2006, Schedule 6, paragraph 11.

30.46   Disclosure requirements are referred to below – see **30.53**.

DISCLOSURE REQUIREMENTS – PURCHASE METHOD

Business combinations during the period

30.47   The following should be disclosed in respect of each business combination effected during the period:

- the names and descriptions of the combining entities or businesses;

- the acquisition date;

- the percentage of voting equity instruments acquired;

- the cost of the combination and a description of the components of that cost (such as cash, debt, and equity instruments);

- the amounts recognised at the acquisition date for each class of the acquiree's assets, liabilities, and contingent liabilities (but see **30.49** below);

- the amount recognised at the acquisition date in respect of goodwill;

- the useful life of goodwill – if this exceeds five years, disclosure is required of the supporting reasons for this; and

- the periods in respect of which 'negative goodwill' (see **30.40** above) will be recognised in profit or loss.

30.48   The Regulations to CA 2006, Schedule 6, paragraph 13(4) state:

'Where the acquisition method of accounting has been adopted, the book values immediately prior to the acquisition, and the fair values at the date of acquisition, of each class of assets and liabilities of the undertaking or group acquired must be stated in *tabular form* (emphasis added), including a statement of the amount of any goodwill or negative consolidation difference arising on the acquisition, together with any significant adjustments made.'

This additional disclosure requirement is reflected in **Example 30.16** below.

Focus

This is another example of 'compliance with FRS 102 alone will often be insufficient to ensure compliance with all the disclosure requirements set out in the Act and the Regulations' (FRS 102, Appendix IV, paragraph A4.10). The FRC does warn that 'FRS 102 is not intended to be a one-stop-shop for all accounting and legal requirements …'.

Note that the reference above to 'any significant adjustments made' could relate to adjustments required to align accounting policy differences, as well as fair value adjustments. Where both of these apply, separate adjustment columns should be presented.

Example 30.13 – Acquisition during the current period: disclosure example

(Please refer back to the information in **Example 30.5.**)

Extract from notes to the financial statements

On 30 June 2019, E Limited acquired 100% of the share capital of F Limited. Both companies manufacture ceramic tiles. The total consideration was £5.9 million made up of fair value of shares £3 million, cash £2.75 million and expenses £0.15 million.

The following table sets out the book values of the identifiable assets and liabilities acquired and their fair value to the group. Goodwill will be amortised over a period of five years as the company is unable to make a reliable estimate of the goodwill's useful life.

	Book value £'000	Fair value adjustments £'000	Fair value £'000
Customer list		440 (note 1)	440
Property, plant and equipment	2,800	100 (note 2)	2,900
Stocks	370	20 (note 3)	390
Debtors	125		125
Cash	65		65
Creditors	(135)		(135)
Loans	(100)		(100)
Deferred tax	(180)	(168) (note 4)	(348)
Net assets	2,945	392	3,337
Goodwill			2,563
Cost of acquisition			5,900

Notes to consolidation adjustments

The following fair value adjustments were made to the carrying amounts of F's assets for the purpose of measuring consolidation goodwill at acquisition date:

1	F's customer list (not previously recognised in its own separate financial statements) has been assessed as £440,000.
2	The fair value of F's property, plant and equipment was assessed as £2.9m as compared with a book value of £2.8 million.
3	The fair value of F's inventories has been assessed at £390,000 compared with a book value of £370,000.
4	Deferred tax of £168,000 has been provided in respect of the above fair value adjustments.

Both companies have identical accounting policies, so no adjustment is required for accounting policy alignments.

30.49 For each material business combination that occurred during the period, the acquirer should disclose the amounts of post-acquisition date revenue and profit of the acquiree which have been included in the consolidated statement of comprehensive income for the reporting period.

For acquisitions which are not individually material, this disclosure may be given in aggregate.

All business combinations

30.50 The notes to the financial statements should include a reconciliation of the movement on positive goodwill between the beginning and the end of the reporting period, showing separately:

- changes arising from new business combinations;
- amortisation;
- impairment losses;
- disposals of previously acquired businesses; and
- other changes.

Note that a comparative reconciliation for the previous year is not required.

30.51 The notes to the financial statements should also include a reconciliation of the movement on 'negative goodwill' between the beginning and the end of the reporting period, showing separately:

- changes arising from new business combinations;
- amounts recognised in profit or loss (see **30.40** above);

- disposals of previously acquired businesses; and

- other changes.

Note that a comparative reconciliation for the previous year is not required.

DISCLOSURE REQUIREMENTS – GROUP RECONSTRUCTIONS

30.52 For each group reconstruction effected during the period, the following should be disclosed:

- the names of the combining entities (other than the reporting entity);

- whether the combination has been accounted for as an acquisition or a merger; and

- the date of the combination.

SUMMARY – WHAT IS DIFFERENT FROM THE PREVIOUS UK GAAP?

- The purchase method (previously referred to as acquisition accounting) is generally required except:

  o FRS 102, paragraph 19.6(a) gives an accounting policy option for group reconstructions to be accounted for using merger accounting (whereas previous UK GAAP imposed restrictions on the use of this method) – see **30.42**; and

  o Public benefit entity combinations that are in substance a gift or that are a merger must be accounted for in accordance with Section 34 of FRS 102.

- FRS 10 has a rebuttable presumption that the useful economic life of goodwill is limited to 20 years (FRS 10, paragraph 19) whereas FRS 102 specifies that if an entity is unable to make a reliable estimate of the useful life of goodwill then that life must not exceed five years.

- The hindsight period is shorter under FRS 102 – it is restricted to 12 months from the acquisition date – whereas FRS 7, paragraph 24 goes as far as the date on which the first post-acquisition financial statements are approved.

- The recognition of intangible assets acquired in a business combination does not have the previous UK GAAP specification that they should be capable of being disposed of, or settled, separately – it is possible that under FRS 102 more intangible assets will be recognised separately from goodwill (as has been the experience under full IFRS).

Chapter 31

Associates and joint ventures

SIGNPOSTS

This chapter deals with two aspects of FRS 102:

- Investments in associates (Section 14).

- Investments in joint ventures (Section 15).

- The definition of associate in FRS 102 (see **31.4**) is similar to that in previous UK GAAP, but does not use the term 'participating interest'. A holding of 20% or more of voting power of the associate is still presumed to give significant influence; a holding below this level is presumed not to give significant influence.

- In group consolidated financial statements, investments in associates should continue to be accounted for using the equity method of accounting. There is one exception – where an investment in an associate is held as part of an investment portfolio, in which case the investment should be measured at fair value, with changes in fair value dealt with through profit or loss (see **31.31**).

- Where an investor's share of the losses of an associate equals or exceeds the carrying amount of the investment, the investor should discontinue recognising its share of further losses (see **31.20–31.21**) – this is different from previous UK GAAP (FRS 9.44 required such losses to continue to be recognised).

- FRS 102 states that joint ventures can take any one of three forms: jointly controlled operations; jointly controlled assets; jointly controlled entities (see **31.38**). These terms differ from those in FRS 9, for example the term 'Joint arrangement that is not an entity' (JANE) is no longer used. Investors should reassess their existing investments to establish which category they fall into under the new requirements.

- Under FRS 102, jointly controlled entities (as defined in the Glossary to FRS 102 – see **31.44**) were described in FRS 9 as joint ventures. FRS 102 requires investments in such entities to be accounted for in the consolidated financial statements using the equity method, same as for investments in associates (see **31.53**). By contrast, previous UK GAAP required the use of the gross equity method (FRS 9.20).

- Associates and joint ventures which are foreign operations are referred to in **Chapter 32** (see **32.4** and **32.5**).

SCOPE

Investments in associates – scope

31.1   Section 14 applies to:

- accounting for associates in consolidated financial statements; and

- accounting for investments in associates in the individual statements of an investor that *is not* a parent (ie which does not have subsidiaries).

31.2   Investments in associates in the individual statements of a parent company are dealt with in FRS 102, paragraphs 9.24 and 9.26 (see **29.37** above).

Investments in joint ventures – scope

31.3   Section 15 applies to:

- accounting for joint ventures in consolidated financial statements;

- accounting for investments in joint ventures in the individual statements of a venturer that *is not* a parent (ie which does not have subsidiaries); and

- accounting for investments in jointly controlled operations and jointly controlled assets·in the separate financial statements of a venture that *is* a parent.

Investments in jointly controlled entities in the individual statements of a venturer that *is* a parent company are dealt with in FRS 102, paragraphs 9.24 and 9.26 (see **29.37**).

DEFINITION OF AN ASSOCIATE

Basic definition

31.4   An associate is an entity – including an unincorporated entity such as a partnership, over which the investor has significant influence – that is neither a subsidiary nor an interest in a joint venture.

Significant influence

31.5   Significant influence is the power to participate in the financial and operating policy decisions of the associate but it is not control, or joint control, over those policies.

31.6   An investor is presumed to have significant influence if the investor holds (either directly, or indirectly – for example, through subsidiaries) 20% or more of the voting power of the associate – unless it can be clearly demonstrated that this is not the case.

31.7   An investor is presumed *not* to have significant influence if the investor holds (either directly, or indirectly – for example, through subsidiaries) *less than 20%* of the voting power of the associate unless such influence can be clearly demonstrated.

31.8   Where a different investor has a substantial or a majority ownership, this does not preclude another investor from having significant influence.

CONSOLIDATED FINANCIAL STATEMENTS AND THE EQUITY METHOD OF ACCOUNTING

Requirement to use the equity method

31.9   An investor that is a parent is required, in its consolidated financial statements, to account for all investments in associates using the equity method. There is no accounting policy choice. However, there is one exception to this requirement – where investments in associates are held as part of an investment portfolio, see **31.32** below.

31.10   The equity method of accounting is well established in UK GAAP and in outline is as follows:

- on initial recognition, the investment in the associate is recognised at the transaction price, inclusive of transaction costs; and

- subsequently, the carrying amount of the investment is adjusted to reflect the investors share of the associate's profit or loss, other comprehensive income, or equity.

31.11   Detailed requirements of the equity method are set out immediately below.

Distributions and other adjustments to carrying amount

31.12   Distributions received from the associate reducing the carrying amount of the investment (offset by cash received of the same amount).

The carrying amount of the investment may also need to be adjusted as a result of changes in the equity of the associate arising from items of other comprehensive income (eg surpluses on revaluation of property, plant and equipment).

Potential voting rights

31.13   Potential voting rights should be taken into account in deciding whether an investor has significant influence. However, such rights should not affect the measurement of the investor's interests in the associate – these should be based on present ownership interests.

Implicit goodwill and fair value adjustments

31.14   On the acquisition of an investment in an associate, any difference between cost of acquisition and the investor's share of the identifiable net assets of the associate should be accounted for as goodwill in accordance with the rules in Section 19, Business Combinations.

This means that the goodwill element of the cost of investment will be amortised in accordance with FRS 102, paragraphs 19.22–19.23.

Example 31.1 – Accounting for investments in associates

The H Limited group has a number of subsidiaries. The group year-end is 31 December. On 1 July 2016, the group acquired a 30% shareholding in A Limited at a cost of £285,000. A Limited is regarded as an associate of H Limited.

At 1 July 2016, the net assets of A limited amounted to £700,000 including plant and equipment of £250,000. The remaining life of this equipment, as from 1 January 2016, was 10 years, with zero residual value.

425

At 1 July 2016, the fair value of A's net assets was assessed as £750,000. The increase in far value of £50,000 was entirely attributable to the plant and equipment referred to above.

The implicit goodwill is calculated as £60,000 (£285,000 – 30% × £750,000). In accordance with Section 19, the implicit goodwill will be amortised over five years in the absence of a reliable estimate of useful life.

Impact on consolidated financial statements at 1 July 2016

The carrying amount of the investment in the associate is £285,000. If a consolidated balance sheet had been presented at this date, the investment would have been presented as a one-line item under the heading of fixed assets.

Consolidated financial statements for the year ended 31 December 2016

In the period from 1 July 2016 to 31 December 2016, the associate's profits before tax amounted to £60,000 and its tax £20,000. No dividends were paid.

The consolidated profit and loss account of H Limited will include the following in respect of its investment in A Limited:

Share of profit

Share of profit before adjustments £18,000 (30% of £60,000)

less amortisation of implicit goodwill of £6,000 (£60,000/5 × 6/12)

less share of additional depreciation (FRS 102, paragraph 14.8(c) of £750 (£15,000 */ 10 × 6/12)

= share of profit £11,250.

* Excess of fair value of A's assets over carrying amount of 30% × £50,000 (£750,000 – £700,000).

Share of tax charge

£6,000 (30% × £20,000).

Effect on consolidated profit and loss reserves and investment in associate

The share of profit after tax of £5,250 (£11,250 – £6,000) will be added to group profit and loss reserves and the carrying amount of the investment increased from £285,000 to £290,250.

Impairment

31.15   If there is an indication that the investment in an associate may be impaired, the investor should test the entire carrying amount (inclusive of any goodwill element which has not yet been amortised) for impairment as a single asset.

Investor's transactions with associates

31.16   Unrealised profits and losses resulting from both upstream transactions (associate to investor) and downstream transactions (investor to associate) should be eliminated.

31.17   Unrealised losses from investor's transactions with associates (see below) may provide evidence of an impairment of the asset transferred.

Date of associate's financial statements

31.18   The financial statements of the associate used in applying the equity method, should be made up to the same date as those of the investor, unless it is impracticable to do so.

Where this is impracticable, the investor should use the most recent available financial statements of the associate, with adjustments made for the effects of any significant transactions or events occurring between these two dates.

Associate's accounting policies

31.19   Where the associate uses accounting policies which differ from those of the investor, the financial statements of the associate should be adjusted to reflect the accounting policies of the investor unless this is impracticable.

Losses in excess of investment

31.20   If an investor's share of the losses of an associate either equals or exceeds the carrying amount of the investment in the associate, the investor should discontinue recognising its share of further losses.

Additional losses should be recognised as a provision, but only to the extent that the investor has incurred legal or constructive obligations, or has made payments on behalf of the associate.

31.21   Any share of subsequent profits should be recognised only to the extent that these equal the share of losses not recognised.

Discontinuing the equity method

31.22   An investor should cease using the equity method from the date that significant influence ceases and provided that the associate does not become a subsidiary or joint venture. Detailed requirements are set out in paragraph 14.8(i).

Gain or loss on disposal of investment in associate

31.23   The gain or loss on disposal should also include those amounts that have previously been recognised in other comprehensive income.

Example 31.2 – Disposal of investment in associate

J Limited acquired a 30% investment in K Limited several years ago at a cost of £100,000. Since the purchase, J's share of profit after tax of K (after making adjustments for implicit goodwill and fair values – see **Example 31.1**) amounted to £45,000.

J has also recognised its share of surpluses on revaluation of property, plant and equipment of K in other comprehensive income. These surpluses net of deferred tax amounted to £60,000.

Immediately before J sold its investment in K for proceeds of £250,000, the carrying amount of the investment was £205,000 (£100,000 + £45,000+ £60,000).

The gain on disposal is £105,000 calculated as £45,000 (£250,000 – £205,000) + the £60,000 previously recognised in other comprehensive income.

Effectively the revaluation reserve account is debited with £60,000 and profit and loss reserves credited with £60,000. In the consolidated profit and loss account, this will be shown as a reclassification adjustment with a bracket amount in the other comprehensive income section of £60,000 and in the profit and loss section at the top a single profit on sale figure of £105,000.

INDIVIDUAL FINANCIAL STATEMENTS OF AN INVESTOR THAT IS A PARENT COMPANY

31.24 The requirements are dealt with in FRS 102, paragraphs 9.24 and 9.26 (see **29.37**).

INDIVIDUAL FINANCIAL STATEMENTS OF AN INVESTOR THAT IS NOT A PARENT COMPANY

Accounting policy election

31.25 An investor that is not a parent must make an accounting policy choice between one of the following three options:

All investments in associates should be accounted for by using either:

- the cost model (cost less accumulated impairment); or
- the fair value model (changes in fair value recognised in other comprehensive income); or
- fair value with changes in fair value recognised in profit or loss.

Cost model

31.26 An investor that is not a parent that makes an accounting policy choice to adopt the cost model, measures its investments at cost less any accumulated impairment losses.

31.27 Dividends and other distributions received from the investment should be recognised as income, whether or not the dividends are from the associate's accumulated profits arising before or after the date of acquisition.

Fair value model

31.28 Note that the term 'fair value model' refers to where gains or losses are recognised in other comprehensive income (not through profit or loss). The fair value model is consistent with the alternative accounting rules in the Regulations to CA 2006.

31.29 Guidance on determining fair value is provided in paragraphs 11.27 to 11.32 of Section 11, Basic Financial Instruments (see **36.30–36.33**).

31.30 In situations where an investor uses the fair value model, but where it is impracticable to measure fair value reliably without undue cost or effort, the cost model should be used.

WHERE AN INVESTMENT IN AN ASSOCIATE IS HELD AS PART OF AN INVESTMENT PORTFOLIO

31.31   Where an investor is a parent and has an associate that is held as part of an investment portfolio, the investment should be measured at fair value, with changes in fair value recognised in profit or loss within the consolidated financial statements.

This is consistent with paragraph 9.9B which refers to subsidiaries held as part of an investment portfolio (see **29.7–29.8**).

PRESENTATION REQUIREMENTS – ASSOCIATES

31.32   Investments in associates should be classified as fixed assets, unless otherwise required under the Regulations to CA 2006.

DISCLOSURE REQUIREMENTS – ASSOCIATES

General requirements

31.33   The following should be disclosed:

- the accounting policy for investments in associates;
- the carrying amount of investments in associates; and
- the fair value of investments in associates accounted for using the equity method for which there are published price quotations.

Investments in associates accounted for in accordance with the cost model

31.34   Disclose the amount of dividends and other distributions recognised in income.

Investments in associates accounted for in accordance with the fair value model

31.35   The disclosure requirements are contained in paragraphs 11.43 and 11.44 of Section 11, Basic Financial Instruments (see **30.36**).

Investments in associates accounted for in accordance with the equity model

31.36   Disclose separately the investor's share of the profit or loss of the associate(s) and its share of any discontinued operations of the associate(s).

Individual financial statements of an investor that is not a parent company

31.37 Disclose summarised financial information about investments in associates, together with the effect of including those investments as if they had been accounted for using the equity method.

Exemption from this disclosure requirement is given to investing entities that are exempt from preparing consolidated financial statements, or that would be exempt if they had subsidiaries.

DEFINITION OF A JOINT VENTURE

31.38 A joint venture is a contractual arrangement whereby two or more parties undertake an economic activity that is subject to joint control.

Joint control is the contractually agreed sharing of control over an economic activity and exists only when the strategic financial and operating decisions relating to the activity require the unanimous consent of the parties sharing control (the venturers).

Joint ventures can take the form of:

- jointly controlled operations; or

- jointly controlled assets; or

- jointly controlled entities.

JOINTLY CONTROLLED OPERATIONS

31.39 Some joint ventures involve the use of assets and resources of individual venturers, as opposed to establishing a separate company, partnership or other entity separate from the individual venturers.

31.40 Each venturer uses its own property, plant and equipment, carries its own inventories, incurs its own expenses, and raises its own finance. The joint venture agreement will usually provide a means of sharing revenues earned less expenses incurred, between the venturers.

Example 31.3 – Jointly controlled operations

Two companies X Limited and Y Limited enter into a contractual arrangement under which they will combine their operations, resources and technical expertise to manufacture, market and distribute aircraft aimed at the high-volume low-cost carrier market.

The two companies will carry out different parts of the manufacturing process. Each company will bear its own costs and be entitled to a share of the revenue from the sale of the aircraft. The basis for allocating revenue is determined in accordance with the terms of the contractual arrangement.

X Limited and Y Limited have joint control over the manufacturing operations as described in paragraph 31.38 above, and the joint venture takes the form of a jointly controlled operation.

31.41   Each individual venturer should recognise the following in its financial statements:

- the assets that it controls, and the liabilities it incurs; and

- the expenses that it incurs and its share of the income that it earns from the sale of goods or services by the joint venture.

JOINTLY CONTROLLED ASSETS

31.42   Some joint ventures involve joint control or joint ownership by the venturers of one or more assets, acquired for and dedicated to, the purposes of the joint venture.

31.43   Each individual venturer should recognise the following in its financial statements:

- its share of the jointly controlled assets;

- any liabilities that it has incurred;

- its share of any liabilities incurred jointly with the other venturers in relation to the joint venture;

- any income from the sale or use of its share of the output of the joint venture, together with its share of any expenses incurred by the joint venture; and

- any expenses that it has incurred in respect of the interest in the joint venture.

Example 31.4 – Jointly controlled assets

P Limited and Q Limited are independent oil production companies operating in the North Sea with adjacent oil wells. They enter into a contractual arrangement to control and operate an oil pipeline jointly.

Each company uses the pipeline to transport oil to an on-shore oil refinery which is owned and operated by R Limited, a third-party oil company. R Limited will take up any surplus capacity of oil stocks. P and Q will each bear an agreed proportion of the expense of operating the oil pipeline.

This is a joint venture which takes the form of jointly controlled assets.

P and Q will each account for its share of the jointly controlled asset, the oil pipeline and for its share of the expenses of maintenance of the pipeline and storage costs, and its share of revenues from sales by R.

The stocks of oil passing through the pipeline are separate assets of P and Q.

JOINTLY CONTROLLED ENTITIES

Definition

31.44   A jointly controlled entity is a joint venture that involves the establishment of a corporation, partnership, or other entity in which each venture has an interest.

31.45   The entity set up for the joint venture operates in the same way as other entities, except that a contractual arrangement between the venturers establishes joint control over the economic activity of the entity.

INDIVIDUAL ACCOUNTS

Individual accounts of a venture that is a parent

31.46   A venture which is a parent should account for its investments in jointly controlled entities in accordance with paragraph 9.26 of Section 9 (see **29.37**).

Individual accounts of a venture that is not a parent

31.47   A venturer that is not a parent must adopt one of the three following policies of accounting for its investments in jointly controlled entities:

- at cost less impairment (the 'cost model'), or

- at fair value with changes in fair value recognised in other comprehensive income (the 'fair value model'); or

- at fair value with changes in fair value recognised in profit or loss.

Cost model

31.48   A venturer that is not a parent and which chooses the accounting policy option of the cost model, should measure its investment at cost less any accumulated impairment losses.

31.49   Dividends and other distributions received from the investment should be recognised as income, whether or not the dividends are from the jointly controlled entity's accumulated profits arising before or after the date of acquisition.

Fair value model

31.50   The term 'fair value model' refers to where gains or losses are recognised in other comprehensive income (not through profit or loss).

31.51   Guidance on determining fair value is provided in paragraphs 11.27 to 11.32 of Section 11, Basic Financial Instruments (see **36.30–36.33**).

31.52   In situations where an investor uses the fair value model, but where it is impracticable to measure fair value reliably without undue cost or effort, the cost model should be used.

CONSOLIDATED FINANCIAL STATEMENTS AND THE EQUITY METHOD OF ACCOUNTING

Requirement to use the equity method

31.53   In its consolidated financial statements, a venturer that is a parent is required to account for investments in jointly controlled entities using the equity method of accounting. An exception is referred to in **31.42** below.

Application of the equity method

31.54   The equity method is applied in accordance with the procedures in paragraph 14.8 of Section 14, Investments in Associates (set out in **31.10** above). In that paragraph, reference to 'significant influence' should be read as 'joint control', and references to 'associate' should be read as 'jointly controlled entity' (see **Example 31.1** above).

Investments held as part of an investment portfolio

31.55 Investments in jointly controlled entities that are held as part of an investment portfolio should not be accounted for under the equity method. They should be accounted for at fair value with changes recognised in profit or loss.

TRANSACTIONS BETWEEN A VENTURER AND A JOINT VENTURE

Contribution or sale of assets by a venturer to a joint venture

31.56 Where the assets are retained by the joint venture, and provided that the venturer has transferred the significant risks and rewards of ownership, the venturer should recognise only that portion of gain or loss attributable to the interests of the other venturers.

Any portion of a gain from the transaction recognised by the venturer should reflect the substance of the transaction.

31.57 When the contribution or sale provides evidence of an impairment loss, the venturer should recognise the full amount of the loss.

Purchase of assets by a venturer from a joint venture

31.58 The venturer should not recognise its share of the profits of the joint venture arising from the transaction until the venturer has resold the assets to an independent party.

INVESTOR WHO DOES NOT HAVE JOINT CONTROL

31.59 If an investor in a joint venture does not have joint control, the investment should be accounted for as follows:

- if the investor has significant influence in the joint venture, the investment should be accounted for as an associate in accordance with Section 14;

- otherwise, the investment should be accounted for in accordance with either Section 11, Basic Financial Instruments, or Section 12, Other Financial Instruments Issues (see **Chapters 36** and **37**).

DISCLOSURE REQUIREMENTS – JOINT VENTURES

General requirements

31.60   The following should be disclosed:

- the accounting policy for recognising investments in jointly controlled entities;

- the carrying amount of investments in jointly controlled entities;

- the fair value of investments in jointly controlled entities accounted for using the equity method for which there are published price quotations; and

- the aggregate amount of its commitments relating to joint ventures, including its share in the capital commitments that have been incurred jointly with other venturers, as well as its share of the capital commitments of the joint ventures themselves.

Investments in jointly controlled entities accounted for in accordance with the equity method

31.61   Disclose separately the investor's share of the profit or loss of the investment in jointly controlled entities and its share of any discontinued operations of such jointly controlled entities.

Investments in jointly controlled entities accounted for in accordance with the fair value model

31.62   The disclosure requirements are contained in paragraphs 11.43 and 11.44 of Section 11, Basic Financial Instruments (see **36.53** and **36.54**).

Individual financial statements of an investor that is not a parent company

31.63   Disclose summarised financial information about investments in jointly controlled entities, together with the effect of including those investments as if they had been accounted for using the equity method.

Exemption from this disclosure requirement is given to investing entities that are exempt from preparing consolidated financial statements, or that would be exempt if they had subsidiaries.

SUMMARY – WHAT IS DIFFERENT FROM THE PREVIOUS UK GAAP?

- The definition of an associate is close to that in FRS 9 – a holding of 20% or more of voting power is presumed to give significant influence. FRS 102 does not use the term 'participating interest'.

- Accounting for associates is the same in principle as under previous UK GAAP except where an investment in an associate is held as part of an investment portfolio, in which case the investment should be measured at fair value, with changes in fair value dealt with through profit or loss (see **31.31**).

- Where an investor's share of the losses of an associate equals or exceeds the carrying amount of the investment, the investor should discontinue recognising its share of further losses (see **31.20–31.21**) – this is different from previous UK GAAP (FRS 9.44 required such losses to continue to be recognised).

- Terminology for joint ventures is very different (see **31.38**). FRS 102 states that joint ventures can take any one of three forms: jointly controlled operations; jointly controlled assets; jointly controlled entities (see **31.38**). These terms differ from those in FRS 9, for example the term 'Joint arrangement that is not an entity' ('JANE') is no longer used. Investors should reassess their investments to establish into which category they fall under the new requirements and ensure that they are referring to the new terminology in financial statements under FRS 102.

- Jointly controlled entities in FRS 102 (see **31.44**) were referred to in previous UK GAAP as joint ventures. FRS 102 requires investments in such entities to be accounted for in the consolidated financial statements using the equity method, by contrast with the previous UK GAAP which required the use of the gross equity method (FRS 9.20).

Chapter 32

Foreign currency translation

SIGNPOSTS

- Section 30 gives guidance on the determination of functional currency, the recording of foreign currency transactions, and the translation of financial statements into a presentation currency.

- It is one of the most complex sections in FRS 102 and needs to be read with great care. The section uses different terminology and concepts compared with SSAP 20 *Foreign Currency Translation,* although for some entities the overall effect on the financial statements may not be greatly different.

- Two areas where the treatment is significantly different from SSAP 20 are foreign exchange forward contracts (see **37.17** and **Example 37.2**) and consolidated goodwill resulting from the acquisition of foreign subsidiaries, associates and joint ventures (see **32.38–32.40**).

- This chapter deals with both transactions in the financial statements of individual entities, as well as the translation of individual financial statements for incorporation within the group consolidated financial statements.

INTRODUCTION AND SCOPE

32.1   The term foreign activities can refer to both transactions in foreign currencies, and foreign operations.

Transactions in foreign currencies

32.2   These could include purchases of goods and materials, sales of goods and services, and acquisitions and disposals of property, plant and equipment with parties external to the reporting entity or group. Transactions could also include trading and long-term loan transactions between group companies.

32.3   In some situations, transactions in foreign currencies could involve contracts for the forward purchase or sale of foreign currencies. These are not dealt with in this chapter – see **Chapter 37**.

Foreign operations

32.4   A foreign operation is defined in the Glossary to FRS 102 as an entity that is a subsidiary, associate, joint venture or branch of a reporting entity, the activities of which are based or conducted in a country or currency other than those of the reporting entity.

32.5   With foreign operations, the degree of involvement of the reporting entity can vary considerably and may include:

- overseas operations, for example subsidiaries, branches, associates and joint ventures which operate in an independent or semi-independent way with a significant degree of autonomy (see **32.26–32.31** below); and

- overseas operations which are essentially an extension of the trading activities of the UK parent (see **32.19–32.22** below).

PRESENTATION CURRENCY

32.6   The term 'presentation currency' is defined simply as the currency in which the financial statements are presented. Although not explicitly stated in FRS 102, entities are permitted to present their financial statements in any currency.

Example 32.1 – Presentation currency £

A UK group has a number of trading subsidiaries operating in Germany and France. As most of the group's turnover and profits are generated by its UK operations, the group chooses to present its consolidated financial statements in £ sterling.

Example 32.2 – Presentation currency €

A UK group has a large number of overseas subsidiaries, trading in Western Europe, Canada and the United States. Approximately 70% of group profit is generated by its Western Europe subsidiaries, whose functional currency is the Euro.

The group has effectively operations with four different functional currencies (see below) – £ sterling, Euros, Canadian $ and US $. Because of the significance of its Western European operations, the group has decided to adopt the Euro as its presentation currency for its consolidated financial statements.

32.7   The financial statements should disclose the presentation currency.

FUNCTIONAL CURRENCY

Functional currency

32.8   Each entity must identify its functional currency. This is defined as the currency of the primary economic environment in which the entity operates. The primary economic environment in which an entity operates is normally the one in which it primarily generates and spends cash.

32.9   The entity's functional currency will be determined by considering the following factors:

- whether the activities of the foreign operation are carried out as an extension of the reporting entity, rather than being carried out with a significant degree of autonomy (see also **32.19–32.22**);

- the currency that mainly influences sales prices for goods and services (often the currency in which sales prices for the goods and services supplied by the entity are denominated and settled);

- whether transactions with the reporting entity are a high or low proportion of the foreign operation's activities;

- the currency of the country whose competitive forces and regulations mainly determine the sales prices of its goods and services;

- the currency that mainly influences labour, material and other costs of providing goods and services;

- whether cash flows from the activities of the foreign operation directly affect the cash flows of the reporting entity and are readily available for remittance to it;

- the currency in which funds from financing activities such as issuing shares and debt instruments are generated;

- the currency in which receipts from operating activities are usually retained; and

- whether cash flows from the activities of the foreign operation are sufficient to service existing and normally expected debt obligations without funds being made available by the reporting entity.

> **Focus**
>
> The reporting entity is the entity that has the foreign operation as its subsidiary, branch, associate or joint venture.
>
> For autonomous foreign operations, the functional currency of the foreign operation is different from that of the reporting entity.
>
> For foreign operations which are an extension of the reporting entity, the foreign operation's functional currency is the same as that of the reporting entity.

Changes in functional currency

32.10   Once the functional currency is determined, it can only be changed where there is a change to the underlying transactions, events and conditions that are relevant to the entity.

A change in the currency that mainly influences the sales price of goods and services may lead to a change in an entity's functional currency.

Section 30.16 of FRS 102 sets out requirements where there is a change in the entity's functional currency.

REPORTING INDIVIDUAL FOREIGN CURRENCY TRANSACTIONS

Introduction

32.11   The following are examples of transactions denominated in a foreign currency, or requiring settlement in a foreign currency:

- purchase or sale of goods or services whose price is denominated in a foreign currency;

- borrowing or lending of funds when the amounts payable or receivable are denominated in a foreign currency; and

- acquisition or disposal of assets or incurring or settlement of liabilities denominated in a foreign currency.

Transaction date

32.12   This is the date on which the transaction first qualifies for recognition. A rate that approximates to the actual rate at the date of transaction is often used. For example, where transactions occur over a period, an average rate for the period might be appropriate.

Initial recognition

32.13   On initial recognition, the transaction should be recorded at the spot exchange rate at the date of the transaction.

Focus

This applies whether or not the transaction is covered by a forward foreign currency contract (contrast with SSAP 20 paragraph 46 which gives a choice between recording the transaction at the spot rate at the transaction date, and the rate specified in the contact).

You only need to worry about the potential complexity, and the hedge accounting option, if a forward exchange contract is in place (for more detail of potential complexities, see **Chapters 37** and **38**).

Example 32.3 – Purchase of machinery from an overseas supplier

A UK company buys a machine from a supplier in the Netherlands for immediate payment on delivery of €550,000. The spot rate at the date the machine is recognised in the accounting records and when payment is made is £1 = €1.28. The company will record the asset at historical cost less accumulated depreciation.

The machine would be recognised at £429,687 (€550,000/1.28). Subsequent depreciation charges will be based on this amount. No other adjustments should be made other than in the event of disposal or impairment.

Settlement within the same accounting period

32.14   Exchange differences should be recognised in profit or loss in the period in which they arise.

Example 32.4 – Purchase of materials from an overseas supplier, payment within current period

A UK company with a 31 December year-end purchases materials from a supplier in France at a cost of €250,000. The materials are received and recorded in the accounting records on 8 November 2015 and payment is due four weeks later.

The spot rate of exchange on 8 November 2015 is £1 = €1.21 and on 8 December 2015 £1 = €1.24.

Purchases would be debited on 8 November 2015 with £206,611 (€250,000/1.21) with a corresponding liability in trade creditors.

On 8 December 2015, the payment of £201,613 (€250,000/1.24) will be debited to trade creditors. The difference on trade creditors of £4,998 representing a gain on exchange will be recorded in profit or loss for 2015.

Reporting at the end of the subsequent reporting period

32.15 Monetary items should be translated from the reporting entity's functional currency into its presentation currency using the closing rate of exchange.

Focus

The term 'closing rate' is defined as the spot rate of exchange as at the end of the reporting period.

Example 32.5 – Purchase of materials from an overseas supplier, payment in following period

Purchases are as in **Example 32.4** above, but instead the company obtains two months' credit, and payment is made after the year-end on 8 January 2016. Respective spot rates of exchange on 31 December and 8 January are £1 = €1.26 and €1.29.

The creditor balance at 31 December 2015 should be translated at the closing rate of exchange giving a figure of £198,412 (€250,000/1.26).

An exchange gain of £8,199 (£206,611 – £198,412) will be recorded in profit or loss for 2015.

The payment on settlement on 8 January 2016 is £193,798 (€250,000/1.29). The exchange gain on settlement of the creditor amounting to £4,614 (£198,412 – £193,798) will be included within profit or loss for 2016.

32.16 Non-monetary items measured in terms of historical cost in a foreign currency should be translated into the presentation currency using the exchange rate at the date of the transaction.

32.17   Non-monetary items measured at fair value in a foreign currency should be translated into the presentation currency using the exchange rate at the date when the fair value was determined.

Subsequent settlements and retranslation

32.18   The following exchange differences should be recognised in profit or loss:

- those arising on the settlement of monetary items at rates different from those at which they were translated on initial recognition (see **Example 32.4**); and

- those arising from translating monetary items at rates different from those at which they were translated on initial recognition during the period or in previous periods (see **Example 32.5**).

TRANSLATING THE FINANCIAL STATEMENTS OF FOREIGN OPERATIONS WHICH ARE CARRIED OUT AS AN EXTENSION OF THE TRADE OF THE REPORTING ENTITY

Introduction

32.19   This part of Section 30 applies where the foreign operations are carried out by entities which operate as a direct extension of the trade of the investing entity. This may include certain subsidiaries and branches. Possible examples of scenarios are referred to at **Example 32.6**.

32.20   The term 'foreign operation' could include a branch of a reporting entity. Although an overseas branch would legally be part of the reporting entity, it could be set up either as an extension of the reporting entity's operations (with the same functional currency) or as a separate foreign operation (with a different functional currency from that of the reporting entity).

32.21   A branch that operates as an extension of the operations of the reporting entity would be accounted for as in **32.23–32.24**.

32.22   A branch which in substance operates as a separate foreign operation with a reasonable degree of autonomy from the reporting entity would be accounted for as in **32.32–32.37**.

Example 32.6 – Foreign operations which operate as extensions of a UK business

The following are examples of foreign operations which effectively operate as extensions of a UK business:

● the foreign operation acts as a selling agency receiving stocks of goods from the reporting entity investor and remits the proceeds to it;

● the foreign operation produces a raw material or manufactures parts or sub-assemblies which are then shipped to the investor for inclusion in its own products; or

● the foreign operation is located overseas for tax, exchange control or similar reasons to act as a means of raising finance for other companies in the group.

Reporting requirements

32.23 Foreign operations which are carried out as an extension of the trade of the operations of the reporting entity should be accounted for as follows.

32.24 At the balance sheet date, assets and liabilities should be dealt with as follows:

● monetary items (debtors, cash, creditors and loans) should be translated into the presentation currency at the closing rate of exchange;

● stocks stated at cost should be translated into the presentation currency at the rate of exchange at the date of acquisition (in many cases, the closing rate of exchange may provide a reasonable approximation);

● property, plant and equipment stated at cost less accumulated depreciation should be translated into the presentation currency at the rate of exchange at the date of acquisition; and

● property, plant and equipment and other non-monetary assets stated at fair value at the balance sheet date should be translated into the presentation currency using the exchange rate at that date.

32.25 All exchange differences should be recognised in profit or loss (ie reflected in profit after tax) and disclosed in accordance with paragraph 30.25(a) of FRS 102.

TRANSLATING THE FINANCIAL STATEMENTS OF AUTONOMOUS FOREIGN OPERATIONS INTO THE PRESENTATION CURRENCY

Introduction

32.26 An entity may present its financial statements in a functional currency which differs from its presentation currency. Such entities may operate as autonomous foreign operations owned by an investor in a different country.

32.27 An example of an autonomous foreign operation is one which accumulates cash and other monetary items, incurs expenses, generates income and arranges borrowings, all substantially in its local currency. Such operations could include certain subsidiaries and branches, as well as associates and joint ventures, as indicated below.

Example 32.7 – Presentation currency for a UK group operating in various countries

A UK group contains individual overseas entities which operate on an autonomous basis and which have functional currencies which differ from the presentation currency of the UK parent (£ Sterling).

The items of income and expense and financial position of each of the individual overseas entities are expressed in a common currency (ie £ Sterling) so that consolidated financial statements may be prepared.

32.28 Autonomous foreign operations may have the following characteristics:

- the parent company's investment is in the net worth of the foreign operation, as opposed to a direct investment in its assets and liabilities;

- the foreign operation will normally have both fixed assets and working capital, and these may be part-financed by local currency borrowings, as opposed to being entirely financed by the parent company or joint venturers;

- in its day-to-day operations, the foreign operation is not usually dependent on the reporting currency of the investing company; or

- the parent company or joint venturer will expect dividends to be paid out of future profits, but their investment will remain until such future time as the foreign operation is disposed of or liquidated.

Subsidiaries

32.29   Overseas subsidiaries may well have characteristics which fit in with those referred to in **32.28** above.

Example 32.8 – Group with autonomous subsidiaries

UK Limited has three overseas subsidiaries in Germany, Poland and Norway.

Each subsidiary operates with significant autonomy from UK Limited. The management of each subsidiary determine selling prices which are influenced mainly by local competition, all products are manufactured locally, with locally employed workforces and locally obtained raw materials.

The functional currency of each subsidiary is Euro, Zloty and Krone, respectively. The presentation currency for the UK consolidated financial statements is £ Sterling.

Each income, expense, asset and liability item for each subsidiary must be translated into £ Sterling for the purpose of presenting the UK group's consolidated financial statements.

Associates and joint ventures

32.30   Associates and joint ventures are likely to operate as separate foreign operations and will normally be accounted for in the same way as autonomous subsidiaries.

Branches

32.31   Branches were referred to in **32.20–32.22** above. Branches may or may not have characteristics similar to those in **32.28** above, depending on the way in which the branch is set up.

Example 32.9 – Autonomous branch

A UK company sets up a branch in Italy. The branch assembles components sourced locally, sells the completed products to customers in the local region and keeps separate accounting records.

The functional currency of the branch is the Euro. The branch's financial statements would be translated into the reporting entity's presentation currency £ Sterling, using the translation method immediately below.

Translating the financial statements

32.32   Procedures for translating the entity's results and financial position into a different presentation currency (eg £ Sterling in **Example 32.6** above) are as follows:

32.33   Assets and liabilities for each statement of financial position presented (including comparatives) should be translated at the closing exchange rate at the date of the statement of financial position (balance sheet).

32.34   Income and expenses for each statement of comprehensive income (including comparatives) should be translated at exchange rates at the dates of the transactions.

Focus

Section 30, paragraph 30.19, states:

'For practical reasons, an entity may use a rate that approximates the exchange rates at the dates of the transactions, for example an average rate for the period to translate the income and expense items. However, if exchange rates fluctuate significantly, the use of the average rate for a period is inappropriate.'

Exchange differences

32.35   All resulting exchange differences should be recognised in other comprehensive income. These exchange differences arise, for example, during the consolidation of overseas subsidiaries as well as from entities not consolidated such as associates and joint ventures whose financial statements are drawn up in functional currencies which differ from the presentation currency of the parent company.

32.36   The exchange differences above reflect the combined effect of:

- translating income and expenses at exchange rates at the date of the transactions and assets and liabilities at the closing rate;

- translating the opening net assets at a closing rate that differs from the previous closing rate; and

- goodwill (see **32.38, 32.40**).

32.37 Such exchange differences should be recognised in other comprehensive income and disclosed in accordance with FRS 102, paragraph 30.25(b).

Focus

Note that there is no requirement to keep the cumulative amount of these exchange differences in a separate component of equity, although some groups may choose to classify these differences in a foreign currency reserve within equity.

Consolidated goodwill

32.38 Any goodwill arising on the acquisition of a foreign operation is to be treated *as an asset of the foreign operation.*

32.39 Any fair value adjustments to the carrying amount of assets and liabilities arising on the acquisition of a foreign operation shall be treated as assets and liabilities of the foreign operation.

32.40 The assets and liabilities referred to in **32.33** above should be expressed in the functional currency of the foreign operation and translated at the closing rate of exchange.

Focus

This treatment is different from the treatment in SSAP 20 where the carrying amount of consolidated goodwill was not changed as a result of subsequent exchange rate changes. SSAP 20 regards consolidated goodwill as an asset of the parent company and not the subsidiary.

Example 32.10 – Retranslation of goodwill

Goodwill relating to the acquisition by a UK company of a company in the Netherlands should be expressed in the Dutch company's functional currency, Euros, and retranslated into £ Sterling at each balance sheet date for consolidation purposes.

Example 32.11 – Preparing consolidated financial statements

Holdings Limited acquired all of the ordinary share capital of Sub SA on 1 January 2016 at a cost of £800,000 paid in cash in £ Sterling. At acquisition, the net assets of Sub amounted to €950,000 and the spot exchange rate was £1 = €1.27. No fair value adjustments were required at acquisition. Holdings has no other subsidiaries. The presentation currency is £ Sterling.

The relevant spot rates of exchange are:

At 31 December 2016: £1 = €1.29

Average for 2016: £1 = €1.28.

Purchased goodwill is calculated at £51,969 (£800,000 – €950,000/1.27). If the company is unable to make a reliable estimate of the useful life, goodwill will be amortised over a maximum period of five years on a straight-line basis (FRS 102, paragraph 19.23(a)).

As indicated above, the goodwill is to be regarded as an asset of Sub, expressed in the functional currency of Euros and translated at the year-end at the closing rate of exchange. The initial goodwill figure expressed in the functional currency is €66,000 (£51,969 × 1.27).

The amortisation charge for the period should be translated at the average rate of exchange (see **32.34** *above). The amortisation charge for 2016 will therefore be £10,313 (€66,000/5 years/1.28).*

The year-end balance is €52,800 (the asset is required to be expressed in the functional currency) and £40,930 (€52,800/1.29) expressed in the presentation currency for consolidation purposes.

The movement on goodwill for the year may be summarised as follows:

	Exchange rate	€ (functional currency)	£ (presentation currency)
Arising on acquisition	1.27	66,000 (W1)	51,969
Amortisation charge	1.28	13,200 (W2)	(10,313) (W3)
Exchange movements		–	(726) (W4)
Balance at 31/12/16	1.29	52,800	40,930

W1	£51,569 × 1.27
W2	€66,000/5
W3	€13,200/1.23
W4	The exchange difference of (£726) consists of the net of the translation differences on:

	£
Opening balance of €66,000: €66,000/1.27 − €66,000/1.29 =	(806)
Depreciation charge of €13,200: €13,200/1.28 − €13,200/1.29 =	80
	(726)

Note that the exchange difference (loss) of £726 above will be separately disclosed within the goodwill note as part of the movement on goodwill. However, the £726 will not be separately disclosed elsewhere in other comprehensive income or equity. It is part of the overall exchange difference of £12,808 (see **Working 6** below), shown as a separate line ('Other comprehensive income') in the consolidated income statement.

The summarised balance sheets and profit and loss accounts of the respective companies are:

Balance sheets at 31 December

	Holdings Limited 2015 (£)	Holdings Limited 2016 (£)	Sub SA 2016 (€)
Investment in subsidiary	–	800,000	–
Other assets less liabilities	1,315,450	1,550,000	1,030,000
Net assets	1,315,450	2,350,000	1,030,000
Share capital	(500,000)	(500,000)	(400,000)
Retained earnings	(815,450)	(1,850,000)	(630,000)
Total	0	0	0

Profit and loss accounts for the year ended 31 December 2016

	Holdings (£)	Sub (€)
Turnover	2,909,560	400,500
Expenses and taxation	(1,875,010)	(320,500)
Retained earnings for the year	1,034,550	80,000
Retained earnings brought forward	815,450	550,000
Retained earnings carried forward	1,850,000	630,000

Translation of balance sheet at 31 December 2016 of Sub SA into presentation currency £

	Sub SA (€)	Exchange rate	Sub SA (£)
Other assets less liabilities	1,030,000	1.29	798,450
Net assets	1,030,000	1.29	798,450
Share capital	(400,000)	1.27	(314,961)
Retained earnings at acquisition	(550,000)	1,27	(433,071)
Retained earnings post-acquisition	(80,000)		(62,500)
Foreign exchange reserve	0		12,082 (W5)
Total	0		0

W5

Foreign exchange reserve (not including goodwill adjustment – see below)

Exchange loss on net assets at acquisition (€950,000/1.27 – €950,000/1.29)	(11,597)
Exchange loss on retained profit (€80,000/1.28 – €80,000/1.29)	(485)
Net exchange loss	(12,082)

W6

Total exchange difference (see **32.36** above).

Foreign exchange difference (W5)	(12,082)
Goodwill adjustment (W4)	(726)
Total loss	(12,808)

Translation of profit and loss account of Sub into presentation currency £

	Sub (€)	Exchange rate	Sub (£)
Turnover	400,500	1.28	312,891
Operating expenses and taxation	(320,500)	1.28	(250,391)
Retained earnings for the year	80,000	1.28	62,500
Retained earnings brought forward	550,000		
Retained earnings carried forward	630,000		

Consolidated balance sheet

	Holdings £	Sub £	Adjustment debit £	Adjustment credit £	Total £
Investment in subsidiary	800,000	0		800,000	0
Goodwill	0	0	800,000	314,961 433,071 10,312(a) 726(b)	40,930
Other assets less liabilities	1,550,000	798,450			2,348,450
Share capital	(500,000)	(314,961)	314,961		(500,000)
Retained earnings at acquisition	0	(433,071)	433,071		0
Retained earnings post-acquisition	(1,850,000)	(62,500)	10,312(a)		(1,902,188)
Foreign exchange reserve	0	12,082	726(b)		12,808
Total	0	0	1,559,070	1,559,070	0

Focus

Note that the foreign exchange reserve need not be disclosed as a separate component of equity – it could be included within profit and loss reserves (but note disclosure requirements in FRS 102, paragraph 30.25(b) of relating to differences arising during the period). The separate presentation above is for the purposes of clarification.

32.41   *Foreign currency translation*

Consolidated profit and loss account

	£
Turnover	
(£2,909,560 + £312,891)	3,222,451
Operating expenses (including depreciation)	
(£1,875,010 + £250,391)	(2,125,401)
Amortisation of goodwill	(10,312)
Retained earnings for the year	1,086,738
Retained earnings brought forward	815,450
Retained earnings carried forward	1,902,188

Consolidated statement of comprehensive income

	£
Profit for the year	1,902,188
Exchange difference on translation of foreign operations	(12,808)
Total comprehensive income for the year	1,889,380

Reconciliation of exchange differences

	£
Exchange loss on net assets at acquisition	(11,597)
Exchange loss on profit for the year ((£485) + (£726))	(1,211)
Total exchange loss arising during the year	(12,808)

INTRA-GROUP TRANSACTIONS (OTHER THAN THOSE WHICH ARE PART OF A NET INVESTMENT IN A FOREIGN OPERATION)

General requirements – separate accounts of individual group companies

32.41   In the separate accounts of the parent and subsidiary companies, the usual rules for dealing with monetary items apply. These are illustrated in **Examples 32.12** and **32.13** below.

General requirements – consolidated financial statements

32.42   Assets, liabilities, income and expenses of a foreign operation should be incorporated with those of the reporting entity using the procedures set out above (see **32.33–32.34**) and follow normal consolidation procedures including elimination of intra-group balances and intra-group transactions.

32.43   However, intra-group monetary assets or liabilities, whether short-term or long-term, cannot be eliminated against the corresponding intra-group items without the results of currency fluctuations being shown in the consolidated financial statements as exchange differences.

32.44   This is because the monetary item represents a commitment to convert from one currency to another and exposes the reporting entity to a gain or loss through currency fluctuations. The exchange differences reflect the risk of transactions with a foreign operation even though that foreign operation is in fact a member of the group.

32.45   Exchange differences will be reflected in profit or loss, unless they arise from the special circumstances of a net investment in a foreign operation (see **32.52–32.58**) in which case they will be presented as part of other comprehensive income.

Example 32.12 – Amount invoiced to subsidiary in functional currency of the parent company

UK Co has a wholly owned subsidiary, Subco whose functional currency is the Euro. One month before the group year-end, UK Co provides services to Subco and immediately invoices the company for £600,000. At the invoice date, the exchange rate is £1 = €1.30. The invoice is still outstanding at the year-end when the exchange rate is £1 = €1.25.

Impact on individual financial statements of UK parent

As the invoice is denominated in £ Sterling, UK Co will debit inter-company debtors and credit income with £600,000. As the debtor is denominated in £ Sterling, UK Co does not make any further adjustment in its own individual accounts.

Impact on individual financial statements of overseas subsidiary

On receipt of the invoice, Subco will translate the £600,000 into its own functional currency of the Euro. Expenses will be debited and inter-company creditors credited with €780,000 (£600,000 × 1.30).

At the year-end, Subco translates the monetary item, the inter-company liability of £600,000 using the year-end rate of €1.25 into €750,000 (£600,000 × 1.25). The exchange gain of €30,000 (€780,000 – €750,000) will be reflected in the individual profit and loss account of Subco, following the usual rules for monetary items.

Impact on consolidated financial statements

On consolidation, the exchange gain of €30,000 will be translated into the presentation currency £ Sterling at the closing rate of exchange of £1 = €1.25 (ie £24,000). This will be recognised in profit or loss in the consolidated income statement (profit and loss account).

Example 32.13 – Amount invoiced to subsidiary in functional currency of subsidiary

The invoice is denominated in Euros so the amount stated on the invoice is €780,000 (£600,000 × 1.30).

Impact on individual financial statements of UK parent

The invoice is denominated in Euros so UK Co will debit inter-company debtors and credit income with £600,000 (€780,000/1.30). At the year-end, the inter-company debtor of €780,000 will be translated into UK Co's presentation currency £ at the closing rate of 1.25, giving an amount of £624,000 (€780,000/1.25). The gain on retranslation of £24,000 will be recognised in UK Co's individual profit and loss account.

Impact on individual financial statements of overseas subsidiary

As the invoice is denominated in Euros, Subco will debit inter-company debtors and credit income with €780,000. As the inter-company creditor is Euros, Subco does not make any further adjustment in its own individual accounts.

Impact on consolidated financial statements

On consolidation, the exchange gain of £24,000 will be will be recognised in profit or loss in the consolidated income statement (profit and loss account).

Inter-company long-term loans

32.46   As indicated in **32.45**, intra-group loans, whether short-term or long-term, cannot be eliminated against the corresponding intra-group items without the results of currency fluctuations being shown in the consolidated financial statements as exchange differences.

32.47   In the case of long-term loans, exchange differences will normally be recognised in profit or loss in both:

- the subsidiary's individual income statement (profit and loss account) (assuming the loan is denominated in the presentation and functional currency of the parent company); and

- in the consolidated income statement (profit and loss account).

If the loan is denominated in the functional currency of the subsidiary, exchange differences will be recognised in the income statement (profit and loss account) of both subsidiary and group.

The exception to this is where a loan is treated as part of a net investment in a foreign operation. This special case is dealt with below (see **32.52–32.58**).

Inter-company dividends

32.48   Dividends paid by the subsidiary to the parent should be translated at the exchange rate at the date of payment. Differences between the exchange rate at this date, compared to the exchange rate at the reporting date, form part of the exchange difference from translation that arises during the year.

Example 32.14 – Inter company dividends

The summarised movement on net assets of Subco for the year ended 31 December 2015 was as follows:

	€
Net assets at 1 January 2015	530,000
Profit after tax for the year	245,000
Dividend paid	(90,000)
Net assets at 31 December 2015	685,000

The exchange rates for 2015 were as follows:

1/1/15: €1.21 = £1

31/12/15: €1.29 = £1

Average for the year: 1.25

At date of payment of dividend: 1.27

The translation difference for the year, recognised as part of other comprehensive income, is calculated as follows:

Component	Calculation	Amount include in consolidated other comprehensive income (£)
Opening net assets	€530,000/1.21 – €530,000/1.29	(27,164)
Profit for the year	€245,000/1.25 – €245,000/1.29	(6,078)
Difference in dividend paid	€90,000/1.27 – €90,000/1.29	1,099
Total translation difference (loss) arising during the year – recognised in other comprehensive income		**(32,143)**

Exchange differences

32.49   Exchange differences will be recognised in profit or loss except where it arises from the circumstances referred to in **32.50** below, in which case it will be recognised in other comprehensive income.

(See **32.59** for disclosure requirement relating to presentation of exchange differences.)

Disposal of a foreign operation

32.50   The profit or loss on disposal is calculated as the difference between the proceeds of sale and the carrying amount at the date of disposal (excluding the cumulative amount of any exchange differences) and presented as part of other comprehensive income.

32.51   The computation of the gain or loss on disposal is set out in FRS 102, paragraph 9.18A.

Focus

This calculation is different from that under full IFRS (see IAS 21, paragraph 48) which takes such cumulative gains/losses into account in determining the profit or loss on disposal of the foreign operation.

NET INVESTMENT IN A FOREIGN OPERATION

Introduction

32.52   The Glossary to FRS 102 defines a net investment in a foreign operation as 'the amount of the reporting entity's interest in the net assets of that operation'. This part of FRS 102, Section 30 deals with certain very specific inter-company monetary items receivable by the reporting entity from or payable to a foreign operation.

Paragraphs 30.12 and 30.13 deals with receivables and/or payables for which settlement is *neither planned nor likely to occur in the foreseeable future* and may include long-term receivables or loans. In substance, these are a part of the reporting entity's net investment in the foreign operation and should be accounted for as set out below.

32.53   The monetary item should be viewed by management as part of the entity's long-term investment. The phrase 'neither planned nor likely to occur in the foreseeable future' needs to be considered by management very carefully.

Judgement may be required in determining whether or not settlement is expected.

The following considerations are relevant:

● the term 'foreseeable' future does not stipulate a particular time period;

● there must be no intention or expectation by either party to the loan that repayment will be made; and

● a long-term loan with a specified maturity will not qualify for treatment as part of 'net investment in a foreign operation' simply because the loan has a long duration. It is necessary to assess management's intention as regards settlement of the monetary item. Management must have expressed an intention to renew the loan at maturity and the foreign operation must not expect to make a repayment.

Note that the monetary items above do *not* include trade receivables or trade payables (see FRS 102, paragraph 30.12).

32.54   **Chapter 38** refers to the foreign exchange risk in a net investment in a foreign operation (see **38.16** and **38.17**).

Accounting requirements – separate financial statements of the reporting entity or the foreign operation

32.55   Exchange differences may arise because the respective items are translated at each reporting date at the closing rate of exchange. Such exchange differences should be recognised in the respective entity's profit or loss.

Accounting requirements – consolidated financial statements

32.56   Section 30, paragraph 30.13 requires that the exchange difference on translation arising during the year is recognised in other comprehensive income and reported as a separate component of equity.

32.57   Recording the exchange gains and losses arising from retranslation is consistent with the treatment required when translating the financial statements of autonomous foreign operations into the presentation currency (see **32.32** onwards above).

32.58   Exchange differences recognised separately as above should not again be recognised in profit or loss on a subsequent disposal of the net investment.

Example 32.15 – Loan regarded as part of long-term investment

The functional and presentation currency of the reporting entity X is £ Sterling. The foreign operation Y (a wholly owned subsidiary of X) is located in Belgium and its functional currency is the Euro (€).

During the year, X made a loan to Y denominated in Euros and amounting to €1 million. At the date of the loan, the exchange rate was £1 = €1.20. At the end of the year, the exchange rate was £1 = €1.26.

Management regards the loan as part of the entity's long-term investment in Y and there is no intention or expectation by either X or Y that repayment will be made.

Financial statements of X

The loan receivable is recorded initially at £833,333 (€1m/1.20). At the year-end the loan will be retranslated to £793,650 (€1,000,000/1.26). The loss on exchange of £39,683 will be recorded in profit or loss.

Financial statements of Y

The loan payable will initially be recorded at €1 million. No further adjustment is required as the loan is denominated in Euros

Consolidated financial statements

On consolidation the inter-company loan is eliminated in full. The exchange loss of £39,683 will be recognised in the consolidated financial statements in other comprehensive income (not in profit or loss).

This will require a simple consolidation adjustment, picking up the exchange loss recorded in the individual profit and loss account of X and recording it as 'other comprehensive income' in the group's consolidated profit and loss account.

The effect of the above transaction on the consolidated balance sheet is as follows:

Assets of subsidiary (€1m Euros)	€793,650
Reduction in assets of parent company	(€833,333)
Net liability	(€39,683)
Foreign currency reserve/profit and loss reserves	(€39,683)

Example 32.16 – Loan regarded as part of long-term investment

The functional and presentation currency of the reporting entity X is £ Sterling. The foreign operation Y (a wholly owned subsidiary of X) is located in Belgium and its functional currency is the Euro.

During the year, X made a loan to Y denominated in £ Sterling and amounting to £833,333. At the date of the loan, the exchange rate was £1 = €1.20. At the end of the year, the exchange rate was £1 = €1.26.

Management regards the loan as part of the entity's long-term investment in Y and there is no intention or expectation by either X or Y that repayment will be made.

Financial statements of X

The loan receivable is recorded initially at £1m. No further adjustment is required as the loan is denominated in £ Sterling.

461

Financial statements of Y

The loan payable will initially be recorded at €1m (£833,333 × 1.20). At the year-end the loan will be retranslated to €1,050,000 (£833,333 × 1.26). The loss on exchange of €50,000 will be recorded in profit or loss.

Consolidated financial statements

On consolidation the inter-company loan is eliminated in full.

The loan payable of €1,050,000 will be translated into the group's presentation currency £ Sterling, to €1,050,000/1.26 = £833,333.

The exchange loss of €50,000 will be translated into £ Sterling at the year-end rate of 1.26 (ie £39,683). This will be recognised in the consolidated financial statements in other comprehensive income (not in profit or loss).

The impact on the group financial statements is the same as in **Example 32.15** *above.*

DISCLOSURE REQUIREMENTS

32.59   The following should be disclosed in the financial statements:

- exchange differences recognised in profit or loss during the period (see **32.14**, **32.18**, **32.25**), with the exception of those arising on any financial instruments required to be measured at fair value through profit or loss;

- the amount of exchange differences arising during the period and classified in equity at the end of the period (see **32.36**);

- the currency in which the financial statements are presented;

- where the presentation currency is different from the functional currency, this fact should be stated together with disclosure of the functional currency and the reason for using a different presentation currency; and

- where applicable, the fact that there has been a change in the functional currency of either the reporting entity or a significant foreign operation, and the reason for the change in the functional currency.

32.60   Section 3, paragraph 3.17(e) requires the notes to the financial statements to include 'a summary of significant accounting policies' and, where appropriate, this would include the entity's accounting policy for foreign currency transactions and translations.

Example 32.17 – Extract from statement of significant accounting policies

Foreign currency translation

(a) *Individual financial statements of entities within the group*

Transactions in foreign currencies are recognised in the individual entity's functional currency at the exchange rates at the transaction dates. At the year-end, monetary items denominated in foreign currencies are retranslated at the year-end exchange rate. Non-monetary items measured in terms of historical cost in a foreign currency are not retranslated. Non-monetary items carried at fair value that are denominated in foreign currencies are retranslated at the year-end exchange rate.

All exchange differences are recognised in profit or loss.

(b) *Consolidated financial statements*

For the purposes of the consolidated financial statements, the results and financial position of each group entity are expressed in £ Sterling which is the functional currency of the parent company and the presentation currency for the consolidated financial statements.

Exchange differences arising from the translation of the financial statements of foreign operations are recognised in other comprehensive income and classified in a separate component of equity, designated as a foreign currency translation reserve in the balance sheet.

Exchange difference arising on a monetary item that forms part of the reporting entity's net investment in a foreign operation are also recognised in other comprehensive income and classified in a foreign currency translation reserve. These will remain in equity even in the event of subsequent disposal of the foreign operation.

All other exchange differences are recognised in consolidated profit or loss in the period in which they arise.

Example 32.18

Note

Operating costs are stated after charging foreign exchange gains of £x and exchange losses of £y relating to operating activities.

Example 32.19

Note y

Other financial expenses includes £z relating to net foreign exchange losses on financing activities.

SUMMARY – WHAT IS DIFFERENT FROM THE PREVIOUS UK GAAP?

- FRS 102 specifically allows an entity to use any currency for its presentation currency.

- As regards foreign currency transactions, SSAP 20 allows a company which has a foreign exchange contract in place for a transaction to record the transaction at either the spot rate at the date of the transaction, or the exchange rate specified in the forward contract. Under FRS 102, the transaction is recorded at the spot rate (see **32.13** above) whilst the forward contract is accounted for as a derivative within the section 'Other financial instruments' (see **Chapter 37**).

- Under FRS 102, consolidation goodwill is regarded as an asset of the subsidiary and must be remeasured in line with exchange rate changes arising after the date of acquisition (see **32.38**).

- The term 'functional currency' used in FRS 102 can be equated to SSAP 20's 'local currency'. However, the guidance is different, therefore the detail needs to be followed carefully.

- For companies currently applying FRS 23 *The Effects of Changes in Foreign Exchange Rates*, the difference to be aware of is regarding FRS 102, paragraph 30.13 (see **32.56** above). Exchange differences initially recognised in other comprehensive income should not be recognised in profit or loss on disposal (FRS 102, paragraph 9.18A).

Chapter 33

Assets held for sale and discontinued operations

SIGNPOSTS

- This chapter covers accounting and disclosure requirements for:

    o   Assets held for sale where there is a binding sales agreement at the balance sheet date;

    o   Impairment issues regarding property, plant and equipment held for sale; and

    o   Discontinued operations.

- Where an entity at the reporting date has a binding sales agreement for a major disposal of assets or a disposal group, it must provide detailed memorandum disclosure in the notes to the financial statements (see **33.1** below).

- FRS 102, paragraph 17.26 refers to impairment indicators in this context (see **33.3**, **33.4** below).

- The presentation of discontinued operations is dealt with in Section 5 which requires a multi-column presentation in the statement of comprehensive income and the income statement (see **33.5** below).

BINDING SALES AGREEMENTS FOR A MAJOR DISPOSAL OF ASSETS

33.1   At the reporting date, if an entity has a binding sales agreement for a major disposal of assets, or a disposal group, the following should be disclosed (FRS 102, paragraph 4.14):

- a description of the asset(s) or the disposal group;

- a description of the facts and circumstances of the sale or plan; and

- the carrying amount of the assets or, for a disposal group, the carrying amounts of the underlying assets and liabilities.

33.2   A disposal group is defined in the Glossary to FRS 102 as a group of assets to be disposed of, by sale or otherwise, together as a group in a single transaction, and liabilities directly associated with those assets that will be transferred in the transaction.

The group of assets and liabilities includes goodwill acquired in a business combination if the group is a cash-generating unit to which goodwill has been allocated in accordance with the requirements of FRS 102, paragraphs 27.24–27.27.

Example 33.1 – Binding sales agreement

The following disclosure example might be appropriate where a group has entered into a binding sales agreement to dispose of certain of its assets at a future date:

Note 28 – Commitment to dispose of assets

In November 2015, the group entered into a binding agreement for the sale of several large items of specialised plant and machinery to an independent third party for £750,000. The group will continue to operate the machinery until it is transferred to the purchasing company on 16 March 2016.

At 31 December 2015, the carrying amount of the machinery to be disposed of is £623,500.

IMPAIRMENT ISSUES REGARDING PROPERTY, PLANT AND EQUIPMENT HELD FOR SALE

33.3   A plan to dispose of an asset before the previously expected date is an indicator of impairment that triggers the calculation of the asset's recoverable amount in order to determine whether the asset is impaired (FRS 102, paragraph 17.26).

33.4   FRS 102, paragraph 27.7 refers to the need for an entity to assess whether there is any indication that an asset may be impaired and the various indicators that must be considered 'as a minimum'.

Specifically, FRS 102, paragraph 27.9(f) refers to the following particular internal source of information:

'Significant changes with an adverse effect on the entity have taken place during the period, or are expected to take place in the near future, in the extent to which, or manner in which an asset is used or is expected to be used. These changes include the asset becoming idle, plans to discontinue

466

or restructure the operation to which the asset belongs, plans to dispose of an asset before the previously expected date, and reassessing the useful life of an asset as finite rather than indefinite.'

DISCONTINUED OPERATIONS

Definition

33.5   A *discontinued operation* is defined in the Glossary to FRS 102 as a component of an entity that has been disposed of and:

- represented a separate major line of business or geographical area of operations;

- was part of a single co-ordinated plan to dispose of a separate major line of business or geographical area of operations; or

- was a subsidiary acquired exclusively with a view to resale.

Presentation of discontinued operations

33.6   Whichever presentation option is adopted, the statement of comprehensive income should present an amount relating to discontinued operations and comprising the total of:

- the post-tax profit or loss of a discontinued operation; and

- the post-tax gain or loss recognised on the impairment or on the disposal of the net assets constituting a discontinued operation.

(FRS 102, paragraph 5.7D.)

33.7   The entity should provide an analysis between continuing operations and discontinued operation for each of the line items on the face of the statement of comprehensive income.

33.8   FRS 102, paragraph 5.7D requires a columnar layout to be adopted.

Example 33.2 – Disposal of subsidiary

A group sold a subsidiary during the year. The disposal is classified as a discontinued operation.

The pre-tax profits of the subsidiary for the period up to the date of sale are £18,000 [£128,000 – £110,000] and the pre-tax profit on disposal (proceeds less net assets at date of sale including goodwill) amounted to £301,000. The tax on these two items amounted to £80,000.

In accordance with the requirements of FRS 102, paragraph 5.7D and the guidance in the Appendix to Section 5, the results would be presented as follows:

	Continuing operations £'000	Discontinued operations £'000	Total £'000
Turnover	4,200	1,232	5,432
Cost of sales	(2,591)	(1,104)	(3,695)
Gross profit	1,609	128	1,737
Expenses	(240)	(110)	(350)
Profit on disposal of operations	–	301	301
Operating profit	1,369	319	1,688
Interest payable	(194)	–	(194)
Tax	(390)	(80)	(470)
Profit for the year	785	239	1,024

RESTATEMENT OF COMPARATIVES

33.9   This relates to all operations that have been discontinued by the end of the latest reporting period being presented. In such cases the disclosures in **33.7** and **33.8** above should be restated and represented for the comparative period.

33.10   The requirement to restate comparatives relates to the comprehensive income statement. Comparatives for the balance sheet should *not* be restated.

33.11   FRS 102 is silent regarding the cash flow statement. In practice, it may be more straightforward to present the cash flow statement in the usual way without distinguishing between cash flows relating to continuing activities and those relating to discontinued operations.

33.12   Particular issues arising on first-time adoption in FRS 102, paragraph 35.9(d) are referred to in **39.16–39.17**.

SUMMARY – WHAT IS DIFFERENT FROM THE PREVIOUS UK GAAP?

- The definition of discontinued operations in FRS 102 is less rigid than that in FRS 3 *Reporting Financial Performance* (see **33.5**) so it is possible that more operations will be reported as discontinued under FRS 102 compared with previous UK GAAP.

- The presentation requirements of FRS 102 are more onerous than those in FRS 3 due to restrictions imposed by the Regulations to CA 2006, in particular a multi-columnar format of presentation is required by FRS 102 (see **33.6–33.8**).

- FRS 3 does not address the issue of assets held for sale. FRS 102 requires memorandum disclosure (see **33.1**).

Chapter 34

Reduced disclosures for subsidiaries and parent companies

SIGNPOSTS

- Certain groups presenting consolidated financial statements may be entitled to disclosure concessions in relation to the individual financial statements of the parent company and its subsidiaries.

- Two alternative sets of reduced disclosure concessions are available – which is more appropriate will depend on the group's circumstances, and in particular whether the consolidated financial statements are prepared in accordance with UK GAAP or EU-endorsed IFRS.

- The concessions may also be available to certain UK subsidiaries which have overseas parent companies but many of the disclosure concessions contain the proviso provided the equivalent disclosures required are included in the consolidated financial statements of the group – it is important to refer to FRS 100 *Application Guidance, The Interpretation of Equivalence*.

- The two sets of disclosure concessions are dealt with below in the following sequence:

  ○ Section 1 of FRS 102 (see **32.6** to **32.10**); and

  ○ FRS 101 *Reduced Disclosure Framework* (see **32.11** to **32.20**).

INTRODUCTION AND SCOPE

Introduction

34.1 Many of the concessions referred to below are given on the basis that particular disclosure information relating to the individual entity is available on an aggregated basis in the consolidated financial statements and disclosure at individual entity level would be of comparatively little benefit to users of financial statements.

Scope

34.2 Disclosure concessions may be available to individual financial statements of *a qualifying entity.*

A qualifying entity is defined as a 'member of a group that prepares publicly available financial statements, which give a true and fair view, in which that member is consolidated'. The term includes qualifying subsidiaries (including those with overseas parent companies) and ultimate parent companies.

Focus

The term 'publicly available financial statements' is not defined in FRS 102.

Where the parent company is registered in the UK, consolidated financial statements will be filed at Companies House.

Where the parent company is registered outside the UK, the key issue is whether anyone who wanted to obtain a copy of the consolidated financial statements could do so relatively easily. This would be so for financial statements filed in a public registry. Alternatively, consolidated financial statements could be regarded as publicly available where the notes to the financial statements of the parent company or subsidiaries gave the address from which the consolidated financial statements could be obtained.

34.3 The subsidiaries need not be wholly owned, but where FRS 102 is used to prepare the financial statements of a partly owned subsidiary, the shareholders must be informed about the exemptions and not object to their use (see **34.9**).

34.4 Financial institutions adopting FRS 102 may adopt the options referred to below, although some of the concessions may not be available to them (FRS 102, paragraph 1.9; FRS 101, paragraph 7).

The reduced disclosure options

34.5 The two options are:

Reduced disclosures under FRS 102

Financial statements which take advantage of these concessions are based on the recognition and measurement principles of the new UK GAAP framework under FRS 102.

34.6 *Reduced disclosures for subsidiaries and parent companies*

Reduced disclosure framework under FRS 101

This framework is based on recognition and measurement principles adopted from full, EU-endorsed IFRS, modified to comply with the requirements of the EU Fourth Directive incorporated in the Regulations to CA 2006.

Although FRS 102 is derived from IFRS, it is regarded as part of UK GAAP and must comply with the format requirements set out in the Regulations to CA 2006.

REDUCED DISCLOSURES UNDER FRS 102

Introduction

34.6 This option may be used by qualifying entities irrespective of whether the consolidated financial statements are prepared on the basis of FRS 102 or EU-adopted IFRS.

Concessions for qualifying entities which are not financial institutions

34.7 The disclosure concessions are set out in paragraph 1.12 of FRS 102 and include exemption from disclosing the following:

- a reconciliation of the number of shares outstanding at the beginning and at the end of the period;

- a statement of cash flows;

- the financial instruments disclosures contained in Sections 11 and 12 provided the equivalent disclosures required by FRS 102 are included in the consolidated financial statements of the group in which the entity is consolidated (but see **32.8** below);

- the total of key management personnel compensation; and

- certain share-based payment disclosures provided the equivalent disclosures required by FRS 102 are included in the consolidated financial statements of the group in which the entity is consolidated.

34.8 The final sentence of FRS 102, paragraph 1.8 states:

'Where the qualifying entity has financial instruments held at fair value subject to the requirements of paragraph 36(4) of Schedule 1 to the Regulations, it must apply the disclosure requirements of Section 11, Basic Financial Instruments to those financial instruments held at fair value.'

For derivatives such as forward foreign currency contracts, this effectively means that all relevant disclosure requirements in Section 11 (eg 11.42, 11.43 and 11.48) must be given in the individual accounts of parents and subsidiaries, even though the reduced disclosure exemption is claimed. FRS 102 cannot reduce disclosures which are required by the Regulations to CA 2006 (in this case Schedule 1, paragraph 55(2)).

Focus

Requirements for determining whether equivalent disclosures required are included in the consolidated financial statements are contained in FRS 100 *Application Guidance, the Interpretation of Equivalence* (AG 1-10).

Where the parent presents consolidated financial statements in accordance with either FRS 102 or EU-endorsed IFRS, this requirement will usually be satisfied.

However, where the parent produces consolidated financial statements in accordance with another GAAP (AG 6(d)) it is important to refer to the *Application Guidance*, particularly paragraphs AG 8 and AG 10.

Example 34.1 – Reduced disclosure requirements under FRS 102

Sub Limited satisfies the requirements to be classed as a qualifying entity. Sub's UK parent company wishes to take advantage of the disclosure concessions in Section 1 of FRS 102.

Sub's balance sheet includes the following financial instruments:

- a bank loan of £850,000 repayable in six-monthly instalments over a period of eight years and secured on the company's freehold property;

- cash at bank of £35,725;

- trade debtors amounting to £1,345,432;

- trade creditors amounting to £834,563;

- a forward foreign currency contract with a fair value of £54,336; and

- an investment in an unlisted company amounting to 1% of its share capital and with a fair value of £213,000.

If Sub takes advantage of the maximum exemption available in respect of financial instrument disclosures, will any disclosure be required in respect of the above?

FRS 102 exempts from disclosure all the requirements of FRS 102, paragraphs 11.39–11.48A provided the equivalent disclosures required by the FRS are included in the consolidated financial statements of the group. Assuming the group consolidated financial statements are prepared in accordance with FRS 102, this is the case. However, the disclosure exemptions do not extend to 'financial instruments held at fair value subject to the requirements of paragraph 36(4) of Schedule 1 to the Regulations'.

Paragraph 36(4) refers to:

'Financial instruments that, under international accounting standards adopted by the European Commission on or before 5 September 2006 in accordance with the IAS Regulation, may be included in accounts at fair value, may be so included, provided that the disclosures required by such accounting standards are made.'

This would include the forward foreign currency contract but none of the other items. Paragraph 1.8 of FRS 102 states that this would be subject to the disclosure requirements of Section 11, and in particular:

- the carrying amount of the derivative contract (11.41(a));

- information that enables users of financial statements to evaluate the significance of financial instruments for its financial position and performance (11.42);

- the basis for determining fair value (11.43); and

- changes in fair value (11.48(a)(i)).

(Note also Schedule 1 to the Regulations, paragraph 55(2).)

Schedule 1 paragraph 61 requires disclosure of details of indebtedness relating to the bank loan:

- amount of any instalments which fall due for payment more than five years from the balance sheet date;

- terms of repayment including rate of interest; and

- aggregate amount of debt for which security given and indication of nature of security.

What conditions have to be satisfied?

34.9   A qualifying entity may take advantage of the respective disclosure exemptions above, provided that:

- its shareholders have been notified in writing about the disclosure concessions and do not object to their use;

- the entity otherwise applies the relevant recognition, measurement and disclosure requirements of FRS 102;

- the entity discloses a brief narrative summary of the disclosure exemptions adopted; and

- the notes state the name of the parent in whose consolidated financial statements its own financial statements have been consolidated, and from where those consolidated financial statements can be obtained. The parent could potentially be an overseas entity.

Focus

The exemption is available to both wholly owned and partly owned subsidiaries. However, FRS 102, paragraph 1.11(a) and FRS 101 both give minority shareholders a right to object. With regard to the first bullet point in **34.9** above, one of the qualifying conditions is that the entity's shareholders must have been notified in writing and do not object to the use of the disclosure exemptions.

The immediate parent of the entity, or an individual shareholder or group of shareholders holding in aggregate 5% or more of the allotted shares can serve notice on the qualifying entity in accordance with reasonable timeframes and format requirements.

Reporting for groups preparing consolidated accounts

34.10   The disclosure concessions above may be used irrespective of whether the consolidated financial statements are prepared in accordance with UK GAAP (FRS 102) or EU-endorsed IFRS.

Example 34.2 – Options for a group which presents consolidated financial statements under UK GAAP

Group A is a large unlisted group whose business is mainly within the UK. The group currently prepares its consolidated accounts in accordance with full UK GAAP. The parent company and most of the subsidiary companies also adopt full UK GAAP, but some small-sized subsidiaries adopt the FRSSE (effective April 2008).

The group may choose to continue to apply UK GAAP to the separate financial statements of the parent and of the subsidiaries, under FRS 102 with or without the reduced disclosure concessions. The separate financial statements of small subsidiaries may alternatively be prepared in accordance with the FRSSE (either the April 2008 version or the January 2015 version).

Example 34.3 – Options for a listed group which presents consolidated financial statements under IFRS but which uses UK GAAP for parent and subsidiaries

Group B is a fully listed group. The consolidated financial statements are prepared under EU-endorsed IFRS, but the separate financial statements of the parent company and subsidiaries are prepared in accordance with UK GAAP.

The group may choose to continue to apply UK GAAP to the separate financial statements of the parent and of the subsidiaries, under FRS 102 with or without the reduced disclosure concessions.

Alternatively, the group may decide in future to adopt the reduced disclosure framework in FRS 101 (see below).

Example 34.4 – Options for an *unlisted* group which presents consolidated financial statements under IFRS but which uses UK GAAP for parent and subsidiaries

Group D is a large privately owned group which, in 2005, decided to adopt full (EU-endorsed) IFRS on a voluntary basis. The group adopts UK GAAP for the individual accounts of the parent company and all of the subsidiaries.

What options are available to the group, parent company and subsidiaries on the basis of the accounting requirements of FRSs 100, 101 and FRS 102?

The group consolidated financial statements may continue to be prepared on the basis of EU-adopted IFRS. Alternatively, as EU-endorsed IFRS is not mandatory for this group, the September 2012 amendments to *CA 2006* will make it possible to change the group's reporting framework and prepare the consolidated financial statements on the basis of the current FRS 102.

Where the group takes advantage of the new *CA 2006* option to revert back to UK GAAP, the individual accounts of the parent company and subsidiaries may be prepared in accordance with FRS 102 taking account of disclosure concessions in Section 1 of FRS 102.

REDUCED DISCLOSURE FRAMEWORK UNDER FRS 101

Introduction and scope

34.11   FRS 101 is effectively a hybrid – full IFRS modified to comply with the requirements of the Regulations to CA 2006. Company law regards financial statements prepared in accordance with FRS 101 as an alternative form of UK GAAP. The legal status of FRS 101 is totally distinct from full, EU-endorsed IFRS.

Focus

EU-endorsed IFRS is authorised by the IAS Regulation and is outside the UK GAAP Regulations to CA 2006. Presentation and format requirements are covered by IAS 1 and not Schedule 1 to the Regulations.

By contrast although FRS 101 has been derived from EU-endorsed IFRS, it has been modified in FRS 101, Application Guidance to make it compatible with EU Accounting Directives and the Regulations to CA 2006. FRS 101 is part of the 'UK GAAP family' and consequently presentation and format rules in FRS 101 are contained in Schedule 1 to the Regulations and not IAS 1.

34.12 In summary, FRS 101 consists of:

- recognition and measurement principles derived from IFRS, but modified to ensure compatibility with the requirements of the Regulations to CA 2006 and the EU Fourth Directive (AG 1, various sub-paragraphs);

- presentation and format requirements in the Regulations to CA 2006 (FRS 101, AG 1 (g) (h)); and

- disclosure requirements of EU-endorsed IFRS as reduced by the concessions in FRS 101.

34.13 The disclosure concessions in paragraph 8 of FRS 101 are detailed and may be difficult to apply without familiarity with EU-endorsed IFRS.

To whom might FRS 101 apply?

34.14 The Summary to FRS 101, paragraph (viii), states: 'A qualifying entity may apply the reduced disclosure framework regardless of whether the financial reporting framework applied in the consolidated financial statements of the group are based on standards and interpretations issued (or adopted) by the International Accounting Standards Board.'

34.15 In practice, it seems more likely that FRS 101 will be adopted by members of groups who already present their accounts in accordance with full EU-endorsed IFRS. However, some of these may instead prefer to adopt FRS 102 with Section 1 concessions as referred to above.

34.16 As with FRS 102, concessions available under FRS 101 differ according to whether or not the qualifying entity is a financial institution.

What conditions have to be satisfied?

34.17   The qualifying conditions are identical to those referred to in **32.9** above.

Recognition and measurement principles under FRS 101

34.18   The amendments to the recognition and measurement rules in EU-endorsed IFRS are set out in the Application Guidance. These are detailed and extensive and include the following:

- first-time adoption issues in IFRS 1 (AG 1(a) and (b));

- amendments to business combination requirements in IFRS 3 dealing with negative goodwill and revisions arising from contingent purchase consideration (AG 1 (c)(d)(e)); and

- various other issues set out in the remainder of AG 1.

Presentation and format requirements under FRS 101

34.19   The amendments to the presentation and format rules in IAS 1 *Presentation of Financial Statements* and IFRS 5 *Non-current Assets Held for Sale and Discontinued Operations* in EU-endorsed IFRS are set out in the Application Guidance and include the following:

- information is to be presented in the statement of financial position/ balance sheet (AG 1 (h));

- information is to be presented in profit or loss (AG 1 (i)); and

- requirement to present discontinued operations in a columnar format (AG 1 (g)).

Disclosure concessions available

34.20   The list is potentially long and detailed. The following is not intended to be comprehensive, but aims to highlight some of the more important concessions:

- where equivalent disclosures are included in the consolidated financial statements of the group in which the entity is consolidated:

  ○ certain share-based payment disclosures;

  ○ certain business combination disclosures;

  ○ cash flows relating to discontinued operations; and

  ○ financial instruments disclosures.

- fair value disclosures;

- related party disclosure exemptions for transactions between members of a group where any subsidiary which is a party to the transaction is wholly owned;

- cash flow statements; and

- disclosure of total of remuneration of key management personnel.

Example 34.5 – IFRS currently used throughout the group

Group B is a fully listed group. The consolidated financial statements are prepared under EU-endorsed IFRS, as are the separate financial statements of the parent company and subsidiaries.

The group may choose to continue to apply EU-endorsed IFRS to the separate financial statements of the parent and of the subsidiaries.

Alternatively, the group may decide in future to adopt the reduced disclosure framework in FRS 101 and use recognition and measurement principles derived from IFRS, thus reducing a number of potential consolidation adjustments. A note of caution – the potential advantages of FRS 101, reduced disclosures plus broadly similar recognition and measurement policies, look tempting. However, FRS 101 is a fairly complex standard to read, and should therefore be used with great care and attention to detail.

Focus

Listed groups have a number of reporting options as regards individual financial statements of parents and subsidiaries:

- EU-endorsed IFRS without taking advantage of any concessions;

- the reduced disclosure framework of FRS 101; and

- the reduced disclosures under Section 1 of FRS 102.

REPORTING OPTIONS FOR UK SUBSIDIARIES OF OVERSEAS PARENT COMPANIES

34.21   A UK subsidiary which is a qualifying entity may prepare its financial statements under UK GAAP (with or without reduced disclosure concessions) or EU-endorsed IFRS or FRS 101. The theoretical choice available is subject to the requirements of the overseas parent.

34.22 *Reduced disclosures for subsidiaries and parent companies*

34.22   If either of the reduced disclosure requirement options is claimed, it is important to consider carefully the Application Guidance, the Interpretation of Equivalence (AG 1–10) in FRS 100 (see Focus Box, **34.8** above).

Example 34.6 – UK subsidiary with overseas parent company

Company E has an annual turnover of around £45m and is wholly owned by a listed US parent company. The company currently adopts UK GAAP.

The company has a 31 December year-end and does not intend to apply FRS 102 earlier than the mandatory date. The first set of FRS 102 financial statements will therefore be in respect of the year to 31 December 2015.

The choices referred to below are subject to any reporting requirements imposed by the US parent (provided these are consistent with the requirements of *CA 2006*):

- As the company currently adopts UK GAAP, the preferred option might be to adopt FRS 102 with Section 1 concessions on disclosure – possibly the preferred option.

- Adopt EU-endorsed (full) IFRS, with full disclosure requirements, with format rules set out in IAS 1.

- Adopt FRS 101 with recognition and measurement principles based on IFRS, but format rules compliant with the Regulations to CA 2006.

- Adopt FRS 102 without reduced disclosures.

SUMMARY – WHAT IS DIFFERENT FROM THE PREVIOUS UK GAAP?

Under the previous UK GAAP, opportunities for parents and subsidiaries included within a consolidation to reduce disclosures have been limited. One of the few examples is the exemptions in FRS 1 *Cash Flow Statements*.

Qualifying entities have a choice between taking the concessions in Section 1 of FRS 102, taking the concessions in FRS 101, or ignoring the concessions altogether.

The exemption in Section 1 of FRS 102 would allow qualifying parents and subsidiaries to reduce disclosures in the notes. The extent of the concessions would depend on whether or not the qualifying parent or subsidiary is a financial institution.

In practice, it is likely that qualifying entities who want to take advantage of the concessions will choose FRS 102 in preference to FRS 101 in view of the complexity of the latter. Entities that decided to opt for FRS 101 are more likely to belong to groups that prepare consolidated financial statements under full IFRS.

Chapter 35

Financial instruments – Introduction

SIGNPOSTS

- FRS 102 divides financial instruments into two broad categories:

  ○ Basic financial instruments, which are dealt with in Section 11, Basic Financial Instruments and defined in paragraph 11.5; and

  ○ Other, more complex, financial instruments, which are dealt with in Section 12, Other Financial Instruments.

- For many entities, financial instruments is likely to be a key area of change – whether or not the entity has previously adopted FRS 26 *Financial Instruments: Recognition and Measurement* (referred to in the remainder of this chapter simply as FRS 26).

- FRS 26 contains measurement rules for current and fixed asset investments, but the standard has been mandatory only for restricted categories of entities, for example individual accounts of listed parent companies, and has been optional for other entities who adopt the fair value rules in the Regulations to Companies Act 2006 (see **7.4**).

- For entities that have previously adopted FRS 26, the approach in Sections 11 and 12 of FRS 102 is significantly different (FRS 26 is based on the old version of IAS 39 *Financial Instruments: Recognition and Measurement* prior to amendment for IFRS 9 *Financial Instruments*).

- Apart from FRS 26, there is no equivalent recognition and measurement standard under previous UK GAAP, although SSAP 20 *Foreign Currency Translation* makes reference to forward foreign exchange contracts, and FRS 4 *Capital Instruments* deals with certain aspects such as the amortised cost method. The Regulations to CA 2006 (see **7.4**) deal with valuation rules affecting investments (Schedule 1, Part B deals with companies and groups other than those relating to banking and insurance).

INTRODUCTION

How FRS 102 deals with financial instruments

35.1   The following sections of FRS 102 deal in whole or in part with financial instruments:

- Section 11 – Basic Financial Instruments (commonly held assets and liabilities include trade debtors and creditors, cash at bank, bank loans and overdrafts, and investments).

- Section 12 – Other Financial Instruments Issues (basically those relating to more complex financial instruments, for example derivatives and hedge accounting).

- Entities who consider that they have only basic financial instruments do need to confirm that they are outside the scope of Section 12 before they assume that it does not apply to them.

- Section 22 – Liabilities and Equity, which deals with classification of financial instruments between debt and equity.

- Section 34 – Specialised Activities (disclosure requirements for financial institutions and retirement benefit plans).

How the chapters are divided up

35.2

- Financial instruments are dealt with in **Chapter 27** and in **Chapters 35 to 38**.

- **Chapter 27** deals with classification of shares and dividends.

- This chapter provides a basic introduction to what is a potentially complex area and does not refer to entities with complex financing arrangement and overseas transactions and operations. It attempts to avoid complex terminology and areas which most trading entities will not need to worry about.

- **Chapter 36** deals with accounting for basic financial instruments, financial assets as well as financial liabilities.

- **Chapters 37** and **38** deal with issues relating to more complex financial instruments.

Definition

35.3   A financial instrument is defined as a contract that gives rise to a financial asset of one entity and a financial liability or equity instrument of another entity.

Examples of basic financial instruments

35.4   Simple examples relating to most companies include:

- cash at bank on current or deposit account;

- trade debtors (receivables);

- trade creditors (payables);

- bank loans and overdrafts; and

- certain investments in shares.

Chapter 36 refers to these and others in detail.

35.5 Investments in shares which are regarded as basic financial instruments include:

- investments in ordinary shares carrying the usual rights and which do not impose any obligation on the entity to buy back the shares at a future date (referred to in Section 11 as 'non-puttable');

- investments in preference shares which do not carry conversion rights and which do not impose any obligation on the entity to buy back or redeem the shares at a future date (referred to in Section 11 as 'non-convertible').

Recognition and measurement under FRS 102 or IAS 39?

35.6 FRS 10, paragraph 11.2 gives entities an accounting policy choice between the following:

- the provisions of both Sections 11 and 12 of FRS 102; or

- the recognition and measurement provisions of IAS 39 *Financial Instruments: Recognition and Measurement* (as adopted for use in the European Union), together with the disclosure requirements of Sections 11 and 12 of FRS 102; or

- the recognition and measurement provisions of IFRS 9 *Financial Instruments* and/or IAS 39 (as amended following the publication of IFRS 9), together with the disclosure requirements of Sections 11 and 12 of FRS 102.

The choice between these two is an accounting policy choice which must be applied to *all* of the entity's financial instruments.

Focus

Sections 11 and 12 are the only sections of FRS 102 which make reference to International Financial Reporting Standards. This is a legacy from the text of the International Financial Reporting Standards for SMEs (IFRS for SMEs) from which FRS 102 has been derived (albeit with significant amendments).

IFRS 9 has not yet been endorsed for use within the EU and cannot presently be adopted by entities such as fully listed companies who present their financial statements in accordance with EU-endorsed IFRS.

For legal reasons, this restriction does not apply to entities who adopt UK GAAP in the form of FRS 102, hence the above references in FRS 102 to IFRS 9. The legal constraint on the use of IFRS 9 within this part of FRS 102 is that its requirements must not conflict with those in Schedule 1 of the Regulations to Companies Act 2006, in particular the fair value rules in paragraphs 36 to 41 of Schedule 1.

Several parts of Sections 11 and 12 are already in line with IFRS 9 (eg the treatment of accounting for investments). The Accounting Council's *Advice to the FRC*, paragraph 58 notes that the requirements for hedge accounting and impairment of financial assets in FRS 102 are based on the requirements of IAS 39. The Accounting Council will issue two exposure drafts on these issues proposing amendments to FRS 102 once the International Accounting Standards Board has updated IFRS 9 on these two issues.

The first of these, dealing with hedge accounting, is likely to be issued in the later part of 2013. (The International Accounting Standards Board published an amendment to IFRS 9 dealing with hedge accounting in November 2013.)

35.7   It is assumed in this chapter and in **Chapter 36** that the accounting policy choice is to apply FRS 102 for recognition and measurement of basic financial instruments (see **36.5**).

Disclosure requirements

35.8   Whichever of the above recognition and measurement options is selected, the applicable disclosure requirements for basic financial instruments are the same and are set out in Section 11.

35.9   Disclosure requirements are also contained in the Regulations to Companies Act 2006 (these are referred to in **Chapters 36, 37** and **38**).

SUMMARY – WHAT IS DIFFERENT FROM THE PREVIOUS UK GAAP?

- For some companies, this will be an important area of change according to whether or not under previous UK GAAP, they adopted FRS 26 (and related standards including FRS 23 *The Effects of Changes in Foreign Exchange Rates* and FRS 29 *Financial Instruments: Disclosures*).

- For previous FRS 26 adopters, the changes will be significant. Key areas of change are highlighted in **Chapters 36–38**.

- For companies who have not been required to, or who have chosen not to, adopt FRS 26, the changes will be less extensive. For some companies there will be little or no changes to the recognition and measurement requirements, but there will be new disclosures required by Section 11 (see **Chapter 36**).

- Other companies with investments in equity shares (see **Chapter 36**) or forward foreign currency contracts (see **Chapter 37**), will need to study the new requirements carefully, including the need to obtain fair value measurements.

Chapter 36

Accounting for basic financial instruments

SIGNPOSTS

Please refer also to SIGNPOSTS in Chapter 35

- **Chapter 35** gives examples of basic financial instruments, including cash, loans receivable and payable, trade debtors, trade creditors, and certain investments in shares.

- Basic financial instruments are generally dealt with on an historical cost basis, with limited exceptions such as certain investments in shares.

- Section 11 of FRS 102, Basic Financial Instruments uses technical terms including 'amortised cost' and 'effective interest' method (see **36.16** onwards) and it is important to become familiar with the jargon.

- Accounting requirements for the amortised cost method are illustrated in **Example 36.7** below.

- FRS 102 refers to impairment and loss events (see **36.22** onwards).

- Straightforward investments in equity shares are basic financial instruments. If the shares are either listed or unlisted but a reliable fair value measure can be obtained, the investments should be included in the balance sheet at fair value, and subsequent changes in fair value reported in profit or loss (see **36.29**).

- FRS 102 has specific derecognition rules – these are referred to and illustrated in **36.39** onwards below.

- Some of the disclosure requirements for basic financial instruments will be new or different – it is important to review these carefully (see **36.50** onwards).

INTRODUCTION

Definition of financial instrument

36.1   A financial instrument is defined as a contract that gives rise to a financial asset of one entity and a financial liability or equity instrument of another entity.

Scope of Section 11 – Basic financial instruments

36.2   Section 11 is a particularly difficult section to read, but essentially the following are examples of basic financial instruments which fall within its scope:

- cash;
- demand and fixed-term deposits when the entity is the depositor (eg bank accounts);
- commercial paper and commercial bills held;
- accounts receivable and payable (ie trade debtors and trade creditors);
- accounts payable in a foreign currency;
- loans from banks and other third parties;
- loans to subsidiaries, associates or joint ventures;
- bonds, and similar debt instruments;
- investments in non-convertible preference shares and non-puttable ordinary and preference shares (see **36.4** and **36.29** below); and
- commitments to receive a loan and commitments to make a loan to another entity that cannot be settled net in cash (see **36.42** below).

Debt instruments are only regarded as basic if they comply with the complex wording of paragraph 11.9 of FRS 102 (see **36.45** below). If they do not, they must be accounted for at fair value in accordance with Section 12.

Overview of requirements

36.3   All basic financial instruments, apart from certain investments, should be accounted for using the amortised cost model (see **36.16** below) – which, in most cases, will simply be the historical cost of the financial asset or financial liability.

36.4   The main exception to this rule is basic investments in shares where the shares are publicly traded or where the fair value of the shares can otherwise be measured reliably which should be stated in the balance sheet at fair value (see **36.8** and **36.29** below).

These are referred to in Section 11 as 'investments in non-convertible and non-puttable preference shares and non-puttable ordinary shares'.

Focus

Investments in the following are not classified as basic financial instruments and are thus outside the scope of Section 11:

- convertible preference shares (ie shares giving the holder a right at a future date to convert the preference shares into ordinary shares); and

- puttable shares which give the holder the right or option to require the company to buy back the shares.

Accounting policy choice

36.5 As indicated in **Chapter 35**, FRS 102, paragraph 11.2 (see **35.6** and **Focus box**) gives entities an accounting policy choice between the following:

- the provisions of both Sections 11 and 12 of FRS 102; or

- the recognition and measurement provisions of IAS 39 *Financial Instruments: Recognition and Measurement* (as adopted for use in the European Union), together with the disclosure requirements of Sections 11 and 12 of FRS 102; or

- the recognition and measurement provisions of IFRS 9 *Financial Instruments* and/or IAS 39 (as amended following the publication of IFRS 9), together with the disclosure requirements of Sections 11 and 12 of FRS 102.

The choice between these three is an accounting policy choice which must be applied to *all* of the entity's financial instruments.

36.6 In practice, entities dealing with basic financial instruments are likely to choose the first option, in view of the complexity of IAS 39/IFRS 9. This is the approach taken in this chapter. No further reference will be made to IAS 39/IFRS 9, although it will be referred to where relevant in **Chapters 37** and **38**.

INITIAL RECOGNITION OF FINANCIAL ASSETS AND LIABILITIES

36.7 Financial assets and financial liabilities should be recognised in the financial statements only when the entity becomes a party to the contractual provisions of the instrument.

INITIAL MEASUREMENT OF FINANCIAL ASSETS AND LIABILITIES

General requirements

36.8 Financial assets and liabilities should be measured initially at transaction price. Transaction price should include transaction costs, except for the initial measurement of financial assets and liabilities that are measured at fair value through profit or loss.

Example 36.1 – Listed and unlisted investments

A company has recently acquired investments in *the equity shares* of two companies.

The investment in A plc, a listed company, should be initially recorded at the cost of investment excluding transaction costs. Transaction costs should be charged immediately to profit or loss. The investment should subsequently be accounted for at fair value through profit or loss (see **36.29**).

The investment in B Limited is initially recorded at cost including transaction costs, as it is considered that it will not be possible to obtain a reliable fair value at subsequent balance sheet dates (see **36.29**).

36.9 An exception to the requirement in **36.8** above is where the arrangement constitutes, in effect, a financing transaction. If the arrangement constitutes a financing transaction, the entity shall measure the financial asset or financial liability at the present value of the future payments discounted at a market rate of interest for a similar debt instrument.

A financing transaction may take place in connection with the sale of goods or services, for example if payment is deferred beyond normal business terms or is financed at a rate of interest that is not a market rate.

Example 36.2 – Loan made to another entity

An entity makes a long-term loan to another entity. This is a financing transaction and should be recognised initially at the present value of cash receivable (including interest payments and repayment of principal) from that entity.

Example 36.3 – Sale of goods on short-term credit

An entity sells goods on normal business terms on short-term credit.

The receivable should be recognised at the undiscounted amount of cash receivable from that entity (normally the invoice price).

Example 36.4 – Sale of goods on interest-free credit terms

An entity sells goods to a customer on interest-free credit terms, offering two-year interest-free credit. If the current cash sales price is known, the receivable should be recognised at that amount. If the current cash sales price is not known, it may be estimated at the present value of the cash receivable discounted using the prevailing market rate of interest for a similar receivable.

Example 36.5 – Loan received from a bank

An entity receives a loan from a bank. A payable is initially recognised at the present value of cash payable to the bank (including interest and repayment of principal).

Example 36.6 – Purchase of goods on short-term credit

An entity purchases goods from a supplier on normal business terms with short-term credit.

A payable is recognised at the undiscounted amount owing to the supplier (normally the invoice price).

SUBSEQUENT MEASUREMENT – DEBT INSTRUMENTS

36.10 Debt instruments that meet the conditions set out in paragraph 11.9 (see **36.45**) shall be measured at the end of each reporting period at amortised cost using the effective interest method (see **36.18–36.20** below).

36.11 These debt instruments will include, for example, trade debtors, trade creditors, loans and deposits.

36.12 Those debt instruments that are classified as current assets or current liabilities shall be measured at the undiscounted amount of the cash or other consideration expected to be paid or received (net of impairment – see **36.17** and **36.22** below).

36.13   If the arrangement constitutes a financing transaction, the debt instrument shall be measured at the present value of the future payments discounted at a market rate of interest for a similar debt instrument.

36.14   Commitments to receive a loan and to make a loan to another entity which meet specified conditions are referred to in **36.42**.

36.15   The fair value option for certain debt instruments is referred to below in **36.46**. This is likely to be relevant only for financial institutions and certain specialised entities.

DEBT INSTRUMENTS: AMORTISED COST AND THE EFFECTIVE INTEREST METHOD

Definition of amortised cost

36.16   The amortised cost of a financial asset or financial liability at each reporting date is defined as the net of the following four amounts:

- the amount at which the financial asset or financial liability is measured at initial recognition;

- *minus* any repayments of principal;

- *plus* or *minus* the cumulative amortisation using the effective interest rate method (see below) of any difference between the amount at initial recognition and the maturity amount; or

- *minus* – in the case of a financial asset – any reduction for impairment or uncollectibility.

36.17   Note that financial assets and liabilities that have no stated interest rate and which are classified as current assets or current liabilities are initially measured at an *undiscounted* amount. These will include trade debtors and trade creditors.

The effective interest method

36.18   This is a method of:

- calculating the *amortised cost* of a financial asset or a financial liability (the carrying amount in the statement of financial position/balance sheet); and

- allocating the interest income or interest expense over the relevant period on an actuarial basis using the *effective interest rate*.

36.19 *The amortised cost* of a financial asset (liability) is the present value of future cash receipts (payments) discounted at the effective interest rate (FRS 102, paragraph 11.16).

*The effective interest rat*e is the rate that exactly discounts estimated future cash payments or receipts through the expected life of the financial instrument (or, where appropriate, a shorter period), to the carrying amount of the asset or liability (FRS 102, paragraph 11.16).

36.20 The interest income or expense in a period equals the carrying amount of the financial asset or liability at the beginning of a period multiplied by the effective interest rate for the period.

Example 36.7 – Application of the effective interest method

A company borrows £110,000 and incurs issue costs of £10,000 giving net proceeds of £100,000.

The loan incurs a fixed interest coupon of £5,900 per annum. The loan is to be repaid at the end of five years at a premium of £15,000 (ie total to be repaid is £125,000).

Total finance costs are: £29,500 (interest) + £15,000 (debt premium) + £10,000 (transaction costs) = £54,500.

* The effective interest rate which discounts the above payments to the initial loan proceeds of £100,000 is approximately 10%. In practice, it would be calculated precisely using a computer program. For the purposes of the illustration, 10% has been used and, because this is not the precise number, the finance cost in 2015 of £11,872 (see table below) is effectively a balancing figure. The relevant balance sheet and profit and loss account entries are as follows.

Year	Amortised cost at start of year £	Finance costs £	Cash flow £	Amortised cost at end of year £
2012	100,000	10,000	5,900	104,100
2013	104,100	10,410	5,900	108,610
2014	108,610	10,861	5,900	113,571
2015	113,571	11,357	5,900	119,028
2016	119,028	*11,872	5,900	125,000
		54,500	29,500	

> *Accounting policy extract – Debt instruments (part of note)*
>
> Debt instruments are initially reported at cost, which is the proceeds received, net of transaction costs. Subsequently they are reported at amortised cost using the effective interest rate method. Any premium on redemption is amortised over the duration of the debt instrument, and is recognised as part of interest expense in the income statement.

36.21   FRS 102 gives detailed guidance which may be relevant in more complex cases (paras 11.17 to 11.20) including:

- the contractual terms of the arrangement (including options) and known credit losses that have been incurred;

- the amortisation period where there are complex arrangements regarding related fees, finance charges, premiums and discounts;

- the impact of changes in interest rates on variable rate financial assets and liabilities; and

- revisions to estimates of payments or receipts.

IMPAIRMENT

General requirements

36.22   An entity shall assess at the end of each reporting period whether there is any objective evidence that a financial asset measured at cost or amortised cost is impaired.

If there is objective evidence of impairment, an impairment loss should be recognised in profit or loss immediately.

Examples of loss events

36.23   Objective evidence that a financial asset or group of assets is impaired includes observable data regarding the following loss events that comes to the attention of the entity holding the asset:

- significant financial difficulty of the issuer or obligor;

- a breach of contract such as a default or delinquency in interest or principal payments;

- the creditor, for economic or legal reasons relating to the debtor's financial difficulty, granting to the debtor a concession that the creditor would not otherwise consider;

- it has become *probable* that the debtor will enter bankruptcy or other financial reorganisation;

- observable data indicating that there has been a measurable decrease in the estimated future cash flows from a group of financial assets since the initial recognition of those assets, even though the decrease cannot yet be identified with the individual financial assets in the group, such as adverse national or local economic conditions or adverse changes in industry conditions; and

- significant changes with an adverse effect that have taken place in the following environments in which the issuer of the financial instrument operates:

  ○ technological environment;

  ○ market environment;

  ○ economic environment; and

  ○ legal environment.

Individual assessment or on a group basis?

36.24 FRS 102 requires the following financial assets to be assessed for impairment on an individual basis:

- all equity instruments regardless of significance; and

- other financial assets that are individually significant.

Measurement – financial instruments measured at amortised cost

36.25 The impairment loss is the difference between the asset's carrying amount and the present value of estimated cash flows discounted at the asset's *original* effective interest rate. If the financial asset has a variable interest rate, the discount rate for measuring any impairment loss is the current-effect interest rate determined under the contract.

Example 36.8 – Calculation of impairment loss

B Limited purchased a debt instrument for £10k (cost is inclusive of transaction costs). The instrument has a principal amount of £12.5k and has five years remaining to maturity. The interest coupon rate is 4.7% per annum – interest of £590 is payable at the end of each year.

The debt instrument schedule is as follows:

	Amortised cost at start of year	Interest income at 10.0%	Cash flows	Amortised cost at end of year
	£	£	£	£
2010	10,000	1,000	590	10,410
2011	10,410	1,040	590	10,860
2012	10,860	1,090	590	11,360
2013	11,360	1,130	590	11,900
2014	11,900	1,190	13,090*	–

*£12,500 + £590

The effective interest rate is calculated as 10% per annum.

At the end of 2010, the amortised cost of the debt instrument is £10,410 (see above). At this point, B Limited assesses that the debt instrument has become impaired and expects that no further interest payments will be paid on the debt, but that the instalments of capital will still be paid.

B Limited recalculates the present value of the principal repayment in four years time as £8,538 (£12,500/1.14).

B Limited recognises an impairment loss of £1,872 (£10,410 – £8,538).

Measurement – Financial instruments measured at cost

36.26   Financial instruments measured at cost as opposed to amortised cost include unlisted investments whose fair value cannot be measured reliably.

36.27   The impairment loss is the difference between the asset's carrying amount and the best estimate that the entity would receive for the asset if it were to be sold at the reporting date.

Paragraph 11.25(b) comments that this amount might be zero.

Reversal of impairment losses

36.28   In some situations, the amount of an impairment loss might decrease in a subsequent period.

If the decrease can be related objectively to an event occurring after the impairment was recognised (eg an improvement in the debtor's credit rating), the entity shall reverse the previously recognised impairment loss and recognise this immediately in profit or loss.

The reversal shall not result in a carrying amount of the financial asset that exceeds what the carrying amount would have been had the impairment not previously been recognised.

SUBSEQUENT MEASUREMENT – INVESTMENTS IN SHARES

General requirements

36.29   Investments that meet the basic financial instruments criteria (investments in non-convertible preference shares and non-puttable ordinary or preference shares) should be accounted for as follows:

- if the shares are publicly traded *or* their fair value can otherwise be measured reliably, the investment should be measured at fair value with changes in fair value recognised through profit or loss; and

- all other such investments should be measured at cost less impairment (see below).

(See **36.8** regarding treatment of transaction costs.)

Investments whose fair value can be measured reliably

36.30   Section 11 contains detailed requirements and guidance regarding the determination of fair value. For non-financial entities, this part of Section 11 will be relevant for entities with investments in shares.

Otherwise, this part will be of far greater importance for entities with more complex financial instruments that fall within the scope of Section 12 (see **Chapters 37** and **38**).

Fair value hierarchy

36.31   An entity is required to use the following hierarchy in order to estimate the fair value of the shares:

- the best evidence of fair value is a quoted price for identical assets in an active market – the quoted price is usually the bid price;

- when quoted prices are not available, the price of a recent transaction for an identical asset provides evidence of fair value as long as there has not been a significant change in economic circumstances or a significant lapse of time since the transaction took place – in certain cases, that price may need to be adjusted; and

- if the market for the asset is not active and recent transactions of an identical asset on their own are not a good estimate of fair value, an entity estimates the fair value using an estimation technique which seeks to estimate what the transaction price would have been on the measurement date in an arm's-length exchange motivated by normal business considerations.

Valuation techniques

36.32   Valuation techniques include the following:

- recent arm's-length market transactions for an identical asset between knowledgeable, willing parties;

- reference to the current value of another asset that is substantially the same as the asset being measured;

- discounted cash flow analysis; or

- option pricing models.

Focus

Detailed guidance on determining fair values, including the hierarchy for estimating fair value and valuation techniques, is set out in FRS 102, paragraphs 11.27 to 11.32.

Where there is no active market

36.33   Paragraph 11.30 sets out the circumstances in which the fair value of unquoted ordinary or preference shares is regarded as reliably measurable:

- the variability in the range of reasonable fair value estimates is not significant for that asset; or

- the probabilities of the various estimates within the range can be reasonably assessed and used in estimating fair value.

36.34 Where a fair value that was previously reliably measurable is no longer available, the last carrying amount becomes the new cost. The asset will then be measured at cost less impairment until a reliable measure of fair value becomes available.

Investments whose fair value cannot be measured reliably

36.35 These investments should be measured at cost less impairment. The requirements for impairment are set out in **36.22** above.

DERECOGNITION OF FINANCIAL ASSETS AND FINANCIAL LIABILITIES

Derecognition of financial assets

36.36 A financial asset should be derecognised (ie removed from the balance sheet) only if one of the following applies:

(a) the contractual rights to the cash flows from the financial assets expire or are settled (eg, a receipt of cash in settlement of the amount owing on a trade debtor); or

(b) the entity transfers to another party substantially all the risks and rewards of ownership of the financial asset (see **Example 36.9** below); or

(c) the entity has retained some significant risks and rewards of ownership, but has transferred control of the asset to another party who:

- has the practical ability to sell the asset in its entirety to another third party; and

- is able to exercise that ability unilaterally, and without needing to impose additional restrictions on the transfer.

In such cases, the entity should:

- derecognise the asset; and

- recognise separately any rights and obligations retained or created in the transfer.

36.37 In situation (c) above, the carrying amount of the transferred asset should be allocated between the rights or obligations retained, and those transferred, on the basis of their relative fair values at the transfer date. Newly created rights and obligations should be measured at their fair values at that date.

Any difference between:

- consideration received; and

● amounts recognised and derecognised in accordance with (c) above should be recognised in profit or loss in the period of the transfer.

36.38 The following is an example of the entity transferring to another party 'substantially all the risks and rewards of ownership of the financial asset'.

> **Example 36.9 – Sale of trade debtors which transfers risks and rewards of ownership**
>
> An entity sells a group of its trade debtors to a bank at less than their face amount. The entity collects payment from the debtor and is required to remit to the bank on a prompt basis all monies collected. The bank pays a market fee for the collection/statement service. The entity has no obligation to the bank for slow payment or non-payment by debtors.
>
> The entity has transferred to the bank 'substantially all the risks and rewards of ownership of the financial asset' and therefore removes the trade debtors from its balance sheet, and shows no liability to the bank in respect of the amounts received from the bank relating to proceeds received on the initial sale of the debtors. (There is a liability to the bank in respect of cash collected from debtors but not yet paid over.)
>
> The entity will recognise a loss in its profit and loss account/income statement, in respect of the differences between the carrying amount of the debtors at the time of sale and the proceeds received from the bank.

36.39 Where an entity has retained significant risks and rewards of ownership of a transferred asset, the transfer does not result in derecognition and the entity should continue to recognise the transferred asset in its entirety, and should recognise a financial liability for the consideration received.

The asset and the liability should not be offset, and the entity should recognise any income on the transferred asset and any expense incurred on the transferred liability.

> **Example 36.10 – Sale of trade debtors which does *not* transfer risks and rewards of ownership**
>
> An entity sells a group of its trade debtors to a bank at less than their face amount. The entity collects payment from the debtor and is required to remit to the bank on a prompt basis all monies collected. The bank pays a market fee for the collection/statement service. The entity has agreed to buy back from the bank any receivables for which the debtor is in arrears as to principal or interest for more than 120 days.

The entity has retained the significant risk of slow payment or non-payment. Therefore the entity does not treat the debtors as sold to the bank, and does not derecognise them from the balance sheet.

The entity treats the proceeds from the bank as a loan, secured by the trade debtors.

Derecognition of financial liabilities

36.40   An entity shall derecognise a financial liability (or part of it) only when it is extinguished. This will be when the obligation specified in the contract is discharged, cancelled or expires.

36.41   Any difference between the carrying amount of the liability and the consideration paid, including any non-cash assets transferred or liabilities assumed, will be recognised in profit or loss.

BASIC FINANCIAL INSTRUMENTS – FURTHER CONSIDERATIONS

Loan commitments

36.42   This is another part of Section 11 which is difficult to read. FRS 102, paragraph 11.5(g) gives as an example of a basic financial instrument 'commitments to receive a loan and commitments to make a loan to another entity that meet the conditions of paragraph 11.8(c)'.

36.43   FRS 102, paragraph 11.8(c) refers to commitments to receive or make a loan to another entity that cannot be settled net in cash, and when the commitment is executed, are expected to meet the conditions in FRS 102, paragraph 11.9 (see **36.45** below).

Example 36.11 – Loan commitment

An entity intends to acquire a new factory and enters into a commitment with a bank to take out a loan in six months' time. Under the terms of the loan agreement, the entity is committed to receiving the loan in 18 equal consecutively monthly instalments.

Under the agreement, the entity is contractually bound to repay the loan five years after the final instalment has been received from the bank. Interest

---

is payable monthly. The loan commitment meets the conditions in **36.45** below.

The loan commitment cannot be settled net (ie the entity is committed to receiving the loan receipts, pay the interest monthly and repay the amount borrowed on the due date).

The loan commitment is a basic financial instrument and should be accounted for in accordance with Section 11 (see below).

36.44   FRS 102, paragraph 11.14(c) requires commitments to receive a loan and commitments to make a loan to another entity to be measured at cost less impairment. The paragraph comments that cost is sometimes nil.

Debt instruments

36.45   FRS 102, paragraph 11.9 is supposed to relate to basic financial instruments, but is far from straightforward.

Fortunately, it will only be necessary to refer to this paragraph in detail in more complex situations. The paragraph says that a debt instrument which satisfies all the following four conditions should be accounted for as a basic financial instrument.

The four conditions in summary are:

Condition 1 – Returns to the holder

Returns to the holder must be:

- a fixed amount, *or*

- a fixed rate of return over the life of the instrument, *or*

- a variable return that, throughout the life of the instrument, is equal to a single referenced quoted or observable interest rate, *or*

- some combination of such fixed and variable rates, provided that both the fixed and variable rates are positive.

Condition 2 – Absence of potentially detrimental contractual provisions

There must be no contractual provision that could result in the holder losing the principal amount or any interest attributable to the current period or a prior period.

Debt that is subordinated to other debt instruments would not be caught by this provision (ie it would be treated as a debt instrument).

Condition 3 – Contractual provisions beneficial to the lender

Any contractual provisions that permit the issuer (the borrower) to prepay a debt instrument or permit the holder (the lender) to put it back to the issuer before maturity must not be contingent on future events, other than to protect the holder or issuer from changes in taxation/law or downgrade in credit or control of the issuer.

There must be no conditional returns or repayment provisions except for the variable rate return described in condition 1 and the prepayments provision described in condition 3.

Focus

In most cases involving non-financial entities, identifying whether debt instruments are 'basic' will not be too difficult, and it will not be necessary to refer to paragraph 11.9 above in detail.

The fair value option for certain debt instruments

36.46 This complicated option derived from detailed requirements in IAS 39 is available to debt instruments that meet the conditions in **36.45** above.

36.47 Note that this option enables an entity, should it so choose, to designate a debt instrument as at fair value through profit or loss, subject to satisfying certain criteria, based on the concept that this treatment would result in more relevant information being provided, because either:

- it eliminates or significantly reduces a measurement or recognition inconsistency (sometimes referred to as an accounting mismatch) that would otherwise arise from measuring assets or debt instruments or recognising the gains and losses on them on different bases; or

- a group of debt instruments or financial assets and debt instruments is managed and its performance is evaluated on a fair value basis in accordance with a documented risk management or investment strategy.

36.48 This is a specialist area likely to be of relevance only to financial institutions, and further reference is outside the scope of this text. Readers requiring further information on this area are recommended to refer to a specialist text on financial instruments.

The relevant disclosures required by paragraph 11.48A of Section 11 are not referred to in the disclosure requirements below, but are covered in **Chapters 37** and **38**.

PRESENTATION – OFFSET OF FINANCIAL ASSETS AND FINANCIAL LIABILITIES

36.49   A financial asset and a financial liability shall be offset and the net amount presented in the balance sheet only when the entity:

- currently has a legally enforceable right to set off the recognised amounts; and

- intends either to settle on a net basis, or to realise the asset and settle the liability simultaneously.

DISCLOSURE REQUIREMENTS FOR BASIC FINANCIAL INSTRUMENTS

Disclosure requirements – Basic financial instruments

36.50   The disclosure requirements below are set out in paragraphs 11.39 to 11.48 of FRS 102.

Please note that any disclosure requirements in Section 11 relating to complex financial instruments and complex situations are not referred to below.

In particular, any disclosure relating to financial liabilities measured at fair value through profit or loss are not included as these are considered to relate to situations involving complex financial instruments, and are not relevant to non-financial assets in sectors such as manufacturing, trading and services.

Note that disclosures relating to share capital are set out in paragraph 4.12 of FRS 102.

Accounting policies

36.51   Disclose the measurement basis (bases) used for financial instruments and the other accounting policies used for financial instruments that are relevant to an understanding of the financial statements.

Example 36.12 – Accounting policy extract

Financial instruments

Financial assets and financial liabilities are recognised on the balance sheet when the company becomes party to the contractual provisions of the financial instrument.

Trade debtors and trade creditors are initially measured at fair value. Subsequent to initial valuation, they are carried at amortised cost using the effective interest method, less any impairment losses.

Interest-bearing borrowings are recognised initially at fair value less directly attributable transaction costs. Subsequent to initial recognition, interest-bearing borrowings are stated at amortised cost with any difference between cost and redemption value being recognised in the profit and loss account using the effective interest.

Investments in equity shares which are publicly traded or where the fair value of the shares can otherwise be measured reliably are initially measured at fair value. Transaction costs are charged to profit or loss. The investments are subsequently remeasured in the balance sheet at fair value with changes in fair value are recognised through profit or loss.

Investments in equity shares which are not publicly traded and where the fair value of the shares cannot be measured reliably are initially measured at cost, including transaction costs. The investment is not remeasured except where impairment has been identified.

Accounting policy examples for derivatives and hedge accounting are included in **Chapters 37** and **38**.

Categories of financial assets and financial liabilities

36.52 The carrying amounts for each of the following categories should be disclosed, either in the statement of financial position/balance sheet or in the notes:

- financial assets measured at fair value through profit or loss (this would apply to quoted investments or to unlisted investments whose fair value can be measured reliably);

- financial assets that are debt instruments measured at amortised cost;

- financial assets that are equity instruments measured at cost less impairment (eg unlisted investments whose fair value cannot be measured reliably);

- financial liabilities that are measured at amortised cost; and

- loan commitments measured at cost less impairment.

Disclosure of information that enables users to evaluate the significance of financial instruments for the entity's financial position and performance

36.53 Examples would be information regarding long-term debt (eg interest rate, maturity, repayment schedule and any restrictions imposes on the entity, or disclosure of loan commitments (see **36.42** above) outstanding at the balance sheet date).

Financial assets measured at fair value

36.54 The notes to the financial statements should disclose the basis for determining fair value (eg quoted market price in an active market or a valuation technique).

When a valuation technique is used, the entity should disclose the assumptions applied in determining fair value.

36.55 Note the disclosure requirements in the Regulations to CA 2006, Schedule 1 Part D paragraphs 55–57.

Those relating to more complex financial instruments are referred to in **Chapter 37**. Those relevant to basic financial instruments such as investments in equity shares include:

- the significant assumptions underlying the valuation models and techniques used;

- the fair value of financial instruments by category; and

- the changes in value included in the profit and loss account by category.

Transfers of financial assets that do not qualify for derecognition

36.56 The following disclosures apply where an entity has transferred financial assets to another party in a transaction that does not qualify for derecognition (see **36.39** above). Disclosures should be given for each class of financial assets (eg trade debtors):

- the nature of the assets;

- the nature of the risks and rewards of ownership to which the entity remains exposed; and

- the carrying amounts of the assets and any associated liabilities that the entity continues to recognise.

Collateral

36.57   This applies where an entity has pledged financial assets as collateral for liabilities or contingent liabilities. Disclosure is required of:

- the carrying amounts of the financial assets pledged as collateral; and

- the terms and conditions relating to its pledge.

These might be relevant in the cases of invoice discounting or debt factoring where loans received are secured by way of charge on trade debtors (see **Example 36.10** above).

Defaults and breaches on loans payable

36.58   Disclosure is required in respect of loans payable recognised at the reporting date for which there is a breach of terms or default of principal, interest, sinking fund or redemption terms *that has not been remedied by the reporting date.*

36.59   The disclosures required are:

- details of that breach or default;

- the carrying amount of the related loans payable at the reporting date; and

- whether the breach or default was remedied, or the terms of the loans payable were renegotiated, before the financial statements were authorised for issue.

Income, expenses, gains and losses

36.60   Disclosure is required of income, expense, gains or losses (including changes in fair value) recognised on the following:

- financial assets measured at fair value through profit or loss;

- financial liabilities measured at fair value through profit or loss;

- financial assets measured at amortised cost; and

- financial liabilities measured at amortised cost.

Total interest income and total interest expense

36.61   This disclosure applies to financial assets or financial liabilities that are *not* measured at fair value through profit or loss.

36.62 Disclosure is required of total interest income and total interest expense (calculated using the effective interest method).

Impairment losses

36.63 Disclosure is required of the amount of any impairment loss for each class of financial asset.

SUMMARY – WHAT IS DIFFERENT FROM THE PREVIOUS UK GAAP?

- Most unlisted companies are not required to and do not choose to adopt FRS 26 *Financial Instruments: Recognition and Measurement* (FRS 26). For these entities, the main recognition and measurement changes for basic financial instruments relate to investments in equity shares (see **36.29**).

- There is no current standard dealing with investments, but the Regulations to CA 2006 (see **7.4**) contain historical cost rules, alternative accounting rules, and fair value rules.

- Under the alternative accounting rules, changes in the market value of investments were dealt with under previous UK GAAP in the Statement of total recognised gains and losses required by FRS 3 *Reporting Financial Performance*.

- Under Section 11, investments in equity shares which are either listed or unlisted where a reliable fair value can be obtained, should be included in the statement of financial position/balance sheet at fair value, with changes in fair value dealt with through profit or loss – this could lead to greater volatility in reported profit/loss from year to year.

- Section 11 contains specific requirements relating to impairment (see **36.22** onwards) but there was no equivalent under previous UK GAAP.

- The disclosure requirements in Section 11 are more extensive than those in Schedule 1 of the Regulations to CA 2006 (which continues to be applicable alongside the FRS 102 regime).

- Qualifying entities which are not financial institutions are entitled to disclosure exemptions relating to financial instruments (see **32.60**).

- For entities who have previously adopted FRS 26, all of the above are relevant, but additional issues are referred to in **Chapters 37** and **38**.

Chapter 37

More complex financial instruments

SIGNPOSTS

- This chapter deals mainly with the requirements of Section 12, Other Financial Instruments Issues (apart from the rules on hedge accounting which are dealt with in **Chapter 38**), with particular reference to their application to entities other than *financial institutions* (see definition in **40.10**).

- FRS 102 allows an accounting policy choice between:

  ○　the provisions of both Sections 11, Basic Financial Instruments and 12 of FRS 102; or

  ○　the recognition and measurement provisions of IAS 39 *Financial Instruments: Recognition and Measurement* (as adopted for use in the European Union), together with the disclosure requirements of Sections 11 and 12 of FRS 102; or

  ○　the recognition and measurement provisions of IFRS 9 *Financial Instruments* and/or IAS 39 *Financial Instruments: Recognition and Measurement* (as amended following the publication of IFRS 9 *Financial Instruments*), together with the disclosure requirements of Sections 11 and 12 of FRS 102.

  (See Focus box below **35.6**.)

- Whichever is chosen must be applied consistently to all classes of financial instruments, whether basic or more complex.

- Disclosure requirements for more complex financial institutions are located in Sections 11 and 12 of FRS 102, as well as in the Regulations to CA 2006.

- Reduced disclosure requirements for qualifying entities which are not financial institutions are referred to in **32.7**.

INTRODUCTION

A health warning!

37.1　　Section 12 contains only just over six pages but, like Section 11, it is a difficult section to read – it covers complex topics, and in many places lacks explanation and detail. It needs to be read in conjunction with the relevant parts of Section 11 (see **Chapter 36**) and also the relevant parts of the Regulations to CA 2006 (see **7.4**).

37.2 In broad terms, complex financial instruments may be grouped into two main categories:

- those that may be encountered by larger companies and groups in business sectors such as manufacturing trading and services, particularly those with extensive overseas transactions and operations; and

- those mainly likely to be encountered within financial sectors such as banking, investment entities and insurance. These specialist areas are also dealt with in Section 34, Specialised Activities (see **Chapter 40**) and the Regulations to CA 2006 (Schs 2 and 3).

This and the following chapter are primarily concerned with the application to the first category above. For some entities with non-basic financial instruments, FRS 102 will represent a significant step change.

Detailed issues specific to financial institutions are outside the scope of this text.

Accounting policy choice

37.3 As indicated in the two previous chapters, entities have an accounting policy choice for basic financial instruments. In principle this choice applies to all financial instruments which fall within the scope of either Section 11 or Section 12.

As a reminder, an entity must choose between the following:

- the provisions of both Sections 11 and 12 of FRS 102; or

- the recognition and measurement provisions of IAS 39 *Financial Instruments: Recognition and Measurement* (as adopted for use in the European Union), together with the disclosure requirements of Sections 11 and 12 of FRS 102; or

- the recognition and measurement provisions of IFRS 9 *Financial Instruments* and/or IAS 39 (as amended following the publication of IFRS 9), together with the disclosure requirements of Sections 11 and 12 of FRS 102.

The above choice between these two is an accounting policy choice which must be applied to *all* of the entity's financial instruments.

37.4 What is important is that if an entity makes the IAS 39 choice, it must be applied to all financial instruments, whether basic or complex. Again, repeating the point made earlier, IAS 39 is extremely complex (leaving aside the eventual transition to IFRS 9), and entities contemplating this option are advised to undertake a thorough and comprehensive review before committing to an accounting policy choice to adopt the requirements of IAS 39.

Example 37.1 – Investments in equity shares

Consider a simple example which illustrates the potential impact of adopting IAS 39. Suppose, for whatever reason, an entity with complex financial instruments decides to choose the IAS 39 option.

This choice impacts not only on the entity's complex financial instruments, but also on accounting for the entity's basic financial instruments.

Suppose the entity has some fixed asset equity investments which are publicly traded or where the fair value can otherwise be measured reliably. If the entity chooses the FRS 102, Sections 11 and 12 option for recognition and measurement, the investment will be measured at fair value with changes in fair value taken through profit or loss (see **36.29**).

Under the IAS 39 option, the investment will be classified as 'available for sale' with changes in fair value recognised in other comprehensive income.

37.5 Where relevant, brief reference to IAS 39 will be made in this chapter and in **Chapter 38**, but readers wishing to explore IAS 39 (and its eventual successor IFRS 9) in detail, are advised to refer to a specialist text on the subject.

Scope of Section 12

37.6 What falls within the scope of Section 12 is defined in terms of which financial instruments are *excluded from its scope*. There are two categories of exclusions:

- those financial instruments which are deemed 'basic' and which therefore fall within the scope of Section 11 (see **Chapter 36**); and

- those financial instruments which are dealt with in other sections – as listed immediately below.

37.7 Section 12 applies to all financial instruments *except for the following*:

- all financial instruments covered by Section 11;

- investments in subsidiaries, associates and joint ventures (see **Chapter 29**);

- employers' rights and obligations under employee benefit plans;

- insurance contracts;

- financial instruments that meet the definition of an entity's own equity;

- leases;

- contracts for contingent consideration in a business combination, from the acquirer's perspective;

- any forward contract between an acquirer and a selling shareholder to buy or sell an acquiree that will result in a business combination at a future acquisition date;

- financial instruments, contracts and obligations to which Section 26, Share-based Payments, applies (with certain exceptions);

- reimbursement assets accounted for in accordance with Section 21, Provisions and Contingencies; and

- financial guarantee contracts (Section 21, Provisions and Contingencies).

37.8   Generally, contracts to buy or sell a non-financial asset such as a commodity or inventory or property, plant and equipment, are outside the scope of Section 12, because they are not financial instruments. However, paragraphs 12.4 and 12.5 do make certain exceptions.

EXAMPLES OF FINANCIAL INSTRUMENTS WHICH ARE NOT BASIC

Those which might relate to entities in manufacturing, trading and services

37.9   The following are examples of complex financial instruments which are outside the scope of Section 11 but within the scope of Section 12.

Section 11, paragraphs 11.6 and 11.11 list a number of examples, including:

- options, rights, warrants, futures contracts, forward contracts and interest rate swaps that can be settled in cash or by exchanging another financial instrument;

- financial instruments that qualify and are designated as hedging instruments in accordance with the requirements in Section 12 (see **Chapter 38**);

- commitments to make a loan to another entity and commitments to receive a loan if the commitment can be settled net in cash;

- investments in another entity's equity instruments other than non-convertible preference shares and non-puttable ordinary and preference shares (see **36.4**);

- an interest rate swap that returns a cash flow that is positive or negative;

- a forward commitment to purchase a commodity or financial instrument that is capable of being cash-settled and that, on settlement, could have positive or negative cash flows;

- options and forward contracts; and

- investments in convertible debt (the return to the holder can vary with the price of the issuer's equity shares rather than just with market interest rates).

Those which might relate to entities in financial sectors

37.10   Section 11.6(a) refers to 'asset-backed securities' such as collateralised mortgage obligations, repurchase agreements and securitised packages of receivables. These financial instruments are not referred to further in this text in view of their specialised nature and application.

37.11   Note that financial institutions (as defined in the Glossary to FRS 102) are also subject to the disclosure requirements of Section 34, paragraphs 34.19 to 34.33 (briefly referred to in **40.12** and Schs 2 and 3 of the Regulations to CA 2006).

37.12   Section 11, paragraph 11.14(b) refers to the fair value option for debt instruments (see **36.46** to **36.47**) together with related disclosure requirements in paragraph 11.48A.

INITIAL RECOGNITION

37.13   An entity shall recognise a financial asset or financial liability only when the entity becomes a party to the contractual provisions of the instrument. On initial recognition, a financial instrument is measured at its fair value (this will usually be the transaction price).

37.14   Transaction price will usually be inclusive of transaction costs except for financial assets and liabilities measured at fair value through profit or loss where the transaction price should be excluded from initial measurement and should be charged as an expense to profit or loss.

37.15   Where payment for an asset is deferred beyond normal business terms or is being financed at a rate that is not a market rate, the financial asset should be measured initially at the present value of the future payments discounted using a market rate applicable for a similar debt instrument.

SUBSEQUENT MEASUREMENT

Basic requirements

37.16   At the end of each reporting period, all financial instruments falling within the scope of Section 12 shall be measured at fair value, with changes recognised in profit or loss.

Exceptions

37.17   These are two exceptions to this rule:

- equity instruments that are not publicly traded and whose fair value cannot otherwise be measured reliably. These should be measured at cost less impairment; and

- hedging instruments (eg forward foreign currency contracts and interest rate swaps) which are in a designated hedging relationship, where hedge accounting is adopted (see **Chapter 38**).

Reliable fair value measurement no longer available

37.18   This applies to equity instruments which are usually measured at fair value through profit or loss, but for which a reliable fair value is no longer available.

37.19   In such cases, the fair value at the last date for which a reliable fair value was obtained is now treated as the 'cost' of the financial instrument. The financial instrument will subsequently be measured at this 'cost' figure less any impairment, until such time as the entity can obtain a reliable fair value.

DETERMINING FAIR VALUE

Basic requirements

37.20 Fair value measurements should be determined by applying the guidance in Section 12. This guidance is referred to below, including guidance from Section 11 repeated here for convenience in view of its particular importance and its relevance to this section.

37.21 Transaction costs should not be included in the fair value of a financial instrument which will subsequently be measured at fair value through profit or loss.

37.22 The fair value of a financial liability that is due on demand is not less than the amount payable on demand, discounted from the first date that the amount could be required to be paid.

Analogy to other sections of FRS 102

37.23 Fair value in other sections of FRS 102 include:

- paragraphs 11.27 to 11.32 of Section 11 (see below); and

- Sections 9, 13, 14, 15, 16, 17, 18, 27, 28 and 34.

37.24 FRS 102, Section 11, paragraph 11.27 states:

'In applying the fair value guidance to assets or liabilities accounted for in accordance with those sections [as in **37.23** above] the reference to ordinary shares or preference shares in these paragraphs should be read to include the types of assets and liabilities addressed in those sections.'

Fair value hierarchy

37.25 This was referred to in **Chapter 36** in the context of investments in shares and is repeated here for convenience.

37.26 An entity is required to use the following hierarchy in order to determine fair value:

- the best evidence of fair value is a quoted price for identical assets in an active market – the quoted price is usually the bid price;

- when quoted prices are not available, the price of a recent transaction for an identical asset provides evidence of fair value as long as there has

515

not been a significant change in economic circumstances or a significant lapse of time since the transaction took place – in certain cases, that price may need to be adjusted; or

● if the market for the asset is not active and recent transactions of an identical asset on their own are not a good estimate of fair value, an entity estimates the fair value using an estimation technique which seeks to estimate what the transaction price would have been on the measurement date in an arm's-length exchange motivated by normal business considerations.

Valuation techniques

37.27   Valuation techniques include:

● using recent arm's-length market transactions for an *identical asset* between knowledgeable, willing parties;

● reference to the current value of another asset that is substantially the same as the asset being measured;

● discounted cash flow analysis; and

● option pricing models.

37.28   The objective of using a valuation technique is to establish what the transaction price *would* have been on the measurement date on an arm's-length exchange motivated by normal business considerations.

37.29   Fair value should be estimated on the basis of results of techniques which make maximum use of market inputs and which rely as little as possible on entity-determined inputs.

37.30   Where there is no quoted price in an active market for the ordinary or preference shares, fair value is reliably measurable if:

● the variability in the range of reasonable fair value estimates is not significant for that asset; or

● the probabilities of the various estimates within the range can be reasonably assessed and used in estimating fair value.

Practical tip

Plan ahead – identify where fair values will be required at transition date.

37.31   Where a reliable measure of fair value is no longer available for an asset previously measured at fair value, the carrying amount of the asset at the last date at which it was reliably measured becomes the asset's new cost.

Subsequently, the asset is measured at this cost amount (less any accumulated impairment) until such time as a reliable measurement of fair value becomes available.

DERECOGNITION OF FINANCAL ASSETS AND FINANCIAL LIABILITIES

37.32   The derecognition requirements of Section 11 relating to financial assets and financial liabilities should also be applied to this section (see **36.36** to **36.41**).

IMPAIRMENT

37.33   The guidance on impairment in Section 11 refers to those financial assets which are measured at cost. This is more likely to be applicable to basic financial instruments which fall within the scope of Section 11, but technically also applies to Section 12 (see paragraph 12.13).

This guidance is set out in paragraphs **36.22** to **36.28** and is not repeated below.

Example 37.2 – Forward foreign currency contract

A UK company is intending to purchase a machine from a supplier in Euroland at a cost of €500.

Delivery is planned for 31 March 2013, with payment on 31 May 2013.

Consequently, on 30 November 1992, the company entered into a forward contract for purchase of €500 on 31 May 2013 at a rate of €1.5 to £1.

The company's year-end is 31 December 2012.

Accounting entries under paragraph 12.8, assuming the company does *not* opt for hedge accounting, are as follows. The derivative asset/liability is accounted for 'at fair value' through profit or loss.

The journal entries would be as follows. *Assumed figures* are used as indicated below for spot rates of exchange and fair values of the forward contract.

The bank has provided fair values for the derivative contract as follows:

At 31 December 2012	£3
At 31 May 2013	£37

Date	Transaction	Dr £	Cr £
30/11/12	Derivative (forward contract)	0	
	Cash		0
	Historical cost of derivative assumed nil		
31/12/12	Derivative	3	
	Profit and loss account/Income statement (*within profit or loss*)		3
	Recording increase in fair value of derivative		
31/3/13	Property, plant and equipment	350	
	Payables		350
	Recording of fixed asset, using spot rate of 1.43 at date of purchase [€500/1.43 = £350]		
31/5/13	Payables	350	
	Income statement	20	
	Cash		370
	Payment to supplier at spot rate of 1.35 [€500/1.35 = £370] and recording of exchange loss on payable between 31/3/13 and 31/5/13 of £20 (FRS 102, paragraph 30.10)		
31/5/13	Derivative	34	
	Profit and loss account/Income statement (*within profit or loss*)		34
	Recording increase in fair value of derivative between 1/1/13 and 31/5/13 of £34 [Note: FV to date of derivative of (£3 + £34 = £37) equals net settlement from bank on forward contract]		
31/5/13	Cash	37	
	Derivative		37
	Net settlement under forward contract [Equals difference between €500 at spot rate of 1.35 and contract rate of 1.5]		

Chapter 38 deals with hedge accounting, and the relevant entries using the information above are in **Example 38.6.**

PRESENTATION – OFFSET OF FINANCIAL ASSETS AND FINANCIAL LIABILITIES

37.34   A financial asset and a financial liability shall be offset and the net amount presented in the statement of financial position/balance sheet only when the entity:

- currently has a legally enforceable right to set off the recognised amounts; and

- intends either to settle on a net basis, or to realise the asset and settle the liability simultaneously.

DISCLOSURE REQUIREMENTS

37.35   All of the disclosure requirements of Section 11 are applicable (see **Chapter 36**). Disclosure requirements in Section 12 regarding hedge accounting are dealt with in **Chapter 38**.

37.36   Paragraph 12.26 specifically excludes derivatives (other than those used in a hedge accounting relationship) from the disclosure requirements of paragraph 11.48A.

37.37   The Regulations to CA 2006 set out explicit disclosures where fair value through profit or loss is used, and these requirements make particular reference to derivatives (Sch 1, Part D, paragraphs 55 and 56), including:

- the significant assumptions underlying the valuation models and techniques used;

- the fair value of financial instruments by category; and

- the changes in value included in the profit and loss account by category.

Specifically, for each class of derivatives, disclosure is required of the nature and extent of the derivative financial instruments, including significant terms and conditions that may affect the amount, timing and certainty of cash flows.

> **Example 37.3 – Accounting policy extract**
>
> *Derivative financial instruments*
>
> The group primarily uses forward foreign currency contracts to manage its exposure to fluctuations in foreign exchange rates. These instruments are accounted for as hedges when they are designated as hedges at the inception of the contract. The group does not hold derivative financial instruments for trading purposes.

Derivatives are initially recognised at fair value on the date a contract is entered into and are subsequently measured at fair value. The fair values of derivatives are measured using observable market prices, or where market prices are not available, fair values are calculated by reference to forward exchange rates for contracts with similar maturity profiles, or by using discounted expected future cash flows at prevailing interest and exchange rates.

Where derivative financial instruments are not designated as effective hedges or do not qualify for hedge accounting, any gain or loss on measurement is taken to the income statement through profit or loss.

(See **Example 38.2** for an accounting policy example where hedge accounting is adopted.)

SUMMARY – WHAT IS DIFFERENT FROM THE PREVIOUS UK GAAP?

- The biggest change relates to the treatment of derivatives such as forward foreign currency contracts and interest rate swaps (except for UK companies who have been required to, or who have chosen to adopt, FRS 26, which requires derivatives to be included on the balance sheet at fair value).

- Existing UK GAAP (apart from FRS 26 and the fair value rules in the Regulations to CA 2006 (see **7.4**)) have derivatives in the balance sheet at historical cost (generally zero) whereas Section 12 of FRS 102 requires them to be stated at fair value.

- Under the previous UK GAAP (assuming FRS 26 was not adopted), derivatives were accounted for on settlement. Under FRS 102 they will be recognised earlier (see **37.17** above), and this is likely to make the trend of reported profits more volatile.

Chapter 38

Financial instruments, the hedge accounting option

SIGNPOSTS

- It is important to appreciate that hedge accounting is *not mandatory*, it is an accounting policy choice which companies can take or leave.

- For those entities who are eligible to adopt hedge accounting and who make the accounting policy choice, there are presently three accounting policy options:

  ○ the requirements of Section 12, Other Financial Instruments, (due to be reviewed later this year – the Financial Reporting Council is expected to issue a Financial Reporting Exposure Draft proposing amendments to Section 12); *or*

  ○ the hedge accounting requirements in IAS 39 *Financial Instruments: Recognition and Measurement* (as adopted for use in the European Union); *or*

  ○ the hedge accounting requirements of IFRS 9 *Financial Instruments,* which were revised in November 2013.

- This chapter refers to IAS 39 where relevant, but does not deal with IAS 39-style hedge accounting.

- In FRS 102, there are two unnamed categories of hedge accounting (see **38.15** and **38.16** below) as compared with IFRS which refers to three categories:

  ○ fair value hedges (corresponding with those listed in **38.15** below);

  ○ cash flow hedges (corresponding with those in **38.16** below); and

  ○ hedges of a net investment (the final bullet point in **38.16** below).

- Some of these requirements may be familiar to companies who are either required to or who have chosen to adopt FRS 26 *Financial Instruments: Recognition and Measurement* (the UK GAAP equivalent of IAS 39).

INTRODUCTION

What is hedge accounting?

38.1   The commercial practice of hedging risk (sometimes referred to as an 'economic hedge') and the accounting practice of 'hedge accounting' are not the same. A company may hedge risk exposures but may either choose not to adopt the option of hedge accounting or not even be permitted to adopt hedge accounting because it is unable to satisfy the demanding criteria in FRS 102 and IAS 39 respectively.

38.2   Hedge accounting is not a defined term, either in FRS 102 or IAS 39, but a hedged item and hedging instrument both have a definition.

38.3   Hedge accounting is a complex topic and is dealt with in detail in IAS 39. This chapter aims to give an overview of the hedge accounting possibilities under FRS 102. Groups wishing to pursue this topic in greater detail are advised to refer to a specialised text dealing with IFRS.

Hedge accounting is optional

38.4   Hedge accounting is an option which many potentially eligible companies/groups may choose not to adopt because of its complexity and administrative cost.

Please note that any references in this chapter to hedge accounting are to the version in FRS 102.

Why adopt hedge accounting?

38.5   Hedge accounting recognises the offsetting effects on profit or loss of changes in the fair values of the hedging instrument and the hedged item, so that the income effects of both hedged items and hedging items are recognised in the same period. This should achieve the effect of reducing volatility of earnings between accounting periods.

Specifically the two main situations in which companies may wish to adopt hedge accounting are to:

- correct accounting recognition and measurement inconsistencies; and

- reflect management of risks associated with future transactions.

Accounting recognition and measurement inconsistencies

38.6 Without hedge accounting, gains and losses on assets and liabilities that are managed together may be recognised in profit or loss in different periods.

Recognition inconsistencies arise when assets and liabilities that are subject to financial risks are recognised on the balance sheet while others are not. Gains and losses on those assets and liabilities are recognised in different periods.

Measurement inconsistencies arise when assets and liabilities that are subject to financial risks are measured on different bases. Gains and losses on those assets and liabilities are recognised in the income statement/profit and loss account in different periods.

Example 38.1 – Interest-rate swap and fixed-rate borrowing

A company has a fixed-rate borrowing which has a further five years to maturity. The borrowing is carried in the balance sheet at amortised cost.

The company anticipates that interest rates are likely to fall and enters into a fixed-to-floating interest rate swap in order to manage the interest rate risk.

Under FRS 102, the derivative (the interest rate swap) must be measured in the balance sheet at fair value.

In the absence of hedge accounting, gains and losses on the derivative would be recognised in the income statement/profit and loss account immediately.

However, gains and losses on the debt are recognised on a different basis, since it is measured in the balance sheet at amortised cost and not fair value. Thus, in the absence of hedge accounting, gains and losses on the derivative, the swap, are included in the income statement/profit and loss account at a different time from corresponding gains and losses on the debt.

Reflecting the management of risks associated with future transactions

38.7 Financial instrument contracts may be entered into in the current period in order to manage risks associated with future transactions (which are not reflected in the balance sheet or income statement/profit and loss account of the current period).

A company may wish to adopt hedge accounting in order to match the current income statement/profit and loss account effects arising from the financial instrument managing the risk, with the future income statement/profit and loss account effect of the future transactions.

Example 38.2 – Forward foreign exchange contract to manage risk of future purchases of services in a foreign currency

A holiday company enters into a forward foreign currency contract to manage the foreign exchange risk relating to committed foreign purchases (cost of hotel rooms etc) which will take place in the following period.

Without hedge accounting, the gain or loss on the derivative would be recognised in the income statement of the current period, whilst the foreign exchange gain or loss on the purchases would not be recognised in the company's income statement until the following period.

Example 38.3 – Forward foreign exchange contract to manage risk of future purchase of capital equipment in a foreign currency

A company intends to purchase equipment in the following accounting period, from an overseas supplier. The company enters into a foreign currency contract to manage the foreign exchange risk related to the anticipated future purchase of the capital equipment. Although a contractual commitment to purchase is not in place, the transaction is classified as 'highly probable' (see **38.16** below).

Without hedge accounting, gains and losses on the derivative are recognised in the income statement immediately. However, the gains and losses on the capital expenditure transaction will be recognised in the period in which the expenditure takes place (the actual sterling cost will determine the depreciation charge).

The application of hedge accounting is illustrated in **Example 38.6** below.

QUALIFYING CONDITIONS FOR HEDGE ACCOUNTING

38.8   An entity must comply with all of the following conditions if it wishes to adopt hedge accounting:

- The entity designates and documents the hedging relationship so that the risk being hedged, the hedged item and the hedging instrument are clearly identified and the risk in the hedged item is the risk being hedged with the hedging instrument.

- The hedged risk is one of the four risks specified in **38.10** below.

- The hedging instrument is as specified in **38.11** below.

- The entity expects the hedging instrument to be highly effective in offsetting the designated hedged risk as specified in **38.12** below.

Designation and documentation of risks

38.9   The following is a simple example of what might be required:

Example 38.4 – Hedging documentation

Hedging documentation could include paragraphs dealing with the following:

- risk management objective and strategy – this should be consistent with the company's internally documented risk management policy, and the description in the notes to the financial statements as required by FRS 102, paragraphs 12.27 to 12.29;

- hedged item – specific details including amounts, dates and cross references to other documentation;

- hedging instrument – details of forward exchange contract, swap document etc;

- hedge risk exposure – description of variability of future cash flows or fair value changes etc;

- term of hedging relationship – relevant dates (eg period covered);

- nature of hedging relationship – type of hedge;

- method of assessing effectiveness – details of prospective assessment method and of retrospective assessment method. This should be very detailed and include: method (eg ratio analysis method or regression method); frequency of testing; data to be used as inputs; whether assessment is period-by-period or cumulative – IAS 39 has more detail on this); and

- effectiveness measurement method.

Restrictions on hedged risks

38.10   Hedge accounting may only be used for *one of the four following risks:*

- Interest rate risk and foreign exchange risk of a debt instrument measured at amortised cost. This could cover the use of interest rate swaps as hedging instruments, for example:

  - pay fixed receive variable (cash flow hedge per IAS 39 terminology); or

  - pay variable receive fixed (fair value hedge per IAS 39 terminology).

- Foreign exchange or interest rate risk in a firm commitment or a highly probable forecast transaction.

- Price risk of a commodity that the entity holds or price risk in a firm commitment or a highly probable forecast transaction to purchase or sell a commodity.

- Foreign exchange risk in a net investment in a foreign operation (see below).

Hedging instrument

38.11   Hedge accounting may only be used if the hedging instrument meets *all* of the following terms and conditions.

Condition 1 – The hedging instrument must be one of the following:

- an interest rate swap;

- a foreign currency swap;

- a cross-currency interest rate swap;

- a forward or future foreign currency exchange contract;

- a forward or future commodity exchange contract; or

- any financial instrument used to hedge foreign exchange risk in a net investment in a foreign operation.

Condition 2

The hedging instrument must involve a party external to the reporting group, segment, or individual entity being reported on.

Condition 3

The notional amount of the hedging instrument must be equal to the designated amount of the principal or notional amount of the hedged item.

Condition 4

There are detailed restrictions on the specified maturity date of the hedging instrument (see FRS 102, paragraph 12.18(d)).

Condition 5

The hedging instrument must have no prepayment, early termination or extension features other than at fair value.

Hedge effectiveness

38.12   The entity must expect the hedging instrument to be highly effective in offsetting the designated hedged risk.

Hedge effectiveness is defined as the degree to which changes in the fair value or cash flows of the hedged item that are attributable to a hedged risk are offset by changes in the fair value or cash flows of the hedging instrument.

38.13   FRS 102 gives no further information but IAS 39 *Application Guidance*, paragraph 105 refers to 'Assessing hedge effectiveness'. Specialist commentaries on IFRS9/IAS 39 give practical guidance.

THE TWO TYPES OF HEDGE ACCOUNTING REQUIREMENTS

38.14   There are two sets of hedge accounting requirements in FRS 102, paragraphs 12.19 and 12.22, according to the particular situation and type of hedge undertaken:

The first set

38.15   The first set (Sections 12.19 to 12.22) covers hedges of the following risks:

*   fixed interest rate risk of a debt instrument measured at amortised cost;

*   foreign exchange risk of a debt instrument measured at amortised cost;

*   commodity price risk of a commodity that it holds; or

*   commodity price risk in a firm commitment.

The second set

38.16   The second set (Sections 12.23 to 12.25) covers hedges of the following risks:

*   variable interest rate risk in a debt instrument measured at amortised cost;

*   foreign exchange risk in a debt instrument measured at amortised cost;

*   foreign exchange risk or interest rate risk in a firm commitment or highly probable forecast transaction;

- the commodity price risk in a highly probable forecast transaction; or

- the foreign exchange risk in a net investment in a foreign operation (see also **Example 38.5**).

38.17 The term net investment in a foreign operation is defined as the amount of the reporting entity's interest in the net assets of that operation; it is referred to in Section 30, Foreign Currency Translation (see **32.53**).

Example 38.5 – Hedge of a net investment in a foreign operation

An example of a hedge of a net investment in a foreign operation would be where a company issues foreign currency debt or enters into a forward foreign exchange contract in order to hedge the risk of foreign currency exchange gains and losses on the net investment.

MEASUREMENT

Basic requirements where hedge accounting is adopted

38.18 Where the hedged risk is one of the risks in **38.10** above, the part of the change in the fair value of the hedging instrument that was effective in offsetting the change in the fair value of the expected cash flows of the hedged item should be recognised in other comprehensive income.

In **Example 38.6** below, the hedging instrument is a forward foreign currency contract. The hedge is considered to be 100% effective in offsetting changes in expected future cash flows, so the whole of the change in the fair value of the derivative is recognised in other comprehensive income.

38.19 The hedging gain or loss recognised in other comprehensive income must be reclassified to profit or loss when the hedged item is recognised in profit or loss or when the hedging relationship ends.

In **Example 38.6** below, the hedged item is a highly probable forecast transaction, the future purchase of plant and machinery. This item is recognised in profit or loss once the machinery starts being depreciated, and this is when the reclassification starts, as illustrated in the example below.

38.20 FRS 102, paragraph 12.23 covers hedge ineffectiveness. This is a complex area and is not analysed further here.

Example 38.6 – Hedge of a foreign exchange risk in a highly probable forecast transaction

This example deals with a hedge of a foreign exchange risk in a highly probable forecast transaction.

A UK company is intending to purchase a machine from a supplier in Euroland at a cost of €500. Delivery is planned for 31 March 2013, with payment on 31 May 2013.

Consequently, on 30 November 2012 the company entered into a forward contract for the purchase of €500 on 31 May 2013 at a rate of €1.50 to £1. The company's year-end is 31 December 2012.

The forecast transaction is assessed as 'highly probable' and the hedging relationship qualifies for hedge accounting. The hedge is determined to be fully effective.

Scenario 1

Chapter 37 (see **Example 37.2**) dealt with the accounting entries assuming that the company did *not* opt for hedge accounting. The derivative asset/liability was accounted for at fair value through profit or loss.

Scenario 2

Using hedge accounting, the journal entries would be as follows. References are to paragraphs in FRS 102.

Date	Transaction	Dr £	Cr £
30/11/12	Derivative (forward contract)	0	
	Cash		0
	Fair value of derivative at date the company becomes a party to the contractual provisions of the derivative contract is nil (any transaction costs would be expenses immediately to profit or loss).		
31/12/12	Derivative	3	
	Other comprehensive income (through hedging reserve in B/S)		3
	Increase in fair value of derivative (**see paragraph 12.23**)		

Date	Transaction	Dr £	Cr £
31/3/13	Property, plant and equipment	350	
	Payables		350
	*Recording of fixed asset, using spot rate of 1.43 at date of purchase (***see paragraph 30.7***)*		
	[€500/1.43 = £350]		
31/5/13	Payables	350	
	Income statement (within profit or loss)	20	
	Cash		370
	Payment to supplier at spot rate of 1.35 [€500/1.35 = £370]		
	*and recording of exchange loss on payable between 31/3/13 and 31/5/13 of £20 (***see paragraph 30.10***)*		
31/5/13	Derivative	34	
	Other comprehensive income (through hedging reserve in B/S)		34
	Recording increase in fair value of derivative between 1/1/13 and 31/5/13 of £34 [Note: FV to date of derivative of (£3 + £34 = £37) equals net settlement from bank on forward contract]		
31/5/13	Cash	37	
	Derivative		37
	Net settlement under forward contract [Equals difference between €500 at spot rate of 1.35 and contract rate of 1.5]		

The associated gain should be reclassified (effectively 'recycled') into profit or loss in the same period(s) during which the asset acquired affects profit or loss, in this case over the periods that depreciation expense is recognised) – assume over five years.

Extract – Statement of comprehensive income – hedge accounting under FRS 102

	2012	2013	2014	2015	2016	2017	Total
Revenue	x	x	x	x	x	x	x
Operating expenses (£37/5 = 7.4)	(x)	7.4	7.4	7.4	7.4	7.4	37
Finance cost/income	(x)	(x)	(x)	(x)	(x)	(x)	(x)
Profit for the year	x	7.4	7.4	7.4	7.4	7.4	37
Other comprehensive income:							
Hedge accounting							
– gains/losses arising during the year	3	34					37
– reclassification adjustments	–	(7.4)	(7.4)	(7.4)	(7.4)	(7.4)	(37)
Other comprehensive income for the year	3	26.6	(7.4)	(7.4)	(7.4)	(7.4)	0
Total comprehensive income for the year	3	34	0	0	0	0	37

38.21 Where the hedged risk is the variable interest rate risk in a debt instrument measured at amortised cost, the entity is required to subsequently recognise in profit or loss the periodic net cash settlements from the interest rate swap in the period in which the net settlements accrue.

Discontinuance of hedge accounting

38.22 Hedge accounting should be discontinued in any of the following situations:

● the hedging instrument expires, is sold or is terminated; or

● the hedge no longer meets the criteria for hedge accounting; or

● in a hedge of a forecast transaction, where the forecast transaction is no longer highly probable; or

● the entity revokes the designation.

DISCLOSURES

General requirements

38.23   For each of the four types of hedges referred to in **38.10** above, disclose:

- a description of the hedge;

- a description of the financial instruments designated as hedging instruments and their fair values at the reporting date; and

- the nature of the risks being hedged, including a description of the hedged item.

Disclosure requirements for first set

38.24   Where hedge accounting is used for one of the hedges in **38.15** above, disclose:

- the amount of the change in fair value of the hedging instrument recognised in profit or loss for the period; and

- the amount of the change in fair value of the hedged item recognised in profit or loss for the period.

Disclosure requirements for second set

38.25   Where hedge accounting is used for one of the hedges in **38.16** above, disclose:

- the periods when the cash flows are expected to occur and when they are expected to affect profit or loss;

- a description of any forecast transaction for which hedge accounting had previously been used, but which is no longer expected to occur;

- the amount of the change in fair value of the hedging instrument that was recognised in other comprehensive income during the period;

- the amount that was reclassified from other comprehensive income to profit or loss for the period; and

- the amount of any excess of the fair value of the hedging instrument over the change in the fair value of the expected future cash flows that was recognised in profit or loss for the period.

Example 38.7 – Accounting policy on financial instruments (part of note)

Derivative financial instruments

The group primarily uses forward foreign currency contracts to manage its exposure to fluctuations in foreign exchange rates. These instruments are accounted for as hedges when they are designated as hedges at the inception of the contract. The group does not hold derivative financial instruments for trading purposes.

Derivatives are initially recognised at fair value on the date a contract is entered into and are subsequently measured at fair value. The fair values of derivatives are measured using observable market prices, or where market prices are not available, fair values are calculated by reference to forward exchange rates for contracts with similar maturity profiles, or by using discounted expected future cash flows at prevailing interest and exchange rates.

Where derivative financial instruments are not designated as effective hedges or do not qualify for hedge accounting, any gain or loss on measurement is taken to the income statement through profit or loss.

Where derivative financial instruments are designated as, and are effective as hedges, any gain or loss on remeasurement is taken to other comprehensive income and held in equity. The gains or losses are then recycled through profit or loss when the designated item is transacted.

SUMMARY – WHAT IS DIFFERENT FROM THE PREVIOUS UK GAAP?

- Existing non-FRS 26 users will probably not find this section of FRS 102 to be particularly relevant. However, it is worth noting that the Financial Reporting Council intends to simplify the qualifying conditions for the adoption of hedge accounting which, if agreed, could lead more entities to adopt it. This may be confirmed when a Financial Reporting Exposure Draft is published later in 2013, proposing amendments to FRS 102.

- For non-FRS 26 adopters, this is completely new territory.

- FRS 26 adopters will compare the present requirements of Section 12, referred to in this chapter, with those in FRS 26, paragraphs 89–102. These adopters should also keep a careful look out for revised proposals from the FRC.

Chapter 39

First-time adoption of FRS 102

SIGNPOSTS

- This section of FRS 102 requires attention at an early stage, particularly as regards both recognition and measurement issues at transition date. FRS 102 is mandatory for accounting periods beginning on or after 1 January 2015.

- If you have a 31 December year-end and don't adopt early, transition date will be 1 January 2014.

- Financial statement formats need reviewing – particularly the statement of comprehensive income and the statement of cash flows.

- Exemptions – Section 35 of FRS 102 offers a number of exemptions from the potentially onerous requirement of retrospective restatement including a general exemption due to being impracticable (see **39.10** and **39.19–39.30** below).

- Exceptions – it must also be noted that Section 35 actually prohibits full retrospective application for five specified areas (see **39.11–39.18** below).

- Disclosures – detailed disclosures are required to explain the impact of the transition (see **39.31–39.32** below).

INTRODUCTION

Overview

39.1   FRS 102 is mandatory for accounting periods beginning on or after 1 January 2015. Earlier application is permitted for accounting periods ending on or after 31 December 2012, with certain restrictions imposed on entities that are within the scope of a SORP.

Entities that apply FRS 102 early must disclose that fact.

39.2   An entity adopting FRS 102 for the first time is required to apply Section 35 of the standard in its first financial statements complying with the standard. The first set of FRS 102 accounts will require comparatives restated in accordance with the standard.

39.3   In general, adoption of FRS 102 requires retrospectively changing the accounting used by the entity under its previous financial reporting framework (ie 'old' UK GAAP). This may involve adjustments to retained earnings as at transition date. This requirement is subject to certain restrictions and concessions – these are referred to below.

39.4   FRS 102 requires the financial statements to explain how the transition from previous GAAP to FRS 102 affected the entity's reported financial position, financial performance and cash flows – see below.

Transition date

39.5   This is defined as 'the beginning of the earliest period for which an entity presents full comparative information under FRS 102 in its first financial statements that comply with this FRS'.

Example 39.1 – Determining transition date

Company X has a 31 December year-end. Assume that its first set of accounts complying with FRS 102 covers the year ending 31 December 2015. Transition date is 1 January 2014.

Compliance statement

39.6   Entities whose financial statements comply with FRS 102 are required to make an explicit and unreserved statement of such compliance in the notes to the financial statements.

Example 39.2 – Compliance statement

These financial statements have been prepared in accordance with the Financial Reporting Standard applicable in the UK and Republic of Ireland (The FRS) issued by the Financial Reporting Council. They are presented in £ sterling.

Before 2015, the financial statements were prepared in accounting with previous UK GAAP as issued by the former UK Accounting Standards Board. The financial effects of the transition to the FRS are set out in Note 3 below (see **Example 39.10**).

The requirement for retrospective restatement at transition date

39.7   Section 35 of FRS 102 deals with the transition from the existing UK GAAP to FRS 102. Generally the FRS requires retrospective restatement so that comparatives should be restated in line with the new reporting requirements.

Exemptions from retrospective restatement (see **39.19** onwards) are there to make transition easier.

Practical tip

It is important to make sure these exemptions are understood earlier rather than later, to avoid wasting resources compiling restatement information that is not necessary.

PROCEDURES AT TRANSITION DATE

39.8   Except as provided below (see restrictions and exemptions) the entity should apply the following four requirements as at transition date:

(a)   recognise all assets and liabilities whose recognition is required by FRS 102;

(b)   not recognise items as assets or liabilities where FRS 102 does not permit recognition (in practice, this is likely to be uncommon for UK companies who have previously adopted UK GAAP);

(c)   reclassify items that it recognised under the entity's previous GAAP as one type of asset, liability or component of equity, but are regarded under FRS 102 as a different type of asset, liability or component of equity (eg different groupings in the cash flow statement); and

(d)   apply FRS 102 in measuring all recognised assets and liabilities.

Example 39.3 – Transition adjustment to reflect fair value of forward currency contracts

An entity has forward foreign currency contracts. Under the previous UK GAAP the entity did not adopt FRS 26 so the contracts were included in the balance sheet at historical cost (ie zero).

Under FRS 102 these should be recognised at fair value. This requires an adjustment at transition date to retained earnings (see (a) and (d) above, and **39.9** below).

Example 39.4 – Reclassification of cash flow statement to comply with Section 7 of FRS 102

An entity has previously presented its cash flow statement in accordance with FRS 1 *Cash Flow Statements*. It is now required to follow Section 7 of FRS 102 which requires cash flows to be reclassified (see (c) above) and the statement to reconcile to cash and cash equivalents.

Example 39.5 –Transition adjustment to reflect fair value of equity investments

An entity recognised fixed asset investments under UK GAAP but measured them at cost. Assuming the investments are either publicly traded or their fair value can otherwise be measured reliably, such investments would be recognised at transition date at fair value, with an adjustment to retained earnings (see (d) above and **39.9** below). Deferred tax would be provided on the adjustment.

Focus

Where assets and liabilities are included in the balance sheet at fair value instead of historical cost, it is always worth asking the question: 'Does this, or might this, have deferred tax implications?'

ADJUSTMENTS AT TRANSITION DATE

Requirements

39.9   FRS 102, Section 35, paragraph 35.8 refers to situations where the accounting policies that an entity uses in its opening balance sheet under FRS 102 differ from the policies used for the same date for its previous reporting framework.

The previous reporting framework will usually be 'old' UK GAAP but, in some cases, could be IFRS following recent changes to the *Companies Act 2006* in *SI 2012/2301* regarding change of accounting framework.

The resulting adjustments should be recognised directly in retained earnings.

39.10   FRS 102, paragraph 35.11 refers to situations where 'it is impracticable for an entity to restate the opening statement of financial position at the date of transition …' and the required disclosures. 'Impracticable' is defined in the Glossary as 'applying a requirement is impracticable when the entity cannot apply it after making every reasonable effort to do so'.

Such situations are likely to be uncommon for UK entities who have previously adopted UK GAAP.

RESTRICTIONS ON RETROSPECTIVE APPLICATION

Requirement

39.11   Paragraph 35.9 states that, on first-time adoption of FRS 102, an entity is not permitted to retrospectively change the accounting that it followed under its previous financial reporting framework for any of the following transactions in **39.12–39.18**.

Derecognition of financial assets and financial liabilities

39.12   Financial assets and liabilities derecognised under the entity's previous reporting framework before the date of transition to FRS 102 should not be recognised on adoption of the FRS.

Conversely, for financial assets and liabilities that would have been derecognised under FRS 102 in a transaction that took place before the date of transition, but that were not derecognised under an entity's previous accounting framework, an entity may choose:

- to derecognise them on adoption of FRS 102; or

- to continue to recognise them until disposed of or settled.

Hedge accounting

39.13   This is a complex area and only likely to be applicable to large groups, including those with significant overseas operations. Hedge accounting cannot be adopted retrospectively.

The designation and documentation of a hedging relationship must be completed on or before the date of transition to FRS 102 if the hedging relationship is to qualify for hedge accounting from transition date.

Hedge accounting is referred to in **Chapter 38** of this book.

Accounting estimates

39.14   Estimates at transition date in accordance with FRS 102 should be consistent with estimates made for the same date in accordance with previous GAAP.

Example 39.6 – Revision of previous estimate

Consider a company that previously adopted UK GAAP and will adopt FRS 102 for the first time for the year to 31 December 2015. Transition date is therefore 1 January 2014.

New information received on 8 July 2014 requires a revision of an estimate made in accordance with UK GAAP for the balance sheet at 31 December 2013. There is no objective evidence that the estimate was in error, the accounting estimate was considered appropriate at the time.

The new information should *not* be adjusted in the FRS 102 balance sheet at transition date (1 January 2014). Instead, it should be reflected in the FRS comparative balance sheet at 31 December 2014. Effectively the revision of the estimate is recognised as income or expense in the period when the entity made the revision (ie the year ended 31 December 2014).

39.15   However retrospective adjustments *are* required in either of the following situations:

- to reflect any differences in accounting policies; and

- if there is objective evidence that the previous GAAP estimates were in error.

Discontinued operations

39.16   A key issue is that the definitions and criteria for discontinued operations in FRS 102 differ from those in previous UK GAAP FRS 3 *Reporting Financial Performance* (see **Chapter 33**). FRS 102, paragraph 35.9(d) simply states 'discontinued operations' without adding any explanation.

39.17   In cases where an entity's previous financial reporting framework had a different definition of a discontinued operation, or specified a different accounting treatment for discontinued operations, no reclassification or re-measurement is required on adoption of FRS 102.

Example 39.7 – Discontinued operation (1)

An entity is adopting FRS 102 for the first time in respect of its 31 December 2015 financial statements.

A discontinued operation was reported in 2014 under its previous GAAP (say FRS 3). This will be reported as a comparative in its 2015 accounts without restatement, but accompanied by an explanatory note.

Example 39.8 – Discontinued operation (2)

An entity is adopting FRS 102 for the first time in respect of its 31 December 2015 financial statements.

No adjustment to previously reported comparatives should be made for any transactions in 2014 that were not reported as discontinued under FRS 3 but which might have been reported as discontinued had FRS 102 been applicable in 2014.

Example 39.9 – Discontinued operation (3)

An entity is adopting FRS 102 for the first time in respect of its 31 December 2015 financial statements.

A discontinued operation was reported in 2015 in accordance with FRS 102. This falls within the usual rules under FRS 102 (see **Chapter 33**) and the comparative statement of comprehensive income should be restated (see **33.10**).

Measuring non-controlling interests (minority interests)

39.18 The following requirements should be applied prospectively from the date of transition to FRS 102:

- to allocate profit or loss and total comprehensive income between non-controlling interest and owners of the parent;

- for accounting for changes in the parent's ownership interest in a subsidiary that does **not** result in a loss of control; and

- accounting for a loss of control over a subsidiary.

EXEMPTIONS FROM FULL RETROSPECTIVE APPLICATION

Introduction

39.19 FRS 102 requires *retrospective application* in most cases, according to the requirements in **39.8** above. The retrospective application requirement is subject to specific restrictions and prohibitions (see **39.11–39.18** above), and exemptions (see **39.20–39.30** below).

Without these exemptions, some companies would be required to carry out complex recalculations relating to transactions that took place some years back.

39.20 Entities may use one or more of the following exemptions (or indeed ignore them altogether if it so chooses). There is potentially a long list of possible exemptions but, in practice, many of these will apply only to specialised transactions and entities in specialised business sectors.

The exemptions most likely to be used by a broad range of entities are referred to below, and the more specialised ones listed only briefly (see **39.30**).

Business combinations

39.21 Paragraph 35.10(a) is likely to be a particularly important part of FRS 102. It is tricky and should be read very carefully. It may also prove to be contentious and be interpreted in different ways by different entities.

39.22 The exemption relates to business combinations that were effected before the date of transition to IFRS. Any business combinations with an acquisition date after transition date must comply fully with Section 19, Business Combinations (see **30.35**).

39.23 For business combinations with an acquisition date before transition date, entities have a choice:

Option 1 – Restate the effects of the business combination retrospectively

This would require recalculating the effects of the business combination as though Section 19 of FRS 102 (see **Chapter 30**) had been applied at transition date. For example, goodwill would be accounted in accordance with paragraph 19.23 (in the absence of a reliable estimate, a useful life of five years would have to be adopted), deferred tax in accordance with paragraph 19.15A, and measurement of acquired intangibles in accordance with paragraph 18.11.

Retrospective restatement would require reliable information that would have been available at acquisition date and this information may not be readily available many years after acquisition date.

Note that, if this route is taken, all subsequent business combinations prior to acquisition date will have to be restated retrospectively.

Option 2 – Elect to apply the exemption in paragraph 35.10(a)

For business combinations effected prior to transition date, the following requirements must be followed to claim the exemption:

- recognise and measure, as at transition date, all the assets and liabilities acquired or assumed applying the rules referred to in **39.8** to **39.17** above, except for the following requirements relating to goodwill and intangibles;

- intangibles subsumed within goodwill under previous GAAP shall not be separately recognised; and

- no adjustment shall be made at the transition date to the carrying value of goodwill, which should subsequently be amortised prospectively after its remaining useful life.

Focus

Section 35.10(a) is silent as regards the remaining useful life of the goodwill. In many cases, where for example, the amortisation period under FRS 10 *Goodwill and Intangible Assets* was determined as 20 years, the remaining life of the goodwill after transition date may exceed five years.

At the time of going to press, recommended practice has not been established. Evidence should be provided at transition date to support the remaining economic life. However, where this is not available, the reader should check current commentary regarding the acceptability of simply ensuring that there is no evidence to suggest the remaining life is shorter than originally estimated.

FRS 102 does not explicitly require the remaining economic life in these circumstances to be reassessed. Some commentators take the view that the entity should provide evidence at transition date to support the remaining economic life of the goodwill.

Example 39.10 – Goodwill at transition date

An entity acquired a business in early 2006 and, in accordance with FRS 10, estimated the useful life of the goodwill at 20 years. The cost of the goodwill was determined as £800,000.

At transition date of 1 January 2014, the carrying amount of the goodwill is £480,000 (£800,000 × 12/20). The entity has reviewed the carrying amount and evidence is available at transition date that the remaining life of the goodwill is at least 12 years. The goodwill at transition date is not adjusted, and is amortised over the remaining 12 years at £40,000 per annum.

Note that paragraph 19.25(g) requires disclosure of the useful life of goodwill and the reasons for using a period in excess of five years.

Revaluation as deemed cost

39.24   A first-time adopter may elect to use a previous GAAP revaluation of an item of property, plant and equipment as its deemed cost at the revaluation date.

The surplus on the previous revaluation should have been transferred to a separate revaluation reserve in accordance with paragraph 35 of Schedule 1 to the Regulations to CA 2006.

Following the establishment of the revaluation reserve, each year annual transfers (equivalent to the difference between the revaluation depreciation and what it would have been had the asset not been revalued) would be made from revaluation reserve to profit and loss reserves.

At transition date, a deferred tax liability must be recognised in accordance with paragraph 35.7(a) of Section 35. paragraph 35 requires this adjustment to be made against retained earnings but, in these circumstances, it would be acceptable to make a subsequent transfer from retained earnings to revaluation reserve, so that, effectively, the revaluation reserve is presented net of deferred tax.

Example 39.11 – Revaluation as deemed cost

A freehold property was acquired on 1 January 2000 at a cost of £140,000 split between land of £100,000 and buildings of £40,000. The life of the buildings was assessed as 50 years, so the annual depreciation charge was £40,000/50 = £800.

The property was revalued on 31 December 2010 at £202,000 (split land £160,000 and buildings £42,000). Subsequently the depreciation charge (rounding to £'000) amounted to £42/39 = £'000 of 1.1. The difference between revaluation depreciation and historical cost depreciation of £'000 0.3 (= £1.1 – £0.8) was transferred each year out of revaluation reserve and into profit and loss reserves.

For simplicity, the above example does not reflect the deferred tax adjustment at transition date.

The effect of the above up to transition date of 1 January 2014 may be summarised as follows (all amounts rounded to £'000):

	Land £	Buildings £	Total £
1/1/2000 – cost	100	40	140
Depreciation 10 years	–	(8)	(8)
1/1/2010	100	32	132
Depreciation 2010	–	(0.8)	(0.8)
Revaluation surplus	60	10.8	70.8
Revaluation 31/12/10	160	42	202
Depreciation 2011 (£42,000/39 years)	–	(1.1)	(1.1)
Depreciation 2012 (£42,000/39 years)	–	(1.1)	(1.1)
Depreciation 2013 (£42,000/39 years)	–	(1.1)	(1.1)
At transition date 1/1/14	160	38.7	198.7

The revaluation reserve of £10.8 would be reduced by annual transfers to profit and loss reserves (see above) of £0.3 so that at transition date it would stand at £10.8 less £3 × £0.3 = £9.9.

After transition date the property would be presented as deemed cost of £198.7 and subsequently reduced by annual depreciation charges over the following 36 years from 2014 to 2049 of £38.7/36 years = £1.1.

Revaluation reserve of £9.9 at transition date would be reduced over the following 36 years to zero by means of annual transfers of £9.9/36 years = £0.3.

Please note – the above example does not reflect deferred tax – this should be put through as an adjustment at transition date.

Fair value as deemed cost

39.25   A first-time adopter may elect to measure an item of property, plant and equipment at fair value at transition date and to use that fair value as its deemed cost at that date.

The surplus on revaluation should be transferred to a separate revaluation reserve in accordance with paragraph 35 of Schedule 1 to the Regulations to CA 2006 (see **7.4**).

On transition, a deferred tax liability must be recognised in accordance with FRS 102, paragraph 35.7(a). FRS 102, paragraph 35.8 requires this adjustment to be made against retained earnings, but in these circumstances, it would be acceptable to make a subsequent transfer from retained earnings to revaluation reserve, so that effectively the revaluation reserve is presented net of deferred tax.

The calculations would be similar to those in **Example 39.9** above.

Deferred development costs as a deemed cost

39.26   A first-time adopter may elect to measure the carrying amount at transition date related to development costs capitalised in accordance with previous UK GAAP SSAP 13 *Accounting for Research and Development* as its deemed cost at transition date.

Lease incentives

39.27   This exemption is only available where the term of the lease commenced before the date of transition to FRS 102. It is available to both lessees and lessors.

Without the exemption, retrospective application is required. For a lessee this would require the aggregate benefit of lease incentives to be recognised as a reduction in lease expense over the lease term.

For a lessee, the exemption would allow the entity to continue to recognise the benefit on the same basis as that applied at the date of transition to FRS 102 (ie following UITF 28 *Operating Lease Incentives*).

Individual and separate financial statements

39.28   This exemption relates to investments in subsidiaries, associates and jointly controlled entities. It allows the entity to elect to adopt the carrying amount as determined under the previous UK GAAP as its deemed cost under FRS 102.

Borrowing costs

39.29 This exemption applies where an entity wishes to adopt an accounting policy of capitalising borrowing costs as part of the cost of a qualifying asset. The entity may elect to treat the date of transition to FRS 102 as the date on which capitalisation commences.

More specialised exemption categories

39.30 In view of their specialised application, these are not further referred to, but the relevant paragraphs in Section 35 are noted in brackets.

- share-based payments transactions (35.10(b));

- compound financial instruments (35.10(g));

- service concession arrangements (35.10(i));

- extractive activities (35.10(j));

- arrangements containing a lease (35.10(k));

- decommissioning liabilities included in the cost of property, plant and equipment (35.10(l));

- dormant companies (35.10(m));

- public benefit entity combinations (35.10(q));

- assets and liabilities of subsidiaries assets and joint ventures – where subsidiaries, associates and joint ventures become first-time adopters later than the parent entity (35.10(r)); and

- designation of previously recognised financial instruments (35.10(s)).

DISCLOSURE REQUIREMENTS FOR THE ENTITY'S FIRST FINANCIAL STATEMENTS PREPARED IN ACCORDANCE WITH FRS 102

General requirement

39.31 Paragraph 35.12 requires an entity to explain how the transition from its previous reporting framework to FRS 102 affected its reported financial position and financial performance.

Specific disclosures

39.32 Assume, for the purposes of illustration, that the previous financial reporting framework was UK GAAP. Paragraph 35.13 requires the following reconciliations and explanations to be included within the entity's first financial statements prepared using FRS 102:

- a description of the nature of each change in accounting policy;

- a reconciliation of its equity determined in accordance with UK GAAP to its equity determined in accordance with FRS 102, in respect of both of the following dates:

  ○ at the date of transition to FRS 102; and

  ○ at the end of the latest period presented in the entity's most recent annual financial statements prepared in accordance with UK GAAP.

- a reconciliation of the profit or loss determined in accordance with UK GAAP for the latest period in the entity's most recent annual financial statements, to its profit or loss determined in accordance with FRS 102.

Format options

39.33 FRS 102 does not specify a particular format. In practice, there are two presentation options:

- *Option 1*: A vertical format which lists the various adjustments in a single column.

- *Option 2*: A columnar method which shows the effects of the adjustments on each line item in the income statement and balance sheet. This presentation method is particularly useful if there are a number of adjustments affecting several line items.

Example 39.12 – Transition disclosure option 1

This sets out Option 1

Extracts from the notes to the financial statements for the year ended 31 December 2015

Note 2 – Basis of preparation and accounting policies

These financial statements have been prepared in accordance with the Financial Reporting Standard applicable in the UK and Republic of Ireland (The FRS) issued by the Financial Reporting Council. They are presented in £ sterling.

Before 2015, the financial statements were prepared in accounting with previous UK GAAP as issued by the former UK Accounting Standards

---

Board. The financial effects of the transition to the FRS are set out in Note 3 below.

Note 3 – Transition to the FRS

These financial statements for the year ended 31 December 2015 are the company's first financial statements that comply with the FRS. The company's date of transition to the FRS is 1 January 2014. Its last financial statements prepared in accordance with previous UK GAAP were for the year ended 31 December 2014.

The transition to the FRS has resulted in a number of changes in the company's accounting policies compared to those used when applying previous UK GAAP.

The following explanatory notes to the financial statements describe the differences between the equity and profit or loss presented under previous UK GAAP, and the newly presented amounts under the FRS for the reporting period ended 31 December 2014 (the restated comparatives), as well as the equity presented in the opening balance sheet at 1 January 2014 (transition date). The notes also describe all the required changes in accounting policies made on first-time adoption of the FRS.

In the table below, equity determined in accordance with the FRS is reconciled to equity determined in accordance with previous UK GAAP at both 1 January 2014 (the date of transition to the FRS) and 31 December 2014 (the end of the latest period presented in the most recent financial statements prepared under previous UK GAAP.

	31/12/14	*1 /1/ 14*
	£	£
Equity according to previous UK GAAP	1,713,794	995,118
Effect of adopting:		
Fair value of forward exchange contracts	16,000	9,500
Fair value of investments	15,000	6,000
Tax on above	(9,300)	(4,650)
Deferred tax on investment property surplus	(59,700)	(36,750)
Equity according to the FRS	1,675,794	969,218

Reconciliation of profit or loss for the year ended 31 December 2014

	£
Profit for the year according to the previous UK GAAP	847,176
Gain on forward exchange contracts	6,500
Gain on investments	9,000
Gain on investment properties	76,500
Taxation	(27,600)
Profit for the year according to the FRS	911,576

Notes to the financial statements – explanation of transition to the FRS

The transition to the FRS (The Financial Reporting Standard applicable in the UK and Republic of Ireland) reporting has resulted in a number of changes in the reported financial statements, notes thereto and accounting principles compared to those presented in previous years in accordance with UK GAAP.

The following explanatory notes explain the differences between the FRS and previous UK GAAP, as referred to in the reconciliations below, required in accordance with the FRS.

(i) Forward exchange contracts

Under UK GAAP, SSAP 20 offers a choice of methods for purchases of goods where the purchases are 'hedged' by a contract for forward purchase of foreign currency. The purchase may be booked at either the spot rate at the transaction date, or at the rate specified in the forward contract.

Under the FRS, purchases must be booked at the spot rate of exchange at the date of the transaction. Forward exchange contracts are accounted for separately and included in the statement of financial position at fair value. Changes in fair value are recognised in profit or loss.

(ii) Fixed asset investments

Under UK GAAP, the fixed asset investments were stated at cost – the company did not adopt the revaluation alternative available under the *Companies Act 2006.*

Under FRS 102, investments are measured at fair value provided that the investments are publicly traded or their fair value can otherwise be measured reliably. Changes in fair value are recognised in profit or loss. Otherwise investments are measured at cost less impairment.

(iii) Investment properties

Under UK GAAP, investment properties must be accounted for in accordance with SSAP 19. The properties are stated in the balance sheet at open market value, with changes in value taken direct to an investment revaluation reserve.

Under FRS 102, investment properties whose fair value can be measured reliably without undue cost or effort on an ongoing basis are included in the statement of financial position (balance sheet) at fair value. Changes in fair value are recognised in profit or loss. All other investment property is accounted for as property, plant and equipment.

(iv) Deferred tax

Under UK GAAP, no deferred tax was provided in respect of revaluation surpluses on investment properties. FRS 102 requires that deferred tax is provided.

Example 39.13 – Transition disclosure option 2

This sets out Option 2:

Extracts from the notes to the financial statements for the year ended 31 December 2015

Note 2 – as in **Example 9.10**

Note 3 – as in **Example 9.10**

Reconciliation of equity at 1 January 2014

	Notes	UK GAAP	Effect of transition to FRS 102	FRS 102
		£	£	£
Assets				
Property, plant and equipment		658,228		658,228
Investment properties	3	312,500		312,500
Goodwill		96,500		96,500
Investments	2	16,000	6,000	22,000
Total non-current assets		1,083,228	6,000	1,089,228

	Notes	UK GAAP	Effect of transition to FRS 102	FRS 102
		£	£	£
Inventories		141,070		141,070
Trade and other receivables		496,755		496,755
Forward contracts	1	–	9,500	9,500
Cash and cash equivalents		75,000		75,000
Total current assets		712,825	9,500	722,325
Liabilities				
Trade and other payables		98,275		98,275
Current tax payable		24,200		24,200
Total current liabilities		122,475		122,475
Net current assets		590,350	9,500	599,850
Total assets less current liabilities		1,673,578	15,500	1,689,078
Long-term borrowings		300,000		300,000
Preference shares		250,000		250,000
Deferred tax		128,460	41,400	169,860
Total non-current liabilities	4	678,460	41,400	719,860
Net assets		**995,118**	**(25,900)**	**969,218**
Equity				
Share capital		450,250		450,250
Retained earnings		422,368	96,600	518,968
Investment property revaluation reserve	3	122,500	(122,500)	
		995,118	**(25,900)**	**969,218**

39.33   *First-time adoption of FRS 102*

Reconciliation of equity at 31 December 2014

	Notes	UK GAAP	Effect of transition to FRS 102	FRS 102
		£	£	£
Assets				
Property, plant and equipment		613,128		613,128
Investment properties	3	389,000		389,000
Goodwill		90,500		90,500
Investments	2	41,000	15,000	56,000
Total non-current assets		1,133,628	15,000	1,148,628
Inventories		169,286		169,286
Trade and other receivables		548,106		548,106
Forward contracts	1	–	16,000	16,000
Cash and cash equivalents		989,513		989,513
Total current assets		1,706,905	16,000	1,722,905
Liabilities				
Trade and other payables		104,824		104,824
Current tax payable		286,425		286,425
Total current liabilities		391,249		391,249
Net current assets		1,315,656	16,000	1,331,656
Total assets less current liabilities		2,449,284	31,000	2,480,284
Long-term borrowings		250,000		250,000
Preference shares		250,000		250,000
Deferred tax		235,490	69,000	304,490
Total non-current liabilities	4	735,490	69,000	804,490
Net assets		**1,713,794**	**(38,000)**	**1,675,794**

	Notes	UK GAAP £	Effect of transition to FRS 102 £	FRS 102 £
Equity				
Share capital		450,250		450,250
Retained earnings		1,064,544	161,000	1,225,544
Investment property revaluation reserve	3	199,000	(199,000)	–
		1,713,794	**(38,000)**	**1,675,794**

Reconciliation of profit or loss for the year ended 31 December 2014

	Notes	UK GAAP £	Effect of transition to FRS 102 £	FRS 102 £
Revenue		5,163,524		5,163,524
Cost of sales	1	(3,157,780)	(9,700)	(3,167,480)
Gross profit		2,005,744		1,996,044
Other operating income	3	25,000	76,500	101,500
Distribution costs		(239,363)		(239,363)
Reorganisation costs		(153,000)		(153,000)
Exceptional bad debt charge		(92,000)		(92,000)
Other administrative expenses		(292,670)		(292,670)
Operating profit		1,253,711		1,320,511
Financial income	2	11,920	9,000	20,920
Financial expense	1	(25,000)	16,200	(8,800)
Profit before tax		1,240,631		1,332,631
Tax	4	(393,455)	(27,600)	(421,055)
Profit for the period		847,176	64,400	911,576

SUMMARY – WHAT IS DIFFERENT FROM THE PREVIOUS UK GAAP?

There is no equivalent standard under existing UK GAAP.

Chapter 40

Specialised activities and other entities

SIGNPOSTS

- Section 34, Specialised Activities of FRS 102 includes some areas not currently covered by existing UK GAAP, for example accounting for agricultural activity (see **Chapter 16**).

- Section 34 will have a major impact on disclosures for those financial institutions who adopt new UK GAAP – some entities will have to give careful consideration as to whether they will fall within the comprehensive definition of 'financial institution'.

- Public benefit entities (not-for-profit entities) will need to consider the requirements of Section 34 and relevant parts of other sections, as well as relevant legislation and Statements of Recommended Practice (SORPs).

INTRODUCTION

Aim of this chapter

40.1   Section 34 of FRS 102 deals with a diverse range of activities, including financial institutions and public benefit entities. The purpose of this chapter is to indicate the coverage of this section of FRS 102, and to indicate where further information might be obtained.

The chapter does not attempt to deal with the detailed requirements of Section 34 – please note that Agriculture is dealt with in **Chapter 16**.

Scope of Section 34 – Specialised activities

40.2   This section covers an extremely diverse range of activities and entities including:

- agriculture;
- extractive industries;

- service concession arrangements;

- financial institutions disclosures;

- financial statements of retirement benefit plans (defined contribution plans and defined benefit plans);

- heritage assets;

- funding commitments (including guidance in Appendix I of Section 34); and

- requirements relevant to Public Benefit Entities including: incoming resources from non-exchange transactions (also Appendix II to Section 34) public benefit entity combinations; and

- concessionary loans.

AGRICULTURE

40.3   Existing UK GAAP does not have a specific standard covering this topic. This issue is dealt with in **Chapter 16**.

EXTRACTIVE ACTIVITIES

40.4   FRS 102 makes brief reference to this – only four paragraphs. However, it does require that entities engaged in the exploration and/or evaluation of mineral resources (extract activities) should apply the requirements of IFRS 6 *Exploration for and Evaluation of Mineral Resources* (see also FRS 102, paragraph 1.7).

FRS 102, paragraph 20.1(a) states that leases to explore for or use minerals, oil, natural gas and similar non-regenerative resources are outside the scope of Section 20, Leases. This scope exclusion, without any further comment or explanation, simply repeats IAS 17.2(a).

40.5   This specialist area is outside the scope of this book and further reference should be made to a specialist text dealing with IFRS 6.

SERVICE CONCESSION ARRANGEMENTS

40.6   FRS 102 defines a service concession arrangement whereby a public sector body or a public benefit entity (see definition below in **40.24**) (the grantor) contracts with a private sector entity (the operator) to construct (or upgrade), operate and maintain infrastructure assets for a specified period of time (the concession period).

40.7   FRS 102 deals with accounting requirements for both grantors and operators, and is more extensive than the equivalent requirements in the IFRS for SMEs, as a result of requests from commentators for more guidance.

FINANCIAL INSTITUTIONS

Introduction

40.8   One of the major issues of debate in recent years is whether financial institutions (apart from those which are fully listed, have subsidiaries and for whom IFRS is mandatory for their consolidated financial statements) should in future have to adopt EU-endorsed IFRS.

At first it appeared as though the answer to this was going to be 'yes' as an early exposure draft regarded financial institutions as 'publicly accountable' but the concept of public accountability proved difficult to define in a satisfactory way and was subsequently dropped.

40.9   FRS 102 now includes a comprehensive (very long) definition, and allows such entities to adopt the new UK GAAP, subject to the additional disclosure requirements of Section 34, as well as those in Sections 11 and 12 of FRS 102.

Furthermore, financial institutions which are qualifying entities (certain parents and subsidiaries) may take advantage of the reduced disclosure concessions in either FRS 101 or FRS 102 (with some restrictions compared with non-qualifying entities (see **Chapter 34**)).

Definition

40.10   A financial institution is defined in the Glossary to FRS 102 as any of the following:

(a)   A bank which is:

    (i)   A firm with a Part IV [*Financial Services and Markets Act 2000, s 40(4)*] permission which includes accepting deposits and:

        (a)   which is a credit institution, or

        (b)   whose Part IV permission includes a requirement that it complies with the rules in the General Prudential sourcebook for Banks, Building Societies and Investment Firms relating to banks, but which is not a building society, a friendly society or a credit union.

    (ii)   An EEA bank which is a full credit institution.

(b)   a building society which is defined in *section 119(1)* of the *Building Societies Act 1986* as a building society incorporated (or deemed to be incorporated) under that Act;

(c)   a credit union, being a body corporate registered under the *Industrial and Provident Societies Act 1965* as a credit union in accordance with the *Credit Unions Act 1979*, which is an authorised person;

(d)   custodian bank, broker-dealer or stockbroker;

(e)   an entity that undertakes the business of effecting or carrying out insurance contracts, including general and life assurance entities;

(f)   an incorporated friendly society incorporated under the *Friendly Societies Act 1992* or a registered friendly society registered under *section 7(1)(a)* of the *Friendly Societies Act 1974* or any enactment which it replaced, including any registered branches;

(g)   an investment trust, Irish Investment Company, venture capital trust, mutual fund, exchange traded fund, unit trust, open-ended investment company (OIEC);

(h)   a retirement benefit plan (see definition below in **40.17**); or

(i)   any other entity whose principal activity is to generate wealth or manage risk through financial instruments. This is intended to cover entities that have business activities similar to those listed above but are not specifically included in the list above.

A parent entity whose sole activity is to hold investments in other group entities is *not* a financial institution.

Presentation and format requirements

40.11   The presentation requirements for financial institutions are set out in Section 4, paragraph 4.2 dealing with the statement of financial position, and Section 5, paragraphs 5.5 and 5.7 dealing with the statement of comprehensive income and the income statement.

These Sections make reference to the Regulations to CA 2006 (see 7.4), in particular Schedule 2 dealing with banking companies, and Schedule 3 dealing with insurance companies.

Disclosure requirements – Financial institutions other than retirement benefit plans

40.12   The disclosure requirements in paragraphs 34.19 to 34.33 apply to:

●   the individual statements of a financial institution (other than a retirement benefit plan – see definition in **40.17** below); and

- the consolidated financial statements of a group which contains a financial institution (other than a retirement benefit plan) – in situations where the financial instruments held by the financial institution are material to the group.

Subject to materiality, these disclosure requirements apply regardless of whether the group's principal activity is that of a financial institution or not. In such cases, disclosures only have to be given in relation to financial instruments held within the group by entities that are financial institutions.

40.13 The disclosure requirements in paragraphs 34.19 to 34.33 are based on those in FRS 29 *Financial Instruments: Disclosures*/IFRS 7 *Financial Instruments: Disclosures* and IAS 1 *Presentation of Financial Statements*.

40.14 In addition, all entities, whether or not they are financial institutions, are required to comply with the disclosure requirements of Section 11 (see **36.50–36.52**).

Further guidance

40.15 The FRC Impact Assessment, March 2013, Appendix II, page 19 (available on www.frc.org.uk) includes case study scenarios relating to the following:

- a building society; and

- a credit union.

40.16 FRC has also issued Staff Guidance Notes on the following:

- Guidance Note 12 – *Financial institutions: Disclosures.*

- Guidance Note 15 – *Credit unions.*

RETIREMENT BENEFIT PLANS

Definition

40.17 A *retirement benefit plan* is defined in the Glossary to FRS 102 as 'an arrangement whereby an entity provides benefits for employees on or after termination of service (either in the form of an annual income or as a lump sum) when such benefits, or the contribution towards them, can be determined or estimated in advance of retirement from the provisions of a document or from the entity's practice'.

Scope exemption

40.18   Section 7, Statement of Cash Flows, does not apply to retirement benefit plans.

Presentation and disclosure requirements – Retirement benefit plans only

40.19   Retirement benefit plans should comply with the presentation requirements in paragraphs 34.34 to 34.38, and the disclosure requirements in paragraphs 34.39 to 34.48.

Statement of Recommended Practice

40.20   The Financial Reporting Council has indicated that most existing SORPs, including Financial Reports of Pension Funds, will be updated to reflect FRS 102.

Entities whose financial statements fall within the scope of a SORP will be required to disclose the title of the SORP and whether the financial statements have been prepared in accordance with the provisions of the SORP.

FRS 102, paragraphs 10.4 and 10.5 sets out the role of SORPs in developing accounting policies for dealing with transactions, other events or conditions not specifically addressed by FRS 102.

The Accounting Council's Advice, paragraph 166, states that 'early application [of FRS 102] should be permitted for entities applying a SORP provided that FRS 102 does not conflict with the requirements of a current SORP or legal requirements for the preparation of financial statements'.

Legislation

40.21   FRS 102, Appendix IV, paragraph A4.42 refers to *The Occupational Pension Schemes (Requirement to Obtain Audited Accounts and a Statement from the Auditor) Regulations 1996 (SI 1996/1975)*.

Further guidance

40.22   The FRC Impact Assessment, March 2013, Appendix II, page 19, includes a case study scenario relating to a pension fund.

HERITAGE ASSETS

40.23   Paragraphs 34.49–34.56 effectively retain the requirements of existing UK GAAP, FRS 30 *Heritage Assets*.

PUBLIC BENEFIT ENTITIES

Definition and examples

40.24   A *public benefit entity* is defined in the Glossary to FRS 102 as 'an entity whose primary objective is to provide goods or services for the general public, community or social benefit and where any equity is provided with a view to supporting the entity's primary objectives rather than with a view to providing a financial return to equity providers, shareholders or members'.

40.25   Examples of PBEs include charities, registered social landlords, further and higher education and local authorities.

Requirements for public benefit entities

40.26   Requirements for public benefit entities are integrated within Section 34 of FRS 102, and most of the relevant paragraph numbers are prefixed by PBE.

40.27   Section 16, Investment Property, paragraph 16.3A states: 'Property held primarily for the provision of social benefits, eg social housing held by a public benefit entity, shall not be classified as investment property and shall be accounted for as property, plant and equipment in accordance with Section 17.'

40.28   FRS 102 has identified the following six issues to be of particular relevance and significance to PBEs:

- Concessionary loans (PBE 34.87–34.97);

- Property held for the provision of social benefits (see **40.27** above);

- Entity combinations (PBE 34.75–PBE 34.86);

- Impairment of assets: public benefit considerations (see Accounting Council's Advice to the FRC, page 251, paragraphs 140–148);

- Funding commitments (PBE 34.57–34.63; Appendix A to Section 34); and

- Incoming resources from non-exchange transactions (PBE 34.64–PBE34.74; Appendix B to Section 34).

Statements of Recommended Practice

40.29   The future role of SORPs was referred to above (see **40.20**). Relevant SORPs for PBEs include those dealing with charities and registered social housing providers.

Legislation

40.30   FRS 102, Appendix IV, Note on Legal Requirements, paragraph A4.41 onwards includes a table containing some relevant legislation which may be relevant.

Further guidance

40.31   FRC Impact Assessment, March 2013, page 19 includes case study scenarios dealing with a registered provider of social housing and a large charity.

40.32   FRC has also issued Staff Guidance Note 13 on incoming resources from non-exchange transactions.

OTHER ENTITIES

Limited Liability Partnerships (LLPs)

40.33   FRS 102 makes specific reference to requirements specific to LLPs, including:

- Section 4, Statement of Financial Position, paragraph 4.2(d); and

- Section 5, Statement of Comprehensive Income, paragraph 5.5(d).

Entities without share capital

40.34   FRS 102, paragraph 4.13 states: 'An entity without share capital, such as a partnership or trust, shall disclose information equivalent to that required by paragraph 4.12(a) showing changes during the period in each category of equity, and the rights, preferences and restrictions attaching to each category of equity.'

Entities whose shares and/or debt are publicly traded

40.35 Paragraphs 1.4 and 1.5 refer to entities whose shares and/or debt are publicly traded. Such entities should apply IAS 33 *Earnings Per Share*, and IFRS 8 *Operating Segments*.

This part of FRS 102 will be of limited relevance to the majority of companies, as most companies operating within the EU whose shares are publicly traded are required to adopt EU-endorsed IFRS.

However, fully listed and AIM-listed companies are only required to apply EU-endorsed IFRS to their consolidated financial statements.

SUMMARY – WHAT IS DIFFERENT FROM THE
PREVIOUS UK GAAP?

- The relevance of Section 34 to different entities will vary hugely, but for those affected, it will be of major significance and will require careful studying. SORPs will continue to play a vital role in providing a link between accounting requirements and relevant legislation.

- LLPs are not specifically referred to in Section 34 of FRS 102, but are referred to elsewhere in FRS 102 (especially in the sections dealing with presentation of financial statements) and are included in this chapter for convenience. The same applies to entities without share capital referred to in Section 4 of FRS 102.

- Entities engaged in extractive activities are referenced to IFRS 6 *Exploration for and Evaluation of Mineral Resources*.

- Service concession arrangements are referred to in current UK GAAP (FRS 5 *Application Note F, Private Finance Initiative and Similar Contracts*).

FRS 102 Appendix VI: Republic of Ireland (RoI) Legal References

Introduction

A1.1   The table below outlines the provisions in the Companies Acts 1963 to 2012 and related Regulations which implement EC Accounting Directives (Irish company law), corresponding to the provisions of the UK *Companies Act 2006* (the 2006 Act) and the UK *Large and Medium-sized Companies and Groups (Accounts and Reports) Regulations 2008* (the 2008 Regulations) (SI 2008/410) referred to in this FRS.

A1.2   The principal Irish companies' legislation referred to in the table below is:

● The Companies Act 1963 (1963 Act);

● The Companies (Amendment) Act 1983 (1983 Act);

● The Companies (Amendment) Act 1986 (1986 Act);

● The Companies Act 1990 (1990 Act);

● The Companies (Amendment) (No 2) Act 1999;

● The European Communities (Companies: Group Accounts) Regulations 1992 – SI No. 201 of 1992 (Group Accounts Regulations 1992 or GAR 1992);

● The European Communities (Credit Institutions: Accounts) Regulations 1992 – SI No. 294 of 1992 (Credit Institutions Regulations 1992 or CIR 1992); and

● The European Communities (Insurance Undertakings: Accounts) Regulations 1996 – SI No. 23 of 1996 (Insurance Undertakings Regulations 1996 or IUR 1996).

A1.3   General references are made in this FRS to UK legislation such as the '2006 Act', 'Companies Act 2006 ('and the Regulations')', 'the Companies Act', 'the Act', 'the Large and Medium-sized Companies and Groups (Accounts and Reports) Regulations, 2008', 'the 2008 Regulations'

and 'the Regulations'. In an Irish context reference should be made to the relevant sections and paragraphs of Irish companies' legislation. Such general references are not dealt with in the table below. References in the text to 'IAS accounts' are equivalent to 'IFRS accounts' in Irish company law.

A1.4   The following Irish legislation is also referenced in the table below:

- The Building Societies Act 1989;

- The Credit Union Acts 1997 to 2012;

- The Central Bank Act 1971;

- The Charities Act 2009;

- The Friendly Societies Acts 1896 to 1977;

- The Friendly Societies (Amendment) Act 1977;

- The Friendly Societies Regulations 1988 – SI No. 74 of 1988;

- The Industrial and Provident Societies (Amendment) Act 1978;

- The Pensions Act 1990; and

- The Occupational Pension Schemes (Disclosure of Information) Regulations 2006 – SI No. 301 of 2006.

Companies Act accounts under Irish company law

A1.5   Certain companies are permitted under Irish company law to prepare their Companies Act accounts using accounting standards other than those issued by the Financial Reporting Council (FRC) and promulgated by the Institute of Chartered Accountants in Ireland in respect of their application in the Republic of Ireland. Specifically:

- Pursuant to the Companies (Miscellaneous Provisions) Act 2009, as amended by the Companies (Amendment) Act 2012, relevant parent undertakings are permitted to prepare 'Companies Act individual accounts' and/or 'Companies Act group accounts' in accordance with US GAAP, as modified to ensure consistency with Irish company law.

- Investment companies subject to Part XIII of the Companies Act 1990 or the European Communities (Undertakings for Collective Investment in Transferable Securities) Regulations 2011 may adopt an alternative body of accounting standards, being standards which apply in the United States of America, Canada or Japan in preparing 'Companies Act individual accounts'.

A1.6   Such companies, therefore, may adopt standards other than those issued by the FRC in preparing Companies Act accounts under Irish company law.

Small companies under Irish company law

A1.7   There is no equivalent to the UK *small companies regime* (see Sections 381 to 384 of the 2006 Act) in Irish company law. Section 8 of the Companies (Amendment) Act 1986 (as amended by the European Union (Accounts) Regulations 2012 (SI No. 304 of 2012)) defines small companies for the purposes of Irish company law. However, whilst Sections 10 and 12 provide certain exemptions for such companies in relation to their financial statements that are filed with the Registrar of Companies, there are no exemptions for individual or group accounts prepared for members. Under Section 8 (as amended) the qualifying conditions for a company to be treated as a small company in respect of any financial year are as follows:

- The amount of turnover for that year does not exceed €8,800,000;

- The balance sheet total for that year does not exceed €4,400,000; and

- Average number of employees does not exceed 50.

A1.8   Except for companies in their first financial year, Section 8(1)(a) provides that companies qualify to be treated as small if, in respect of that year and the financial year immediately preceding that year, the company satisfies at least two of the above criteria. Section 9 provides that where a company has qualified as small, it continues to be so qualified until it does not meet two of the above three criteria for two consecutive years. Similarly, where a company no longer qualifies as small, two consecutive years of meeting two of the three criteria are required to qualify again as small.

A1.9   The following do not qualify as small under Irish company law:

- Companies subject to the European Communities (Credit Institutions: Accounts) Regulations 1992;

- Companies subject to the European Communities (Insurance Undertakings: Accounts) Regulations 1996; and

- Private companies whose securities are admitted to trading on a regulated market.

A1.9 *FRS 102 Appendix VI: Republic of Ireland (RoI) Legal References*

SECTION 1: SCOPE

Paragraph	UK references: 2006 Act and the 2008 Regulations (unless otherwise stated)	RoI references						
		1963 Act	1983 Act	1986 Act	1990 Act	GAR 1992	CIR 1992	IUR 1996
1.3(b) (Footnote 6)	Section 395(1)(a)	Section 148(2)(a)					Regulation 5(1)	Regulation 5(1)
1.3(b) (Footnote 6)	Section 395(1)(b)	Section 148(2)(b)					Regulation 5(1)	Regulation 5(1)
1.8	Paragraph 36(4) of Schedule 1			Paragraph 22AA of Part IIIA of the Schedule		Regulation 15 (applying the Schedule to the 1986 Act)	Paragraphs 46A(4A) and 46A(4B) of Part I and paragraph 1 of Part II of the Schedule	
1.10	Section 399	Section 150(1)				Regulations 5 and 7	Regulation 7(3)	Regulation 10(3)
1.10	Sections 400 to 401					Regulations 8, 9 and 9A	Regulations 8 and 8A	Regulations 12 and 12A
1.10	Section 402	Section 150(1A)*					Paragraph 2 of Part II of the Schedule	Regulation 10(1A)*

*Section 150(1A) of the 1963 Act and Regulation 10(1A) of the IUR 1996 contain an exemption from preparing group accounts which is similar but not identical to Section 402.

SECTION 3: FINANCIAL STATEMENT PRESENTATION

Paragraph	UK references	RoI references						
	2006 Act and the 2008 Regulations (unless otherwise stated)	1963 Act	1983 Act	1986 Act	1990 Act	GAR 1992	CIR 1992	IUR 1996
3.5 (Footnote 9)	Section 396(5)			Section 3(1)(d) and (e)		Regulation 14(3) and (4)	Regulation 5(1A)(d) and (e) and Regulation 7(7)(d) and (e)	Regulation 5(1A)(d) and (e) and Regulation 10(7)(d) and (e)

SECTION 4: STATEMENT OF FINANCIAL POSITION and SECTION 5: STATEMENT OF COMPREHENSIVE INCOME AND INCOME STATEMENT

Paragraph	UK references — 2006 Act and the 2008 Regulations (unless otherwise stated)	RoI references						
		1963 Act	1983 Act	1986 Act	1990 Act	GAR 1992	CIR 1992	IUR 1996
4.2, 5.5 and 5.7	Part 1 *General Rules and Formats* of Schedule 1 to the Regulations			Part 1 of the Schedule				
4.2, 5.5 and 5.7	Part 1 *General Rules and Formats* of Schedule 2 to the Regulations						Chapter 1 of Part I of the Schedule	
4.2, 5.5 and 5.7	Part 1 *General Rules and Formats* of Schedule 3 to the Regulations							Part I of the Schedule
4.2, 5.5 and 5.7	Schedule 6 to the Regulations					Regulation 15 (applying the Schedule to the 1986 Act)	Paragraph 1 of Part II of the Schedule (applying Part I of the Schedule)	Paragraph 1 of Part IV of the Schedule (applying Part I of the Schedule)
4.2, 5.5 and 5.7	Schedule 1 and Schedule 3 to the LLP Regulations	There is no equivalent Irish LLP legislation.						

SECTION 7: STATEMENT OF CASH FLOWS

| Paragraph | UK references | | | | | RoI references | | | |
	2006 Act and the 2008 Regulations (unless otherwise stated)	1963 Act	1983 Act	1986 Act	1990 Act	GAR 1992	CIR 1992	IUR 1996
7.20A	Part 1 *General Rules and Formats of* Schedule 2 to the Regulations						Chapter 1 of Part I of the Schedule	

SECTION 9: CONSOLIDATED AND SEPARATE FINANCIAL STATEMENTS

Paragraph	UK references 2006 Act and the 2008 Regulations (unless otherwise stated)	RoI references 1963 Act	1983 Act	1986 Act	1990 Act	GAR 1992	CIR 1992	IUR 1996
9.3(a) and (b)	Section 400(2)					Regulations 8(3) and 9	Regulation 8(3)	Regulation 12(3)
9.3(b)	Section 400(1)(b)					Regulations 8(1) and 9	Regulations 8(1), (2) and (6)	Regulations 12(1), (2) and (6)
9.3(c) and (d)	Section 401(2)					Regulation 9A(3)	Regulation 8A(3)	Regulation 12A(3)
9.3(d)	Section 401(1)(b)					Regulation 9A(1)(b)	Regulation 8A(1)(b)	Regulation 12A(1)(b)
9.3(e)	Section 383	Please refer to the note above in the introduction to this table – Size exemptions from the preparation of group accounts under Irish company law.						
9.3(e)	Section 384	Please refer to the note above in the introduction to this table – Size exemptions from the preparation of group accounts under Irish company law.						
9.27B	Paragraph 36(4) of Schedule 1 to the Regulations			Paragraph 22AA of Part IIIA of the Schedule		Regulation 15 (applying the Schedule to the 1986 Act)	Paragraphs 46A(4A) and 46A(4B) of Part I and paragraph 1 of Part II of the Schedule	

SECTION 35: TRANSITION TO THIS FRS

	UK references	RoI references					
Paragraph	**2006 Act and the 2008 Regulations (unless otherwise stated)**	**1963 Act**	**1983 Act**	**1986 Act**	**1990 Act**	**GAR 1992**	**CIR 1992**	**IUR 1996**
35.10(m)	Companies Act definition of a dormant company	There is no equivalent definition in Irish company law.						

A1.9 *FRS 102 Appendix VI: Republic of Ireland (RoI) Legal References*

THE ACCOUNTING COUNCIL'S ADVICE TO THE FRC TO ISSUE FRS 102

	UK references	RoI references							
Paragraph	2006 Act and the 2008 Regulations (unless otherwise stated)	1963 Act	1983 Act	1986 Act	1990 Act	GAR 1992	CIR 1992	IUR 1996	
36	Section 467(1)			Sections 2 and 8					
49	Section 405(3)					Regulation 11	Paragraph 2(3) of Part II of the Schedule	Paragraph 2(3) of Part IV of the Schedule	

APPENDIX I: GLOSSARY

Paragraph	UK references	RoI references						
	2006 Act and the 2008 Regulations (unless otherwise stated)	**1963 Act**	**1983 Act**	**1986 Act**	**1990 Act**	**GAR 1992**	**CIR 1992**	**IUR 1996**
'financial institution' and footnote 25	Part IV permission; Section 40(4) of the Financial Services and Markets Act 2000	There is no equivalent legislation in Ireland to the Financial Services and Markets Act 2000. Banks in Ireland are licensed under Section 9 of the Central Bank Act 1971.						
'financial institution'	Section 119(1) of the Building Societies Act 1986	Section 2(1) of the Building Societies Act 1989.						
'financial institution'	Industrial and Provident Societies Act 1965 and Credit Unions Act 1979	Credit Unions Act 1997 to 2012.						
'financial institution'	Friendly Societies Act 1992; section 7(1)(a) of the Friendly Societies Act 1974	Friendly Societies Acts 1896 to 1977.						
'individual financial statements'	Section 394	Section 148						

APPENDIX I: GLOSSARY – contd

Paragraph	UK references 2006 Act and the 2008 Regulations (unless otherwise stated)	RoI references						
		1963 Act	1983 Act	1986 Act	1990 Act	GAR 1992	CIR 1992	IUR 1996
'individual financial statements'	Section 132 of the Charities Act 2011	Section 48 of the Charities Act 2009 provides that all charities are to prepare an annual statement of accounts, the form and content of which can be prescribed by Regulations of the Minister. Section 48 is, at the date of publication of this FRS, not commenced and no Regulations regarding the form and content of charities' annual statements of accounts have been published. Charity companies are required to prepare financial statements which give a true and fair view in accordance with the Companies Acts. Sections 148(3) and 150(4) of the 1963 Act require that companies "not trading for the acquisition of gain by the members" must prepare Companies Act accounts (ie not IFRS accounts), and this definition may apply to many Irish charity companies.						
'individual financial statements'	Section 72A of the Building Societies Act 1986	Section 77 of the Building Societies Act 1989 requires the preparation of (a) an income and expenditure account giving a true and fair view of its income and expenditure for that year, (b) a balance sheet giving a true and fair view of the state of its affairs as at the end of that year, and (c) a statement of the source and application of funds giving a true and fair view of the manner in which its business has been financed and in which its financial resources have been used during that year.						
'LLP Regulations'	The Large and Medium-sized Limited Liability Partnerships (Accounts) Regulations 2008 (SI 2008/1913)	There is no equivalent Irish LLP legislation.						
'qualifying entity' (footnote 29)	Section 474(1)					Regulation 3(1)	Paragraph 1 of Part IV of the Schedule	

574

APPENDIX II: SIGNIFICANT DIFFERENCES BETWEEN FRS 102 AND THE IFRS FOR SMEs

Paragraph	UK references — 2006 Act and the 2008 Regulations (unless otherwise stated)	RoI references						
		1963 Act	1983 Act	1986 Act	1990 Act	GAR 1992	CIR 1992	IUR 1996
Section 9	Paragraph 2(2) of Schedule 6 to the Regulations					Regulation 26(2)	Paragraph 3(3) of Part II of the Schedule	Paragraph 3(3) of Part IV of the Schedule
Section 9	Paragraph 13(a) of Schedule 1 to the Regulations			Section 5(c)(i)		Regulation 28 (applying Section 5 of the 1986 Act)	Paragraph 19(a) of Part I and paragraph 1 of Part II of the Schedule	Regulation 7(c)(i) and paragraph 13 of Part IV of the Schedule
Sections 14 and 15	Paragraph 27 of Schedule 1 to the Regulations			Paragraph 14 of Part II of the Schedule		Regulation 15 (applying the Schedule to the 1986 Act)	Paragraph 36 of Part I of the Schedule and paragraph 1 of Part II of the Schedule	Paragraphs 7 to 8 of Part II of the Schedule and paragraph 13 of Part IV of the Schedule
Sections 14 and 15	Section C of Schedule 1 to the Regulations			Part III of the Schedule		Regulations (applying the Schedule to the 1986 Act)	Paragraphs 39 to 44 of Part I of the Schedule and paragraph 1 of Part II of the Schedule	Chapter 2 of Part II of the Schedule and paragraph 13 of Part IV of the Schedule
Sections 14 and 15	Paragraph 36 of Schedule 1 to the Regulations			Paragraphs 22A and 22AA of Part IIIA of the Schedule		Regulation 15 (applying the Schedule to the 1986 Act)	Paragraph 46A of Part I and paragraph 1 of Part II of the Schedule	

APPENDIX IV: NOTE ON LEGAL REQUIREMENTS

A1.9   *FRS 102 Appendix VI: Republic of Ireland (RoI) Legal References*

Paragraph	UK references		RoI references						
	2006 Act and the 2008 Regulations (unless otherwise stated)	Charities Act 2011 and Regulations made thereunder	1963 Act	1983 Act	1986 Act	1990 Act	GAR 1992	CIR 1992	IUR 1996
A4.1		Charities Act 2011 and Regulations made thereunder	Section 48 of the Charities Act 2009 provides that all charities are to prepare an annual statement of accounts, the form and content of which can be prescribed by Regulations of the Minister. Section 48 is, at the date of publication of this FRS, not commenced and no Regulations regarding the form and content of charities' annual statements of accounts have been published. Charity companies are required to prepare financial statements which give a true and fair view in accordance with the Companies Acts. Sections 148(3) and 150(4) of the 1963 Act require that companies 'not trading for the acquisition of gain by the members' must prepare Companies Act accounts (ie not IFRS accounts), and this definition may apply to many Irish charity companies.						
A4.3	Schedule 1 to the Regulations				Sections 4, 5 and 6 and the Schedule				
A4.3	Schedule 2 to the Regulations							Part I of the Schedule	
A4.3	Schedule 3 to the Regulations								Regulations 6, 7 and 8 and Parts I, II and III of the Schedule

576

A4.3	Schedule 6 to the Regulations				Regulations 15 to 35 & the Schedule	Part II of the Schedule	Regulations 6, 7, 8 and 10 and Parts I, II and III, as modified by Part IV of the Schedule
A4.6	Section 395(1)	Section 148(2)				Regulation 5	Regulation 5
A4.6	Section 396	Section 149	Section 3			Regulation 5	Regulation 5
A4.6	Section 403(2)	Section 150(3)					
A4.6	Section 404	Section 150A and 151			Regulation 14	Regulation 7	Regulation 10
A4.7	'Accounts prepared in accordance with FRS 102 are ... required to comply with the applicable provisions of Parts 15 and 16 of the Act and with the Regulations'	Sections 148, 149, 150, 150A, 150C, 151, 152, 153, 156, 161D and 191	Sections 3 to 6, 16, 16A and 17 and the Schedule	Sections 41 to 43 and Section 63	Regulations 2 to 35 and the Schedule	Regulations 2, 5, 7, 8, 8A, 9 and 10 and the Schedule	Regulations 2, 5, 6, 7, 8, 10, 11, 12, 12A and 13 and the Schedule
	See also Section 33(4) of the Companies (Amendment) (No.2) Act 1999						

APPENDIX IV: NOTE ON LEGAL REQUIREMENTS – contd

Paragraph	UK references	RoI references						
	2006 Act and the 2008 Regulations (unless otherwise stated)	1963 Act	1983 Act	1986 Act	1990 Act	GAR 1992	CIR 1992	IUR 1996
A4.8	Section 407	Section 150C						
A4.12	Paragraph 36 of Schedule 1 to the Regulations			Paragraphs 22A and 22AA of Part IIIA of the Schedule		Regulation 15 (applying the Schedule to the 1986 Act)	Paragraph 46A of Part I of the Schedule and paragraph 1 of Part II of the Schedule	
A4.13	Paragraph 36(4) of Schedule 1 to the Regulations			Paragraph 22AA of Part IIIA of the Schedule		Regulation 15 (applying the Schedule to the 1986 Act)	Paragraphs 46A(4A) and 46A(4B) of Part I and paragraph 1 of Part II of the Schedule	

A4.13	Paragraph 36(3) of Schedule 1 to the Regulations		Paragraph 22A(3) of Part IIIA of the Schedule	Regulation 15 (applying the Schedule to the 1986 Act)	Paragraph 46A(4) of Part I and paragraph 1 of Part II of the Schedule	Regulation 9(4)
A4.15	Section 434(2)		Section 19(3A)		Regulation 6(4)	
A4.15	Section 408	Sections 148(8) and (9)	Sections 7(1A) and (1B)	Regulation 11	Paragraph 2(3) of Part II of the Schedule	Paragraph 2(3) of Part IV of the Schedule
A4.16	Section 405(3)					
A4.17	Paragraph 36 of Schedule 1 to the Regulations		Paragraphs 22A and 22AA of Part IIIA of the Schedule	Regulation 15 (applying the Schedule to the 1986 Act)	Paragraph 46A of Part I and paragraph 1 of Part II of the Schedule	
A4.17	Paragraph 10(2) of Schedule 1 to the Regulations		Section 6	Regulation 28 (applying Section 6 of the 1986 Act)	Paragraph 22 of Part I and paragraph 1 of Part II of the Schedule	Regulation 8
A4.18	Paragraph 9 of Schedule 6 to the Regulations			Regulation 19	Paragraph 10 of Part II of the Schedule	Paragraph 9 of Part IV of the Schedule

APPENDIX IV: NOTE ON LEGAL REQUIREMENTS – contd

Paragraph	UK references 2006 Act and the 2008 Regulations (unless otherwise stated)	RoI references 1963 Act	1983 Act	1986 Act	1990 Act	GAR 1992	CIR 1992	IUR 1996
A4.21	Section 404(5)					Regulation 14(3) and (4)	Regulation 7(7)(d) and (e)	Regulation 10(7)(d) and (e)
A4.22 and A4.23	Paragraph 8 of Schedule 1 to the Regulations			Section 4(11)		Regulation 15 (applying Section 4 of the 1986 Act)	Paragraph 5 of Part I and paragraph 1 of Part II of the Schedule	Regulation 6(9) and paragraph 3(1) of Part IV of the Schedule
A4.24	Sections 611–615	There are no corresponding Irish provisions to Sections 611–615 (group reconstruction and merger relief)						
A4.25 and A4.27	Paragraph 13(a) of Schedule 1 to the Regulations			Section 5(c)(i)		Regulation 28 (applying Section 5 of the 1986 Act)	Paragraph 19(a) of Part I and paragraph 1 of Part II of the Schedule	Regulation 7(c)(i) and paragraph 13 of Part IV of the Schedule

A4.26	Paragraph 36(4) of Schedule 1 to the Regulations		Paragraph 22AA of Part IIIA of the Schedule		Regulation 15 (applying the Schedule to the 1986 Act)	Paragraphs 46A(4A) and 46A(4B) of Part I and paragraph 1 of Part II of the Schedule	
A4.26	Paragraph 39 of Schedule 1 to the Regulations		Paragraph 22CA of Part IIIA of the Schedule		Regulation 15 (applying the Schedule to the 1986 Act)	Paragraph 46BA of Part I and paragraph 1 of Part II of the Schedule	
A4.27	Paragraphs 40 and 40(2) of Schedule 1 to the Regulations		Sections 22D and 22D(2) of Part IIIA of the Schedule		Regulation 15 (applying the Schedule to the 1986 Act)	Paragraphs 46C and 46C(1) of Part I and paragraph 1 of Part II of the Schedule	
A4.30	Paragraph 10 of Schedule 6 to the Regulations	Sections 62 and 149(5)*			Regulation 21	Paragraph 11 of Part II of the Schedule	Paragraph 10 of Part IV of the Schedule
		*Please refer to the note above in the introduction to this table – merger accounting					
A4.32	Sections 690 to 708	Section 72		Part XI			
A4.32	Sections 724 to 732		Section 43A	Section 209			

APPENDIX IV: NOTE ON LEGAL REQUIREMENTS – contd

Paragraph	UK references	RoI references						
	2006 Act and the 2008 Regulations (unless otherwise stated)	1963 Act	1983 Act	1986 Act	1990 Act	GAR 1992	CIR 1992	IUR 1996
A4.33	Paragraph 36 of Schedule 1 to the Regulations			Paragraphs 22A and 22AA of Part IIIA of the Schedule		Regulation 15 (applying the Schedule to the 1986 Act)	Paragraph 46A of Part I and paragraph 1 of Part II of the Schedule	
A4.34	Section C of Schedule 1 to the Regulations			Part III of the Schedule		Regulation 15 (applying the Schedule to the 1986 Act)	Section B of Chapter II of Part I of the Schedule and paragraph 1 of Part II of the Schedule	Chapter 2 of Part II of the Schedule
A4.35	Paragraph 24(1) of Schedule 1 to the Regulations			Paragraph 11(1) of the Schedule		Regulation 15 (applying the Schedule to the 1986 Act)	Paragraph 33(1) of Part I of the Schedule and paragraph 1 of Part II of the Schedule	Paragraph 5(2) of Part II of the Schedule and paragraph 13 of Part IV of the Schedule

Ref	Legislation	Paragraph 19(5) of the Schedule	Regulation 15 (applying the Schedule to the 1986 Act)	Paragraph 41(4) of Part I of the Schedule and paragraph 1 of Part II of the Schedule	Paragraph 15(2) of Part II of the Schedule and paragraph 13 of Part IV of the Schedule
A4.35	Paragraph 32(5) of Schedule 1 to the Regulations				
A4.38	LLP Regulations	There is no equivalent Irish LLP Regulation.			
A4.42	Building Societies Act 1986	Building Societies Act 1989, Part VII, Section 77(1).			
A4.42	Charities Act 2011 and Regulations made thereunder	Section 48 of the Charities Act 2009 provides that all charities are to prepare an annual statement of accounts, the form and content of which can be prescribed by Regulations of the Minister. Section 48 is, at the date of publication of this FRS, not commenced and no Regulations regarding the form and content of charities' annual statements of accounts have been published. Charity companies are required to prepare financial statements which give a true and fair view in accordance with the Companies Acts. Sections 148(3) and 150(4) of the 1963 Act require that companies 'not trading for the acquisition of gain by the members' must prepare Companies Act accounts (ie not IFRS accounts), and this definition may apply to many Irish charity companies.			
A4.42	Friendly and Industrial and Provident Societies Act 1968	Section 30 of Part IV of the Industrial and Provident Societies (Amendment) Act, 1978; Regulation 4 of the Friendly Societies Regulations 1988, pursuant to Section 3 of the Friendly Societies (Amendment) Act 1977.			

APPENDIX IV: NOTE ON LEGAL REQUIREMENTS – contd

| Paragraph | UK references | RoI references | | | | | | |
	2006 Act and the 2008 Regulations (unless otherwise stated)	**1963 Act**	**1983 Act**	**1986 Act**	**1990 Act**	**GAR 1992**	**CIR 1992**	**IUR 1996**
A4.42 and Footnote 36	Friendly Societies Act 1992 and Friendly Societies (Accounts and Related Provisions) Regulations 1994 (as amended)	Regulation 4 of the Friendly Societies Regulations 1988, pursuant to Section 3 to the Friendly Societies (Amendment) Act 1977.						
A4.42	The Occupational Pension Schemes (Requirement to obtain Audited Accounts and a Statement from the Auditor) Regulations 1996	Section 56 of the Pensions Act 1990; Regulation 5 and paragraphs 1 and 2(a)(ii) of Schedule A of the Occupational Pension Schemes (Disclosure of Information) Regulations 2006.						

APPENDIX V: PREVIOUS CONSULTATIONS

Paragraph	UK references 2006 Act and the 2008 Regulations (unless otherwise stated)	RoI references					
		1963 Act	1983 Act	1986 Act	1990 Act	GAR 1992	CIR 1992	IUR 1996
A5.11	'small companies' regime'	There are no equivalent provisions in Irish company law to the UK small companies' regime or to the Small Companies and Groups (Accounts and Directors' Report) Regulations 2008. Small companies are defined in Section 8 of the 1986 Act. Please refer to the note above in the introduction to this table.					

Index

(All references are to paragraph number)